The Americanization
of Social Science

The Americanization of Social Science

Intellectuals and Public Responsibility in the Postwar United States

DAVID PAUL HANEY

TEMPLE UNIVERSITY PRESS
Philadelphia

For Patrick and Eric

TEMPLE UNIVERSITY PRESS
1601 North Broad Street
Philadelphia PA 19122
www.temple.edu/tempress

∞ The paper used in this publication meets the requirements of the American National Standard for Information Sciences—Permanence of Paper for Printed Library Materials, ANSI Z39.48–1992

Library of Congress Cataloging-in-Publication Data

Haney, David Paul, 1963–
    The Americanization of social science : intellectuals and public responsibility in the postwar United States / David Paul Haney.
      p. cm.
    Includes bibliographical references and index.
    ISBN 13: 978-1-59213-713-8 (cloth : alk. paper)
    ISBN 10: 1-59213-713-X (cloth : alk. paper)
      1. Sociology—Study and teaching—United States.   2. Sociology—United States—History—20th century.   3. Sociologists—United States.   I. Title.
    HM477.U6H36 2008
    301.0973'09045—dc22   2007024415

2 4 6 8 9 7 5 3 1

Contents

Preface

Almost exactly twenty years ago, Herbert J. Gans used his presidential address at the Annual Meeting of the American Sociological Association (ASA) to exhort his colleagues to pay greater attention to nonsociologists and to serve the lay public. "We play a smaller role in the country's intellectual life than we should," he observed, and he demanded that sociologists pay greater attention to "salient subjects and issues" of concern to ordinary Americans, that undergraduate sociology curricula emphasize concrete issues and current events rather than abstractions, that the profession "recruit and encourage" among its membership those who possessed the skill and enthusiasm for writing for lay readers, and that scholars renew a commitment to the practice of social criticism that sociology had ceded, by default, to "journalists, essayists, literary critics, and philosophers."[1] Utilizing the historian Russell Jacoby's idea of the public intellectual, he gave the name "public sociologist" to the scholar who would fulfill one or more of those roles.

Recently, growing numbers of American sociologists have responded enthusiastically and productively to this public sociology ideal, making it

---

[1] Herbert J. Gans, "Sociology in America: The Discipline and the Public." Presidential Address to the American Sociological Association. *American Sociological Review* 54, 1 (February, 1989): 1, 6–7.

the focus of extensive professional debate, constructing the means for its realization institutionally, and establishing new and productive relationships with lay publics. Nevertheless, the promise of the current commitment to public sociology raises the question of why it has taken the profession so long to generate a significant measure of discussion of its possibilities and prospects. The most recent efforts on behalf of public sociology represent but the latest in a succession of demands for such a commitment extending back to 1939, when Robert S. Lynd castigated social scientists for neglecting the social value of social research in *Knowledge for What?* Twenty years later, C. Wright Mills returned to the theme in *The Sociological Imagination,* in which he famously defined the larger role of sociologists in terms of their success in transforming "private troubles" into public issues. In 1976, Alfred McClung Lee issued a similar call for publicly relevant sociological work in his own ASA presidential address. The recurrence of these earnest appeals for such a commitment reveals the durability of professional impediments, both institutional and cultural, to its fulfillment.

For at least the last half-century, academic intellectuals in the United States have maintained a greater separation of their research and communication from broader publics than tends to exist internationally. American sociology, in particular, entered the academic mainstream and began its ascent to a position of great influence over the identity of sociology as a profession worldwide amid the social, cultural, and political circumstances prevailing by the mid-twentieth century both within and outside of the United States; these circumstances exerted a powerful influence over the "Americanization" of sociology and served as powerful catalysts of a disciplinary identity that militated against public engagement. The postwar mystique of science and scientific work; the emergence of brilliant and assertive disciplinary leaders who would articulate a common vision for sociology as an emergent means to the evolution of a "science of society"[2]; the translation and professional assimilation of key works of classical European social theory and research; the traumatic experiences of totalitarianism abroad and McCarthyism at home, both of which appeared to obviate prospects for the forging of productive relationships with interested publics; and even the frequent hostility of lay observers to the social sciences' aspirations toward scientific legitimacy all combined to reinforce sociologists' tendency toward private communication and highly circumscribed, incrementalist research during the postwar period.

---

[2] Each of these scholars would serve as president of sociology's national professional organization between 1948 and 1963 and produce a substantial quantity of the discipline's programmatic statements.

This book maintains that the confluence of conditions that accompanied American sociology's ascent into the academic mainstream offer insight not only into this matter of the discipline's historical hesitancy in embracing public sociology, but also into the obstacles that subsequent generations of scholars have struggled to overcome. It therefore explores the postwar history of the discipline in terms of the postwar period's monumental impact upon sociology's professional evolution, and in terms of what this history reveals about the tension between social science professionalization and the social roles and responsibilities of academic intellectuals that persists to the present day.

Acknowledgments

S everal people have in one way or another contributed greatly to the conception and substance of this book. Mark C. Smith of the American Studies program at the University of Texas at Austin played a central role in the development of my intellectual and scholarly interests, and his guidance has been especially essential over the course of my investigations into the history of social science. In addition, his strong commitment to undergraduate teaching has encouraged me to aspire to the same. I owe a special debt of gratitude to Gideon Sjoberg of the University of Texas Department of Sociology; his enthusiasm for this project, his generous sharing of his knowledge and insights, and his willingness to engage in many late-night phone conversations about sociology—and ideas in general—were instrumental in making this project come to fruition. William H. Goetzmann has been a unique source of ideas and inspiration. His enthusiasm for my writing and his sense of humor have served as reminders that the study of history should be not only rigorous and critical but playful as well, and his broad intellectual curiosity is exemplary. I am especially grateful for the guidance of two former teachers at the University of California, Davis, the late Roland Marchand and the late Eugene Lunn, who first introduced me to the richness and life-affirming joy of historical study and teaching. All who were fortunate enough to have known and learned from them remember vividly their passion, creativity, and humanity.

Joli Jensen revealed to me the contemporary relevance of pragmatism, and the philosophical foundations of this study reflect her influence. In addition, her boundless intellectual ebullience and broadminded critical perspectives encouraged me to forge ahead at a critical juncture in my graduate years. David Crew, Toyin Falola, Kevin Gaines, Robert Abzug, Aline Helg, and Atietie Tonwe read all or parts of the manuscript and supplied valued feedback.

A special offering of thanks is extended to Michael Burawoy for his support and contributions of critical insights and suggestions. His belief in the worth of the manuscript, and his judicious reading and thoughtful assessments of it, have been of inestimable value and significance, and I am deeply grateful to him for these.

Micah Kleit, my editor at Temple University Press, offered tremendous encouragement and invaluable perspectives throughout the publication process, and I am very grateful for his generosity in sharing his time and expertise. Pat Cattani provided expert and comprehensive copyediting of the manuscript. I also thank my students at Austin Community College, St. Edward's University, and the University of Texas, whose receptivity to my teaching efforts continues to help make my academic commitments worthwhile. Karla, my wife, has tolerated my histrionics during both my epiphanies and frustrations and has helped me keep my sense of humor during much of the course of this effort. I thank her for these blessings and much more.

Finally, I wish to thank Ann Marie and William Paul Haney, both of whom have always expressed the utmost support and encouragement for my endeavors.

1

Introduction

A society is possible in the last analysis because the individuals in it carry around in their heads some sort of picture of that society.

—Louis Wirth

I t is something of an historical peculiarity that American sociology, an academic discipline charged with the objective of illuminating the substance of everyday life, has possessed such a comparatively low public profile among the social sciences. Sociologists' valuable investigations of and insights into the nature of work and the workplace, parenting and childhood, consumerism, sexuality and sexual identity, race and race relations, public health, economic inequality, criminality, substance abuse, gender roles, aging, athletic competition, and artistic expression have yet to receive the degree of public attention that is accorded the work of psychologists, economists, and political scientists. Moreover, the very awareness of sociological study and its contributions remains comparatively limited within American public life, so that the ordinary citizen's access to the formulation of social issues in sociological terms, and with the support of sociological findings and concepts, remains unnecessarily attenuated.

This book investigates the origins of this public marginalization of American sociology within the particular challenges its practitioners have faced since the end of World War II in defining who they are and what they do. Social scientists in general have of course struggled since their respective disciplines' professionalization amid the turmoil of late nineteenth-century industrialization and the bureaucratization of intellectual endeavor to determine their proper roles within the discourse on and challenges of modernity, and in each instance they have sought to forge symbols and standards to validate their professional competence. In the case of American sociology, especially since 1945, scholars have relied upon particular conceptions of science and scientific work to provide that professional legitimation. As revolutionary postwar developments in the natural and physical sciences fortified science with a mystique that had grown steadily since the Enlightenment, the Comtean ideal of a "science of society" came to exercise a dramatic influence over the social scientist's professional identity.

This study examines the forging of that scientific identity within American sociology in the years following the end of World War II, and through the professional struggles and public and private misunderstandings that this process engendered, it explores the scientific ideal's consequences and implications for sociology's role within broader public conversations about life and society in the United States. During that critical period of the late 1940s through the early 1960s, many of the most influential members of the profession not only discussed and debated their discipline's scientific status in terms of the potential meanings and benefits of scientific work for professional social research, but they also addressed the matter of how the particular scientific identity they envisioned would define sociology's relationship to the wider public sphere.[1] Ultimately, their pronouncements and prescriptions contributed profoundly to the diminution of academic scholars' perceived responsibility for addressing public issues publicly in the name of an informed citizenry and healthy democratic institutions.

---

[1] This issue of scholars' public responsibilities has become a salient one in the intellectual history of the United States, as historians, political scientists, journalists, philosophers, theologians, and others have attempted to clarify the proper roles of academic intellectuals and assess the prospects for their active engagement in the public discussion of public issues. Thomas Bender has written extensively on the relationship between academic intellectuals and the public sphere, particularly the institutionalization of twentieth-century intellectual life in universities, which he argues has exacerbated a rift between the two. See especially *Intellectuals and Public Life: Essays on the Social History of Academic Intellectuals in the United States* (Baltimore: Johns Hopkins University Press, 1993). The contributions of "public intellectuals" is also the theme of Richard H. Pells's survey of the "New York intellectuals," *The Liberal Mind in a Conservative Age: American Intellectuals in the 1940s and 1950s* (New York: Harper & Row, 1985). Michael Walzer, in *The Company of Critics: Social Criticism and Political Commitment in the Twentieth Century* (New York: Basic Books, 1988), explores the contributions of a diverse range of publicly engaged intellectuals, including Randolph Bourne, Martin Buber, Antonio Gramsci, George Orwell, Albert Camus, Simone de Beauvoir, Herbert Marcuse, and Michel Foucault. Russell Jacoby, in *The Last Intellectuals: American Culture in the Age of Academe* (New York: Noonday Press, 1987), laments the disappearance of the autonomous public intellectual with the expansion of universities and institutionalized financial rewards and forms of prestige. Richard Posner, in *Public Intellectuals: A Study of Decline* (Cambridge, MA: Harvard University Press, 2001), cites a diminution in the merit of academic intellectuals' contributions to public discourse.

By 1945 the quest to define American sociology's professional identity had reached a new level of significance and urgency, as the discipline had then entered a highly consequential stage in its professional and intellectual maturation. Sociological researchers' participation in the New Deal and in the development and implementation of war-related programs in particular had provided a powerful impetus for its professional legitimation within the academic mainstream. Beginning with the release of *Recent Social Trends in the United States* in 1933 and culminating in the publication of *The American Soldier* in 1949 (Stouffer and Suchman 1949), sociologists demonstrated their utility to government as the United States confronted the economic challenges and social dislocations of the Great Depression and the threat of fascism. The social sciences' participation in such New Deal programs as Social Security, the Works Progress Administration, and the Department of Agriculture, together with President Roosevelt's enthusiasm for policy-oriented social science research, lent them new professional credibility.[2] The war, in turn, demonstrated the applications of social science research to the challenges of war mobilization, the management of troop and civilian morale, and wartime bureaucratic organization.[3] With the war's end, the social sciences stood to benefit greatly from the windfall of economic recovery, new funding sources, the G.I. Bill and the expansion of American colleges and universities, and new defense-related service in the struggles of the nascent Cold War. This rapid expansion of opportunities and commitments thrust sociology, a young discipline lacking a sufficiently clear self-conception, into a position of increasing influence and responsibility. Its practitioners, anxious both to advance such achievements and to protect the discipline's successes from its detractors, articulated a vision of sociology as an emerging science that would both clarify and legitimate sociology's new role in American professional life.

A variety of postwar conditions influenced the character such a legitimation would assume, chief among which was the ascendance of scientific values themselves within American life. By the end of the war, the culmination of the American romance with science and scientific expertise most closely

---

[2]See Gene M. Lyons, *The Uneasy Partnership: Social Science and the Federal Government in the Twentieth Century* (New York: Russell Sage Foundation, 1969), 50–79; Mark C. Smith, *Social Science in the Crucible: The American Debate Over Objectivity and Purpose, 1918–1941* (Durham, NC: Duke University Press, 1994), 116–17.

[3]See Lyons, *The Uneasy Partnership*, 80–123; Christopher Simpson, *Science of Coercion: Communication Research and Psychological Warfare, 1945–1960* (New York: Oxford University Press, 1994), 22–30; Ellen Herman, *The Romance of American Psychology: Political Culture in the Age of Experts* (Berkeley: University of California Press, 1995), 17–123; Jean M. Converse, *Survey Research in the United States: Roots and Emergence, 1890–1960* (Berkeley: University of California Press, 1987), 162–236.

associated with 1950s American culture was well under way. The institutional growth the war had accelerated within government, the military, universities, and corporations combined with scientific revolutions in the realms of medicine, agriculture, consumer-product research and innovation, computer technology, and weapons-systems innovation to impose immense pressure upon the social sciences for methods and results consistent with the values of the age. The postwar sociological assertions of scientific status began apace amid the popular outlook expressed most emphatically six years earlier by the commercial exhibitors at the 1939 World's Fair, who proclaimed that scientific and technological innovation bequeathed by benevolent national corporations would usher in a new era of efficiency, social harmony, and personal freedom, and even more famously and succinctly that same year by the DuPont Corporation, when it initiated its promise of "Better Things for Better Living... Through Chemistry."[4] Such fervently evangelistic assertions of the promise of science, combined with the advent of atomic and then nuclear technology, established modern science's supreme position within American civilization and its status as an emulative ideal for a myriad of institutionalized professional pursuits. By the mid-1950s, the laboratory scientist in the white lab coat had become the ultimate possessor of the latest tools and techniques for the objective investigation and illumination of phenomena, as well as the purveyor of linear human progress.[5]

A substantial generational shift within American sociology after 1945 also helped to solidify a common professional identity. During the Depression, employment opportunities in academic sociology were meager, the production of Ph.D.'s declined substantially, and membership in the American Sociological Society declined by a third. Moreover, the United States' entry into the war, although a boon to social researchers in need of employment, nevertheless interrupted the training of sociology graduate students entirely.[6] Then, after 1945, the number of professionally trained sociologists grew

---

[4] Roland Marchand traces the origins of DuPont's elevation of the laboratory scientist to the status of "today's Prometheus" to the 1920s, in a campaign which General Electric, Western Electric, General Motors, and Ford quickly imitated. See pp. 194–96 of his *Creating the Corporate Soul: The Rise of Public Relations and Corporate Imagery in American Big Business* (Berkeley: University of California Press, 1998).

[5] At the same time, of course, this image carried connotations of a darker sort, as it was also modern science that had made human survival and human freedom open questions with the development of atomic weapons and the techniques of manipulation and control associated with totalitarianism, and these negative associations with science became liabilities for scientific sociology as well, as is indicated in a subsequent chapter.

[6] Nicholas C. Mullins, *Theories and Theory Groups in Contemporary American Sociology* (New York: Harper & Row, 1973), 49.

exponentially. Membership in the society increased two and one-half times between 1940 and 1949, and by the end of the 1950s, the number stood at 6,500, over six times the 1940 membership total.[7] American sociology's rapid postwar expansion thus reveals a generational lacuna between the prewar sociologists and the much larger body of scholars who rose to prominence with the expansion of American universities and social science funding.[8] The postwar generation of sociologists was therefore able to assert not only its theoretical and methodological orientations but also its professional identity over the various sociological visions of the leading prewar scholars. The sheer numbers of young sociologists joining the profession after the war helped produce a new orientation toward the perceived purpose of sociology itself.

Substantial institutional shifts played a key role in this vision's ascendance. By the war's end, the sociology departments at Columbia and Harvard had come to articulate the vision of sociology's identity and purpose that would dominate the discipline throughout the 1950s. These prestigious departments and their nationally recognized scholars began to exert an ever-greater influence over the meaning of sociological work, whereas the Chicago School of Sociology's dominance over the discipline's identity, which had peaked during the interwar years, began by the mid-1930s to recede.[9] Thus, the prominent theorists and methodologists at both Harvard and Columbia, through their respective institutions' prestige and the training of large numbers of graduate students, forged sociological "schools" that became principal sources not only of sociology's major theoretical and empirical orientations, as Nicholas Mullins has shown, but also of its very identity as a profession and, in turn, of its role within American life.[10] Leading scholars in these

---

[7] Martin Bulmer, "The Growth of Applied Sociology after 1945: The Prewar Establishment of the Postwar Infrastructure," in Terence C. Halliday and Morris Janowitz, eds., *Sociology and Its Publics: The Forms and Fates of Disciplinary Organization* (Chicago: University of Chicago Press, 1992), 319–20.

[8] Stephen Park Turner and Jonathan H. Turner, *The Impossible Science: An Institutional Analysis of American Sociology* (Newbury Park, CA: Sage, 1990), 86–87. Matilda White Riley finds that 61 percent of the members of the American Sociological Association in 1959 had received their Ph.D.s during the 1950s. See Riley, "Membership in the American Sociological Association, 1950–1959," *American Sociological Review* 25, 6 (December 1960): 914–26.

[9] Mullins, *Theories and Theory Groups,* 42–43, 45–46; Norbert Wiley describes Chicago's fall from preeminence during the early 1930s and, ultimately, with the founding of *The American Sociological Review* in 1936. See his "The Rise and Fall of Dominating Theories in American Sociology" in William E. Snizek, Ellsworth R. Fuhrman, and Michael K. Miller, eds., *Contemporary Issues in Theory and Research: A Metatheoretical Perspective* (Westport, CT: Greenwood Press, 1979), 57–63.

[10] Edward A. Tiryakian, "The Significance of Schools in the Development of Sociology," in William E. Snizek, Ellsworth R. Fuhrman, and Michael K. Miller, eds., *Contemporary Issues in Theory and Research* (Westport, CT: Greenwood Press, 1979). Tiryakian argues that a school solidifies around

departments not only played vital roles in normalizing functionalism and particular statistical methods of research throughout the discipline, but their programmatic statements in articles, presidential addresses, and books served to galvanize the profession behind a set of common principles, the most important of these being the idea that sociology was evolving into a true science.

Philanthropic foundations provided another institutional framework for this ascendant scientific identity, operating not only as "gatekeepers" by defining the contours of research but also by necessitating the defining of the nature of sociology itself. By the 1940s, the Rockefeller Foundation and the Ford Foundation in particular had forged personal relationships with particular sociological researchers in order to facilitate funding decisions in the absence of an established peer review process, and thus particular sociologists, such as Samuel Stouffer at Harvard and Robert Lazarsfeld at Columbia, became critical liaisons between the discipline and its private funding sources.[11] A relatively small number of scholars, especially those at large private universities like Harvard, Columbia, and Chicago, therefore bore a disproportionate influence upon sociology's postwar self-conception as they became the "brokers" of much of the research funding during this critical period of sociology's formal expansion.[12]

Indeed, historical studies of this critical period of sociology's postwar evolution have emphasized the primacy of Harvard and Columbia and have explored the ways in which their scholars' theoretical and methodological orientations and innovations became disciplinary norms.[13] Thus, a central theme of such studies has been that of sociology's theoretical development, in particular the ascendance of functionalist theory, from its roots in Durkheimian sociology and the anthropological work of Bronislaw Malinowski and Alfred Radcliffe-Brown to its dominant position in postwar sociological theory with

---

a charismatic leader, who formulates the school's ideas and attracts "interpreters" and "converts" who promote and pursue these ideas further, thereby elevating them to paradigm status. In his short history of the Columbia department, Seymour Martin Lipset observes that most leading sociology departments had by the mid-1950s hired Columbia students, which illustrates the process of diffusion of Columbia sociology throughout the sociological profession as a whole. See Lipset, "The Department of Sociology," in Lipset, ed., *A History of the Faculty of Political Science, Columbia University* (New York: Columbia University Press, 1955), 299.

[11] Turner and Turner, *The Impossible Science*, 94.

[12] Ibid., 94–96.

[13] A significant divergence from the consensus on the postwar Harvard-Columbia dominance of sociology is Gary Alan Fine, ed., *A Second Chicago School? The Development of a Postwar American Sociology* (Chicago: University of Chicago Press, 1995), which notes the impact of postwar symbolic interactionism on the profession, especially by the late 1950s.

the work of Talcott Parsons and Robert K. Merton.[14] Similarly, the critiques of functionalism's preeminence have then taken sociology's theoretical character as their starting point and, since the mid-1950s, they have presented alternative theoretical models that range from an emphasis on social conflict to the Chicago School theory of symbolic interactionism, both of which challenge functionalism's putatively static conception of social systems and the values that exist within them.[15]

Another central theme in the historiography of postwar sociology has been that of the discipline's methodological development. Historical studies of social science survey research and public opinion polling in particular trace the development of sampling methods, scale analysis, significance testing, pattern variables, and other quantitative research techniques.[16] Methodological innovators, the successful construction of new research institutes, and groundbreaking studies have provided the historical substance for such studies as they have explicated sociology's methodological evolution.

Consequently, both the historiography of and the challenges to mainstream postwar sociology have understood theory and methods to lie at the center of the discipline's identity. Postwar sociology tends to be studied according to its success in reconciling theory and empirical research, the scientific validity of its empirical methods, the degree to which the theories generated actually describe modern social conditions, and other questions rooted in

---

[14]Don Martindale, *The Nature and Types of Sociological Theory* (Boston: Houghton Mifflin, 1960); Mullins, *Theories and Theory Groups*; Robert Bierstedt, *American Sociological Theory: A Critical History* (New York: Academic Press, 1981).

[15]Conflict theory's challenge to functionalism's primacy began with the publication of Lewis Coser's *The Functions of Social Conflict* (New York: Free Press, 1956), and Ralf Dahrendorf's *Class and Class Conflict in an Industrial Society* (Stanford, CA: Stanford University Press, 1958). See Randall Collins, *Three Sociological Traditions* (New York: Oxford University Press, 1985) for a concise overview of the conflict tradition's evolution. Theoretical challenges continued with Dahrendorf's essay "Out of Utopia: Toward a Reorientation of Sociological Analysis," *American Journal of Sociology* 64, 2 (September 1958): 115–27, and George Homans's 1964 ASA presidential address, "Bringing Men Back In," *American Sociological Review* 29, 5 (December 1964): 809–18. By the end of the 1960s, attacks on functionalism had begun to focus on its professed value neutrality, culminating in Robert W. Friedrichs's *A Sociology of Sociology* (New York: Free Press, 1970), and especially Alvin W. Gouldner's *The Coming Crisis of Western Sociology* (New York: Basic Books, 1970). On symbolic interactionism, see J. David Brown, "Elaboration, Revision, Polemic, and Progress in the Second Chicago School," in Fine, ed., *A Second Chicago School?*

[16]John Madge, *The Origins of Scientific Sociology* (New York: Free Press, 1962) examines pivotal quantitative postwar research projects, including the landmark government studies of army morale and the Frankfurt School's study of fascism. Converse, in *Survey Research in the United States*, provides a thorough history of opinion polling and attitude surveys from their nineteenth-century origins to their modern commercial and academic institutionalization. A particularly critical overview of postwar quantitative research can be found in Turner and Turner, *The Impossible Science*, 114–18.

epistemology rather than in the flux and contingency of knowledge rooted in history.

This study does not attempt to test the validity of these aspects of modern sociology. It foregoes the analysis of postwar sociology's theoretical and methodological contours and instead examines the social and historical meaning of the professional ideology that accompanied them. Thus, it approaches sociology's postwar history in a manner similar to that employed in the major studies of prewar social science, which have analyzed the values social scientists have constructed or internalized to legitimate their work.[17] These studies emphasize the centrality of the roles social scientists wished to assume in modern American life, dissecting the language, institutional arrangements, and research techniques they constructed in order not only to reveal the meaning of particular social phenomena but, equally important, to demonstrate the social scientist's social utility and professional competence.

This study examines how postwar sociology's professional discourse forged a scientific identity that could legitimate sociology as a distinct realm of professional competence and cumulative knowledge. Like the first generation of American sociologists who, as Thomas Haskell argues, sought to preserve their genteel class and moral authority through the institutionalization of scientific social inquiry, postwar sociologists articulated a professional identity that would insure the discipline's institutional autonomy and growth.[18]

---

[17]Thomas Haskell, *The Emergence of Professional Social Science* (Chicago: University of Chicago Press, 1977) traces social science's identity to the creation of the American Social Science Association (ASSA) during the industrial expansion of the late nineteenth century. The "crisis of authority" brought about by the dynamics of mass society and the decline of traditional patterns of deference led to the creation of formal institutions to certify and professionalize the study of society. The ASSA was thus created in 1865 to protect the prestige of experts, or "professional men," and the integrity of social science itself. Mary Furner, in *Advocacy and Objectivity: A Crisis in the Professionalization of American Social Science, 1865–1905* (Lexington: University Press of Kentucky, 1977) sees social science's entrance into the American university as creating a conflict between social scientists' desire to reform society and their self-conception as objective, disinterested experts. Like Haskell, Furner understands their concern over the maintenance of social status to have determined their choice of the latter identity. Dorothy Ross, in *The Origins of American Social Science* (Cambridge: Cambridge University Press, 1991), argues that professional social scientists' belief in American exceptionalism, or an exaggerated sense of America's uniqueness, led them to cultivate an ahistorical vision of scientifically derived knowledge about society. Mark C. Smith, in *Social Science in the Crucible*, examines the 1920s and 1930s struggle between "objectivist" social scientists, who believed in the objective, technical application of scientifically derived knowledge to social problems, and "purposivist" scholars, who insisted upon a moral framework for social science and the social scientist's active engagement in defining important social problems and offering solutions.

[18]The Victorian motivations behind the first generation of American social scientists' desire to retain genteel authority is also analyzed by David A. Hollinger in "Inquiry and Uplift: Late Nineteenth-

However, unlike these nineteenth-century progenitors, American sociologists have over the last century concerned themselves not with preserving deference to traditional class authority but with creating a new pattern of deference based on institutionalized scientific technique in a culture of highly refined professional expertise. By the end of World War II, as an expanding middle class accelerated the bureaucratization of social status and professional prestige, sociologists recognized that their fortunes were tied to their success in asserting for themselves the social status of the scientist. They therefore articulated for themselves a common vision for their profession that emphasized its ever-closer approximation of the status of a science akin to modern physics or biology.[19] Thus, whereas the nineteenth-century social scientist perceived the scientific identity as the means to the preservation of traditional moral authority, the twentieth-century sociologist, particularly after the war, perceived it largely as the means to the attainment of the decidedly nontraditional status of the modern white-collar professional, embodied in the professionally trained scientist.

Of central significance to the scientific identity that sociology was forging for itself was the corollary that the discipline's scientific endeavors could only flourish if they took place in isolation from public discourse and insulated from publics. For many leading sociologists of the postwar period, performing truly scientific sociological work implied not merely the circumscribing of sociological communication to exclude laypersons, journalists, activists, and political officeholders but also the view that these groups constituted skeptical and potentially obstructionist adversaries of the discipline. This study thus follows Thomas Kuhn's conceptualization of modern science's evolution from a corpus of practical, common-sense knowledge with immediate applications to the world outside of the scientific community, to a rather hermetic activity practiced in greater isolation from that community.[20] Rather than attempting to determine whether postwar sociology, or social science in general, constituted a true science, this study explores the larger consequences of sociol-

---

Century American Academics and the Moral Efficacy of Scientific Practice," in Thomas Haskell, ed., *The Authority of Experts: Studies in History and Theory* (Bloomington: Indiana University Press, 1984).

[19] Florian Znaniecki, co-author of the pathbreaking 1914 empirical study, *The Polish Peasant in Europe and America,* even compared the discipline to oceanography, "from the point of view of methods and results," in an effort to demonstrate a more appropriate natural science parallel to social science research. See "The Proximate Future of Sociology: Controversies in Doctrine and Method," *American Journal of Sociology* 50, 6 (May 1945): 520.

[20] Thomas S. Kuhn, *The Structure of Scientific Revolutions* (Chicago: University of Chicago Press, 1962).

ogy's scientific ethos as this movement away from public discourse and engagement with publics became the discipline's dominant self-conception.

One particular consequence as the scientific identity solidified into the
prevailing postwar orientation of sociologists to their work and their society
was the emergence of a growing body of dissenters and detractors within sociology itself. By the mid-1950s, the struggle over sociology's vision and purpose, which until then had received its most compelling statement in Robert S.
Lynd's *Knowledge for What?* in 1939, intensified as dissenting sociologists such
as Pitirim Sorokin and C. Wright Mills attacked sociology's scientific aspirations and, especially in the case of Mills, pondered the broader consequences of
sociology's scientific self-conception for individual freedom and enlightenment in a mass society. These critics of the profession's ascendant identity
emphasized frequently and sometimes emphatically the importance of an
active engagement with nonsociologists over such crucial postwar issues as
racial inequality, the intractability of entrenched urban and rural poverty,
nuclear technology and the nuclear arms race, totalitarianism, consumerism,
commercial mass media, youth culture, and the resurgence of radical rightist
politics—issues that received astonishingly scant attention from mainstream
sociologists.[21]

As the debate over sociology's self-image intensified within the discipline, a
chorus of nonprofessional critics attacked it more publicly in newspapers,
opinion journals, mass-circulation magazines, and other publications accessible to lay readers. Sociology's detractors seized upon a fundamental weakness
in the sociological self-conception: as the profession distanced itself from
public discourse in the name of science, it diminished its ability to communicate its *raison d'être* to the very groups to which it appealed for financial
support and, equally important, intellectual and philosophical approval. As
Henry W. Riecken, a member of the Program Analysis Office of the National
Science Foundation, observed, social scientists seeking funding and professional
respectability addressed clients and elites who lacked a clear understanding of
the nature of social science work or even an remote awareness of methodological issues with which the social science disciplines concerned themselves.

---

[21]Patricia Wilner, in "The Main Drift of Sociology Between 1936 and 1982," *History of Sociology* 5, 2
(Spring 1985): 1–20, provides an inventory of articles published in the *American Sociological
Review* and reveals that the journal neglected profound events and developments throughout its
first 46 years of existence. Between 1936 and 1941, only 6.4 percent of the articles dealt directly
with the Depression; between 1947 and 1956, only 1 percent of the articles addressed the Cold War
and McCarthyism; and, perhaps most remarkably, between 1947 and 1975, only 2.6 percent of the
articles dealt with citizen activism and demands for social or political change. Hans Gerth,
meanwhile, observed that only two articles on Nazism appeared in *The American Journal of
Sociology* between 1933 and 1947. See his "The Relevance of History to the Sociological Ethos,"
Studies on the Left 1, 1 (Fall 1959): 7–13.

Thus, the debate within sociology over its scientific character, which depended heavily upon the clarification of methodological standards, made little sense to potential allies of the discipline. The goal of operationalizing sociological concepts, for example—the building of a scientific terminology usable in repeatable experiments—appeared to many lay critics as an attempt to disguise the triviality of research subjects and conclusions rather than as the foundation of a truly scientific mission. Thus, Riecken observed:

> Very few people outside of social science care about the "methodology" of social research. Not only are they not convinced by discussion of methods, but it usually makes their eyes glaze over. It may indeed be appropriate for the social sciences to resemble "natural" science in analytic methods, standards of proof, techniques of inquiry, and the like, but this does not materially abet their claim to valid knowledge in the eyes of legislators and the public at large.[22]

The skepticism the discipline faced from other professionals—lawyers, legislators, administrators, financiers, and others—compounded its dilemma, for these could accuse sociology of belaboring the obvious. "As men of affairs," Riecken noted, "members of the audience are likely to consider themselves well-informed about how society works and skillful at analyzing human behavior. Often, they are puzzled at the social scientist's interest in what, to them, is obvious."[23] By the early 1960s, these attitudes and perceptions had made their way into newspapers and magazines, as journalists and academics ridiculed sociology for its obscure terminology, its apparent obsession with trivia, and its tendency to belabor social questions that seemed amenable to common-sense interpretation. A science of society that, unlike the natural or physical sciences, existed more clearly *within* society, therefore faced legitimation obstacles unique unto itself.[24] The language postwar sociologists relied upon in constructing their profession's postwar identity both solidified that identity within the profession and also constituted a political liability in sociology's negotiations with the public sphere.

---

[22] Henry W. Riecken, "Underdogging," in Samuel Z. Klausner and Victor M. Lidz, eds., *The Nationalization of the Social Sciences* (Philadelphia: University of Pennsylvania Press, 1986), 222.

[23] Ibid., 221–22.

[24] Riecken observed, "When social science is not concerned with public issues, when it goes about its own business of adding to the store of basic knowledge about human behavior and society," critics indict it for its "frivolous expenditure of public funds on useless, pointless research" (Riecken, "Underdogging," 223).

This study, in focusing on that language, shares elements of the hermeneutical, "postmodern" critiques of social science initiated by Michel Foucault, in which discourses are understood to operate as mechanisms that confer power and authority and exclude competing claims to that authority. However, whereas postmodern critiques focus on how language constructs these modes of domination instead of capturing the essence of the phenomena it purports to understand, this study concurs with pragmatist and neopragmatist critiques of language that retain a sanguinity about language's liberating potential.[25] Richard Rorty in particular has shown that pragmatism offers a way out of postmodernism's philosophical dilemma of power *versus* indeterminacy. Rorty's pragmatism shares postmodernism's rejection of the Cartesian dualisms that came to dominate Western philosophy with Kant—especially the separation of the "thing-in-itself" from humanity's representation of it—but it rejects its capitulation to indeterminacy. Rorty agrees with the postmodernists that such dualisms lack any essential validity, but he transcends postmodernism's pessimism to argue that they have also become an obstacle to the real business of intellectual inquiry, that of identifying and attempting to solve social problems. Denying an *a priori* world "out there" and another world consisting of human concepts, a decision which he terms the "end of Philosophy," would liberate rather than defeat humanity's attempts to construct meaningful, usable philosophical concepts.[26] Following William James and John Dewey, Rorty agrees that an idea's truth and value, though possessing no distinct basis in some absolute "reality," nevertheless possesses validity if it works in practice. The questions pragmatism asks of existence, Rorty argues, pave the way for a "post-Philosophical culture" which would require a new form of commitment from intellectuals. Who would have to renounce the search for conclusions with universal validity and instead accept the provisionality and, indeed, negotiability, within a democratic discursive context, of their every scholarly conclusion.

The contingency of all knowledge about society presents the prospect for a social science that negotiates over which questions address important social questions and which answers can resolve them, in a process Rorty describes

[25] A succinct summary of pragmatism's origins and its modern incarnations is James T. Kloppenberg, "Pragmatism: An Old Name for Some New Ways of Thinking?" *The Journal of American History* 83, 1 (June 1996): 100–38. Robert Westbrook offers a useful critique of Rorty's antifoundationalism in *John Dewey and American Democracy* (Ithaca, NY: Cornell University Press, 1991), 539–42, as does John Patrick Diggins in *The Promise of Pragmatism: Modernism and the Crisis of Knowledge and Authority* (Chicago: University of Chicago Press, 1994), 453–56.

[26] Richard Rorty, *Philosophy and the Mirror of Nature* (Princeton, NJ: Princeton University Press, 1979).

as "simply casting about for a vocabulary that might help."[27] The post-philosophical approach would require that social scientists question both the validity and the efficacy of the scientific identity, because its reliance upon such dualisms as science and speculation, experts and laypersons, and professional discourse and democratic deliberation to demonstrate the social scientist's special realm of professional competence has inhibited not only the vitality of public debate about social questions but also the broader utility of sociological work itself.

Neopragmatists like Rorty have embraced Dewey's ideas not only as an antidote to poststructuralist nihilism but also because it offers a normative basis for valid understanding. The pragmatist denial of the idea of social science *qua* science has been criticized, as have the postmodern attacks, for having thrown all intellectual activity into a subjective realm that denies the validity of expert opinion and, more broadly, verifiable truths, so that all understanding becomes dangerously relativized. In fact, Dewey's appeal to rational consensus offers an alternative to this epistemological dead end. In *The Public and Its Problems,* published in 1927, Dewey declared that generating useful ideas, or ideas that work in practice, requires the public's active engagement in defining itself, its interests, and its relationship to the political institutions that represent it.[28] By refusing to dichotomize such concepts as "the public" and "the state," Dewey demands that the relationship between the two be continually renegotiated so that the former continually legitimates the latter and, in so doing, actually becomes a part of the latter. Dewey's argument responded to those of democratic realists, most notably Walter Lippmann, who had come to advocate a separation between the public sphere and the corps of experts who must manage its complex functioning. For Dewey, to exclude the public from the negotiation of usable knowledge was to deny the very existence of a public. "There can be no public," he insisted, "without full publicity in respect to all consequences which concern it."[29] Dewey's public therefore exists when open channels of communication, the essence of democratic practice, also exist, much as Jurgen Habermas's community of rational consensus exists with the removal of obstacles to an open community of inquiry. Habermas's concept of the "ideal speech situation," to

---

[27] Ibid., 63.

[28] Westbrook's *John Dewey and American Democracy,* Chapter 9, provides an account of how Dewey's public philosophy responded to the democratic realist rejection of participatory democracy during the 1920s.

[29] John Dewey, *The Public and Its Problems* (Athens, OH: Swallow Press, 1954), 167.

which all communication must aspire, requires the same Deweyan acceptance of democratic testing of claims to truth.[30]

American sociology, however, had by the end of World War II accepted Cartesian dualisms as necessary for defining social science as a scientific endeavor. The discipline embraced the goal of constructing a "science of society," which leading sociologists defined as a cumulative process of assembling small-scale and repeatable empirical studies to form a larger whole. Sociology's identity therefore depended upon an incrementalist and verificationist conception of science that adhered to the tradition of Western positivism.[31] The discipline thereby accepted and proulgated the presumption that a realm of scientific work and communication existed separately from the nonscientific sphere of public discourse, a presumption which often contained a concomitant perception of the public and its elected representatives as obstructionist naysayers, necessarily passive beneficiaries of sociological research, or some combination thereof.

The scientific identity helped shape some of the salient theoretical and ideological currents in postwar sociology as well. Theoretically, functionalism's primacy after the war de-emphasized the role of human agency in human affairs in favor of an emphasis on society as a system, in which individuals interacted according to prevailing norms and values rather than on the basis of independent, subjective interests and perceptions. On an ideological level, many American sociologists came to perceive the ideal of participatory democracy as untenable, adopting instead variations of the democratic realism that had emerged in American social science during the interwar years.[32] Buttressed by empirical studies revealing high levels of public apathy and the presence of a working-class authoritarianism, they constructed theories that conceived of American politics as a competition between institutionalized elites and of decision making as informed optimally by service intellectuals rather than by public input or citizen activism. Allied with studies of apathy were various non-Marxian concepts of alienation that became more prevalent in sociological analysis by the 1950s and often deepened sociologists'

---

[30]For connections between Habermas's theory of communicative action and pragmatism, see Kloppenberg, "Pragmatism: An Old Name for Some New Ways of Thinking?" 135–36; Diggins, *The Promise of Pragmatism*, 444–45; and Richard J. Bernstein, *The New Constellation: The Ethical-Political Horizons of Modernity/Postmodernity* (Cambridge, MA: MIT Press, 1992), 48.

[31]For a useful critique of positivist assumptions in postwar American sociology, see Christopher G. A. Bryant, *Positivism in Social Theory and Research* (London: Macmillan, 1985), chap. 5.

[32]Edward A. Purcell Jr. explores the ascendance of naturalistic conceptions of democracy, which abandoned traditional, participatory democratic ideals in favor of a scientifically derived, technocratic conception that placed far greater emphasis on expert-informed decision making. See Purcell, *The Crisis of Democratic Theory* (Lexington: University Press of Kentucky, 1973).

suspicion of participatory democracy and the potential of individuals to understand and defend their own interests. The scientific sociological identity, the functionalist paradigm, and sociological conceptions of a rarefied democracy thereby reinforced one another.

Professional sociology's postwar identity also fostered the active censure of nonsociologists who appropriated the language, research results, and theories of sociology for public consumption, as well as of academic sociologists who published texts for lay consumption. Popularization, already stigmatized by the late 1930s, was further discouraged as a growing network of university presses came to represent for social scientists an intellectual alternative to the larger commercial publishing houses and their production of mass-circulation paperback books. Journalists were thus discouraged from trespassing into professional sociology's turf, and sociologists' vigorous condemnations of their peers who addressed a broader, nonprofessional readership served to reinforce sociology's identification with scientific standards rather than with satisfying public curiosity about the nature and consequences of modernity.

American sociology's choice of moving away from the sphere of public discourse represented more than simply an institutional *fait accompli*, determined solely by funding sources' priorities, foundation directors' liberal-technocratic ideologies, or practical political considerations.[33] The sociologists who played vital roles in forging the discipline's postwar identity were as anxious to insulate their scholarly research from outside institutional pressures as they were to attract funding. As will be shown, leading scholars like Talcott Parsons were determined to legitimate sociology before the professional community and decision-making elites not only to guarantee the discipline's survival and funding but also sought to protect its autonomy against those who would interfere with its pursuit of scientific objectives. Similarly, Paul Lazarsfeld's interest in consumer preferences and public opinion led him to devise strategies for acquiring research funding that would not only satisfy clients but also pay for objective, disinterested studies that would add to the existing scientific understanding of society. The sociological commitment to scientific status transcended the practical need for public and private institutional support because this status was understood to depend upon sociology's independence

---

[33] On the ties between sociology and its public and private funding sources, see Loren Baritz, *Servants of Power: A History of the Use of Social Science in American Industry* (Middletown, CT: Wesleyan University Press, 1960); Donald Fisher, "American Philanthropy and Cultural Imperialism: The Reconstruction of a Conservative Ideology," in Robert F. Arnove, ed., *Philanthropy and Cultural Imperialism: The Foundations at Home and Abroad* (Boston: G.K. Hall, 1980); and Donald Fisher, "The Role of Philanthropic Foundations in the Reproduction and Production of Hegemony," *Sociology* 17, 2 (May 1983): 206–33.

from the priorities and values of nonscientists. Foundations, for example, sought practical results from sociological research, not a cumulative body of knowledge about society and social behavior. They were policy-oriented and problem-focused, yet leading postwar sociologists persisted in defining their discipline's scientific progress in terms of its dedication to basic research.

Postwar sociology's retreat from concrete problem solving and the broader public sphere into a realm of "true science" cannot therefore be explained simply through the analysis of a hegemonic discourse shaped by funding sources. Sociologists' programmatic statements regarding sociology's proper identity and their professional secession from public discourse reflected more than merely the pressures exerted by interested parties. Rather, as Robert Bannister observes of prewar sociology's quest for objective knowledge, the quest itself took place within a context of rapid social change and a loss of faith in the individual's capacity to reason and thereby to reach meaningful conclusions about society. Sociology, with its short history, lack of a distinct body of subject matter, and absence of any long-standing theoretical or methodological traditions, approached the challenge of securing professional status by appealing to the relatively new authority of science and scientific expertise in an age of political and cultural uncertainty. As Bannister observes of American sociologists during the interwar years, their "creed" reflected "a distrust of self and alienation from society":

> The result was an important difference between the "fact-gathering" of naive empiricism and a consensualist quest for "hard data," however much the two blurred in the sociologists' own discussions of the issue. In the first, the test of truth was the perception of the individual; in the second, it was the agreement of experts.... For the objectivists, as the sociologist Michael Schudsen has written of journalism in the same period, a "person's statements about the world can be trusted [only] if they are submitted to established rules and values deemed legitimate by a professional community." Implicit in this view was a distrust of individual judgment, whether exercised in the voting booth or in the market place.[34]

The postwar scientization of American sociology thus suggests a response to the condition Max Weber termed the "disenchantment of the world," in which "precisely the ultimate and most sublime values have retreated from public life," so that the social scientist must commit to rigorous, disinterested

---

[34]Robert C. Bannister, *Sociology and Scientism: The American Quest for Objectivity, 1890–1940* (Chapel Hill: University of North Carolina Press, 1987), 237.

inquiry and avoid the premodern patterns of thought and discourse characteristic of the public sphere.[35] Postwar sociology in turn retreated from a public life that it perceived to have remained in the prescientific realm of superstition, prejudice, and nonempirical, common-sense responses to social questions.[36] The advance of a university-based culture of intellectual expertise therefore offered a way out of competing claims to truth and promised to reveal the connections between social phenomena that modernity had obscured from public perception.[37] As early as the 1880s, Thomas Bender has observed,

> Valid social knowledge, formerly concretized in individual relationships or institutions, now seemed to call for definition in terms of processes and interconnections one step removed from direct human experience. The perceived need for such esoteric knowledge served, as it always has, as the basis for the creation of privileged intellectual authority.[38]

It was thus a particular kind of knowledge that postwar social science sought, one that reveals its practitioners' faith in a particular form of social progress. Attaining such progress required the application of professional expertise to the specific problems of modernity. These problems, the social scientist declared, demanded not the reassertion of traditional values or a resort to transformative, revolutionary action, but rather the application of specialized scientific technique.[39] The social scientist, as the authority on the processes of

---

[35] Max Weber, "Science as a Vocation," in Hans H. Gerth and C. Wright Mills, eds., *From Max Weber: Essays in Sociology* (New York: Oxford University Press, 1946), 155.

[36] It is in fact a common practice within contemporary sociology textbooks to contrast the results of persuasive sociological inquiry into the nature of particular social problems with widely accepted and putatively "common-sense" understandings of those problems to illustrate the degree to which the public's understanding of social reality is suffused with myth and distortion.

[37] Thomas Bender, "The Erosion of Public Culture: Cities, Discourses, and Professional Disciplines," in Bender, ed., *Intellect and Public Life: Essays on the Social History of Academic Intellectuals in the United States* (Baltimore: Johns Hopkins University Press, 1993), 44. For the European context of the struggle for the intellectual restoration of connections severed by industrialization, see Bruce Mazlish, *A New Science: The Breakdown of Connections and the Birth of Sociology* (University Park: Pennsylvania State University Press, 1989).

[38] Ibid., 45.

[39] Christopher Lasch, *The True and Only Heaven: Progress and Its Critics* (New York: W.W. Norton, 1991). In Chapter 4, "The Sociological Tradition and the Idea of Community," Lasch describes the sociological abandonment of preindustrial world views based upon shared sentiments and provincial, prescientific values in favor of a cosmopolitan, scientific outlook and an unqualified faith in incremental social progress achieved through impersonal scientific and technological innovation.

modernity, therefore enjoyed a privileged status as the source of society's understanding and, ultimately, control and direction of those processes.

By 1945, the expansion of universities and university culture, methodological innovation, broadening public and private institutional ties, and an explosion of professional communication through professional journals and associations increased the momentum of this separation of intellectual work and public life. During the 1950s, the high degree of disciplinary consensus in American sociology caused this separation to deepen, as sociologists promised society and themselves that they would create order out of the chaos of social experience through the autonomous cultivation of professional expertise.

Of course, sociology did not exist separately from public life at all after World War II. During the 1950s, foundation, government, and corporate largesse fostered the rapid growth of applied sociology, in which academic researchers provided clients with useful information in policy making, market research, labor relations, and other endeavors unrelated to the project of constructing a science of society. That the scientific ethos and sociology's increasing interaction with interests outside the formal confines of the university existed side-by-side made the discipline's assertion of autonomy from the public sphere a problematic one. Postwar sociology thus professed a particular kind of public commitment, one which engaged a growing web of institutionalized interests like its own, but which generally eschewed communication with the disparate audiences of the wider public sphere. As Lewis Coser has observed, the audience for sociological communication had changed between the Progressive Era and the end of World War II from one consisting of "lawyers, reformers, radicals, politicians" to a professional clientele of "social workers, mental health experts, religious leaders, educators, as well as administrators, public and private."[40]

The timing of American sociology's professional secession from public communication is compelling also for the fact that it coincided with a variety of other postwar changes that that actually improved the prospects for a lively public debate about sociological issues germane to postwar American life. Nonacademic opinion journals such as *Partisan Review, Politics, Dissent, Harper's, The Nation, The New Republic,* and *Commentary* offered nonacademic readers access to a growing national forum for the discussion of salient political, economic, social and cultural concerns, while expanded local channels of communication offered yet-another communicative forum, as well as the opportunity to create one's own organ of opinion. The nation's literacy rate increased markedly after the war, as did the percentage of Americans with at least some college background, thereby enlarging the potential popular readership for sociology. The attention the mass media gave sociology during

---

[40]Lewis A. Coser, *The Functions of Social Conflict,* 29.

the 1950s, moreover, stimulated and also reflected public interest in socio-logical questions, as the success of both scholarly and journalistic best sellers such as *The Lonely Crowd* and *The Status Seekers* attests. Such trends ran counter to the identity sociology was articulating for itself, revealing a public hunger for illumination of contemporary social life and social issues.

Responding to this need, many prominent sociologists did in fact acquire a significant popular readership after World War II. C. Wright Mills, Lewis Coser, Edward Shils, Seymour Martin Lipset, Daniel Bell, and others published reg-ularly in the opinion journals of the 1950s, addressing the intractability of the Cold War arms race, suburbanization, the affluence of the new middle class, the implications of postwar liberalism, and other issues of interest to nonprofes-sional readers of social science, much as current scholars like Amitai Etzioni, Robert Bellah, William Julius Wilson, Theda Skocpol, Herbert J. Gans, Charles Derber and Todd Gitlin address for such readerships issues such as imperiled community life, the class dynamics within racial communities, downclassing, corporate power and globalization, and the ownership and control of the mass media. Their examples demonstrate that the postwar sociological identity in-deed constituted a fragile consensus whose significant fissures finally engulfed it in the disciplinary crises and reassessments of the 1960s, in struggles that ultimately produced both greater leverage for public-spirited sociologists and a continued insistence on scientific, and therefore exclusive, patterns of identity.[41]

This study confines itself to the critical period of sociology's struggle for a coherent identity that lasted roughly from 1945 to 1963. The latter date marks the ascendance of competing sociological visions that challenged the scientific paradigm and its standards of objectivity, the dominance of quantitative re-search methods, the theoretical primacy of functionalism, and behaviorism's minimizing of the importance of social structure.[42] Moreover, as political

---

[41] On these 1960s struggles within sociology, see Alan Sica and Stephen Turner, eds., *The Disobedient Generation: Social Theorists in the Sixties* (Chicago: University of Chicago Press, 2006). A broader intellectual view of the period is provided in Howard Brick, *Age of Contradiction: American Thought and Culture in the 1960s* (Ithaca, NY: Cornell University Press, 2001). It was during the 1960s that quantitative sociology—a primary emblem of the scientific identity forged in the 1950s—experienced its greatest expansion under the influence of such prominent practitioners of statistical analysis as Otis Dudley Duncan and William H. Sewell. See, for example, Peter M. Blau and Duncan, *The American Occupational Structure* (New York: Wiley, 1967).

[42] Irving Horowitz's early 1960s critiques of sociology following the death of C. Wright Mills helped to stimulate the aggressive 1960s challenges to the prevailing postwar sociological assumptions, particularly with his publication of *Professing Sociology* in 1963, which contained "Sociology for Sale," his analysis of money-driven research priorities. In 1964, he edited *The New Sociology: Essays in Social Science and Social Theory in Honor of C. Wright Mills* (New York: Oxford University Press, 1964), an anthology of the writings of "radical sociologists."

consensus broke down in the United States with the escalating commitment in Vietnam and the disjuncture between the promise and the limitations of the Great Society, radical sociologists challenged their discipline's faith in the efficacy of liberal social policy and interest group–based political decision making, which they insisted were grounded not in empirical certitudes but in ideology. Another dissenting group demanding a more humanistic sociology emerged at roughly the same time and called for a less technical, bureaucratic approach to sociological discovery in favor of one that would address such moral concerns as humanity's need for expanded opportunities for freedom and creativity.[43] Meanwhile, as journalism adopted a more sociological orientation and even began appropriating sociological research in its reportage and analysis, dissenting sociologists called for a reciprocal turn in sociology, demanding a more participatory, journalistic sociology that would restore the investigator's personal engagement with ordinary people's experience and that understood the heart of the discipline's mission to include active confrontations with pressing social problems. American sociology's experience of the 1960s thus reflects its movement from consensus into fragmentation, in which the breakdown of the dominant theoretical and empirical paradigms of the 1950s dissolved disciplinary consensus into competing and often hostile theoretical, methodological, and political factions.

The study of sociology's professional and intellectual history involves inevitably the consideration of its contemporary roles and responsibilities, both of which have remained unnecessarily limited as a consequence of its exclusionary professional identity. Recent developments within the profession, however, suggest a sea change with regard to the public role of the discipline. Over the last few years, public-spirited scholars have produced fruitful statements and formulations of the promise of public sociology that have fostered a growing awareness of its achievements and future potential. They have dedicated entire conferences and symposia to the issue, and in 2004, American Sociological Association president Michael Burawoy made public sociology the theme of the association's annual meeting.[44] The ASA

---

[43] Robert A. Nisbet, considered an exemplar of the humanistic outlook, articulated his perspective in the mid-1960s in *The Sociological Tradition* (New York: Basic Books, 1966). In it, he advocated a more community-centered, morally committed sociology akin to those of Tönnies, Weber, Durkheim, and Simmel. Other statements included Peter Berger and Thomas Luckmann's *Invitation to Sociology: A Humanist Perspective* (New York: Anchor Books, 1963) and Alfred McClung Lee's ASA presidential address, "Sociology for Whom?" *American Sociological Review* 41, 6 (December 1976): 925–36.

[44] See Michael Burawoy, "For Public Sociology," address to the American Sociological Association, San Francisco, August 15, 2004; *American Sociological Review* 70 (February 2005): 4–28; Burawoy, William Gamson, Charlotte Ryan, Stephen Pfohl, Diane Vaughan, Charles Derber, and Juliet Schor,

subsequently added a Task Force on Institutionalization of Public Sociology, and, since 2002, it has published a quarterly journal, *Contexts*, to disseminate, in readily accessible forms, analyses of contemporary social issues of discernible public interest and of immediate national and often global importance, such as Social Security reform, poverty policy, the balancing of work and home life, English-only initiatives, the exportation of American popular culture, incarceration and economic inequality, Islamic radicalism, corporate conduct, social activism, and the politicization of scientific research. Significantly, the journal promptly won the American Association of Publishers' prestigious award for the best journal in the social sciences for 2002, an auspicious beginning for this effort to build bridges between sociological research and a general audience. Sociologists have also promoted the ideal of public sociology, as well as particular projects, on Web sites and blogs.

As the debate over the sociology's public role evolves and expands, the historical investigation of the scientific professional ideology that still informs the discipline's identity sheds light on both the avenues taken in the past and those that remain available. The historian's task is to explore the origins, contours, and meaning of ideas that have given form to particular identities and have provided the legitimation for particular roles and courses of action over time. In the case of American sociology, C.P. Snow's warning regarding the gulf between scientific and humanistic cultures illuminates the contemporary challenge of surmounting obstacles to American society's improved self-understanding.

"Public Sociologies: A Symposium from Boston College," *Social Problems* 51, 1 (February 2004): 103–30. An extended discussion of Burawoy's conception of "public sociologies" is available in *Social Forces* 82, 4 (June 2004): 103–30. An international discussion of Burawoy's presidential address is published in the *British Journal of Sociology* 56, 3 (September 2005): 333–524. Craig Calhoun, the president of the Social Science Research Council, advocates a broader public role for the social sciences writ large in "Toward a More Public Social Science" (president's report, Social Science Research Council, 2004), 13–17; available at http://www.ssrc.org/programs/publications_editors/publications/PresReport/SSRC_PresReport.pdf (accessed 25 September 2005).

2

The Postwar Campaign
for Scientific Legitimacy

rguments supporting sociology's possession of its own realm of
scientific integrity have existed as long as the very idea of sociology
itself. When Auguste Comte formulated his "positive sociology"
in the 1830s, he envisioned a social and intellectual order in which the
bearers of a new "science of society"—the most complex of all the sciences—
would bring order and harmony to the human community. Emile Durkheim, similarly, sought to make sociology a true science by establishing
consistent and reliable definitions of social facts, the substance of the discipline. To obtain such facts and thereby to advance sociology's progress
toward "intellectual maturity," he asserted in 1885, the sociologist would
have to "assume the state of mind of physicists, chemists, and physiolo-
gists" in order to overcome the temptation to provide facile or dogmatic
explanations of social phenomena that, unlike those of the natural world,
seemed "immediately clear to the mind."[1]

Moreover, the empirical methods that provided much of the foundation for the twentieth-century social sciences' claims to scientific status
were themselves not new, having emerged before the Civil War. The implementation of the U.S. Census in 1790 and the private publication of

---

[1] Emile Durkheim, *The Rules of Sociological Method*, trans. W. D. Halls (New York: Free Press,
1982), 37–38.

social and economic statistics during the first half of the nineteenth century provide early examples of the growing awareness of the value of social data. Reform organizations such as the American Statistical Association predicated the success of their efforts to uplift society upon their access to meaningful statistics on social and moral conditions. In Europe, Adolphe Quetelet, a Belgian mathematician and astronomer, had by the end of the 1820s formalized procedures for gathering, analyzing, and presenting census figures, and in 1834 he participated in the creation of the Statistical Society of London. The growing interest in the social changes that accompanied industrialization in Britain spawned several organizations like the Statistical Society that devoted their energies to the observation of social conditions and the gathering and analysis of social data for such purposes as factory inspection and regulation. By the end of the nineteenth century, Friedrich Engels, Charles Booth, and Beatrice and Sidney Webb had produced monumental contributions to the "scientific" study of social conditions in an industrial society.[2]

What therefore became most significant for the professionalization of the social sciences in the United States was neither the novelty of the concept of social science as science nor the introduction of statistical analysis, but rather the central role these aspects of social research played in the formation of a professional social science identity. As the social science disciplines professionalized themselves following the Civil War with the building of national associations, standards of membership, and scholarly journals, assertions of the scientific ideal represented an urgent response to the rapid industrial and urban transformation of American society and the crisis of order and authority this transformation had wrought, which knowledge professionals hoped the application of their expertise—consisting of, in Dorothy Ross' words—the "quantitative and technocratic manipulation of nature," could ameliorate in the name of social harmony, order, and control.[3] Social science would embrace not only these broader social objectives but also legitimate social scientists as the possessors of the specialized knowledge and scientific techniques essential to social health. As Thomas Haskell reveals, American social science's postbellum institutionalization began not merely in the spirit of social reform but also "as a measure to preserve professional unity and reestablish the authority of all professional men" in the face of an

---

[2] Mark C. Smith, *Social Science in the Crucible: The American Debate Over Objectivity and Purpose, 1918–1941* (Durham, NC: Duke University Press, 1994), 16; Nathan Glazer, "The Rise of Social Research in Europe," in Daniel Lerner, ed., *The Human Meaning of the Social Sciences* (New York: Meridian Books, 1959).

[3] Dorothy Ross, *The Origins of American Social Science* (Cambridge: Cambridge University Press, 1991), xiii.

emergent mass society that was quickly eroding traditional patterns of deference to authority.[4] Therefore, the role of the American Social Science Association (ASSA), founded in 1865 under the leadership of Frank Sanborn, would be to "defend authority, to erect institutional barriers against the corrosive consequences of unlimited competition in ideas and moral values in an interdependent society."[5]

As Haskell observes, the status of the leaders of the movement to professionalize social science was of great significance. As "men of the gentry and professional class," they feared the loss of authority as cultural and intellectual leaders as the emerging industrial society eliminated traditional patterns of authority.[6] Like Alexis de Tocqueville, these individuals perceived that the emergence of a mass society of relative equality in the United States would allow mass opinion and uncontrolled competition to eliminate tradition-sanctioned distinctions between people. Doctors and lawyers, for example, had begun to experience "a painful breakdown of the institutional mechanisms for conferring authority upon new recruits," as new professional schools began to offer degrees that competed with the older sanctioners of competence, such as bar associations and medical societies, and state medical associations began removing barriers such as certification and licensing to entrance to the professions.[7] In the face of these threats to professional status, the ASSA emerged as its protector, conferring authority upon the social scientist—indeed upon all professionals, as every profession was to be represented in the organization—according to its own criteria.

As a movement to establish this professional authority within universities began by the 1880s to supersede the rather inchoate professional objectives of the ASSA, the social sciences began to evolve, in Mary O. Furner's words, into "a professional subculture," apart from existing callings such as theology, medicine, and law, and thereby came to develop their own specialized concepts, language, and networks of exclusive communication within specialized journals and associations.[8] While the university-based social scientists shared the existing anxiety over the amelioration of social disorder in the industrial age, they sought new bases for prestige than had the genteel

---

[4]Thomas Haskell, *The Emergence of Professional Social Science: The American Social Science Association and the Nineteenth Century Crisis of Authority* (Chicago: University of Illinois Press, 1977), 64, 89.

[5]Ibid., 63.

[6]Ibid., 64.

[7]Ibid., 79–80.

[8]Mary O. Furner, *Advocacy and Objectivity: A Crisis in the Professionalization of American Social Science, 1865–1905* (Lexington: University Press of Kentucky, 1975), 5.

professionals of the ASSA: their status would depend not upon traditional patterns of deference to those possessive of class privilege and high levels of social and cultural capital but upon their success in demonstrating their competence as knowledge specialists. In contrast to their immediate predecessors, who had conceived of broadly intelligible social science activity that could readily transmit research on practical subjects to laypersons in "everyday language," these academic social scientists emphasized the separateness of their methods and modes of communication, and they retreated from the open advocacy of the amateurs they supplanted in the name of distinguishing themselves from ideologically motivated social reformers. "With professionalization," Furner observes, "objectivity grew more important as a scientific ideal and also as a practical necessity. After a good deal of experimentation with other positions, professional social scientists based their claims to competence in social analysis on the authority conferred by scientific methods and attitudes."[9]

The new discipline of sociology possessed little that would stand in the way of this scientific identification. Ross, in her study of the American social sciences' early history, notes that sociology, unlike economics, lacked a coherent, paradigmatic intellectual framework that would give the discipline a clear identity. Economics' intellectual roots lay in classical theory, whereas those of sociology resided in a myriad of practical activities that included social work, Protestant social activism, and progressive reformism, as well as in the philosophical rejection of social Darwinism. Moreover, early sociologists proved willing to risk embracing a diffusive, open-ended definition of their discipline's subject matter in order to overcome the deficiencies they found in other disciplines. As Bruce Mazlish observes, early sociologists countered the reductionism they found in classical economics, with its distillation of human activity into its supposed essences of self-interest and the cash nexus, as they sought to "rediscover the multi-stranded web" that was society through the application of science.[10] An expansive subject matter would allow the fledgling discipline to construct a holistic intellectual framework that would require scientific rigor, not simplistic homilies, moral appeals, or monocausal explanations, for its mastery. In addition, the foundations that funded such sociological research sought to legitimate their programs by characterizing their objectives in terms of scientific progress, and thus as early as the 1920s, Beardsley Ruml, the director of the Laura Spelman Rockefeller Memorial, characterized his institution's ultimate goal as that of becoming

---

[9] Ibid., 322–23.

[10] Bruce Mazlish, *A New Science: The Breakdown of Connections and the Birth of Sociology* (University Park: The Pennsylvania State University Press, 1989), 137–38.

like the natural sciences.[11] As these foundations then came to serve as what Lewis Coser has called the "gatekeepers" of social research, they encouraged the scientific identity with their objective of social problem solving through the application of scientific social research.

The succeeding decades saw this scientific momentum increase. During the interwar years, as the historical tradition of science building within social research combined with philanthropy's increasing funding contributions and new partnerships with government, influential and scholars such as Luther Bernard, Howard Odum, F. Stuart Chapin, and William F. Ogburn asserted an objective, scientific philosophy in support of the statistical methods they championed.[12] Then, during World War II, sociologists strengthened the legitimation of their discipline through wartime service in government, lending their expertise to such wartime agencies as the Office of War Information, the Office of Price Administration, the War Production Board, the Budget Bureau's Division of Statistical Standards, and the Office of Strategic Services.[13]

With the massive demobilization following the war's conclusion, however, American social scientists faced the challenge of providing national decision makers with a compelling rationale for sustained government support of social science research during peacetime. The natural sciences, meanwhile, enjoyed vastly increased government funding due to the new exigencies of the Cold War, which demonstrated more readily than social science the utility of applied scientific research. New government agencies such as the Office of Naval Research and the Atomic Energy Commission operated or

[11] Donald Fisher, "American Philanthropy and the Social Sciences: The Reproduction of a Conservative Ideology," in Robert F. Arnove, ed., *Philanthropy and Cultural Imperialism: The Foundations at Home and Abroad* (Boston: G. K. Hall, 1980), 234–35; Smith, *Social Science in the Crucible*, 26.

[12] On the scientific sociological ideas of Ogburn, Bernard, and Chapin, see Bannister, *Sociology and Scientism*. On Ogburn's objective orientation to his participation in the Hoover administration's Committee on Social Trends, which produced the research for *Recent Social Trends*, see Smith, *Social Science in the Crucible*, 72–75. Characteristic statements include Ogburn's "The Folkways of a Scientific Sociology," *Publications of the American Sociological Society* 24 (1929): 1–11, and Carl C. Taylor, "The Social Survey and the Science of Sociology," *American Journal of Sociology* 25, 6 (May 1920): 731–56. John L. Gillin, in "The Development of Sociology in the United States" (presidential address) *Publications of the American Sociological Society* 21 (1927), asserted the importance of a scientific sociology to combat reformist elements that had made sociology "a mess of undigested, unsystematized, and unscrutinized generalities, which made a popular appeal to sophomores and attendants at chautauquas" (24).

[13] See Gene M. Lyons, *The Uneasy Partnership: Social Science and the Federal Government in the Twentieth Century* (New York: Russell Sage Foundation, 1969); Ellen Herman, *The Romance of American Psychology: Political Culture in the Age of Experts* (Berkeley: University of California Press, 1995).

provided funding to national laboratories and university science programs, and the budgets of the Department of Defense and the National Aeronautics and Space Administration became, until the mid-1960s, a seemingly inexhaustible source of funds for scientists.[14] Scientists themselves had also proven adept at making the case for greater funding through increased political involvement and institution building.[15] The natural sciences therefore presented postwar social science with an inspiring example of the possibilities within reach of those disciplines that could successfully demonstrate their usefulness to both public and private institutions.

In this environment of uncertainty and new potential immediately following the war, the prewar generation of sociologists resumed their assertions of their discipline's scientific status. George Lundberg and Read Bain, both longtime advocates of the separation of science from values, again defended the scientific ideal by insisting, much as the Progressive Era generation had, that sociology needed to clarify its social function in order to ensure its social legitimation. Significantly, both perceived the need for providing such a clarification within the public sphere. In nearly identical arguments, they cautioned that the American public had developed a problematic perception of sociologists. Lundberg asserted in 1945 that the term "social scientist" called forth for many the image not only of "honest social workers and scientists," but also of "a tremendous conglomeration of uplifters, do-gooders, evangelists, and crackpots."[16] Two years later, Bain cautioned that as the popular media had afforded sociology a new presence in the popular consciousness, the public had thereby received "a very unclear idea of what scientific sociology is," often confusing sociology with "socialism, social work, social reform, birth control and divorce, the coddling of criminals, or whatever they may favor or condemn." Perhaps even worse, physical and natural scientists seemed to look down on the sociologist and regard him or her as "a pseudo-scientist at best and as a crackpot radical at worst."[17]

Bain concluded that in the face of public skepticism, sociology's professional legitimation depended on its success in establishing and solidifying the source of its identity in its methodology. "It is *method* rather than subject

---

[14]Bruce L. R. Smith, *American Science Policy Since World War II* (Washington, DC: Brookings Institution, 1990), 48–49. Lyons, ibid., 266.

[15]Gideon Sjoberg and Ted R. Vaughan, "The Bureaucratization of Sociology: Its Impact on Theory and Research," in Ted R. Vaughan, Gideon Sjoberg, and Larry T. Reynolds, eds., *A Critique of Contemporary American Sociology* (Dix Hills, NY: General Hall, 1993), 62.

[16]George Lundberg, "The Proximate Future of American Sociology: The Growth of Scientific Method," *American Journal of Sociology* 50, 6 (May 1945): 510.

[17]Read Bain, "Sociology as a Natural Science, *American Journal of Sociology* 53, 1 (July 1947): 9.

matter that differentiates the scientific from other modes of knowledge," he insisted, and indeed, sociology would succeed in asserting its own method because, like the natural and physical sciences, its subject matter was amenable to "predictive and descriptive generalizations that go beyond common sense in accuracy and usefulness."[18] Bain dismissed critics who contended that social scientists could never achieve scientific detachment from their subject by virtue of their membership in the very society they studied, or due to its sheer complexity, and he asserted boldly that, in fact, "common sense experience testifies to the relative orderliness and predictability of much social behavior."[19] Ironically, when it came to sociological inquiry itself, common sense, with its connotations of intuitive thinking and reliance upon time-honored beliefs, would then have to yield to the scientific method. "Natural science," Bain concluded, "is a stronger staff to lean upon than the broken reed of common sense or the shattered straw of hysterical appeals to hypothetical gods."[20] By following the example of natural science, social science would transcend the superstitions and illogic of the public sphere.

Lundberg offered a similar prescription for sociology's legitimation by contrasting sociology's "time-tested methods of scientific advance" to what he perceived to be a vogue of social science popularization and activism. Many sociologists had succumbed to the passions of wartime commitments, Lundberg insisted, and had sacrificed their scientific integrity by engaging the public sphere in unacceptable ways. In an assessment suggestive of the classic indictments of mass society, he alleged:

> The favorite argument of the exponents of this view is that, unless scientists leave their laboratories to join the appropriate "Independent Committees" of sculptors, movie stars, columnists, astronomers, and politicians, science itself will be put out of business. What they actually mean is that people like themselves, engaged in ordinary pressure-group activity while masquerading as scholars or scientists, would be exposed for what they are.[21]

---

[18] Ibid., 9, 13.

[19] Ibid., 13.

[20] Ibid., 16.

[21] George A. Lundberg, "Sociology Versus Dialectical Immaterialism," *American Journal of Sociology* 53, 2 (September 1947): 85. Seymour Martin Lipset and Neil Smelser would echo this particular perspective in an essay assessing the scientific trajectory of modern sociology, comparing its impact to the secularizing effects of scientific discoveries by Darwin, Einstein, and others. Each of these discoveries diminished the influence of "the representatives of older moral and intellectual traditions." Scientific sociology, similarly, thwarted the moralists, or "the people who incline

Truly scientific sociology, Lundberg concluded, transcended the temporal realms of politics and ideology and accepted the objective standards of natural science, such as the strict methodological standards of quantification and scientific detachment from practical affairs. Anything else, Lundberg implied repeatedly, placed one in the same camp as Marxists and other "evangelical" thinkers. Scientific status required that the sociologist separate scholarly activity from his or her role as a citizen; in fact, upon reporting "the consequences and the costs of alternate possible courses of action," sociologists' scientific function came to an end: "What they further may wish to do in the fields of citizenship, propaganda, family life, or sport," he declared, "is not dictated by any scientific canons."[22]

Although the arguments of Bain and Lundberg in the years immediately following the war echoed prewar assertions of sociology's scientific status, it was not the outspoken proponents of scientific sociology, communicating in rather polemical fashion to professional peers, who made the largest impact on sociology's scientific self-identification after World War II. Defenses of sociology as an emergent science became less common in the profession's major journals after the war, and the postwar generation's leading departments refused to engage in such debates. The Chicago, Harvard, and Columbia scholars, in fact, honored a tacit agreement to avoid them, which led in turn to their institutionalized suppression.[23] Instead, leading sociologists' pronouncements on the subject began to suggest that sociology's scientific character was an established fact, and that all that remained was for lawmakers, foundation committees, and other elites to accept it as such and to promise their political and financial support. Increasingly, therefore, arguments for sociology-as-science began to be directed outward, toward a lay audience of sociologically untrained but vitally important opinion and decision makers.

---

toward political sensitivity and broad moral concerns," who "experience a sense of loss as sociological thought strives—with varying degrees of success—for a closer approximation to standards of scientific adequacy." See Seymour Martin Lipset and Neil Smelser, eds., *Sociology: The Progress of a Decade* (Englewood Cliffs, NJ: Prentice-Hall, 1961), 8.

[22]Lundberg, "Proximate Future," 513. Lundberg elaborated upon this position in a 1947 essay entitled *Can Science Save Us?* 2nd ed. (New York: Longmans, Green, 1961). He concluded that science was the only hope for civilization and that "the best hope for man in his present social predicament lies in a type of social science strictly comparable to the other natural sciences" (147). Christopher G. A. Bryant notes the strong Comtean strain in Lundberg's scientism in his *Positivism in Social Theory and Research* (London: Macmillan, 1985), 147–48. Like Comte, Lundberg perceived the modern social malaise to be a product of theological and metaphysical thinking, which scientific values and methods would supplant.

[23]Stephen Park Turner and Jonathan H. Turner, *The Impossible Science: An Institutional Analysis of American Sociology* (Newbury Park, CA: Sage, 1990), 109–10.

Equally important, these new formulators of the scientific ideal replaced the polemical arguments proffered by Bain and Lundberg with more temperate and sophisticated ones. In particular, they did not focus upon the alleged similarities between the social and natural sciences or assert the predictability of their respective subject matter, and neither did they stress the difference between their work and moral commitment or policy advocacy, as had generations of earlier proponents of an objective or scientific sociology. Instead, they emphasized sociology's steady process of maturation, its importance to society, and its meticulous refinement of its theories and methods—the fundamentals of science. Finally, and crucially, they understood the impediments to such scientific pursuits to be no longer simply the pretenders to professional legitimacy—the amateur social researchers and lay reformers of the half century previous—but, potentially, anyone and everyone outside the social sciences who doubted their integrity or remained suspicious of their motives and objectives. In the view of these scholars, professional and institutional autonomy became the essential prerequisite for a scientific sociology's maturation.

These campaigners' legitimation of the social sciences as scientific became more urgent after World War II, as sociologists faced considerable resistance or even outright hostility from a variety of quarters in their attempts to secure the burgeoning institutional funding to which the natural sciences enjoyed access. Many adversaries in the natural sciences, fearing competition for research funding, declared publicly that the social sciences possessed neither the necessary corpus of generally accepted theoretical and methodological achievements to be considered truly scientific nor the longstanding social or institutional sanctions for the pursuit of anything approaching scientific work. Others questioned whether social scientists could attain the necessary objectivity toward their research given the controversial nature of social issues. In the face of such skepticism, foundation administrators confronted the matters of whether social science could produce the kind of clearly demonstrable and practical achievements of the natural and physical sciences and of whether their funds would be better spent on the tried-and-true fields of "hard science."

American sociology encountered these particular sources of opposition in stark configuration when in early 1945 the social sciences began to seek entry into what would ultimately become the National Science Foundation (NSF). After World War I, the National Academy of Sciences had excluded sociology from its membership precisely because its leadership believed that sociology was not a science.[24] The debate over social science's inclusion in a new

---

[24]Henry W. Riecken, "Underdogging: The Early Career of the Social Sciences in the NSF," in Samuel Z. Klausner and Victor M. Lidz, eds., *The Nationalization of the Social Sciences* (Philadelphia: University of Pennsylvania Press, 1986), 209.

national foundation for the support of scientific research similarly reflected each of the oft-heard objections of politicians, scientists, and spokesmen for professional societies as diverse as the American Medical Association and the American Chemical Society.[25] To dispel the prejudices and defensiveness of these interests and to win them over to social science, a special committee of the Social Science Research Council (SSRC) in late 1946 asked Talcott Parsons to prepare a paper in support of the inclusion of social science within the NSF. His task required the creation of a compelling statement of the practical value and scientific integrity of the social sciences that would convince influential natural scientists, in particular, to support the inclusion of the social sciences in the NSF on an equal footing with the natural sciences. If they could be persuaded, the social sciences would have a better chance of enjoying adequate funding and patent protection through the foundation's governing board, which natural scientists would inevitably dominate.[26]

Parsons had begun to participate in the debate over the social sciences' inclusion in the spring of 1946 and had subsequently provided an account of the deliberations in the *American Sociological Review*.[27] In the summer of 1947, he published an article in the *Political Science Quarterly* that presented a glimpse of the principles and appeals he would offer on behalf of the social sciences in the paper he had been asked to write for the SSRC. In this article, he attempted to provide convincing arguments for the importance of the social sciences to the future harmony and development of the United States. "The urgency of the practical needs for rational control of social processes is so great and so obvious as scarcely to need discussion," he declared. In fact, he continued, this control had assumed greater importance by mid-century relative to the older human concern for the mastery of the natural world. "Most scientists, as well as other intelligent citizens," he insisted, "would agree that the great problems of our time are not those of the control of nature but of the stability and adequacy of the social order."[28] Parsons then suggested that it was time for the social sciences to receive the kind of support and respect accorded the natural sciences by virtue of the former's greater importance in the confrontation of profound social challenges. Though the latter had provided solutions to many of humanity's immediate material concerns,

---

[25] Ibid., 211.

[26] Samuel Z. Klausner, "The Bid to Nationalize American Social Science," in Klausner and Lidz, eds., *The Nationalization of the Social Sciences*, 15.

[27] Talcott Parsons, "The Science Legislation and the Role of the Social Sciences," *American Sociological Review* 11, 6 (December 1946): 653–66.

[28] Talcott Parsons, "Science Legislation and the Social Sciences," *Political Science Quarterly* 62, 2 (June 1947): 241.

American society lacked a framework through which to address its fundamental social concerns. The NSF, he noted, must help cultivate that framework by its full inclusion of the social sciences in its mandate.

Parsons then ascended to a more theoretical plane to reinforce the importance of the social sciences to the progress of civilization. "All science," he declared, "is a fundamental unity. It simply is not possible to draw sharp clearcut lines between the natural and the social sciences." Although he acknowledged that the social sciences possessed their own unique research methods and areas of inquiry, he also insisted that their autonomy was "relative." Because human beings were living organisms, the psychological, biological, and sociological explanations of their behavior were interdependent, so that "it is not in the interest of science to attempt to set up watertight compartments between these different aspects."[29] By arguing for the unity of all science, Parsons hoped to refute social science's detractors who maintained that social science was not a true science. If they could be convinced that social science was part of a larger corpus of endeavor called "science," they might accept social science on an equal footing with the other sciences in the NSF. In particular, Parsons hoped to avoid the creation of a separate division for the social sciences within the NSF, a decision that would serve to ghettoize, and thereby stigmatize, the social sciences. A separate classification for them would brand them as inferior to the natural sciences. Parsons therefore sought to minimize the distinctions between them so that natural scientists would resist their inclination to deny the social sciences their rightful place within the foundation.

Nevertheless, Parsons still faced the perennial counterargument of those who perceived social science research as political activism disguised by a veneer of scientific respectability. Conservatives in Congress who participated in the NSF debate and opposed social science's inclusion in the organization characterized social science as politically motivated and as possessing hidden ideological agendas. Senator Thomas C. Hart, Republican from Connecticut, asserted that "no agreement has been reached with reference to what social science really means. It may include philosophy, anthropology, all the racial questions, all kinds of economics, including political economics, literature, perhaps religion, and various kinds of ideology."[30] Another Republican, Senator Robert A. Taft of Ohio, offered an even bolder assertion of social science's supposed political underpinnings when he ventured that its research "means a political board. It means someone may want all the housing legislation . . . and all the other matters which come in under the all-inclusive

---

[29]Ibid., 242–43.

[30]U.S. Senate, *The Congressional Record*, vol. 92, pt. 7 (July 3, 1946): 8230.

term of 'social sciences.'... Social sciences are politics."[31] Senator H. Alexander Smith, Republican of New Jersey, reiterated Senator Taft's conception of social research as fundamentally different from the disinterested, "pure" scientific research he deemed appropriate to the NSF's purpose: "We are trying to subsidize pure science, the discovery of truth," he proclaimed. "This has nothing to do with the theory of life, it has nothing to do with history, it has nothing to do with law, it has nothing to do with sociology. I am all for those sciences, and I call them sciences, but they do not belong in this bill."[32]

Other congressional critics associated social science with socialism or meddlesome "social engineering." In a declaration anticipatory of the anticommunist hysteria that would emerge only a year later, and which foreshadowed the corrosive ideological associations against which sociologists would labor throughout the following decade, Ohio Republican congressman Clarence Brown announced:

The average American just does not want some expert running around prying into his life and his personal affairs and deciding for him how he should live, and if the impression becomes prevalent in Congress that this legislation is to establish some sort of an organization in which there would be a lot of short-haired women and long-haired men messing into everybody's personal affairs and lives, inquiring whether they love their wives or do not love them and so forth, you are not going to get your legislation.[33]

Brown's images of a culturally radical social science bent on weakening or overthrowing traditional American institutions and values reflected widespread suspicions of the social science professions as merely covers for a constellation of ideologies that would, with governmental financial support in this case, provide the impetus for radical reformist agendas.

These vociferous objections to the inclusion of the social sciences in the NSF, all of which were rooted in the denial of the social sciences' scientific integrity, required that social scientists marshal an argument on behalf of their scientific status. Their rejoinder would require assertions of social science's capacity for value neutrality, commitment to basic research, and disinterested application of specialized technique understood to exist in the

---

[31] Ibid., 8145.

[32] Ibid., 8231.

[33] Quoted by J. Merton England in *A Patron for Pure Science: The National Science Foundation's Formative Years, 1945–57* (Washington, DC: National Science Foundation, 1982), 50.

other sciences. Most important, social scientists would have to demonstrate the practical utility of their fields in promoting social progress.

Parsons therefore characterized social science as scientific by virtue of its application of value-neutral technical expertise, and he promised the same quality of results the other sciences had delivered. In an argument consistent with those of earlier generations of social scientists, he asserted that the very fact of modernity, with its complexity and resultant confusion, required the expertise of the social scientist. "We live in a technological age," he reminded his readers, and such an age required "scientifically trained personnel" for its perpetuance. Modern industry and modern medicine required such expertise for the solution of problems "which can be solved only by the techniques of scientific research with the personnel and equipment necessary for their use." Social problems were no different, yet social scientists confronted unwarranted opposition to their claims to expertise in studying them. Parsons then made the critical argument for the scientific—that is, technical—competence of social scientists and for their autonomous professional authority over pressing social issues:

> It is a widespread idea that the common man is his own social scientist; that any ordinary intelligent person is qualified to understand the operation of social processes. Even so far as the current situation is concerned, this is very far from the truth. To a very substantial and rapidly increasing degree, the actual functioning of our social order is dependent on a social technology which is in fact applied social science. Technically trained persons are playing a larger and larger part, for instance, in the administrative process, in the adjustment of industrial relations, in the field of communications, in the control functions of the economy as through the central banking system, in the operation of foreign trade, and various such fields. Great as it is, the difference between the two aspects is one of degree—not of kind.[34]

Parsons thereby made the argument for a social science that would serve as the source of scientific material to public and private decision makers, and conspicuous by its absence was any acknowledgment that this endeavor could involve socially useful exchanges with larger publics. By applying their expertise to the management of the nation's "social technology," social scientists would find their proper role in the maintenance of healthy social

---

[34]Ibid., 243–44.

institutions on behalf of, rather than through the enlistment of the active participation of, the American public.[35]

Having substantiated social science's importance to society, Parsons then made a case for aggressive financial support of social science research on empirical grounds. "Until recently," he observed, "social science has been essentially a library discipline." New circumstances and values, however, had drawn social scientists into field research, which required a new commitment to the creation of the necessary infrastructure for social research. Parsons concluded, "The fact that the social sciences have reached this stage of development has created a need for facilities which have the same function as laboratory equipment in the natural sciences." He then suggested rather boldly that social research would require facilities "even more elaborate and expensive though of a different character from those used in the other fields."[36] Social science research had not only been overlooked in the past, but it also required an even larger commitment of resources than the natural sciences had recently come to enjoy.

Parsons's three basic arguments—that social science was part of the larger whole that constituted modern science, that it offered insights into social problems that were beyond the common-sense perspectives of laypersons, and that it could offer its "social technology" to government to solve social problems—became the focus of his paper on behalf of the SSRC's bid to have social science included in the NSF. Parsons began the paper with broad declarations regarding the nature of science itself. Once again, he defined scientific activity as distinct from the realm of common-sense thinking, as instead "the pursuit of empirical knowledge by technical means, that is, means which cannot be commanded by the ordinary 'layman,' the common-sense actor, but only by the person specially equipped by training and experience to solve problems in the particular area of inquiry."[37] This time, however, he added that such

---

[35] In his account of the SSRC deliberations over the content of Parsons's paper on behalf of the social sciences' inclusion in the NSF, Klausner quotes Parsons as having agreed with a committee of the council "that we should not attempt to reach the general reading public but should aim at producing a document which would be a source of information and reference for highly intelligent persons wanting a relatively nontechnical statement of the status of social science research and the kinds of problems with which it can deal . . . in addition it was thought that the report should be addressed to an important degree to social scientists themselves" (*The Nationalization of the Social Sciences,* 26). Thus, Parsons and key participants in the deliberations envisioned neither the institutional goals nor the hoped-for research findings of postwar social science being made substantially available for public consumption.

[36] Parsons, "Science Legislation and the Social Sciences," 244–45.

[37] Talcott Parsons, "Social Science: A Basic National Resource," in Klausner and Lidz, eds., *The Nationalization of the Social Sciences,* 46. This is an edited version of the 1948 draft Parsons submitted to the SSRC.

specially trained individuals required autonomy sufficient to insulate them from the pressures of everyday prejudice and opposition borne of ignorance. Science depended upon internal discipline and agreed-upon standards of conduct, and nonscientists must be denied the opportunity to corrupt them. "People carrying out these peculiar activities," Parsons warned, "must, if they are to be effective, be adequately protected from undue interference on the part of others who fail to understand or approve of what they are doing."[38] In making this argument, Parsons hoped to convince the future leaders of the NSF that social science, as an endeavor that possessed its own unique realm of competence, required the same respect and independence that the natural sciences demanded.

Parsons then formulated an argument that would become critical to the postwar scientific identity of social science: the social sciences, like the natural sciences, possessed the potential to amass meaningful conclusions about society in a cumulative fashion, so that each new discovery added to an ever-more meaningful whole. It was this promise that Parsons believed the social sciences' detractors continued to frustrate by their opposition to institutional support. If social research required institutionalization and funding comparable to or even greater than that accorded the natural sciences, the lack of these essential resources would explain the social sciences' "relative backwardness" and their failure to produce results of the same significance as those produced by the other sciences. Parsons concluded:

> On the one hand, it is the practical man who most urgently needs the results of scientific advance. On the other, he is often found to be either indifferent or positively hostile to them when they become available. It is only through the institutionalization of scientific and technological progress as an integral part of the social structure itself that this fundamental difficulty can be overcome on a large scale. This institutionalization is well advanced for the fields of applied natural science, but by no means complete. It has proceeded considerably less far in the social field, a fact which primarily explains the greater degree of indifference and positive resistance in that area.[39]

Thus, Parsons argued, the institutionalization of the social sciences would allow the process of cumulative development to proceed, and as a consequence, the social sciences' detractors would have to acknowledge their scientific integrity. Specific empirical investigations into social questions would

---

[38] Ibid., 45.

[39] Ibid., 53.

lead to meaningful theories, and these theories would, in turn, legitimate the social sciences by fostering a growing body of commonly accepted theoretical knowledge. "The many partial theoretical achievements" resulting from empirical work, Parsons insisted, "may be brought to converge into wider and wider complexes, tending toward organized generality of theoretical knowledge and not simply a disconnected multiplicity of particular theories."[40] With the removal of the interference of laypeople, the social sciences, like the natural sciences, would improve society by offering an ever-increasing store of useful knowledge. Empirical investigation would fuel theory building, and new theories would initiate further empirical inquiry.

Before turning to the specific activities and wartime accomplishments of the social sciences, Parsons made a final argument in support of their scientific integrity by assuring his readers—particularly, of course, those within the larger scientific community—that the social sciences themselves constituted a community. In spite of inevitable theoretical and methodological differences and divergences, the social sciences enjoyed a consensus as to their basic operating principles. "The war among competing 'schools' of overall interpretation of social life has greatly subsided, if not entirely disappeared," he proclaimed. "It has to a large extent been replaced by a substantive interest in particular ranges of problems, empirical and theoretical, approached within a relatively agreed upon general framework."[41] Parsons thereby provided a vision of the social sciences that anticipated Daniel Bell's "end of ideology." In the absence of a Marxian social science that emphasized class conflict or a Durkheimian vision of nascent social solidarity, Parsons could make the case for the existence of a generally agreed-upon sociological perspective that eschewed divisive ideological orientations. The system builders of the nineteenth century and the monumental theorists of the early twentieth had not found significant representatives within postwar social science; instead, knowledge workers in these disciplines, striving together toward a common purpose, contributed to a greater whole that enjoyed broad professional acceptance.

Parsons's paper for the SSRC was never published. The first draft received criticism from a host of SSRC participants in the NSF debate, as well as others who were close to the proceedings. Sixty-nine individuals reviewed the manuscript, and responses to it came from a broad range of disciplines. Economists, political scientists, mathematicians, psychologists, and others presented

---

[40] Ibid., 61.

[41] Ibid., 66. A year earlier, in a paper presented before the annual meeting of the American Sociological Society in New York, Parsons had asserted that the variety of theories produced within sociology would "converge into a single developmental structure." See Parsons, "The Position of Sociological Theory," *American Sociological Review* 13, 2 (April 1948): 157.

their misgivings, and many expressed concern that Parsons had produced a document that was too stylistically complex and too technical for nonscientists to understand, thereby undermining the desired consensus that would provide the necessary support for the social sciences.[42] Parsons, of course, had set out above all to convince natural scientists of the value of the social sciences on the assumption that "the subtle resistances by people who accept the basic values of science seems to be the more formidable obstacle" than the intransigence of laypersons and their "'doctrinal' opposition to the general attitudes of science."[43] By focusing on natural scientists' objections, Parsons neglected to pay sufficient attention to the interest of the educated public, including lawmakers, in the debate. Parsons promised a revision, but the criticism he had received ultimately drove him from the debate, and the revision never materialized. In 1950, Congress finally passed legislation creating the NSF, and the social sciences were left out of the new institution.[44]

Despite this disappointing result, Parsons's conception of science, as expressed in the *Political Science Quarterly* article and the SSRC paper, would become critical to the postwar sociologist's self-conception. Parsons's belief in the fundamental unity of science and the social sciences' place within it, his assertion of the social sciences' ability to replace common-sense thinking with the mastery and application of scientific technique, his faith in the cumulative nature of social science research achievements, and his claim that consensus had replaced fundamental ideological and value differences within the social sciences became powerful influences upon the self-conceptions of many of the prominent sociologists of the postwar period. Finally, his insistence on a social science enterprise possessive of both professional autonomy and specialized technique legitimated a sociological perspective that excluded nonsociologists from sociological discourse. A given inquiry could be declared to be scientific only if it employed particular techniques. These techniques were, of course, unique to scientific work, and they remained generally inaccessible and incomprehensible to nonsociologists. Thus, the sociologist's primary responsibility was to the cumulative scientific enterprise of sociology, not to active participation and communication in the public sphere.

---

[42] Klausner, "The Bid to Nationalize American Social Science," 22–26.

[43] Parsons, "Social Science: A Basic National Resource," 53.

[44] Klausner, "The Bid to Nationalize American Social Science," 27–32. In an article on the Senate debate in the May 1947 issue of *The Scientific Monthly*, Lundberg suggested that the vote "should perhaps not be taken as reflecting any considered hostility or opposition on the part of the Senate, but simply as a reflection of the common feeling that the social and the physical sciences have nothing in common and that at best the social sciences are a propagandist, reformist, evangelical sort of cult," and he blamed social scientists themselves for failing to protect themselves from such perceptions (399).

Parsons's scientific sociological vision, with its emphasis on the central role of social science research in the maintenance of order in contemporary civilization and its insistence on the social sciences' institutionalization to protect them from popular misunderstandings and prejudices, also found expression throughout the academic career of Robert K. Merton. As a student of Parsons at Harvard during the 1930s, Merton had become deeply interested in the sociology of science, a subject that had received little scholarly attention from sociologists. In his dissertation, in particular, which examined the institutionalization of science in seventeenth-century England, he argued that the maturation of scientific work had depended upon the separation of scientific activity from everyday concerns, immediately practical applications, and demands for "useful" results.[45] Science thus achieved its legitimation as an endeavor of intrinsic value, and its independence from outside pressures remained essential to scientific progress.

Merton's conception of science reflected larger intellectual currents in the interwar years involving the struggle of reason and freedom against totalitarianism, in which the latter threatened to destroy the free and open inquiry science depended upon for its very existence. As David Hollinger has shown, this conception coalesced during the struggles of the 1930s and 1940s, as Merton and other intellectuals defended scientific inquiry against fascism with the assertion that the former could only exist in a democratic political culture that necessarily respected intellectual autonomy and the free exchange of ideas.[46] In Merton's formulation in particular, Hollinger relates, science existed as a "cultural system, a pattern of attitudes actually embodied in a community," so that it required independence from "external influences and demands."[47]

---

[45] See Robert K. Merton, *Science, Technology and Society in Seventeenth Century England* (New York: Howard Fertig, 1970). This work was first published in *Osiris: Studies on the History and Philosophy of Science, and on the History of Learning and Culture* 4, 2 (1938).

[46] David A. Hollinger, "The Defense of Democracy and Robert K. Merton's Formulation of the Scientific Ethos," in *Science, Jews, and Secular Culture: Studies in Mid-Twentieth Century American Intellectual History* (Princeton, NJ: Princeton University Press, 1996), 81.

[47] Hollinger, "The Defense of Democracy," 85. Hollinger draws particularly upon Merton's 1938 article on the ways in which totalitarianism inhibited and manipulated scientific activity, "Science and the Social Order," *Philosophy of Science* 5, 3 (July 1938): 321–34. In "A Note on Science and Democracy," *Journal of Legal and Political Sociology* 1 (1942): 115–26, Merton continued this analysis with a focus on the necessary relationship between democratic institutions and scientific advancement. As Hollinger summarizes ("The Defense of Democracy," 84–85), Merton characterized the "scientific ethos" as possessing four basic characteristics: "universalism," or the application of findings across cultural, national, and racial lines; "disinterestedness," or the scientist's renunciation of all personal interests in his scientific pursuits; "communism," or the "common ownership" of scientific discoveries; and "organized skepticism," or a commitment to "insistent questioning."

Nazism and Soviet totalitarianism, however, displayed the same profound hostility towards open scientific inquiry that they exhibited toward divergent political ideas and cultural expression. These systems required the subordination of science and its essential conditions of free inquiry to overarching systems of domination. Science, as Hollinger explains, existed therefore as a cultural state rather than merely a set of conditions for empirical discovery, and World War II represented its struggle for survival, a *Kulturkämpf* between democratic, scientific exploration and the forces of its subjugation.[48] Thus the culture of Nazism represented the antithesis of Merton's scientific culture and posed a mortal threat to science itself. Parsons, too, perceived this dichotomy when he wrote in 1938 that, as a "cultural movement," Nazism "is deeply hostile, in particular to the spirit of science and the great academic tradition, and more generally to the whole great cultural and institutional tradition of which these are an integral part."[49]

As Merton's professional reputation grew after the war, and as he became the foremost American sociologist of science, his conception of the autonomy that scientific work required for viability affirmed Parsons's concern for protecting social science from ideological attack and lay skepticism. Just as European fascism had threatened to deny science its independence, the ideological pressures of interested groups and of totalizing systems within the heritage of Western social thought—systems also present within sociology itself—threatened sociology. As a scientific community, professional sociology would therefore require a culture that committed its scholars to the modest purpose of constructing theories and researches of limited scope, scholarship that would provide the building blocks of scientific progress rather than broad, philosophical conclusions or satisfying answers to larger social questions. In this way, sociology, as a nascent and therefore especially vulnerable science, would achieve a salutary—indeed, necessary—distance from the nonscientific features of life and thought in the larger culture.

This Mertonian conception of science suggested that scientific development and the advancement of civilization were inextricably connected, if not synonymous, and therefore the obstacles they faced constituted obstacles to critical rationality itself. Just as Nazi pseudoscience threatened to destroy the very essence of scientific inquiry, all "prescientific" understandings stood as obstacles to reason. Bernard Barber, a Columbia sociologist and student of both Merton and Parsons at Harvard during the late 1940s, affirmed this

---

[48] Hollinger, "Science as a Weapon in *Kulturkämpfe* in the United States During and After World War II," in *Science, Jews, and Secular Culture*, 157.

[49] Talcott Parsons, "Nazis Destroy Learning, Challenge Religion," in Uta Gerhardt, ed., *Talcott Parsons on National Socialism* (New York: Aldine de Gruyter, 1993), 83.

perspective when he wrote in *Science and the Social Order* that the development of social science in the West constituted evidence of "how much better it is than what is available in other societies," be they "civilized" or "primitive."[50] Not only should this superiority provide the basis for optimism in spite of the great distance social science would have to travel in order to "catch up" with the natural sciences, Barber insisted, but it must fortify the social scientist against ignorant naysayers like Congressman Brown and their fears of "short-haired women and long-haired men" invading Americans' privacy. The social scientist, as the possessor of the means for the rational understanding of human affairs, stood against the forces of the outside world, in which lay observers languished in the same prescientific realm inhabited by unenlightened politicians.[51] Indeed, Barber observed of Brown that "the vigor and color of his phrasing suggests that his attitudes are a little more like those of the general public than of the academic groups we have heard from."[52] The basic incompatibility between scientific and prescientific understanding was clear, and sociology required a means for both separating and protecting itself from the pressures and prejudices of the latter.

Merton's sociological vision provided a prescription for disciplinary conduct that would secure for it sufficient autonomy from the public sphere, but also intellectual independence from sociology's own classical tradition. In his *Social Theory and Social Structure*, a 1949 volume of many of his key articles since the mid-1930s, including his studies of the role of science in modern society, Merton supplied an introductory statement that called for a new theoretical focus for sociology, one that affirmed the scientific-sociological viewpoint of Parsons. Modern sociology, Merton observed, had supplanted the ideas of its predecessors by virtue of its cumulative nature; unlike Comte and Herbert Spencer, modern sociologists eschewed system building, which, as an inevitably speculative endeavor, rendered the various resulting systems incompatible with one another. Such sociological systems, he explained, "are

---

[50] Bernard Barber, *Science and the Social Order* (New York: Free Press, 1952), 316–17.

[51] Merton would, like Parsons, supply an argument for winning over a skeptical professional audience in his essay in *The Student-Physician*, a collection of Bureau of Social Research studies of the training of medical students. In it, he noted physicians' history of opposition to sociology's participation in medical issues, which he believed were based usually upon their inattentiveness to the social contexts of health care and their suspicion that sociologists favored socialized medicine. To these doubters, he responded that medicine, a "polygamist" science, became "wedded to as many sciences as prove their worth." Sociology, its most recent suitor, would be welcomed as well, "as the burden of work plainly becomes more than can be managed by the present members of the household." Robert K. Merton, "Some Preliminaries to a Sociology of Medical Education," in Robert K. Merton, George G. Reader, and Patricia L. Kendall, eds., *The Student-Physician* (Cambridge, MA: Harvard University Press, 1957), 32.

[52] Ibid., 323.

typically laid out as alternative and competing conceptions rather than consolidated and extended into a cumulative product."[53] Consequently, these systems failed to yield an ever-expanding understanding of society, leaving sociology with nothing but a congeries of disparate ideas. Merton therefore concluded that "little of what these early forerunners wrote remains pertinent to sociology today."[54] As Stephen P. Turner has contended, this act of separating the discipline's present progress from its historical roots represented the critical post-1945 assertion of independence from putatively nonscientific models of theory and research. In the course of this act of "mutilation," he argues, Parsons and Merton "disdained and ridiculed those of their contemporaries and near predecessors who considered the appreciation of the insights of past scholars to be valuable in itself, or valuable as a mirror of the present, as a means of recognizing the nature of the inferences that we today tacitly make."[55]

Merton's conception of the theoretical orientation appropriate to modern, cumulative sociology, in contrast to the separate theoretical systems of the past, involved "logically interconnected conceptions which are limited and modest in scope, rather than all-embracing and grandiose."[56] To these conceptions Merton gave the name "theories of the middle range." Such theories would accommodate empirical research because their very existence would depend upon empirical verification. Whereas the grand sociological systems had prevented or frustrated attempts at such verification, a middle-range theory's survival would depend upon it; otherwise, it could not be added to the existing accumulation of "valid" theories upon which modern sociology was built. The cumulative project thus established and theoretically validated provided the basis for investigating specific social problems scientifically. Whereas the system builder worked in isolation from the rest of the intellectual community, the middle-range theorizer contributed to a meaningful scientific whole. "We cannot expect any individual to create an archi-

---

[53] Robert K. Merton, *Social Theory and Social Structure* (Glencoe, IL: Free Press, 1949), 5. Merton would later explain the nineteenth-century sociologists' devotion to system building as itself part of the mission of establishing sociology's legitimacy. Because each sociologist was defining the new discipline for himself or herself, each sought to construct a fairly comprehensive system by which he or she could claim to have discovered the essence of sociology. See Robert K. Merton's "Social Conflict Over Styles of Sociological Work," in Larry T. and Janice M. Reynolds, eds., *The Sociology of Sociology* (New York: David McKay, 1970), 176.

[54] Ibid., 5.

[55] Stephen P. Turner, "The Maturity of Social Theory," in *The Dialogical Turn: New Roles for Sociology in the Postdisciplinary Age*, ed. Charles Camic and Hans Joas (Lanham, MD: Rowman & Littlefield, 2004), 154–56.

[56] Merton, *Social Theory and Social Structure*, 5.

tectonic system of theory providing a manual for the solution of problems, social and sociological," Merton insisted. "Science, even sociological science, isn't that simple."[57] Middle-range theorizing, then, would offer more realistic prospects for problem solving by grounding sociology in empirical methods that would seek specific, testable answers to finite questions.

Merton's middle-range proposal therefore placed him firmly within the sociological framework Parsons sought to construct. It would later appear, especially after C. Wright Mills's indictment of Parsonian "grand theory," that Merton's sociology conflicted with that of Parsons. Indeed, Merton had insisted that theoretical system building "has the same large challenge and the same small promise as those all-encompassing philosophical systems which have fallen into deserved disuse."[58] There appeared to be no room for broad, general theorizing in Merton's pragmatic sociological universe. However, Merton went on to explain that such theorizing would in fact serve to consolidate the smaller, middle-range theories. Accommodating Parsons's recent theoretical statements, he declared that theory "must advance on these interconnected planes: through special theories adequate to limited ranges of social data, and through the evolution of a more general conceptual scheme adequate to *consolidate* groups of special theories."[59] Thus, just as middle-range theories would yield cumulative empirical results, sociological theorizing itself was cumulative because the limited, specific theories Merton endorsed would fill in the gaps in the broader, more general theories.[60]

Parsons agreed with Merton's recommendation, affirming its utility in his presidential address before the 1949 meeting of the American Sociological Society. First, he lamented the fact that, thus far, sociology's empirical research had failed to yield meaningful cumulative results. He then asserted that "general theory," or broad, encompassing conceptualizations, would make sociology a cumulative science. General theory served the function of gathering

---

[57] Ibid., 7.

[58] Ibid., 5–6.

[59] Ibid., 10.

[60] In the 1968 edition of *Social Theory and Social Structure,* Merton would discourage broad, abstract theorizing in favor of middle-range work until sociology had reached the level of "maturity" that scientific disciplines such as physics and chemistry had already attained. In so doing, Bernard Phillips asserts, Merton constructed a "self-fulfilling prophesy," a concept that, ironically, he himself had coined. "By defining sociology as immature and unable to employ 'abstractions of high order,'" Phillips argues, "we create that very situation of immaturity." In his view, the Mertonian emphasis on limited abstract theorizing has contributed to a "Babel" of sociological subdisciplines that cannot communicate with one another with a shared language of sufficient abstraction to unite them all. See Phillips's *Beyond Sociology's Tower of Babel: Reconstructing the Scientific Method* (New York: Aldine de Gruyter, 2001), 8.

together what he called the "islands" of more specific theoretical work to form a meaningful whole. Although he acknowledged that only physics had succeeded in attaining such a state—in which the majority of "actual hypotheses of empirical research are directly derived from a general system of theory"—he nevertheless expressed optimism that, for sociology, "*any* real step in that direction is an advance."[61] In particular, he hoped that Harvard's new interdisciplinary Department of Social Relations would further the cause by "considerably increasing the number of theoretically known islands in the sea of social phenomena and thereby narrowing the stretches of uncharted water between them."[62] Sociologists, working together with anthropologists and psychologists, might gradually close gaps in humanity's understanding of itself, thereby paving the way to a more holistic theory of society.[63] Like Merton, then, Parsons expressed his faith in an incremental, cumulative path to enlightenment.

Parsons also reiterated his firm belief that sociology was a scientific enterprise that, in turn, depended upon empirical methods for its scientific legitimation. "If it is to be *scientific* theory" that sociologists articulated, he insisted, "it must be tied in, in the closest possible manner, with the techniques of empirical research by which alone we can come to know whether our theoretical ideas are 'really so' or just speculations of peculiar if not disordered minds."[64] Scientific method, in the form of repeatable investigations with independently verifiable results, would guide sociology to an ever-increasing understanding of society through valid theoretical conclusions, and it would at the same time nullify the kinds of unfavorable perceptions of sociologists that Bain and Lundberg had identified among nonsociologists. Sociology-as-science would offer both enlightenment and professional legitimation.

By wedding empiricism to theory, Merton and Parsons sought an accommodation that avoided the extreme, on the one hand, of abstract theorizing

---

[61] Talcott Parsons, "The Prospects of Sociological Theory," *American Sociological Review* 15, 1 (February 1950): 7.

[62] Ibid., 8. Parsons's hopes for the Department of Social Relations had also shaped his arguments in his SSRC paper, in which he excluded political science and economics from his assessment of the social sciences, ostensibly because they lacked adequate scientific credentials, but also, according to Klausner, because they were not included in the Department of Social Relations. See Klausner, "The Bid to Nationalize the Social Sciences," 27.

[63] Indeed, the Department of Social Relations, whose chairmanship Parsons held for its first ten years, inculcated the scientific vision within students from a variety of social science backgrounds, as its interdisciplinary character reached out to affect professional norms in psychology and anthropology. See Nicholas C. Mullins, *Theories and Theory Groups in Contemporary American Sociology* (New York: Harper & Row, 1973), 50.

[64] Ibid., 14.

that neglected to ground itself in empirical research, and, on the other, of antitheoretical work that focused solely on research technique. Theory and empirical research were equally important and, furthermore, were synergistic. Fruitful, cumulative results depended upon them both. Nevertheless, if leading theorists were aware of the need for mutual accommodation, they advocated it in the context of an explosion of methodological innovation that outpaced theory's ability to keep up with, much less shape or direct, empirical research. Moreover, empirically oriented sociologists were often loath to articulate or even address the theoretical implications of their work, particularly as the social survey movement, and its emphasis upon the accumulation of quantitative data, matured. As a result, the conception of sociology-as-science came to depend more upon the discipline's technical innovations than upon the validity and applicability of its theories.

3
Quantitative Methods and the Institutionalization of Exclusivity

As disciplinary leaders asserted their conceptions of sociology's scientific integrity after World War II, the methodological infrastructure and innovation that would support their claims gained powerful momentum, lending to academic sociology the mien and accoutrements of the professional authority of hard science. Shortly after the war, institutes of survey research emerged at major American universities—the National Opinion Research Center at the University of Chicago, the Survey Research Center at the University of Michigan, the Bureau of Applied Social Research at Columbia, the Institute for Social Science Research at UCLA, the Survey Research Laboratory at the University of Illinois, and the Survey Research Center at Berkeley—and these contributed significantly to sociology's institutionalization within the structure of the postwar university.[1] Their growing federal and private funding, as well as their bureaucratic formalization within the university and within American society at large, meant that the values of their

---

[1] Gideon Sjoberg and Ted R. Vaughan, "The Bureaucratization of Sociology: Its Impact on Theory and Research," in Ted R. Vaughan, Gideon Sjoberg, and Larry T. Reynolds, eds., *A Critique of Contemporary American Sociology* (Dix Hills, NY: General Hall, 1993), 72–73. Jean M. Converse provides a thorough and meticulously researched history of the social survey movement in *Survey Research in the United States: Roots and Emergence, 1890–1960* (Berkeley: University of California Press, 1987).

directors and researchers exerted a powerful influence over the formation of American sociology's identity. With the institutes' establishment and growth, survey techniques came to dominate sociological research to such a degree that, as Richard H. Wells and Steven J. Picou have determined in a content analysis of *The American Sociological Review,* they accounted between 1950 and 1964 for 70.5 percent of the empirical research techniques used in American sociology.[2] In particular, their command of such techniques served to support the kinds of legitimations Merton and Parsons had conceived, which called for a dramatic methodological evolution to facilitate the construction of modern sociological theory. At the same time, however, those techniques and their practitioners pushed sociology in the direction of a legitimation based more heavily upon empirical methods than on theory construction or the maintenance of social order in the modern age. In this way, statistical social research, especially social survey research, became essential to the professional legitimation of sociology as a whole.

The application of these new research methods to the American military experience of World War II would constitute the first major postwar assertion of American sociology's scientific status, in a demonstration of technical accomplishment and social utility that would, it was hoped, lend credence to the promises the discipline's defenders had made. This effort produced in 1949 and 1950 a four-volume series entitled *Studies in Social Psychology in World War II* The study originated in the War Department under Henry L. Stimson, which had commissioned a Research Branch within the Information and Education Division to study the life of the American soldier during wartime. Following the war, the results, which included hundreds of thousands of interviews, were given to a team of researchers selected by the Social Science Research Council (SSRC)—and including Robert Merton and his colleague Paul Lazarsfeld—for analysis, who published their formulations and analyses in the first two volumes of the series under the title *The American Soldier.* As John Madge observes in his history of modern empirical sociology, this study indicated the extent to which social science had achieved professional credibility in the United States, for it signified social science's first attainment of large-scale governmental support.[3] The resulting four volumes therefore represented a crucial opportunity for postwar social science to demonstrate its scientific viability by providing the Army with useful, factual information and at the same time to garner respect for social research within American society in general.

---

[2] Richard H. Wells and Stephen J. Picou, *American Sociology: Theoretical and Methodological Structure* (Washington, DC: University Press of America, 1981), 115. Their analysis covers the content of *The American Sociological Review* from its inception in 1936 to 1978.

[3] John Madge, *The Origins of Scientific Sociology* (London: Tavistock, 1963), 287–88.

Indeed, although the Army was the primary audience for the study, the research team understood clearly the relevance of their efforts to the enhancement of scientific sociology's reputation. Samuel A. Stouffer, Harvard professor of sociology and the study's technical director, explained in the introduction to the first volume, *The American Soldier: Adjustment During Army Life*, that social psychologists and social scientists represented the study's "main audience," as the research team's objective was "to speed up the process of development of the science of man" by revealing its potential to other professional social scientists.[4] Thus, he declared, "If the examples in these volumes, both of the inadequacies of our present knowledge and of the possible remedies for these inadequacies, stimulate a few of the new generation of social scientists to do things better, the labor will not have been in vain."[5]

Stouffer's statements reflected the emergent Harvard-Columbia faith in the promise of a sociology with scientific legitimacy. During the 1920s, Stouffer had studied at the University of Chicago with William Ogburn, the most influential proponent of value-neutral scientific sociology during the interwar years.[6] In his dissertation, Stouffer had asserted the advantages of survey work over the traditional Chicago research technique of the case study. The latter, initiated by Albion Small, W. I. Thomas, and Robert Park, required that researchers descend into particular social milieus, drawing upon observations among groups of individuals within particular sets of social circumstances in order to illuminate larger patterns of social activity and to construct ideal types.[7] Stouffer had challenged this participant-observer, case study approach with the argument that opinion surveys offered a more rigorous means to the scientific understanding of social life by virtue of their use of statistical analysis. His argument, arriving just as the Columbia and Harvard sociology programs had begun their ascendance, and that at Chicago its decline in influence, proved significant in reorienting sociological research—and, in turn, the sources of disciplinary identity—to its postwar form.[8]

---

[4] Samuel A. Stouffer, Edward A. Suchman, Leland C. DeVinney, Shirley A. Star, and Robin M. Williams, Jr., *The American Soldier: Adjustment During Army Life*, Studies in Social Psychology in World War II, vol. 1 (Princeton, NJ: Princeton University Press, 1949), 5.

[5] Ibid., 51.

[6] Robert C. Bannister, *Sociology and Scientism: The American Quest for Objectivity, 1890–1940* (Chapel Hill: University of North Carolina Press, 1987), 161.

[7] Norbert Wiley, "The Rise and Fall of Dominating Theories in American Sociology," in William E. Snizek, Ellsworth R. Fuhrman, and Michael K. Miller, eds., *Contemporary Issues in Theory and Research: A Metatheoretical Perspective* (Westport, CT: Greenwood Press, 1979), 56.

[8] Ibid., 60.

Stouffer's introductory statements to *The American Soldier* affirmed both the essence and the particulars of the scientific vision of sociology that Parsons and Merton had promulgated. "Science, unlike art or literature, is cumulative," he proclaimed, "in the sense that *a scientific achievement is most successful when it stimulates others to make the concepts and techniques it has used look crude and become obsolete as rapidly as possible.*"[9] Scientific sociology, like the other sciences, would have to prove capable of evolving ever-more refined and useful methods of investigation. Its progress would have to be linear by definition, if it was to experience the maturation exemplified by the natural and physical sciences. Again, scientific sociological discovery was to be an incremental, cumulative journey. "We know that the road of social science will be steep and dark," Stouffer admitted, "but men of vision and courage will try to climb it. Perhaps these volumes will add for a time to the light available until, higher up along the path, brighter torches illumine broader and more secure footways."[10]

Stouffer also prescribed middle-range theorizing in order to ensure that sociology's scientific findings would be cumulative. Sociological theories, he argued, should be "at least of some limited generality, which can be operationally formulated such that verification is possible, and from which predictions can be made successfully to new specific instances."[11] "Such theories," he continued, "demand that the objects of study be isolated and accurately described, preferably by measurement," as "the test of the adequacy of the theory, in comparison with alternative theories, must be rigorous, preferably evidenced by controlled experiment, and preferably replicated."[12]

Stouffer's programmatic statements in *The American Soldier* demanded that social researchers retain a certain Mertonian modesty about their enterprise, because the attainment of scientific legitimacy would require a patient, methodical approach to the study of society. In a 1948 paper presented to the American Association for the Advancement of Science, Stouffer had argued that sociology must retain a proper sense of limits and avoid an inflated sense of its capabilities. Although social scientists were "all too eager, with inadequate equipment in theory or techniques, to try to solve the great practical problems of the day," sociology's scientific success would depend upon social researchers' acceptance of their humble place in the universe.[13]

---

[9] Stouffer, et. al., *The American Soldier: Adjustment During Army Life*, 5.

[10] Ibid., 52–53.

[11] Ibid., 51.

[12] Ibid., 51.

[13] Samuel A. Stouffer, *Social Research to Test Ideas* (Glencoe, IL: Free Press, 1962), 2.

Their desire to "save the world" had encouraged the lay public and foundation directors in their already unrealistic expectations for social transformation through social investigation, he warned. "Much of the support now pouring in upon social science," he observed, "is based upon a false conception of what social science is able to deliver, and, unless those of us who see this threat have the vision and courage to reply resourcefully, our best talent will be drawn off, bribed if you will, to work on big, spectacular practical problems that social science as such is not now equipped to solve."[14]

Stouffer's assertion that scientific social investigation was an incremental endeavor, dependent upon the small steps already taken toward new understandings of society for its ability to take still more small steps, not only ruled out transformative accomplishments but also reinforced the postwar vision of the social researcher's proper public identity. A particular kind of social responsibility would have to characterize the sociologist's public role. Although particular lay interests had come to expect scientific miracles from a young profession whose scientific maturity lay well ahead of it, social scientists would have to cultivate a new and more realistic perception of their science as an ever-evolving pursuit, unfolding in a slow and perhaps imperceptible maturation process. Nonsociologists would have to be discouraged from expecting from science that which was impossible for science to provide.

The content of *The American Soldier* reflected this sense of the provisionality of sociology's initial attempts to build an empirically based science of society. The wartime army represented a unique opportunity for analyzing a set of circumstances to which the social scientist could not ordinarily gain access. It resembled a laboratory, in which such sociological phenomena as primary groups, reference groups, obedience to authority, attitude formation and adjustment, and social control could be studied under uncommonly strict conditions and with captive subjects whose experiences followed more regularized patterns than those of civilians. Like a controlled experiment, the war offered unique glimpses into situations for which civilian life offered no equivalents. Effective empirical analysis of the life of the soldier could therefore demonstrate the efficacy of social science research for the measurement of broader realms of human experience.

The American Soldier volumes of the study consisted of chapters on the relationship between soldiers' personal backgrounds and their adjustment to army life, the experiences of soldiers in different branches of the army, the dynamics of the army's status system and "problems of social mobility" within it, attitudes toward leadership, "the ideology of the soldier," the black soldier's experience of army life, and the social psychology of combat. In

---

[14]Ibid., 3.

many instances, the Stouffer group offered confident conclusions on the dynamics of army life and often promised that their initial research had provided foundations for a myriad of future investigations. In the chapter on social mobility within the military, for example, the group suggested that the challenge of selecting the right men for the right responsibilities "will take many years and could use some of the best skills of psychologists and other social scientists."[15] The chapter on soldiers' attitudes toward army leadership concluded with the suggestion that this area of inquiry "lends itself well to experimental study in a peacetime army."[16] The final volume in particular, which dealt with the methodology of the entire study, began with an optimistic assertion of the potential of statistical methods to forge truly scientific social investigation:

> As must be apparent from the preview presented in the present chapter, there is still relatively little which has sufficiently passed out of the realm of controversy to reach a definitive textbook stage. In the history of science, only a small fraction of the proposed scientific models, even including many which have certain initial attractions, find a permanent place. As more and more of the younger psychologists and social scientists, aware of the central importance of the problems here investigated, put their minds to investigation of these problems, we may expect models to take shape which will hold their place in science. Among those models may be some whose development has been furthered by the Research Branch and by the discussion, criticism, and creative inventiveness which it is hoped these chapters will stimulate.[17]

As in Stouffer's other programmatic statements, the message was clear: empirical research of the sort *The American Soldier* represented would supply the building blocks for future research, offering refinements in measurement and prediction that would enable subsequent studies, similarly modest in scope and intent, to take place.

Among sociologists, praise for *The American Soldier* reinforced a growing consensus over the reality of this scientific evolution. Reviewers in *The American Journal of Sociology* and *The American Sociological Review* lauded the studies' methodological innovations, as well as the research team's appropriate sense of

---

[15] Stouffer, et. al., *The American Soldier: Adjustment During Army Life*, 283.

[16] Ibid., 429.

[17] Samuel A. Stouffer, Louis Guttman, Edward A. Suchman, Paul F. Lazarsfeld, Shirley A. Star, and John A. Clausen, *Measurement and Prediction*, Studies in Social Psychology in World War II, vol. 4 (Princeton, NJ: Princeton University Press, 1949), 45.

humility about the practical limits of their achievements. Most significantly, both journals interpreted these achievements in terms of the progress of social research toward fully scientific status. *The American Sociological Review* commented that the studies "constitute as impressive a piece of scientific reporting as we are likely to see in a long time," and it praised the studies' commitment to replicable findings.[18] *The American Journal of Sociology* reviewer similarly found the fourth volume of the series, which described the studies' methodology, to be its most significant contribution of new knowledge, insisting that it was in the project's "development and exploration of new techniques of measurement rather than in any insights which it may have tried to give us into the nature of group behavior in the American army" that represented its most valuable contributions to social science.[19] Such reactions suggested that the study's success in furthering sociology's scientific maturation compensated for its failure to accomplish anything of immediate sociological significance.

Among more skeptical scholars within sociology, however, *The American Soldier* evinced strong objections regarding the purposes to which such a science might be applied in the absence of any clear statement of social science's proper ends. In his review of *The American Soldier*, Alfred McClung Lee of Brooklyn College agreed that the Stouffer group's major achievement was metholodogical in nature, but rather than viewing this as evidence of progress in social science, he expressed deep reservations about its implications for the future of social inquiry. Lee charged that "assembly line" social science of this sort, in which a large team of researchers took responsibility for only small parts of the whole enterprise, sabotaged meaningful theorizing by fostering "committee thinking," which "places a premium on the plausible, the pat, and the salable."[20] He insisted that meaningful theories were the products of individual effort, and that the Stouffer group's attempt to achieve them by enlisting a virtual army of researchers with various areas of expertise had simply eliminated the prospect for anything beyond the most simplistic theoretical conclusions. "Theoretical integration," he declared, "arises from long and careful working and reworking of data by an individual scientist, and this work has far less of such integration than would satisfy many of the outstanding social scientists who are its co-authors."[21]

---

[18]John W. Riley, Jr., review of *The American Soldier*, by Samuel A. Stouffer et al., *American Sociological Review* 14, 4 (August 1949): 557.

[19]Ethel Shanas, review of *Measurement and Prediction*, by Samuel A. Stouffer et al., *American Journal of Sociology* 57, 4 (January 1952): 388.

[20]Alfred McClung Lee, review of *The American Soldier*, vols. 1 and 2, by Samuel A. Stouffer et al., *Annals of the American Academy of Political and Social Science* 265 (September 1949): 174.

[21]Ibid., 174.

Lee thereby challenged Stouffer's assumption that *The American Soldier* would offer a foundation, albeit a small one, upon which subsequent studies might build, and he doubted that the studies' modest methodological and theoretical innovations might contribute to the cumulative project that was social science. If middle-range theorizing was to take place within the context of group research, it would fail to build more general theories. If the various findings that constituted *The American Soldier* were intended to support or even generate middle-range theories, Lee insisted, they had accomplished neither. Lee disagreed with a fundamental tenet of the scientific idealism behind the study, that social scientists could hope for a linear progression of their discipline toward superior methods, testable results, and theories that could explain ever-expanding realms of human experience.

Nevertheless, Lee took the Stouffer group's methodological contributions seriously enough to consider their possible implications for American democracy. Noting the "high selectivity" social researchers exercised in their choice of social problems to investigate, he warned that if the kind of research ideals *The American Soldier* represented came to dominate social science, "the value orientation of the managerial technician rather than the value orientation of the social science educator will dominate what evolves and is called social science." He concluded that, under such circumstances, "the emphasis can thus shift from service to citizens in a democracy to service for those who temporarily control and who wish to continue to control segments of our society."[22] Although he acknowledged that the Stouffer group clearly did not intend to utilize their findings for such purposes, he nevertheless saw the potential for their abuse by those interested in "authoritarian human engineering" rather than democracy. The values of the technician, who, "concerned willy-nilly with morale, control, and efficiency," would sacrifice all other human values, and thus, "the anti-authoritarian tradition of faith in reasonability and dignity of the person becomes an obstacle that must be exorcised with such labels as 'positivistic materialism.' "[23]

Indeed, the Stouffer group had provided such detractors with ample ammunition for their charges of a social science capitulation to interests dedicated to mass manipulation. One of the study's most profound conclusions had concerned the strikingly low level of ideological commitment among the American forces. Beyond simply resenting the subordination of his will to the authority of the military apparatus and wishing above all to remain out of danger, the American soldier had proved remarkably bereft of strong feelings

---

[22] Ibid., 174.

[23] Alfred McClung Lee, letter to the editor, *Annals of the American Academy of Political and Social Science* 267 (January 1950): 252.

about the enemy and of convictions of the rightness of his country's cause. The Stouffer group had addressed this problem several times throughout *The American Soldier* volumes, which, after all, featured the theme of personal adjustment most prominently to begin with. Thus, in the first volume, the researchers had concluded on the basis of officers' testimony that "with proper planning," the military could succeed in "mobilizing informal group pressures such that men induce their least motivated fellows to work for a group goal."[24] On the American serviceman's lack of ideological commitment to the Allied cause, the researchers speculated that this defect had "increased the psychological cost of the war," noting that army psychiatrists and the Surgeon General's Office had "cooperated energetically" with the Information and Education Division in "seeking to help men merge personal desires with the issues of the war," a practice known in nonprofessional circles as indoctrination or, more pejoratively, brainwashing.[25] In the chapters concerning the soldier's service immediately following the war, the researchers emphasized the importance of controlling men's attitudes in the absence of an enemy upon which to focus resentment and aggression, noting rather disingenuously that the study's predictions complemented the military's own efforts in cultivating "the field of democratic management and leadership."[26]

In the face of such troubling implications, Robert Lynd, reviewing *The American Soldier* in the *New Republic*, joined Lee in voicing similar warnings about social science's moral confusion, lamenting that "these volumes depict

---

[24] Stouffer et. al., *The American Soldier: Adjustment During Army Life*, 429.

[25] Ibid., 485.

[26] Samuel A. Stouffer, Arthur A. Lumsdaine, Marion Harper Lumsdaine, Robin M. Williams, Jr., M. Brewster Smith, Irving L. Janis, Shirley A. Star, and Leonard S. Cottrell, Jr., *The American Soldier: Combat and Its Aftermath*, Studies in Social Psychology in World War II, vol. 2 (Princeton, NJ: Princeton University Press, 1949), 595. The study's predictions, they emphasized, "were not made simply as a matter of scientific interest. They were made to be used as a basis for planning measures to counteract the anticipated problems" associated with low morale after the war (595). In the third volume, *Experiments on Mass Communication*, Studies in Social Psychology in World War II (Princeton, NJ: Princeton University Press, 1949), written not by the Stouffer group but by an Experimental Section of the Research Branch consisting of Carl Iver Hovland, Arthur A. Lumsdaine, and Fred D. Sheffield, a team of researchers analyzed the impact of propaganda films—the *Why We Fight* series in particular—on troop morale. The group declared, "The methods used in these studies and the results obtained are described here in the belief that there will be increasing use of such procedures for determining whether motion pictures and similar media really do succeed in attaining their objectives and for modifying the products in accordance with the results obtained by research" (3). Ultimately, the researchers perceived their role as that of "developing a body of scientific principles to assist producers of educational films in achieving products with maximum educational effectiveness" (19). That the researchers of *The American Soldier* series expressed so unabashedly their intent in aiding the efforts of military officials and propaganda filmmakers in managing individuals and attitudes helps explain the bitter reaction of Lee and others to the studies.

science being used with great skill to sort out and to control men for purposes not of their own willing." Accepting the Stouffer group's claims to scientific achievement, he focused his review on the question of the objectives to which such research would be put:

It is a significant measure of the impotence of liberal democracy that it must increasingly use its social sciences not directly on democracy's own problems, but tangentially and indirectly; it must pick up the crumbs from private business research on such problems as how to gauge audience reaction so as to put together profitable synthetic radio programs and movies, or, as in the present case, from Army research on how to turn frightened draftees into tough soldiers who will fight a war whose purposes they do not understand. With such socially extraneous purposes controlling the use of social science, each advance in its use tends to make it an instrument of mass control, and thereby a further threat to democracy.[27]

As in *Knowledge for What?* a decade earlier, Lynd warned that the absence of a moral foundation for the technical and theoretical innovations in social research could only lead to the erosion of individual freedom and the degradation of democracy. *The American Soldier,* in its lack of reflection upon the larger significance of its techniques, exemplified the subordination of moral ends to scientific means.

For Stouffer's detractors within the profession, then, the validity of social science's claims to technical progress warranted less consideration than did the unresolved question of what would be done with the techniques themselves. Lee and Lynd, while skeptical of the Stouffer group's claims that their research had provided a foundation for future empirical work, nevertheless shared the assumption of the proponents of sociology-as-science that refinements in empirical research would produce more sophisticated, accurate, and usable results. They dissented from the peers primarily on the issue of ends, particularly where the ends chosen threatened to erode democratic institutions. Their concern over the antidemocratic potential of postwar social research thus reflected their belief that social science could indeed reach the levels of technical achievement its practitioners and promoters promised.

---

[27] Robert S. Lynd, "The Science of Inhuman Relations," review of *The American Soldier,* by Samuel A. Stouffer et al., *New Republic* (August 29, 1949): 22. A decade later, C. Wright Mills would make a similar charge against the Stouffer group, that *The American Soldier* studies "prove that it is possible for social research to be of administrative use without being concerned with the problems of social science." C. Wright Mills, *The Sociological Imagination* (New York: Grove Press, 1959), 53.

Lay critics skeptical of *The American Soldier's* optimistic tone, on the other hand, questioned the whole scientific enterprise the study claimed to have furthered. Nathan Glazer, who had recently finished the collaborative work with David Riesman on what would be published a year later as *The Lonely Crowd* (1950), noted in his regular social science column in *Commentary* that "the overpowering obsession with the physical sciences and their great achievement makes its mark on every page, and defines the general aim" of the study.[28] Glazer, however, found *The American Soldier* to be scientific only in technique. Like Stouffer, he acknowledged the cumulative character of scientific discovery, but he nevertheless found that *The American Soldier* "forms no part of a cumulative record of science in this sense. It rests on no hypotheses or laws established by previous social science, nor does it pass on any. No one will ever in the future begin a scientific article with the words, 'As Stouffer et al. have *established...*' They will have to use instead words like '*suggested*' or '*illustrated*.'"[29]

Glazer proceeded to question the research group's assumptions about the efficacy of their methods, pondering whether the rush to apply questionnaires to sociological issues might have begun to undermine the sociologist's active consideration of what constituted a sociological problem worth investigating. "Without the questionnaires," he mused, "it would hardly be possible to make such extensive use of The Machines, and it is perhaps not unfair to suggest that this is one of the reasons we have had the increasing emphasis on questionnaires in recent years."[30] If technique provided the impetus for research, research would become that which was technically possible. "In short," Glazer warned, "questions that would otherwise never have come to trouble the human mind can now be asked and answered by the machines."[31] Unlike Lee and Lynd, however, Glazer remained unimpressed by *The American Soldier's* machine-driven results, finding not the tools for the technical manipulation of human beings but merely a mass of trivia. "If *The American Soldier* is not, strictly speaking, science," he asked, "is it at least useful? To the Army, I think hardly at all."[32] He claimed that the attitudes the Stouffer group had discovered among America's fighting men bore little relation to their performance of their duties and that, consequently, the generals who had supported

---

[28] Nathan Glazer, "*The American Soldier* as Science: Can Sociology Fulfill Its Ambitions?" *Commentary* (November 1949): 488.

[29] Ibid., 489.

[30] Ibid., 490.

[31] Ibid., 491.

[32] Ibid., 495.

the study had in the end received little more than the satisfaction of their curiosity. "Indeed," he concluded, "one might say that rarely was so little information about so large a question spread over so many pages. All because the aim was science, not understanding."[33]

Arthur Schlesinger, Jr., provided the most scathing assessment of the study. Like Glazer, he questioned the very premise of the Stouffer group's research, complaining that "sociology has whored after the natural sciences from the start," in this most recent case sabotaging meaningful intellectual inquiry by allowing its investigative techniques, which were themselves of dubious value, to dominate the investigation. Scientific aspirations had thus impoverished the study's living, breathing subject matter, removing it from any human or historical context. "One comes to feel," he lamented, "that the American soldier existed, neither in life nor in history, but in some dreary statistical vacuum."[34] Even more distressing, Schlesinger lamented, was the fact that social scientists' bogus claims to scientific status had hoodwinked universities, foundations, and government agencies to support its research projects:

> Bursting onto university campuses after the war, overflowing with portentous if vague hints of mighty wartime achievements (not, alas, to be disclosed because of security), fanatical in their zeal and shameless in their claims, they persuaded or panicked many university administrations into giving their studies top priorities. Needless to say, they scored an even more brilliant success with the foundations.[35]

Like Glazer, Schlesinger found that *The American Soldier*'s achievements had failed to realize its creators' claims and that most of its findings were accessible to common-sense observation. Bill Mauldin's recently anthologized wartime cartoons, he observed, provided a more succinct and perceptive source of insight into soldiers' attitudes than did the study's array of statistics. While social science perhaps did not pose a threat to American life, "except as it engrosses money and energy which might be put more wisely to other uses," Schlesinger worried that "it might eventually do great harm in obscuring from ourselves the ancient truths concerning the vanity of human wishes, and the distortions worked by that vanity upon the human performance."[36] Sensitive, creative social critics would continue to provide insights into the human

---

[33] Ibid., 496.

[34] Arthur Schlesinger, Jr., "The Statistical Soldier," *Partisan Review* (August 1949): 852, 855.

[35] Ibid., 852.

[36] Ibid., 855.

condition that research bureaus, distracted by statistical models and mountains of data, would fail to notice, much less understand.

Unfortunately, Schlesinger charged, social science had begun to encroach upon the communicative space social critics and social philosophers traditionally occupied. Sociologists, in their professional vanity, had created a language of exclusion. Social researchers' "remorseless jargon" and "barbarous patois" promoted not greater understanding but rather organized meaninglessness, which, considering their institutional sources of support, threatened to suffocate intellectual discourse and inquiry, ultimately "carrying to triumphant completion" the foundations' "ancient hope of achieving the bureaucratization of American intellectual life."[37] Schlesinger thereby implied that sociology's scientific aspirations were antidemocratic, sabotaging free intellectual debate and removing social inquiry from the public sphere. Schlesinger simply lamented that bureaucratic discourse threatened to replace public discourse, as specialized methods and pseudoscientific terminology rendered the results of institutionalized social investigation intelligible only to social scientists.

Significantly, Stouffer himself acknowledged the threat that an overemphasis on technique posed to the social scientist's other intellectual commitments. A year after the publication of the first two volumes of *The American Soldier*, he noted that although the studies had demonstrated the possibilities within empirical research, they also made clear the new and larger rewards available to those embarking upon such projects. As research technique came to receive more generous funding than theoretical work, social scientists might have difficulty retaining their commitment to ideas. "The very success of social science in application is also a grave danger," Stouffer admitted. "There is a danger that our best minds will be drawn away from theory making and theory testing by the greater rewards available in applied research."[38] Stouffer concluded that only the social scientist's commitment to the marriage of theory and methodology could prevent this trend and that each would have to play a central role in the research enterprise in order to prevent a descent into attenuated scholarly activity. Sterility in academic research, Stouffer noted, "is traceable, in part, to the traditional separation of theory and empirical research."[39] Researchers would have to overcome that separation if social science was to progress.

---

[37] Ibid., 853.

[38] Samuel A. Stouffer, "Some Afterthoughts of a Contributor to 'The American Soldier,'" in Robert K. Merton and Paul F. Lazarsfeld, eds., *Continuities in Social Research: Studies in the Scope and Method of "The American Soldier"* (Glencoe, IL: Free Press, 1950), 201, 203.

[39] Ibid., 204.

Despite his ambivalence, Stouffer thus downplayed the implications of the scientific ideal as sociology became a major academic discipline. If productive social research depended mainly upon retaining a proper balance between theory and technique, the larger question of whether the sociological enterprise should conceive of itself as a science could be considered resolved. To Stouffer, sociology's scientific aspirations were a given, and thus sociology simply needed to find the proper relationship between its theories and its empirical findings to become like the natural and physical sciences. Stouffer's emphasis on this relationship echoed his agreement with Merton and Parsons that sociology, a cumulative project, would progress as modest theories of limited scope were tested—or even generated—by the evolving empirical research methods exemplified by *The American Soldier*.

The contentious discussion that *The American Soldier* had stimulated signaled the advent of a struggle that would continue throughout the 1950s over the validity of a scientific sociology, one that would metastasize sufficiently to draw in journalists, academic professionals from the humanities, and renegade sociologists like C. Wright Mills. One group would warn that by neglecting important issues of values and larger social objectives, methodologically driven social investigation threatened to undermine cherished humanistic ideals, whereas the other would insist that quantitative sociological research had yet to demonstrate anything of great significance in spite of its growing methodological sophistication. Thus, ten years after the publication of *The American Soldier*, Paul Lazarsfeld would write, "Tired social scientists and hostile outsiders sometimes ask: what has social research all added up to in the last fifty years? Is there any sociological finding that has not been anticipated by philosophers or novelists?" His answer, that "parsimonious organization of knowledge through systematic theory," as opposed to a primary focus upon pressing social problems and active communication with publics, reflected the impact of scientific idealism upon the conduct of survey research.[40]

Over the course of the 1950s, while survey practitioners such as William H. Sewell at the University of Wisconsin–Madison and Otis Dudley Duncan at the University of Chicago remained vital contributors to the evolution of survey research, it was Lazarsfeld who would, by example and through basic programmatic statements of the sort issued by Parsons and Merton, become the most influential contributor to a sociological identity shaped by research technique. Lazarsfeld, an Austrian émigré, developed his devotion to quantitative research methods while studying at the University of Vienna, and as

---

[40]Paul F. Lazarsfeld, "Problems in Methodology," in Robert K. Merton, Leonard Broom, and Leonard S. Cottrell, eds., *Sociology Today: Problems and Prospects* (New York: Basic Books, 1959), 39.

a member of the Young Socialist League he had gravitated to the study of social psychology to understand the Austrian public's attraction to nationalism rather than socialism. After taking courses toward degrees in both mathematics and *Staatswissenschaft*, which combined the study of law, economics, and political theory, he earned his doctorate in the latter. In the late 1920s, he directed the applied studies of the social psychology division of the psychology institute at the university, and his study of unemployment in the village of Marienthal then brought him to the attention of the Paris representative of the Rockefeller Foundation. In 1932, he received a traveling fellowship to the United States, arriving the next year.[41]

The dire political climate in Austria by early 1934, in the midst of which most of Lazarsfeld's family was imprisoned, led Lazarsfeld to seek to remain in the United States beyond the duration of his fellowship, and, with the help of Robert Lynd, he received a position within the New Deal's National Youth Administration, headquartered at the University of Newark. This position soon led to his appointment in 1937 to the directorship of the Rockefeller Foundation–sponsored Office of Radio Research (ORR), which performed studies into the preferences and reactions of radio listeners and magazine readers for private clients.[42] In 1941, Lazarsfeld and Merton received associate professorships at Columbia and subsequently launched a long-lasting partnership as director and associate director, respectively, of the radio project's new incarnation as the Bureau of Applied Social Research. The bureau, which analyzed such diverse topics as consumer preferences, voter apathy, voting patterns, and the class bases of audience tastes in mass-communication media, proved vital in solidifying the connection Lazarsfeld would articulate between small-scale quantitative research and the construction of a scientific sociology.

Lazarsfeld's energy and fund-raising skills allowed the bureau to garner increasing research funding from private and, later, government sources. In the 1940s and 1950s, Lazarsfeld formulated a highly successful technique for the bureau of providing practical data to business clients while using the funds generated to build upon that data and thereby channel it simultaneously into academic research projects. This strategy, however, posed problems for the

---

[41] Paul Lazarsfeld, "An Episode in the History of Social Research: A Memoir," in Donald Fleming and Bernard Bailyn, eds., *The Intellectual Migration: Europe and America, 1930–1960* (Cambridge, MA: Belknap Press, 1969), 270–76.

[42] Lazarsfeld's offer of appointment to the ORR directorship came from Hadley Cantril, a social scientist at Princeton and collaborator with the Gallup polling organization, and Frank Stanton, the research director and later president of CBS. Their crucial role in building the links between public opinion polling and social science is explored in Converse, *Survey Research in the United States*, chap. 4.

bureau's early relationship with Columbia. First, the bureau's research for business clients presented the possibility that the university's reputation would suffer from a perceived capitulation to commercial interests. Moreover, in 1944, Lazarsfeld published a series of articles in *The Nation* on that year's national election, and the articles ran not with Lazarsfeld listed as their author but rather with the bureau's full name and that of its sponsoring institution, Columbia University. After the university provost expressed his concern over the bureau's increasing involvement in business and political activity and its potential threat to Columbia's autonomy, the university's Sociology Department formed a new governing committee for the bureau, which then issued a series of policies designed to retain university control over the identity and purpose of the bureau. Above all, the university would insist upon the primacy of scientific values within all research activity for commercial clients.[43] The bureau's identity would be linked directly to the idea of quantitative social research as hard science.

At the same time, the bureau committed itself to the kind of limited investigation that Merton and Stouffer had advocated. The studies that its researchers produced would be considered bases for future empirical inquiry rather than as providing conclusive insights into sociological phenomena.[44] To Lazarsfeld, innovations in methodology remained of paramount importance, regardless of the subjects under investigation. Consequently, the bureau's studies amounted largely to a congeries of diverse projects with little or no theoretical unity. As Allen Barton, the bureau's director during the 1960s, explains, the bureau failed to institutionalize Merton's ideal of assembling larger theories out of middle-range endeavors as a guiding force for its research projects, despite the fact that government had by the late 1950s supplanted the private sector as the primary source of the bureau's funding.[45] Quantification seemed in this sense to be self-justifying.

Because of this disjuncture between the bureau's research projects and the middle-range theories Merton had advocated, the Lazarsfeldian vision of

---

[43] Converse, *Survey Research in the United States*, 273–74.

[44] Converse describes how Lazarsfeld and Merton defended the bureau's policy of not implementing "significance tests," or the statistical evaluation of the population samples used in its studies for possible errors in sample selection. Her description conforms to the incrementalist vision of scientific sociology Merton and the others had articulated: "They argued that in these early stages of scientific work, it was desirable to assemble a wide array of evidence, even if some of it was not conclusive, lest 'possibly productive lines of investigation' be cut short (that is, by losing interesting leads). Later, as they wrote, hypotheses could be subjected to more rigorous tests" (Converse, *Survey Research in the United States*, 285).

[45] Allen H. Barton, "Paul Lazarsfeld and Applied Social Research," *Social Science History* 3, 3 (October 1979): 22.

sociology promoted a bias toward a sociological identity based upon methods rather than substantive problems. As quantitative empirical sociology enjoyed dramatically increased institutional and financial support, which strengthened the case offered on behalf of sociology's scientific status, a technically driven definition of sociology became more tenable, and the sociologist's ability to perform sociological research with techniques resembling those of the natural and physical sciences meant that sociology-as-science no longer remained simply a philosophical proposition.

As president of the American Sociological Association in 1962, Lazarsfeld also articulated a philosophical rationale for quantitative research. In his presidential address at that year's ASA meeting, he defended his fellow methodologists with a formulation that echoed those of Merton and Parsons. Sociological research, he argued, should proceed according to a "utility spectrum" that would help the researcher determine the proper scope and application of particular research projects. "At one end," he argued, "you have the idea, most clearly represented by contemporary Soviet opinion, that the only justified use of social research is the advancement of social revolution." At the other end, he continued, "one finds utility in the narrowest sense," or applied sociology, such as government- or business-financed research.[46] These extremes of theoretical and ideological activity on the one hand and practical activity on the other had little relevance for contemporary sociology, for "the exponents of basic social change and the people who want guidance for immediate policy and action are most often disappointed."[47] Like Parsons in his paper for the SSRC, Lazarsfeld saw the necessity for shielding sociological research from external demands to protect its scientific integrity. Middle-range theorizing, alternatively, offered the greatest prospects for meaningful discovery, as it possessed a fruitful relation to empirical methods, which Lazarsfeld illustrated with one of his early Austrian studies on consumer behavior. These, he claimed, demonstrated how a number of small, precise studies had "permitted important generalizations."[48]

Lazarsfeld thereby repeated the tenets of the emergent scientific-sociological ideal: new knowledge arose through the accumulation of modest,

---

[46]Paul F. Lazarsfeld, "The Sociology of Empirical Social Research," *American Sociological Review* 27, 6 (December 1962): 765.

[47]Ibid., 766.

[48]Ibid., 766. Barton has argued that, despite the prevalence of national attitude surveys, Lazarsfeld achieved his best results in surveys of very small numbers of communities or milieus, and that his colleagues and students have had similar success. See Barton, "Paul Lazarsfeld and Applied Social Research," 6–7. Such a pattern is consistent with his assertion of the value of small-scale, limited investigation.

specific research projects whose discoveries, when considered together, created a greater and more meaningful whole. Unlike Merton and Parsons, however, Lazarsfeld seemed to subordinate theory to empirical activity. Whereas the two theorists had considered theory—appropriately circumscribed, to be sure—to be the force behind effective research, Lazarsfeld implied that empirical research could provide the direction for effective theorizing. In effect, empirical findings would allow meaningful theory to exist. Lazarsfeld, like Merton and Parsons, acknowledged theory's dependence upon empirically valid results and embraced a definition of sociology that was dependent upon the scientific method. His utility spectrum was, however, a prescription for the primacy of empiricism: "There probably would not be much theory of the middle range," he asserted, "without the steady supply of specific studies, a growing proportion of which comes from various social research institutes."[49] Whereas Parsons and Merton envisioned a give-and-take between empirical activity and theorizing, in which empirical investigation would be used to test theories and new theories would lead to further empirical investigation, Lazarsfeld conceived of empirical activity as the primary source of theoretical innovation. Whereas pioneers of empirical research in the United States such as Robert Lynd came by their statistical methods in an effort to address what they considered to be the pressing social and cultural problems of his day, Lazarsfeld explained his field as one that first sought to measure a phenomenon and then, if appropriate, evaluated the significance of that which was measured.

Lazarsfeld presented his defense of empirical sociology within the context of a defense of research institutes, for which he served as a leading representative. These institutes shared a focus on the measurement of public attitudes and, as methodological innovators, they brought the empiricist orientation to the matter of sociology's identity. World War II had accelerated the growth of these institutions dramatically, and, as Stephen and Jonathan Turner observe in their history of postwar American sociology, increased funding of survey research encouraged sociology's scientific idealism markedly, as "it was natural to conclude that these changes signaled a coming breakthrough, and that the path to making sociology into a science was to be through the improvement of measurement."[50] For Lazarsfeld, the Turners argue, and for the many survey workers he trained, "the domain of empirical work was a separate domain, with its own rules and strategies that were not

---

[49] Ibid., 766.

[50] Stephen Park Turner and Jonathan H. Turner, *The Impossible Science: An Institutional Analysis of American Sociology* (Newbury Park, CA: Sage, 1990), 106.

dependent on any particular vision of sociology as a theoretical discipline."[51] In keeping with this belief, Lazarsfeld sought to disengage empirical social research from questions of funding sources, objects of study, and the relevance of its findings. "There is hardly any difference," he insisted, "between the academic and the commercial study as far as methods and content go; they differ only with respect to purpose and finances."[52]

Lazarsfeld's contribution to the debate over scientific sociology, then, was to assert for empirical research a separate realm of authority, in which it would not necessarily have to have anything to do with the progress of civilization, human needs, or public enlightenment. To adopt such broad expectations for social research would be to misunderstand the nature of scientific work, which was inevitably incremental and necessarily autonomous from practical, everyday concerns. In recounting his partnership with Merton, he would assert later that "we were quite willing to accept virtually any contract that would give us financial support and so prolong our existence. There was no need to stipulate that the study should have scientific relevance, as we were sure that this would be the case."[53] Scientific relevance would be determined by scientists themselves and by the act of investigation itself. Like Parsons, Lazarsfeld's reflections revealed the assumption that the scientific viability of social research depended on the researcher's freedom from external judgments as to what was scientific and what was not. The social researcher's autonomy would allow research to proceed without the impediments of skeptics and those impatient for immediately meaningful or useful research results.

Lazarsfeld's argument on behalf of scientific social science thus reflected the new exigencies of bureaucratized social research. As the foremost academic entrepreneur within American social science, Lazarsfeld understood better than most the importance of formulating a vision for sociology that accommodated the discipline's sources of sustenance. Funding sources, both public and private, expected from their grant applicants a better-than-reasonable hope of success in their proposed research endeavors. Increasingly, social researchers came to recognize that their research proposals required a kind of credibility that was derived not so much from the social or political importance of their research subjects but upon the probability that their research would yield valid results, results that conformed to the rigorous

---

[51] Ibid., 107.

[52] Paul F. Lazarsfeld, "The Activities of the Bureau of Applied Social Research as Reflected in Its Budget," 3, quoted in Jean M. Converse, *Survey Research in the United States,* 271.

[53] Paul F. Lazarsfeld, "Working With Merton," in Lewis Coser, ed., *The Idea of Social Structure: Papers in Honor of Robert K. Merton* (New York: Harcourt Brace Jovanovich, 1975), 38.

standards of science. Successful research therefore depended upon the re-searcher's access to complex quantitative techniques that could minimize the prospect of unanticipated research results and, thereby, help ensure that research objectives were fulfilled and hypotheses confirmed. In turn, the successful researcher was one who understood that the limits of attainable knowledge about a particular social phenomenon were defined by that which could be verified independently through the application of those quantitative techniques. Inevitably, the researcher would find it necessary to turn to more circumscribed, microscopic subjects, which were more amenable to quanti-fication than larger, more complex subjects.[54] Lazarsfeld's articulation of the importance of standardized methods and his belief in the incremental accu-mulation of new knowledge was therefore in part a reflection of the realities of a new age of highly bureaucratized and institutionally funded social research.

By the beginning of the 1950s, the scientific-sociological ideal had become the dominant professional paradigm in American sociology. The Harvard and Columbia scholars who propounded it had provided the basis for professional consensus regarding sociology's scientific character, an identity that defined science in such a way as to discourage macroscopic thinking, negotiated truths that lay outside the incremental continuum of social research, and, by ne-cessity, the engagement of public issues publicly. Parsons's publication in 1951 of *The Social System* and, with Edward Shils, *Toward a General Theory of Action* placed functionalism at the theoretical center of postwar sociological research.[55] Parsons's strong relationships with his Harvard graduate students during the 1930s and 1940s had produced a loyal corps of followers com-mitted to his vision of the construction of a science of society, a group which, in addition to Merton, included such 1950s luminaries as Kingsley Davis, Robin Williams, Wilbert E. Moore, and later, Neil Smelser. Meanwhile, em-pirical social research of limited scope, Merton's building blocks for pro-ductive theorizing, became the norm throughout the 1950s, as the training of graduate students in Lazarsfeldian quantitative research and sociology's funding sources solidified the norm of small-scale rather than large-scale research.[56]

---

[54]Sjoberg et al., 84.

[55]Shils, a leading scholar in the Chicago department and a friend of Parsons, had become the consulting editor at the Free Press, a small publishing company that subsequently became Par-sons's publisher, reprinting *The Structure of Social Action*, Parsons's essays, and his major postwar works. See Nicholas C. Mullins, *Theories and Theory Groups in Contemporary American Sociology* (New York: Harper & Row, 1973), 52, 59–62; Robert W. Friedrichs, *A Sociology of Sociology* (New York: Free Press, 1970), 20.

[56]Ibid., 59.

These assertions of a sociology that achieved meaningful progress through the assembling of researches of limited scope reflected important larger trends in American intellectual life after World War II. As Edward Purcell observes, the liberal consensus among the majority of American intellectuals after the war led them to insist upon incremental rather than transformative social progress, achieved through the efforts of enlightened individuals working within established institutions. In *The Crisis of Democratic Theory*, Purcell characterizes postwar liberalism as embodying a pluralist conception of American society, which led it to accept and help legitimate existing institutions such as universities, government bureaucracies, and private foundations. These institutions, under the guidance of experts, would produce social improvement through social and political fine-tuning, avoiding the excesses and calamities of the ideologically driven experiments of the first half of the century that had engulfed the industrial West in revolution and war. Thus, according to Purcell, postwar intellectuals, by accepting a pluralist, consensus conception of American society, legitimated established institutions and perceived them as essentially good. Theirs was a "relativist" conception of ideas and institutions, for to accept ideas as absolute had proven to lead to totalitarianism.[57] For their part, American sociologists had embraced these principles by avoiding grand theories that sought to transform social and political life, adopting instead a modest conception of their discipline's potentialities that required patient, incremental steps toward social progress through application of the scientific method to social problems. Like liberalism in general, scientific sociology opted to work within the world of things-as-they-were.

The implications of postwar liberalism and the scientific ideal for American democracy were clear. Together, they made public engagement in social and political discourse less crucial to the success of either democracy or sociology itself. Operating within a larger liberal intellectual consensus, the sociologist, applying the methods and values of hard science to carefully circumscribed research topics, would provide the empirical bases for decision makers to apply minute adjustments to particular spheres of social activity. There would be no direct engagements with publics, which, without the proper expertise, lacked the intellectual tools with which to become participants in making the very decisions that affected them. Finally, the liberal consensus could excuse this exclusion of such publics because they contained the assumption that American democracy was already a reality. As Purcell notes, America itself had become a normative concept for postwar political and

---

[57] Edward A. Purcell, Jr., *The Crisis of Democratic Theory: Scientific Naturalism and the Problem of Value* (Lexington: University Press of Kentucky, 1973), 256–57.

intellectual leaders, who tended to "translate existing institutions into political and moral norms."[58] American democracy's success, then, followed logically from the success of American institutions. This conclusion freed the sociologist from public engagement, for to attempt to communicate with a lay audience was to misunderstand the knowledge worker's proper institutional role: the sociologist promoted American democracy not by enlightening and empowering American citizens but by refining and improving American institutions. Moreover, this self-conception fit perfectly with the growing emphasis on quantitative methodology. The specialized language and putatively scientific techniques of the professional social researcher served not only to facilitate sociological inquiry but to define the sociologist as a sociologist. As an institutionally connected expert, the sociologist required the language and tools that expressed his or her professional status. The "barbarous patois" and "bureaucratization of American life" that Schlesinger had lamented had become the substance and institutional sustenance of professional sociology.

Although the early 1950s marked the emergence of a decidedly skeptical or even hostile array of sociological detractors, prominent sociologists were in turn reaching conclusions about the broader public sphere that exacerbated sociology's estrangement from broader, nonprofessional communities of discourse. At Columbia in particular, the students of Robert Lynd and Robert Merton confronted the theories of European social theorists, particularly Georg Simmel, Max Weber, Karl Mannheim, Emile Durkheim, and Robert Michels, in the contentious atmosphere of the McCarthy era. Ultimately, they added to the scientific identity and its overprofessionalized distance from relationships and dialogue with nonsociologists a profound suspicion of the values and opinions of the nonscientist, which served in turn to reinforce their profession's sense of separation from the rest of society. Sociology's scientific idealism proved resistant not only to the democratization of sociological discourse but also to participatory conceptions of democracy itself.

---

[58] Ibid., 270.

4

Social Theory and the Romance
of American Alienation

The conception of sociology as a hard science ascended to become a primary element of professional sociological identity just as particular critiques of modernity came to enjoy widespread credence among the postwar generation of American sociologists. Influential scholars from leading departments, particularly those of Harvard and Columbia, subsumed the United States and Europe under the common rubric of "mass society," so that by 1956 Daniel Bell would observe that, aside from Marxism, this paradigm constituted "probably the most influential social theory in the Western world today."[1] This conception of mass society, more an indictment of modernity than merely a framework for the kind of dispassionate analysis scientific work seemed to demand, carried implications which exacerbated the estrangement from public discourse that the scientific identity had fostered.

Sociology-as-science, in the Parsonian conception, had meant that sociology would require autonomy from lay pressures and concerns sufficient to allow for the patient, methodical accumulation of results and the building of theory. As scholars adopted the mass-society conception of modernity, their work seemed to validate Parsons's perspective, particularly in the context of the recent global cataclysm of Stalinism and

---

[1]Daniel Bell, "The Theory of Mass Society: A Critique," *Commentary* 22, 1 (July 1956): 75.

Nazism in the 1930s and 1940s, which, when after it combined with the hysterical pathology of McCarthyite anticommunism, left many American sociologists, particularly those at Harvard and Columbia, with a Spenglerian outlook that solidified their professional retreat from public discourse. Thus, the scientific sociological identity combined with the welter of postwar philosophical currents, statistical survey findings, and global and national political events to leave little doubt in the minds of many scholars that ordinary individuals not only lacked the ability to comprehend the complexities of social structure but might, if given the opportunity, collectively inhibit the efforts of others to do so. In the nascent sociological consensus of the postwar period, America's transformation into a mass society meant that, in the words of the *fin-de-siècle* French intellectual Gustave Le Bon, the "crowd-man" threatened to overwhelm the "man of science."[2]

Postwar theories of mass society asserted that modern economic, technological, demographic, and political changes had produced a transformation in the social life of the industrial West. Revolutions in transportation and communication had eroded or in fact ruptured the association of individuals in primary groups and subjected them to a new realm of impersonal communication and anonymous social interaction in urban industrial centers. These same forces eroded regional differences, thereby absorbing and transforming individual consciousness into an undifferentiated mass consciousness that erased community, memory, and tradition. The factory system, meanwhile, had reduced individuals to the status of mere servants of faceless industrial machines, depriving them of any control over their labor and emptying labor itself of meaning and satisfaction. Although such theories of modernity owed a great deal to Marx, they derived even more inspiration from continental philosophers such as Karl Jaspers, Martin Buber, and especially Hannah Arendt, who warned that these sweeping changes had ushered in a new and dangerous political centralization that allowed the modern state to administer to its alienated and, therefore, highly manipulable citizens as an inchoate mass, thereby obliterating the legal guarantees established under the liberal-democratic institutions of the nineteenth century.[3]

By the mid-1950s, theories of mass society and the examination of its psychological consequences had come to occupy prominent places in

---

[2]Gustave Le Bon, *The Crowd: A Study of the Popular Mind* (New York: Viking Press, 1960).

[3]In *The Human Condition* (Chicago: University of Chicago Press, 1958), Arendt wrote that modern industrial society produced a leveling of the human personality, so that it demanded a "normalized" mode of behavior from individuals, "to make them behave, to exclude spontaneous action or outstanding achievement" (40). "With the emergence of mass society," she concluded, "the realm of the social has finally, after centuries of development, reached the point where it embraces and controls all members of a given community equally and with equal strength" (41).

American sociology's theoretical and empirical investigations, with crucial consequences for the relationship between the sociologist and the rest of American society. The work of many prominent American sociologists engaged in the study of mass society took on a decidedly psychological, behavioristic orientation that engendered among them a profound suspicion of the character and inclinations of the American people. In numerous studies of individual alienation, political apathy, racial and ethnic intolerance, public indifference or outright opposition to the protection of civil liberties, and even latent authoritarianism within the American personality, these scholars claimed to have located dangerous pathologies among the general population that quickly came to imply a general malaise within the body politic itself. Not coincidentally, this suspicion of the "masses" increased as sociologists' assertions of their discipline's scientific character increased. Social scientists' rising social status was accompanied by their flagging confidence in the ability of ordinary people to grasp their own interests and to protect those interests through effective participation in a liberal-democratic political order.

The mass society theory—the West's transition from a traditional, communal, and comparatively static social structure to a modern order of atomization and greater social and psychic fluidity—lay at the heart of turn-of-the-century sociological inquiry, as the first European academic sociologists drew a myriad of contrasts between preindustrial and industrial ways of life. Ferdinand Tönnies wrote in 1887 on the transition from the organic, communal life of *Gemeinschaft* to the artificial, "associative" *Gesellschaft* of modern industrial society.[4] Emile Durkheim characterized traditional societies as sharing a "mechanical solidarity," in which "ideas and tendencies common to all members of the society are greater in number and intensity than those which pertain personally to each member,"[5] whereas industrial society, with its complex division of labor, placed individuals in an increasingly differentiated social order that made possible a new, "organic" solidarity based upon mutual dependence. Max Weber contrasted traditional societies' mystical, charismatic bases of authority and cohesion with the depersonalized, regimented "bureaucratic rationality" of corporate capitalism and the modern state. Georg Simmel, in "The Metropolis and Mental Life," described the city's routinization of social activity, its anonymity, and its "objectification" of individuals as "cogs" within a highly organized and impersonal social order.[6]

---

[4] Ferdinand Tönnies, *Community and Civil Society* (Cambridge: Cambridge University Press, 2001).

[5] Emile Durkheim, *The Division of Labor in Society* (New York: Free Press, 1956), 129.

[6] Georg Simmel, "The Metropolis and Mental Life," in Donald N. Levine, ed., *On Individuality and Social Forms* (Chicago: University of Chicago Press, 1971).

In the United States, Charles Horton Cooley drew upon European theoretical models to introduce the concepts of "primary" and "secondary" group life to distinguish between the former's intimate, face-to-face interaction with the latter's impersonal, bureaucratized social relations characteristic of modernity.[7] Louis Wirth used Cooley's concepts to describe urban life as necessarily devoid of primary-group affiliations, which made it susceptible to crises of social disorganization.[8] Robert Park, whose studies in Germany with Simmel had introduced him to the theory of mass society, wrote his dissertation on crowd behavior, exploring how modernity's conditions of interdependence, its breaking down of local group ties, and atomization of the individual produced new forms of collective behavior.[9] For these founders of modern American sociology, mass society and its transformative consequences represented the essence of the study of modernity.

By the late 1930s, with the publication of Parsons's *The Structure of Social Action* and the appearance after the war of English translations of works by Durkheim and Weber, American sociologists began to confront the theories of classical sociology.[10] In turn, they assimilated the European formulation of the concept of mass society and its concomitant thesis of social alienation. This latter concept of significant imprecision and of varied meaning, rooted in the writings of Rousseau, Hegel, and especially the young, pre-*Capital* Marx, became in the hands of American sociologists an amalgam of the various conceptions of these early formulations and the later interpretations of the classical European sociologists. From Durkheim's scholarship of the 1890s in particular, American scholars appropriated the idea of mass society as subject to crises of "anomie," or states of "normlessness" in which reliable regulators of human conduct ceased to provide the individual with reliable means for the achievement of meaningful goals.[11] Robert Merton, as a young professor

---

[7]Charles Horton Cooley, *Social Organization: A Study of the Larger Mind* (New York: Schocken Books, 1962).

[8]Lewis Wirth, "Urbanism as a Way of Life," in Albert J. Reiss, ed., *On Cities and Social Life* (Chicago: University of Chicago Press, 1964).

[9]Robert Ezra Park, "The City as a Social Laboratory," in Ralph H. Turner, ed., *On Social Control and Collective Behavior* (Chicago: University of Chicago Press, 1967); see also "The City: Suggestions for the Investigation of Human Behavior in the Urban Environment," and "Human Migration and the Marginal Man," in Richard Sennett, ed., *Classic Essays on the Culture of Cities* (New York: Appleton-Century-Crofts, 1969).

[10]A significant exception to this pattern of discovery of classical European sociology was Georg Simmel, whose work Robert Park had championed at the University of Chicago.

[11]Durkheim presented the thesis of the social disorganization wrought by modernity's increasingly complex division of labor in *The Division of Labor in Society* (New York: Free Press, 1997), and he explored its pathological consequences in *Suicide: A Study in Sociology* (New York: Free Press, 1997).

at Harvard, popularized Durkheim's concept in his famous 1938 essay, "Social Structure and Anomie," when he applied it to the conflict between American norms of competitive success and the practical obstacles to their fulfillment, suggesting that some forms of criminal behavior represented attempts to fulfill those norms in the absence of accessible, socially sanctioned means.[12]

Parsons's theoretical focus on anomie, combined with Merton's late-1950s publication of a revised version of his 1938 article in *Social Theory and Social Structure*, moved anomie to the center of postwar sociological discourse.[13] As Philippe Besnard has shown, the concept of anomie became far more significant in American sociology than it had ever been in Durkheim's thought. It had figured most prominently in Durkheim's famous study of suicide, but it disappeared from his later works, never occupying the center of his thought but rather appearing during a period of "crisis, if not rupture" in his career.[14] In the United States, however, anomie not only inspired significant intellectual interest, but it also served as a "tactical weapon" in the struggle between Harvard and Columbia for supremacy in the field of sociology after the war, so that even the French spelling—the *ie* rather than a *y* at the end—served the Harvard scholars in their efforts to demonstrate a familiarity with Durkheim's writings in the original French and, by implication, their mastery of the European sociological tradition itself.[15] Exploring anomie became, in Besnard's words, a "marketing strategy" for the Harvard department in its competition with Columbia, for, as a concept lying outside of lay usage, it became "a password for the initiated," conferring intellectual status upon the user.[16] The appearance of neo-Freudian psychological studies in sociology journals during the 1930s and 1940s, in turn, provided a crucial

---

[12] Robert K. Merton, "Social Structure and Anomie," *American Sociological Review* 3, 6 (October 1938): 672–82.

[13] Besnard points to Parsons's 1930s lectures and his *Structure of Social Action* (New York: McGraw Hill, 1937) as the first studies of Durkheim's work to contain a focus on anomie. The republication of Merton's article in *Social Theory and Social Structure* inspired a Durkheimian discussion of the relationship between anomie and deviance in the April 1959 issue of *American Sociological Review*. In *ASR* 24, 2, see Robert Dubin, "Deviant Behavior and Social Structure: Continuities in Social Theory," 147–64; Richard A. Cloward, "Illegitimate Means, Anomie, and Deviant Behavior," 164–76; and Merton's response, "Social Conformity, Deviation, and Opportunity-Structures: A Comment on the Contributions of Dubin and Cloward," 177–89.

[14] Philippe Besnard, "The Americanization of Anomie at Harvard," *Knowledge and Society: Studies in the Sociology of Culture Past and Present* 6 (1985): 46. Besnard also points to Parsons's emphasis on Durkheim's concept in *The Structure of Social Action* as critical in drawing attention to it.

[15] Ibid., 48.

[16] Ibid., 48–49.

psychological orientation for the postwar studies of alienation that emerged from Harvard and Columbia. From the social-psychological writings of the German émigré scholars Karen Horney and Erich Fromm, influential sociologists derived the idea that individual neurosis could be understood as the product of cultural norms. In her 1930s articles in *The American Sociological Review* and *The American Journal of Sociology*, Horney had revised the Freudian definition of neurosis as stemming from particular pivotal incidents in individual development, arguing instead that the conflicting social and cultural demands modernity imposed upon the individual produced a neurotic personality.[17] Erich Fromm, the émigré psychologist of the Frankfurt School's Institute for Social Research, also contributed crucial explorations of the links between culture and neurosis. In *Escape from Freedom*, he described the transformation of social relationships wrought by the Reformation as having cast the individual into a dilemma of greater independence but also a new loneliness and anxiety, a state of alienation that capitalist society then compounded, thereby making imminent a mass "escape" into irrational, sadomasochistic social and political activity.[18] Fromm expanded on these themes in his 1955 work, *The Sane Society*, proposing that capitalist society's objectification of social existence produced a dangerous society of "idolatry," in which humanity devoted its energies to the alienated worship of the estranged products of its own efforts. Existence then became an impoverished realm of "things" rather than life-affirming "productive human powers."[19] The young Marx's observation that industrial society placed increasing value on "the world of things" and devalued "the world of men," so that individuals experienced a "loss of self," became for Fromm an estrangement from life that encompassed not only productive relations but also humanity's spirituality and its capacity to love.[20]

---

[17] In "Culture and Neurosis," *American Sociological Review* 1, 2 (April 1936): 221–35, Horney proposed that accepted values of Christianity conflicted with the immense cultural pressure upon the individual to attain "success" and thus contributed to neurosis. In *The Neurotic Personality of Our Time* (New York: W.W. Norton, 1937), Horney continued this emphasis on the cultural sources of neurosis. The November 1939 issue of *The American Journal of Sociology* was devoted entirely to the relationships between Freudian concepts and sociology. In her contribution, Horney defined a particular variety of neurosis as a "character disorder" produced by the individual's deviation from social and cultural norms, and she called for a rethinking of the narrow, clinical definition of neurosis proffered by mainstream psychiatry. See Horney, "What Is a Neurosis?" *American Journal of Sociology* 45, 3 (November 1939): 426–32.

[18] Erich Fromm, "Individual and Social Origins of Neurosis," *American Sociological Review* 9, 4 (August 1944): 380–84; *Escape from Freedom* (New York: Farrar and Rinehart, 1941).

[19] Erich Fromm, *The Sane Society* (New York: Henry Holt, 1955), 123.

[20] Karl Marx, "Economic and Philosophic Manuscripts of 1844," in Robert C. Tucker, ed., *The Marx-Engels Reader* (New York: W.W. Norton, 1978), 71.

Harold Lasswell also contributed significantly to this psychological orientation. In 1934, he had observed that different civilizations produced different varieties of mental disorder, and that in the United States the increasingly problematic transition to adulthood—especially the perpetuance of "stringent mores" combined with the child's growing confusion as to the basis of moral authority within the family—would produce "a relatively large incidence of neurosis, psychosis, psychopathic personality formation, together with such crude efforts at adjustment as excessive alcoholism and sexual promiscuity."[21] Lasswell warned that, with the specter of fascism looming over the West, such pathologies posed dire threats to American democracy, and he predicted that "increasing external and domestic insecurity will head the United States along the road of rigid centralization, revolutionary upheavals, and international war, unless the emotional tensions of the nation are handled with skill, luck, and persistence."[22]

The postwar generation of sociologists at Harvard and Columbia also adopted this rather individualized, psychological orientation to the study of mass society. They agreed with the assessment of Karl Mannheim, the German émigré sociologist and former student of Max Weber, who had written in 1940 that "it is only possible to understand the real extent of sociological influence on civilization as a whole if we call attention also to the psychological effects of the elementary social processes."[23] In this view, sociological interpretations of the modern personality had placed undue scholarly emphasis upon social structure at the expense of psychological understanding. Sociological analysis of alienative social structures would have to give way to the study of alienated individuals.[24]

---

[21] Harold Lasswell, *World Politics and Personal Insecurity* (Glencoe, IL: Free Press, 1950), 230.

[22] Ibid., 231.

[23] Karl Mannheim, *Man and Society in an Age of Reconstruction* (London: Kegan Paul, Trench, Trubner, 1940), 20. Mannheim sought to challenge the Marxian contention that economic and political factors constituted the mechanisms of social change, and he insisted that the sociologist must consider social relationships—mere epiphenomena to the Marxist—as of primary importance and understand their psychological effects. "These relationships," he argued, "which are neither economic nor political but social, form the real centre of the drama, in which social changes are directly transformed into psychological changes" (21). His *Man and Society in an Age of Reconstruction,* like the 1930s and 1940s psychoanalytic interpretations of mass personality, became a vital influence on 1950s sociology, and it too was cited repeatedly in studies of mass society and its effects.

[24] C. Wright Mills stood practically alone among the Harvard-Columbia scholars in focusing on the social-structural sources of modern alienation. In *White Collar* (New York: Oxford University Press, 1950), Mills defined alienation as a malaise produced by the shift from an entrepreneurial society to a society of employees. Although he located the individual's alienation from the results of his productive efforts not merely in the capitalist market economy's expropriation of it but in

Several such individualized models of alienation appeared in 1950. In his final year as chairman of the Columbia Sociology Department, Robert MacIver used Durkheim's concept of anomie in his 1950 work, *The Ramparts We Guard*, adopting the mass-society thesis that the condition stemmed from such conditions as "culture clash," and "the violence of change."[25] However, whereas Durkheim had characterized anomie as a characteristic of social structure, MacIver described individuals themselves as anomic. MacIver defined *anomy*—again, the Americanized spelling contrasted with the French rendering that would come to dominate 1950s usage—as a psychological condition, the "state of mind" of the individual "who has been pulled up from his moral roots, who has no longer any standards but only disconnected urges, who has no longer any sense of continuity, of folk, of obligation."[26] MacIver had behaviorized Durkheim's concept, thereby making it amenable to the analysis of anomic personality types. These types, he asserted, included those who had lost their moral "compass" and therefore abandoned themselves to a directionless existence in the immediate present; others responded to this crisis by directing their energies to "extrinsic values"; and a third group experienced this values vacuum as "a fundamental and tragic insecurity."[27] That same year, Robert Lynd, who with Merton would exert a decisive influence over the graduate students in the Columbia department throughout the 1950s, shared the same dark view of the individual personality in the modern age. Mass society, he asserted, caused "the attrition of strong spontaneous ties among men," so that modern individuals suffered the "loss of durable, autonomous standards of thinking and feeling and acting." It reduced individuals to "social atoms suspended in insignificance, acted upon but incapable of initiative save in the narrowest personal sense."[28]

David Riesman similarly popularized a psychological variation on Durkheim's concept of anomie, a glimpse of which surfaced prior to the release of his best-selling *The Lonely Crowd*. In a 1948 letter to Merton, Riesman questioned Merton's agreement with the majority of social scientists on the

---

the larger bureaucratization of labor, Mills's indictment nevertheless resembled that of the young Marx. "The more and harder men work," Mills observed, "the more they build up that which dominates their work as an alien force, the commodity; so also, the more and the harder the white-collar man works, the more he builds up the enterprise outside himself, which is, as we have seen, duly made a fetish and thus indirectly justified" (226).

[25] Robert M. MacIver, *The Ramparts We Guard* (New York: Macmillan, 1950), 139.

[26] Ibid., 84.

[27] Ibid., 85–87.

[28] Robert S. Lynd, foreword to Seymour Martin Lipset, *Agrarian Socialism: The Cooperative Commonwealth Federation in Saskatchewan* (Berkeley: University of California Press, 1950), viii.

perceived high level of individualism in American society, countering that "we are so damn socialized that there is little individuality left except of an anomic sort" and observing the significance of "anomic behavior" and "anomic types."[29] Riesman's use of the term departed from that of Durkheim in that he characterized individuals, rather than social structures, as anomic, and then, in *The Lonely Crowd*, he constructed an anomic character type rather than a pattern of anomic social conditions. There, he expanded Durkheim's conception of anomie to render it "virtually synonymous with maladjusted," and he referred to "the anomics" in much the same manner as he had referred to "inner-" and "other-directeds."[30] While he identified changes in social structure as central to the prevalence of modern anomie, he subordinated them to his exploration of the effects these had had on Americans' personalities. Collectively, these personalities could be understood as what he called "social character," after the usage of the concept found in the work of Fromm, Horney, Erik Erikson, Ruth Benedict, Margaret Mead, and others.[31]

Merton, too, embraced the conception of anomie as a psychological condition. In the 1957 edition of his *Social Theory and Social Structure*, he cited MacIver and Riesman as having demonstrated the possibilities within this new conception, and he insisted that studying anomie as "a condition of individuals" could effectively broaden and complement Durkheim's original concept. The next step, he asserted, required the establishment of "objective" criteria with which to measure the presence of anomie. As recent empirical work had demonstrated, scaling techniques could assess the individual's own subjective perception of his or her own lack of integration within the social order. Sociology now needed, according to Merton, to go beyond this kind of haphazard "social bookkeeping" to establish a compendium of social variables—income levels, residential patterns, age groupings, racial patterns, and so on—against which to test those individual perceptions. The concept of anomie, in its sociological and psychological dimensions, would thereby become amenable to "systematic study."[32]

Indeed, as these individualistic interpretations of alienation took hold, scholars sought to "operationalize" the concept of alienation, to formalize its definition, and to render it amenable to empirical testing through opinion and attitude surveys, the primary postwar techniques of social measurement.

---

[29] David Riesman to Robert Merton, April 21, 1948, David Riesman Papers, Harvard University Archive HUG (FP) 99.12, Box 32.

[30] David Riesman, *The Lonely Crowd: A Study of the Changing American Character* (New Haven, CT: Yale University Press, 1961), 242.

[31] Ibid, 4.

[32] Robert K. Merton, *Social Theory and Social Structure*, rev. ed. (Glencoe, IL: Free Press, 1957), 166.

This process of quantifying and psychologizing existing sociological concepts reflected postwar sociology's turn away from the analysis of social structure and toward that of individual attitudes and behavior. Whereas prewar sociology had involved the former, as epitomized in studies like Robert and Helen Lynd's *Middletown* studies, Lloyd Warner's "Yankee City" series, August B. Hollingshead's *Elmtown's Youth,* and a plethora of other community studies, postwar sociology embraced what Christopher G. A. Bryant has characterized as an individualistic approach to the study of society. Under the influence of Merton and Lazarsfeld, he argues, postwar sociologists accepted that social structure could be understood as simply the sum of its separate individual members, and they had done so because their methods offered rather easy—and, more importantly, scientifically credible—access to the attitudes and behavior of those individuals. This "methodological individualism," then, sustained an instrumental positivist sociology in which "individual attitudes and self-avowed behavior, which are readily ascertainable by means of impressive-looking research instruments, command more attention than the formation and transformation of social structures, which are not; how people respond to situations seems to matter much more than what gives the situations their structure and distribution in the first place."[33]

Clearly, statistical methods of measuring individual attitudes played a primary role in postwar sociology's turn away from the analysis of social structure. However, because the 1950s generation of American sociologists also perceived the mass character of that social structure to be engulfing the individual, the role of sociological theory in shaping the scholarship of the decade appears equally significant. In particular, the preponderance of postwar studies that focused on the values and behavior of individuals but, paradoxically, often minimized their social importance or their possession of historical agency, demands an investigation of the formative influence of classical European sociological theory upon the 1950s generation of sociologists. In James S. Coleman's own assessment of his years as a graduate student in the Columbia program during the 1950s, he describes how the Sociology Department turned away from the study of communities out of a sense that they no longer played the primary role they once had in the socialization and

---

[33]Christopher G. A. Bryant, *Positivism in Social Theory and Research* (London: Macmillan, 1985), 140–41. Bryant quotes a similar argument by Richard H. Wells and J. Steven Picou, who characterize Merton-Lazarsfeld sociology as having "provided an intellectual basis for a directional shift in the content and structure of American sociology to conceptual units of analysis (i.e., individuals and roles) that were operationalizable in terms of empirical indicators and techniques (i.e., survey samples and multivariate analysis." See their *American Sociology: Theoretical and Methodological Structure* (Washington, DC: University Press of America, 1981), 154.

status placement of the individual and that, instead, larger forces outside the community shaped the individual's identity.[34] At Columbia, the graduate students who flocked to Robert Merton's seminars and lectures would receive theoretical validations of this idea in the works of Europeans such as Durkheim and Weber, whose theories suggested that radical social change had produced an individual who lacked the traditional ties of place and kinship.

Seymour Martin Lipset articulated these impressions as a young associate professor in Columbia's graduate program. Lipset had earned his doctorate at Columbia, where, under the influence of Lynd and Merton, he had cultivated a theoretical focus on problems of power, class, social change, and functionalist theory, including the classical theories of mass society. From Lazarsfeld, he acquired the statistical methods he utilized in his dissertation, a study of the success of the agrarian socialist Cooperative Commonwealth Federation party in Saskatchewan. Lipset found in the Canadian province a set of social conditions that departed significantly from the trends of mass society. A single-crop economy, a "one-class society," a multitude of private associations, and political decentralization had fostered in Saskatchewan a far more democratic environment than could be found in the United States. Citizens participated actively in local politics through ubiquitous citizens' boards, so that politics became a part of daily life rather than a ritualized activity at election time. "The relatively large number of farmers' organizations, coöperatives, and other civic-interest organizations encourages common citizens to share in the government of their communities as a normal routine of life," Lipset observed.[35] Because Saskatchewan lacked some of the primary elements of a mass society, it preserved earlier Tocquevillian forms of popular democratic engagement, in that local associative connections nurtured individuals' political awareness and fostered their active participation in political affairs.

However, Lipset foresaw in the province the same clash between increasing bureaucratization and community that every modern society faced. In Saskatchewan, the civil service bureaucracy inhibited the reformist inclinations of the public and its elected representatives. The popular will, as expressed in the election of progressive officials to public office, conflicted with the bureaucratic inertia of a nonelective and highly bureaucratized civil service sector that sought to preserve the status quo. Following Robert Michels, who decades earlier had perceived oligarchical bureaucratic momentum to have developed

---

[34] James S. Coleman, "Columbia in the 1950s," in Bennett M. Berger, ed., *Authors of Their Own Lives: Intellectual Autobiographies of Twenty American Sociologists* (Berkeley: University of California Press, 1990), 90–91.

[35] Lipset, *Agrarian Socialism*, 218.

in even the social-democratic political movements of Europe, Lipset concluded that Saskatchewan, despite its political uniqueness, would ultimately exhibit the same mass-society characteristics as other communities, particularly the bureaucratic erosion of participatory political culture.[36]

Six years later, in *Union Democracy* (1956), a collaborative effort with Columbia students Martin Trow and James S. Coleman, Lipset theorized that nongovernmental organizations faced the same fate. In this study of political decision making in the International Typographical Union, he observed that the associative connections Tocqueville had recognized as essential bulwarks against overreaching state power had deteriorated not only in society in general but also in bureaucratic institutions such as unions.[37] Just as democracy in a mass society suffered under the deterioration of mediating institutions between the state and the individual, modern unions lost their democratic culture as their "autonomous suborganizations" disappeared, depriving union members of "centers of opposition" and "independent sources of organization communication."[38] As Michels had theorized, bureaucratic organizations succumbed inevitably to the "iron law of oligarchy," in which organizational leaders came inevitably to achieve autonomy and to dominate the members. Lipset found the ITU to be a significant exception to Michels's iron law, but an exception that proved the rule. Michels's law itself received only an untested theoretical summary in *Union Democracy*, which revealed Lipset's commitment to a foundation of the mass society thesis. Mass society's deleterious effects on political relationships were then twofold: it eroded the individual's secondary attachments, and those that remained, like unions, exhibited the same situation in microcosm. The associative connections valued by Tocqueville and Durkheim ceased to exist on both levels.

Another Columbia Ph.D., Maurice Stein, tied this deterioration of the individual's secondary attachments to the psychological conditions of alienation and anomie in his 1960 study, *The Eclipse of Community*. As a graduate student, Stein had rejected the Merton-Lazarsfeld social-survey approach to sociological research that dominated the Columbia program in favor of ethnographic community study, but he shared the pervasive sense that

---

[36] Michels' analysis of this oligarchical process can be found in *Political Parties: A Sociological Study of Oligarchical Tendencies of Modern Democracy* (New York, Free Press, 1962).

[37] Lipset recounted this research project a decade later in "The Biography of a Research Project: *Union Democracy*," in Phillip E. Hammond, ed., *Sociologists at Work: Essays on the Craft of Social Research* (New York: Basic Books, 1964).

[38] Seymour Martin Lipset, Martin A. Trow, and James S. Coleman, *Union Democracy: The Internal Politics of the International Typographical Union* (Garden City, NY: Anchor Books, 1956), 86.

classical European theory helped explain the human costs of the transition from traditional to modern communities.[39] In the late 1940s, he had assisted Alvin Gouldner in Gouldner's dissertation research of industrial relations in a gypsum mine and plant, and this formative experience among working-class miners confirmed his belief that the classical sociologists' conceptions of modernity explained the ambivalence he felt toward suburban middle-class culture. That culture's lack of spontaneity and emotional authenticity, he concluded, stemmed from the processes of modernity and the psychic toll they exacted upon the individual.

Stein therefore adopted a "social psychiatric perspective" on the subject of suburbanization, arguing that it had produced most markedly those pathologies of the human personality that the neo-Freudians Fromm, Erikson, and Harry Stack Sullivan had identified and that he believed derived from the conditions of mass society.[40] Suburbia represented for Stein the best environment in which to study the personality characteristics mass society had engendered, as it contained a plethora of psychically damaging conventions and expectations. Of these, the most "grievous human loss" suburbanites experienced stemmed from their "status-dominated life style" that forced them "into a rigid mold from within which they can see only limited aspects of human reality." Suburbia dehumanized them, so that "other people become threats or objects to be used." Emotionally, Stein argued, suburbanites languished in the "juvenile phase" that Harry Stack Sullivan had described, for, in the suburbs, "the identity struggles of adolescence are resolved through stereotypes that simplify reality rather than through fresh perceptions that provide a basis for expanding contact with personal and interpersonal realities."[41]

As for the prospects for autonomous individual self-realization in a mass society, Stein held out little hope. The "exurbanites," he wrote, "purchased" their individuality through their submission to their careers, so that "all opportunities for genuine expression" remained imprisoned within "the bounds dictated by commercial necessities."[42] They had confused the assertion of individuality with the attainment of status, thereby sacrificing broader, more

---

[39] Stein recalls his attitude toward the articles of faith of the Columbia department and his gravitation to community studies as a viable alternative in "The Eclipse of Community: Some Glances at the Education of a Sociologist," in Arthur J. Vidich, Joseph Bensman, and Maurice R. Stein, eds., *Reflections on Community Studies* (New York: John Wiley, 1964).

[40] Maurice R. Stein, *The Eclipse of Community: An Interpretation of American Studies* (Princeton, NJ: Princeton University Press, 1960), 285.

[41] Ibid., 286–87.

[42] Ibid., 226.

creative avenues to self-expression. The result, Stein declared, left the modern individual without a personality at all:

> Role personalities in modern urban society easily become objectified clichés. They congeal personal idiosyncrasies into networks of formalized expectations. When the pace of change is so rapid that the expectations themselves are no longer stable, then even the cliché identities that they are capable of engendering cannot be sustained. Thus the last source of identity, role personality, is shattered, leaving only a vague self-image of "flexibility" and powerful unconscious control by one's security system as guides through the social wasteland.[43]

In its denial of the primary-group influences of healthy community life and its neo-Freudianism, Stein's conception of suburbia as exemplifying the soul-crushing pressures of mass society reflected neatly the broader 1950s sociological conceptions derived from individualistic interpretations of Durkheim and Tönnies. If modernity signified the eclipse of community, the individual personality necessarily became the primary object of investigation for sociology.

Thus, the Americanization of the idea of alienation represented an assimilation of the various intellectual antecedents, especially the theories of Durkheim, and their scientization into empirically testable propositions, all of which would validate the existence of alienation as an objective condition by concentrating on alienation's psychological, rather than sociological, dimensions. Quantitative studies of alienation and anomie therefore concentrated on the psychological dimensions of these modern maladies, treating them as character expressions of individuals' lack of integration within societies whose structural features received only cursory analysis or assessment.

The quantification and individualization of alienation had taken a decisive step forward in 1951, with a paper presented by Leo Srole at the annual meeting of the American Sociological Society. Srole, a University of Chicago Ph.D. in sociology and social anthropology, had co-authored a volume of Lloyd Warner's influential Yankee City community studies, and in the late 1940s he served as division director of the Bureau of Applied Social Research. In a precedent-setting 1956 article, he submitted a set of measurement techniques for the establishment of an operationalized conception of anomie, in which, once again, the focus became anomie's individual psychological

---

[43] Ibid., 267–68.

manifestations. Srole noted that Merton, MacIver, and Laswell had initiated a "diversification" of the concept of anomie to make it amenable to new forms of empirical inquiry. To extend this model of analysis, Srole offered his own psychological formulation of anomie, hypothesizing that it reflected "social malintegration," or what he termed "anomia," explaining his choice of the latter term as a means of distinguishing his molecular approach from that of Durkheim. Although the Durkheimian approach to anomie involved the macroscopic analysis of social structure, it presented "formidable operational problems" to the researcher, problems that could be avoided with a molecular approach, which, Srole noted, "has the advantage of being readily fitted to the established operational apparatus of the sample survey."[44] With the concept of "anomia" and its opposite, "eunomia," Srole asserted, individuals' relative levels of social integration could be measured on a "eunomia-anomia" continuum.

To measure this condition of anomia, Srole and his research team constructed five ideational "components," expressed as opinion statements, which reflected what he believed to be its basic elements. The first opinion item expressed the idea that community leaders existed detached from the individual's ability to influence or benefit from their decisions. The second item proposed that the individual perceived the social order as "essentially fickle and unpredictable," an "orderless" situation that discouraged his or her faith in any meaningful realization of "future life goals." The third item expressed the idea that the individual's lot in life was "retrogressing," that things were getting worse for him or her. The fourth item concerned "the deflation or loss of internalized social norms and values, reflected in extreme form in the individual's sense of the meaningless of life itself." Finally, the fifth item asserted that the individual's "framework of immediate personal relationships, the very rock of his social existence, was no longer predictive or supportive."[45] With these items, the Srole group created an "anomia scale," following the scaling models of Louis Guttman, and applied it to the specific question of whether individuals suffering from "anomia" harbored hostile attitudes toward minority groups.

---

[44]Leo Srole, "Social Integration and Certain Corollaries: An Exploratory Study," *American Sociological Review* 21, 6 (December 1956): 710–11.

[45]Ibid., 712–13. Srole's questions, which requested an "agree" or "disagree" response, consisted of such statements as "Nowadays a person has to live pretty much for today and let tomorrow take care of itself," to which an "agree" response would indicate one's loss of faith in his or her ability to realize life goals; and "In spite of what some people say, the lot of the average man is getting worse, not better," to which an "agree" response would indicate a perceived separation of the ordinary individual from his or her community leaders.

Srole's operational definition of anomia and his anomia scale influenced subsequent 1950s studies of alienation and anomie, studies that also accepted the prevailing definition of these conditions as personal, psychological phenomena to be studied and measured with the techniques of survey research. Wendell Bell, in a 1957 article in the journal *Sociometry,* used the Srole scale to measure the instance of anomie in various San Francisco neighborhoods, separated according to socio-economic status and "family characteristics," such as the percentages of working women and of single-family dwellings. Bell found that anomie existed in an inverse relationship to economic status and correlated directly with "social isolation" among men, a concept understood to represent the individual's infrequent participation in "informal" and "formal groups."[46] In a subsequent article, Bell and Dorothy L. Meier drew upon the San Francisco study to apply Srole's anomia scale to measure the presence of "utter hopelessness and discouragement" among individuals who lacked access to the achievement of their life goals.[47]

Other sociologists created their own scaling procedures to measure alienation as a phenomenon of the personality. Dwight Dean created an "alienation scale" consisting of components of "powerlessness," "normlessness," and "social isolation," which he appropriated from Marx, Durkheim, and Horney, and he concluded that advancing age and decreasing social status produced higher incidences of these three components in a "general syndrome" of alienation.[48] In another study, Gwynn Nettler presented the results of a study of alienation—which he defined as "self-estrangement from society"—among a sample of the general population. Like Srole and the other survey researchers of anomia, Nettler asked his interview subjects to read and consider "paradigmatic expressions of alienation" that he had drawn from "the psychological literature and belles-lettres."[49] He then used his subjects'

---

[46]Wendell Bell, "Anomie, Social Isolation, and the Class Structure," *Sociometry* 20, 2 (June 1957): 114.

[47]Dorothy L. Meier and Wendell Bell, "Anomia and Differential Access to the Achievement of Life Goals," *American Sociological Review* 24, 2 (April 1959): 189–202.

[48]Dwight G. Dean, "Alienation: Its Meaning and Measurement," *American Sociological Review* 26, 5 (October 1961): 753–58. That Dean and others derived theoretical grounding from such diverse sources indicated their lack of a clear normative or ideological framework for the study of mass psychology. The research methods they employed, which occupied the center of these studies, marginalized such concerns.

[49]Gwynn Nettler, "A Measure of Alienation," *American Sociological Review* 22, 6 (December 1957): 670–77. Nettler's paradigmatic statements included an Edmund Wilson excerpt from *A Piece of My Mind* (1956), in which Wilson professed a greater sense of belonging in the eighteenth century and rejected many activities central to modern life, such as driving, listening to the radio, watching television, and attending movies. Wilson concluded, "And am I, too, I wonder, stranded? Am I, too, an exceptional case? When, for example, I look through *Life* magazine, I feel that I do

responses to select those individuals "thought to approximate such an alien orientation" for further interviewing with questions about voting habits, consumerism, the media, family life, and spirituality. Nettler found that the subjects selected for their "alienated" outlook displayed "a consistent maintenance of unpopular and averse attitudes toward familism, the mass media and mass taste, current events, popular education, conventional religion and the telic view of life, nationalism, and the voting process."[50] They tended to remain unmarried, harbored decidedly "Schopenhauerian" attitudes about the family, shared a deep suspicion of politics and a minimal interest in current events, and lacked faith in God. Finally, they expressed "a vocal disdain of American mass culture," particularly such hallmarks of modernity as cars, TV, radio, the media, advertising, and spectator sports. Once again, social structure remained implicit and undigested, and Nettler speculated at the conclusion of his article that a relationship existed between this kind of alienation and a variety of social and psychological pathologies, such as mental illness, drug addiction, marital discord, and crime—a rather curious diagnosis, considering that prominent public intellectuals of the 1950s had themselves undertaken the disparaging of "mass culture," and with singularly self-satisfied zeal, which may help explain Nettler's subsequent decision to back away from it.[51]

Indeed, as American sociologists explored the psychological manifestations of mass society, their collective vision of the American personality bore a strong resemblance to the bleak outlook expressed within broader intellectual currents. Prominent postwar writers, led by the "New York intellectuals" around opinion magazines such as Partisan Review and Dissent, displayed a profound suspicion of ordinary people as victims of pathologies peculiar to modernity and politically and culturally dangerous in their effects. In Partisan Review, writers as various as Dwight Macdonald, Melvin Lasky, Clement Greenberg, and Irving Howe detected a kind of psychological malaise amidst modern conditions of mechanized production, high geographic mobility, and bland prosperity, and they perceived a stultifying mass culture

---

not belong to the country depicted there, that I do not even live in that country" (673). Nettler also drew upon an interviewer's reflections upon a conversation with George Santayana, which characterized Santayana as having "no beliefs and no loyalties," "denying the worth of any action," and irritating "everyone who believed in anything" (673). The selection of such profound expressions of estrangement from modern life seem to reveal more about the outlook of the researcher than about those interviewed.

[50] Ibid., 674.

[51] Nettler explored the relationship between alienation and crime subsequently in "Antisocial Sentiment and Criminality," American Sociological Review 24, 2 (April 1959): 202–08. He found that the link between the two had been overemphasized and that the "moderate conformist," rather than a society's most alienated individuals, proved to be the most crime-prone.

to be the end product of these.[52] Contributing to this pattern of indictment were the émigré scholars of the Frankfurt School, particularly Theodor Adorno, Max Horkheimer, Leo Lowenthal, and Herbert Marcuse, who condemned popular forms of entertainment as sources of false consciousness and of satisfactions devoid of human meaning that encouraged the accomodation of the capitalist order.[53] By the end of the 1950s, a coherent body of literature and scholarship attacking America as a mass society with a pernicious mass culture had taken shape and decried American civilization's descent into mediocrity, conformity, isolation, and self-estrangement.

However, what set American sociology apart from this larger intellectual discourse on modernity was its practitioners' rather limited exposure to the breadth of the New York and Frankfurt School critiques and their greater familiarity with the classical European sociological theories. At Columbia, the program from which most of the influential sociological critiques of mass society emanated, most of the graduate students received their theoretical background within a rather insular intellectual environment, at the center of which stood Robert Merton. As James Coleman recalls:

To the graduate student, there was no discipline of sociology outside Columbia. Instead we saw a self-confidence, a looking inward coupled with inattention to the outside. There was a sociological literature of some importance, a literature to which Merton especially directed our attention, but except for the work of Talcott Parsons, which Merton admitted to it, that literature was all written by Europeans no longer

---

[52] For an inventory of the various intellectual assaults against mass culture, see Richard Pells, *The Liberal Mind in a Conservative Age: American Intellectuals in the 1940s and 1950s* (New York: Harper & Row, 1985), chap. 4. Of particular significance was the 1952 *Partisan Review* series, *Our Country and Our Culture*, which brought together leading American writers in a symposium on the state of American culture and the intellectual's place within it. The concept of mass society was prominent in many of the critiques presented. For an interpretation of the evolution of Dwight Macdonald's ideas toward a paternalistic aesthetic elitism, see Paul R. Gorman, *Left Intellectuals and Popular Culture in Twentieth-Century America* (Chapel Hill: University of North Carolina Press, 1996), chap. 7. Bernard Rosenberg's co-edited collection, with David Manning White, *Mass Culture: The Popular Arts in America* (Glencoe, IL: Free Press, 1957), brought together a host of influential critics of mass culture, including Irving Howe, Leslie Fiedler, and Dwight Macdonald. In *No Respect: Intellectuals and Popular Culture* (New York: Routledge, Chapman and Hall, 1989), Andrew Ross offers a critique of the elitist tendencies in the volume similar to that of Gorman.

[53] See Adorno, "On Popular Music," *Studies in Philosophy and Social Sciences* 9, 1 (1941); "A Social Critique of Radio Music," *Kenyon Review* 7, 2 (Spring 1945): 17–48; Marcuse, "Some Social Implications of Modern Technology," *Studies in Philosophy and Social Sciences* 9, 3 (1941): 414–39; Horkheimer, "Art and Mass Culture," *Studies in Philosophy and Social Sciences* 9, 2 (1941): 290–304; Lowenthal, "Historical Perspectives of Popular Culture," in Bernard Rosenberg and David Manning White, eds., *Mass Culture: The Popular Arts in America* (Glencoe, IL: Free Press, 1957).

alive. The effective absence of a discipline west of the Hudson River was most strongly emphasized by the absence of interest in reading or publishing in the journals. Graduate students were not encouraged to read the professional journals; no self-respecting graduate student at Columbia entertained the thought of journal publication as a goal. To us, Lazarsfeld and Merton had no such interests (no matter that they did publish in the journals); the world of sociology was confined to Columbia. Graduate students followed suit, with no interest other than having a paper read by Merton or Lazarsfeld. Once *that* had occurred, there was little interest in having it read by others.[54]

Merton's pedagogical and intellectual focus on classical European scholarship meant that his students received substantial exposure to exclusively sociological theories of mass society and alienation. The Columbia students' effective isolation from broader New York intellectual and even sociological currents, this Mertonian focus meant that Columbia scholars—with the exception of those like Daniel Bell and Nathan Glazer, who had written extensively for opinion magazines—formulated theories that contained the classical dismay over cultural leveling and general mass mindlessness but which lacked the post-Marxist, culturally elitist fatalism of a Macdonald or Irving Howe. Indeed, while the *Partisan Review* intellectuals made frequent use of the concept of alienation, particularly in referring to the intellectual's estrangement from mainstream society, postwar Ph.D.'s who graduated from the Harvard and Columbia programs applied alienation only to the subjects of their theoretical and empirical investigations, not to themselves. The scientific identity forged by Merton, Lazarsfeld, Stouffer, and Parsons had pointed many prominent young sociologists in the direction of a scientific elitism that was of dire consequence for the relationship between American sociology and the nonacademic social realm that it supposedly served. The quantification and theoreticization of the individual psyche in a mass society exacerbated the rift between the layperson and the sociologist-as-scientist.

This professional self-estrangement from lay discourse became most evident in the profoundly pessimistic political outlook that the postwar generation of sociologists shared with the broader American intellectual community. Stein's exegesis on suburbia, for instance, described a pervasive intellectual incapacity among the American people that amounted to a requiem for democratic culture. Under contemporary conditions of status striving, role confusion, and impoverishment of the creative personality, individuals appeared to be losing their ability to participate effectively as

---

[54]Coleman, "Columbia in the 1950s," 79.

citizens. Stein concluded that modern American society's "minor irrationalities" endangered democracy itself by "weakening the capacity for rational social thought." A polity incapable of critical thought could not participate effectively in democratic decision making, thereby rendering the whole society vulnerable to political confusion and decay. "Men who cannot separate fact from fiction in the local political struggles that go on around them will hardly be able to make effective decisions during a real national crisis," Stein warned. "The very fabric of democratic society is weakened when men can no longer understand their everyday worlds."[55]

As Stein's analysis indicates, the bleak prognosis he and many other sociologists offered for the individual's psychological autonomy in a mass society intersected with their growing concern over the survival of democratic institutions. Whether these perceptions stood as valid assessments of their time remains less important than that they reflected a new political pessimism that set postwar sociologists apart from previous generations of social scientists. The theories of alienation and anomie prominent in 1950s sociological scholarship—and the operationalized concepts and survey and scaling techniques that accompanied them—combined with the postwar generation's profound anxieties about threats to political freedom and the prospects for liberal democracy in an age of mass society, particularly in light of challenges from fascist and communist movements. Postwar sociologists' perceptions of pervasive alienation and anomie therefore became the basis for the construction of attenuated conceptions of democracy within postwar sociology, as the apparent evidence of broad patterns of intolerance, prejudice, apathy, and conformity within American society seemed to call into question the average American citizen's capacity for direct participation in a democratic political order.

---

[55] Stein, *The Eclipse of Community*, 328.

5

Theories of Mass Society
and the Advent of a New Elitism

The roots of the postwar American sociologists' linking of modern
mass society and alienation to the threat of political tyranny lay in
the works of conservative European social thinkers such as Gustave Le Bon and José Ortega y Gasset. Le Bon's 1895 essay *The Crowd*
popularized the Nietzschean idea of the modern individual as an irrational creature whose absorption into the mass rendered him incapable of
independent judgment or will. The mass therefore constituted a "servile
flock" that was "ever incapable of doing without its master," an authority
inevitably despotic in its exercise.[1] Ortega, in his 1930 essay, *The Revolt of
the Masses*, wrote of the twentieth century as the age of the "average man,"
the "spoiled child of human history," who had rejected arrogantly and
effortlessly the traditions and institutions that had sustained civilization
and had replaced them with "spiritual barbarism." The modern condition
of "superabundance," Ortega claimed, had impoverished the souls of
ordinary individuals, destroying their respect for civilization's noblest
values and institutions. "The mass," he lamented, "crushes beneath it everything that is different, everything that is excellent, individual, qualified,
and select."[2] Mass man succumbed to obsessions with games and sports,

---

[1]Gustave Le Bon, *The Crowd* (New York: Viking, 1960), 118.

[2]José Ortega y Gasset, *The Revolt of the Masses* (New York: W. W. Norton, 1932), 18.

"the cult of the body," debased, unromantic relations with women, and an arrogant anti-intellectualism. Worst of all, mass man preferred autocratic government over liberal democracy, uniformity of opinion over freedom of discussion, and individual conformity over political liberty. For Ortega, the revolt of the masses led directly to fascism. Ortega perceived in his time "the triumph of a hyperdemocracy in which the mass acts directly, outside the law, imposing its aspirations and its desires by means of material pressure."[3]

The calamitous experiences of fascism and Stalinism during the 1930s and 1940s solidified for many American intellectuals and social scientists the connections Ortega had perceived between mass society, alienation, and totalitarian threats to freedom and to civilization itself, particularly as refugees from Nazism arrived in the United States. German émigré scholars Emil Lederer, Hannah Arendt, and Karl Mannheim—all of whom were cited repeatedly in postwar American social science analyses of mass society— theorized that totalitarianism filled the void left by mass society's leveling of the class and political structures that had formerly protected rational political discourse and practice. Lederer described masses as aggregations of individuals whose particular ties to social groups no longer mattered; they had become "united by emotions, never by reason," and their incapacity for independent critical thought made possible the rise of modern dictatorship and in turn sustained its control.[4] In *The Origins of Totalitarianism,* Arendt asserted that mass society was a prerequisite of totalitarian movements, in that it provided them with the human raw material—a mass of isolated, rootless, politically disengaged, "superfluous" citizens—necessary for success.[5] Mannheim as well observed that mass society's failure to integrate individuals into the social structure meant that dangerous "irrationalities" normally controlled or neutralized by that structure threatened to "force their way into political life." Democratic political life, which depended upon "rational direction" for its survival, might then succumb to those irrationalities and "produce its own antithesis," dictatorship.[6]

---

[3]Ibid., 17.

[4]Emil Lederer, *The State of the Masses: The Threat of the Classless Society* (New York: W. W. Norton, 1940), 30–31.

[5]Hannah Arendt, *The Origins of Totalitarianism* (Cleveland, OH: World Publishing, 1958). Significantly, Arendt observed the emergence of a European "mass man," but she doubted that such an individual existed in the social conditions of the United States: "America, the classical land of equality of condition and of general education with all its shortcomings, knows less of the modern psychology of masses than perhaps any other country in the world" (316).

[6]Karl Mannheim, *Man and Society in an Age of Reconstruction* (London: Kegan Paul, Trench, Trubner, 1940), 63.

American sociologists thus integrated their readings of classical sociology with their heightened concern over the new threat that totalitarianism seemed to pose to democracy, adopting Ortega y Gasset's lament that the alienated masses now possessed control over history, erasing vital cultural traditions and challenging haphazardly the "normal" channels of authority. Talcott Parsons wrote in 1942 that fascism and other forms of radicalism constituted movements in which "large masses of the 'common people' have become imbued with a highly emotional, indeed often fanatical, zeal for a cause."[7] These latter were the poorly integrated victims of the "rationalization" of the modern world, especially susceptible to the fascist appeals of well-situated elites who successfully tapped into the fanaticism that social disorganization had awakened in them. Robert MacIver wrote in 1950 that "the presence of anomy in modern society is evidenced by the spread of violently divisive doctrines, doctrines of all-or-nothing, doctrines that loudly preach a reactionary or a revolutionary authoritarianism, doctrines that appeal to men not as human beings but as de-individualized masses in motion."[8] The voice of the alienated was that of the fascist, one who lacked the spirit of toleration, a sense of moral complexity, or respect for democratic institutions. The pervasiveness of authoritarian ideas during the first half of the twentieth century, then, evidenced the pervasiveness of alienation.

Robert Nisbet provided the most salient example of such an indictment in his 1953 work, *The Quest for Community*. Nisbet, then a professor in the new sociology program at the University of California at Berkeley, perceived in mass society a fatal "atomization of all social and cultural relationships within which human beings gain their normal sense of membership in society." Mass society rendered individuals "insecure, basically lonely, and ground down, either through decree or historical circumstance, into mere particles of social dust."[9] Under such circumstances, the state appeared to the alienated to be their savior from powerlessness and isolation. Nisbet asked, "What remains, then, but to rescue the masses from their loneliness, their hopelessness and despair, by leading them into the Promised Land of the absolute, redemptive State?"[10] Like Tocqueville in his study of the roots of the French Revolution, Nisbet feared the kind of state power that emerged out of

---

[7] Talcott Parsons, "Some Sociological Aspects of the Fascist Movements" (presidential address, Eastern Sociological Society, Asbury Park, NJ, April 25, 1942); *Social Forces* 21, 2 (December 1942): 138.

[8] Robert M. MacIver, *The Ramparts We Guard* (New York: Macmillan, 1950), 89.

[9] Robert A. Nisbet, *The Quest for Community: A Study in the Ethics of Order and Freedom* (New York: Oxford University Press, 1953), 198–99.

[10] Ibid., 199.

the breakdown of community life and local sources of political and social authority, a power that centralized itself as it abolished or simply supplanted those institutions and traditions that had declined. The associative organizations Tocqueville had recognized as serving a vital mediating function between the state and the individual had ruptured, leaving society vulnerable to political domination by a powerful state.[11]

Nisbet's conservative analysis of mass society, which Daniel Bell characterized as "at heart a defense of an aristocratic cultural tradition,"[12] reflected a profound dilemma within the plethora of postwar incarnations of the mass society theory, as each sought to reconcile presumptions of the death of traditional institutions with a redeeming faith in a kind of democracy that could carry on without them. As Leon Bramson observed in his important interpretation of this dilemma, *The Political Context of Sociology*, American sociologists faced the challenge of reconciling a theory with powerfully elitist implications with their commitments to democratic liberalism.[13] Among the immediate postwar generation of new sociology Ph.D.'s, particularly those from Columbia, scholarly interpretations of mass society, alienation, and democracy conveyed a collective loss of faith in the ordinary citizen, combined with a defense of the institutional autonomy and scientific authority of sociology that Parsons, Merton, Lazarsfeld, and Stouffer had advanced in the name of sociology's professional success. The theory of mass society, when

---

[11]Significantly, the thorough influence of Tocqueville evident in the work of Nisbet and, as James Kloppenberg notes, David Riesman, was conspicuously absent from the work of Harvard and Columbia sociologists and their students. In books and essays that virtually all 1950s graduate students and young scholars read, Merton, and particularly Parsons in *The Structure of Social Action*, identified Weber and Durkheim, and, to a lesser degree Gaetano Mosca and Vilfredo Pareto, as the scholars who liberated social investigation from inherited values and ideological prejudices, thereby providing the foundation for making sociology "scientific." As for Tocqueville, *The Structure of Social Action* contains not a single reference, nor does Parsons's 1951 work, *The Social System*, nor his work of the same year, co-authored with Edward Shils, *Toward a General Theory of Action*. In Parsons, Shils, Naegle, and Pitts, eds., *Theories of Society*, (New York: Free Press, 1961), a 1500-page collection of sociological essays by prominent scholars, only Shils refers to Tocqueville, and then only twice. Of Merton's total of two references to Tocqueville in his *Social Theory and Social Structure*, rev. ed. (Glencoe, IL: Free Press, 1957) essays, one is particularly illuminating, for it acknowledges Tocqueville's doubt that the democratic culture of the United States could provide an environment for the maturation of science superior to that of the Old World. Merton, of course, insisted the opposite, that democracy represented the only suitable context for scientific progress. In sum, the Parsons-Merton conception of sociology omitted Tocqueville and thereby helped ensure his omission from the work of much of the rest of the scholarship of their generation. On Tocqueville's influence on Riesman's *The Lonely Crowd*, see Kloppenberg's *The Virtues of Liberalism* (New York: Oxford University Press, 2004), chap. 5.

[12]Daniel Bell, "The Theory of Mass Society: A Critique," *Commentary* 22, 1 (July 1956): 78.

[13]Leon Bramson, *The Political Context of Sociology* (Princeton, NJ: Princeton University Press, 1961).

combined with postwar sociology's scientific aspirations, produced a decidedly Hamiltonian fear for the maintenance of order in the face of perceived political challenges by the mob, rather than a Jeffersonian faith in participatory democracy.

James Coleman's *Community Conflict,* a study of the various ways in which different communities resolved controversy, exemplified this use of the mass-society theory to contrast traditional societies' high levels of continuity and long-standing norms of social practice with modern communities' state of flux and confusion. "In our changing society," he wrote, "such slow diffusion can never keep pace with events; communities continually face problems unique in their own history and for which no precedent exists in the experience of the community leaders."[14] His study, produced under a Twentieth Century Fund grant to the Bureau of Applied Social Research, reflected in turn the Columbia scholars' tendency to link social disorganization to new and complex social and psychological pathologies. In the event of a crisis of collective purpose, modern communities faced a popular revolt against established administrative authority, he asserted, as the "ordinarily inactive" majority succumbed to "a completely new atmosphere of suspicion," in which "values which were well accepted only a short time ago are liable to attack."[15] Public irrationality forced the administrative authority into a defensive position, in which even "one tiny misstep" would bring the wrath of the activated majority down upon it.

Philip Selznick's 1950s writings exemplified the postwar Columbia scholars' linking of mass society, its psychological toll on the individual, and the threat of tyranny. Selznick was a young socialist during the 1940s, at which time he also became a Columbia student of Lynd and Merton. At Columbia, Selznick, like many of his peers, made what Nathan Glazer would later describe as the transition "from socialism to sociology," a loss of faith in democratic avenues to socialism and a growing interest—kindled significantly by readings in European social theory—in the obstacles mass society had placed before democracy itself.[16] In his dissertation, a study of the New Deal's Tennessee Valley Authority (TVA) project that he conducted in the early 1940s, Selznick had examined how mass society's democratizing tendencies compelled governments to confront the political excesses of the "mass man," a challenge that New Deal programs like the TVA had been carefully tailored to meet. In a 1951 article, "Institutional Vulnerability in Mass Society," which was based on work he had performed as a research associate in the Rand

---

[14]James S. Coleman, *Community Conflict* (New York: Free Press, 1957), 2.

[15]Ibid., 8.

[16]Nathan Glazer, "From Socialism to Sociology," in Bennet M. Berger, ed., *Authors of Their Own Lives* (Berkeley: University of California Press, 1990), 190–91.

Corporation's Social Science Division, Selznick drew upon Ortega to assert that the emergence of mass society had rendered American institutions vulnerable to attack by the masses. Mass society had produced a "cultural vacuum," he argued, as elites lost their moral and institutional influence over the rest of the society's members. As modernity's "powerful solvents" of science, technology, and urbanization eroded the primary bonds of family and local community, they destroyed the "sacred quality" of traditional institutions as sources of values. Their disintegration served to "warp the self-confidence of the culture-bearers," opening them to "the pressures of an emergent mass."[17] Mass society, an *Ersatzgemeinschaft* of rootlessness and confusion, thus became for Selznick "one which does not permit elites to carry out their cultural functions."[18]

Selznick asserted that these corrosive conditions exposed democratic societies to grave totalitarian threats. Borrowing neo-Freudian concepts from Erich Fromm, he explained that the combination of a rootless mass and a hobbled elite allowed totalitarian elements to make inroads into the polity with appeals to the individual's "need to belong." Fascist elements exploited the masses' "readiness for manipulation by symbols, especially those permitting sado-masochistic releases," compelling their submission to an authority characterized by "aggression against the weak, nihilism, and conformity."[19] The theory of mass society thus became for Selznick an element of Cold War strategy.

Selznick connected his theory of a crisis in elite cultural leadership to the exigencies of the Cold War a year later, in *The Organizational Weapon*. The proliferation of studies of alienation and anomie and the new national policy of containment of Soviet communism pointed directly to the importance of organizational effectiveness in the face of pressure from the irrational general population. In *The Organizational Weapon,* Selznick theorized that institutional instability threatened to allow communist infiltrators to make inroads into American institutions, as exemplified in Bolshevism's successful "internal subversion" in Russia. Totalitarianism had triumphed in Russia due to the social dislocations and moral confusion modernity had produced. The

---

[17] Philip Selznick, "Institutional Vulnerability in Mass Society," *American Journal of Sociology* 51, 4 (January 1951): 322–23.

[18] Ibid., 321. Here, Selznick also sought to clarify the insights of "antiegalitarians" such as Ortega and Mannheim, who he believed were not criticizing the competence of the masses to make decisions or exert a primary cultural influence but rather simply their participation in roles previously confined to elites. Mass society represented not an instance of the relative competence of masses and elites for leadership; rather, it involved the deterioration of roles. The masses had, in effect, forgotten their place.

[19] Ibid., 324.

Bolsheviks made effective use of what he termed "organizational weapons" against social institutions—"the institutional receptacles of social power"— weakened by the social turmoil and economic uncertainty mass society had wrought. The Bolsheviks' success, far from constituting a simple seizure of political power, reflected a thorough penetration of a myriad of social institutions central to Russian life.

In such a state of institutional instability and decline of elite authority, Selznick argued, communist movements could exploit weaknesses in churches, media organs, labor unions, universities, and governmental bodies in the United States and infiltrate them. They received vital assistance in this effort from mass society's alienated victims, especially those of the American middle class. Selznick referred to these vulnerable individuals as possessing a "Stalinoid" outlook, a term he understood to be in use ordinarily as a "rough synonym for 'fellow traveler'" but which was to be employed as a "psychological category" in his study.[20] These individuals had been drawn into the "communist orbit," but they had not abandoned their ties to mainstream social institutions, so they served for the communists as crucial inroads into those institutions, "political vacuums" through which the party could infiltrate them.[21] Middle-class alienation thus provided the breach through which communism might threaten American democracy.

Selznick's identification of a Stalinoid personality exemplified the diagnosis many sociologists would formulate by the end of the 1950s to describe the ordinary American's psychological condition. The Stalinoid typified the alienated individual, one who experienced "the feeling of isolation, of anxiety, of the need to find some substitute for older rejected values."[22] The Stalinoid's desire for moral order and commitment thus explained communism's appeal. Its promise of transformative change and a social environment of renewed solidarity and justice exploited the alienated individual's sense of moral confusion and estrangement. At the same time, however, the Stalinoid's commitment to communism proved tenuous, for this individual's alienated character rendered him or her incapable of solid commitments of any kind. The Stalinoid's assistance to the cause could only be halfhearted, for it originated not in heartfelt sympathy for communist ideals but merely in "feelings of cynicism, frustration, and an unfulfilled need for social solidarity."[23] The

---

[20] Selznick, *The Organizational Weapon: A Study of Bolshevik Strategy and Tactics* (Glencoe, IL: Free Press, 1960), 297.

[21] Ibid., 298; 175.

[22] Ibid., 299.

[23] Ibid., 299.

alienated individual, a superficial being who "moves from one fad to another," never acquired a deep sense of attachment to anything. Ironically, this very superficiality proved vital to the communists, for the Stalinoid's refusal to abandon his or her participation in mainstream institutions provided the opening for communist infiltration. Selznick observed, "Precisely because he is not withdrawn from his institutional environment—because he looks, dresses, talks like a conventional middle-class individual, because he has not compromised himself legally—he can serve the party well in gaining access to areas of influence so long as effective organizational controls are maintained in the hands of reliable personnel."[24]

Another Columbia Ph.D., Herbert Krugman, constructed a similar assessment of the appeal of communism to socially estranged individuals. In a 1952 article in *Public Opinion Quarterly*, he published the results of fifty interviews with former Communist Party members conducted as part of the Appeals of Communism Project sponsored by Princeton's Center of International Studies. Like Selznick, Krugman conceived of a connection between participation in the Communist Party and particular personality disorders associated with modernity. Membership in the party, which he characterized as a "highly deviant" group, addressed certain of these participants' needs that the larger society had failed to satisfy. It therefore fulfilled particular "functions," both conscious and unconscious, in the lives of its members, all of which Krugman associated with the "release of anxiety" the individuals required due to their maladjustment to modern life. Communism's unconscious functions in particular reflected Krugman's assimilation of the mass society–alienation paradigm. He identified six manifestations of this maladjustment—"hostility," "unworthiness," "weakness," "apathy," "confusion," and "isolation"—which resembled the language of the alienation theories.[25]

Krugman's findings appeared to reveal the same kinds of connections between individuals' lack of secondary-group attachments and alienation prevalent in his fellow Columbia scholars' studies. He had separated his interview subjects into two categories—"intellectuals," whom he defined to include "journalists, writers, artists, professionals, students, etc.," and trade unionists. Unlike the trade unionists, the "intellectuals" had never belonged to any voluntary organizations before joining the Communist Party, which

---

[24] Ibid., 301. In a cryptic footnote, Selznick suggested a relationship between the kind of alienation he described and that explored by Riesman in *The Lonely Crowd*: "It may be well to re-emphasize here the point made above that the 'Stalinoid type' is not the only kind of individual who has been influenced by communism. In addition, on a general level, David Riesman's analysis of the 'other-directed' political style is illuminating" (299).

[25] Herbert E. Krugman, "The Appeal of Communism to American Middle Class Intellectuals and Trade Unionists," *Public Opinion Quarterly* 16, 3 (Fall 1952): 336.

Krugman interpreted as evidence of their "isolation" and a lack of "social relatedness."[26] As in Selznick's conception of mass society, the individual's social estrangement again seemed to increase his or her susceptibility to dangerous political appeals. Krugman concluded that although communism fulfilled "rational interpersonal needs" for trade unionists, for intellectuals "the relevant needs are less rational, intra-personal factors." Communism therefore represented "a more pronounced political deviation for intellectuals than for trade unionists."[27]

William Kornhauser echoed these diagnoses of mass society's links to antidemocratic predispositions among the American people. Kornhauser, a University of Chicago Ph.D. and a colleague of Selznick and Lipset at Berkeley, combined the conservative indictment of modernity with a palpable disillusionment with the self-governing capacities of ordinary people. In *The Politics of Mass Society*, Kornhauser contended that the masses had gained an increasingly direct control over elites, thereby usurping the political and cultural controls that elites had formerly exercised over the society. As a result, elites could no longer act effectively to preserve the moral and institutional continuity necessary for a democratic society's survival. The masses' "direct access" to elites, he observed, weakened the latter's "inner resources" and rendered them incapable of acting "with decisiveness and independence." As elites became weaker and the masses more assertive, the latter tended to reject elites' moral authority, and they became increasingly attracted to "populist values," which Kornhauser defined as including "anti-elitist and strongly egalitarian sentiments."[28] Elites, meanwhile, lost their sense of themselves as elites, as they inevitably internalized the populist sentiments of the masses. Gradually, they became tools of the masses.

The masses, however, lacked the ability to wield power effectively and democratically. Like the other critics of alienation, Kornhauser conceived of the human personality under mass conditions as mired in isolation and moral confusion. In the absence of "differentiated and stable norms," any action the masses might take would jeopardize vital institutions and values, for alienated individuals lacked the capacity for proper judgment. As individuals estranged from "proximate objects" such as community and work, the masses would inevitably seek to express themselves politically in dangerous, radically new ways, often seeking "remote sources of attachment and allegiance."[29] In short,

---

[26] Ibid., 339.

[27] Ibid., 339, 341.

[28] William Kornhauser, *The Politics of Mass Society* (Glencoe, IL: Free Press, 1959), 59–60.

[29] Ibid., 60.

alienated individuals would support demagogues and totalitarian ideals. "Self-alienated attitudes," Kornhauser warned, "heighten the individual's susceptibility to mass appeals" such as those of a Hitler or a Stalin.[30]

While Selznick and Kornhauser explored the masses' supposed vulnerabilities to communism, other prominent American sociologists linked mass alienation to the threat of fascism, a connection the intellectuals of the Frankfurt School proved crucial in explicating. In addition to the theoretical impact of Fromm's *Escape from Freedom* and its concept of mass sadomasochism, the Frankfurt School's joint exploration of fascist attitudes with the University of California's Berkeley Public Opinion Study, which resulted in the publication of *The Authoritarian Personality*, provided American sociology with an allegedly scientific basis for the statistical analysis of the modern personality as vulnerable to the extreme intolerance and antidemocratic sentiments characteristic of fascism. This study, headed by Theodor Adorno of the Institute for Social Research and R. Nevitt Sanford of the University of California, lent both theoretical and empirical credence to the idea that the citizens of the United States possessed potentially fascist sensibilities.

The Adorno group formulated a host of variables that were understood to be part of a larger "syndrome" of authoritarianism, which together formed a fascist disposition measurable with the "F-scale."[31] *The Authoritarian Personality* had introduced several other scales, including an "A-S," or anti-Semitism, scale, an "E-scale" to measure ethnocentrism, and a "Politico-Economic scale" to measure "the individual's general readiness to express conservative ideology."[32] The F-scale was to serve as a device for measuring not the more obvious manifestations of prejudice that the scales for ethnocentrism and anti-Semitism had measured but rather the "deeper, often unconscious forces" within the human personality that might explain the individual's prejudiced outlook. That is, the researchers surmised that ethnocentrism and anti-Semitism might simply exist as manifestations of a deeper personality structure, one with dangerously antidemocratic potential. The racist or anti-Semitic personality might reveal an underlying fascist disposition.

---

[30] Ibid., 115.

[31] These variables included "conventionalism," or "rigid adherence to conventional, middle-class values; "authoritarian submission" to "idealized moral authorities of the ingroup"; "authoritarian aggression" toward "people who violate conventional values"; "anti-intraception," or "opposition to the subjective, the imaginative, the tenderminded"; "superstition and stereotypy"; "power and toughness"; "destructiveness and cynicism"; "projectivity," or "the disposition to believe that wild and dangerous things go on in the world"; and "exaggerated concern with sexual 'goings-on'" (228).

[32] T. W. Adorno, Else Frenkel-Brunswick, Daniel J. Levinson, and R. Nevitt Sanford, *The Authoritarian Personality* (New York: W. W. Norton, 1950), 51.

Like so many other social science investigators of the postwar personality, the researchers of *The Authoritarian Personality* derived the F-scale from their conception of modern society's normlessness. They asserted that the individual with a "prefascist disposition" possessed a personality that lacked a "fully established individual conscience." This individual conformed to "conventional values" not in the healthy manner of the well-adjusted citizen but instead due to "contemporary external social pressure," or the pathologies of mass society.[33] He or she possessed consequently a weak or ineffectual ego. "Weakness in the ego," these researchers concluded, "is expressed in the inability to build up a consistent and enduring set of moral values within the personality."[34]

The nature of the modern, mass society that fostered dangerously prejudiced and antidemocratic personalities remained largely implicit in *The Authoritarian Personality*. Adorno provided but a semblance of such a conception in the midst of a justification of the study's classification of personalities into types. Adorno characterized modernity as a ruthlessly standardizing force that eradicated differences between individuals. He described an "inhuman" society "whose intrinsic tendency towards the 'subsumption' of everything shows itself by the classification of people themselves," so that "large numbers of people are no longer, or rather never were, 'individuals' in the sense of traditional nineteenth-century philosophy."[35] Social processes, which he called "tickets," produced by virtue of their "standardized, opaque, and overpowering" nature individuals who enjoyed "little freedom for action or true individuation" and instead succumbed to predictable, homogeneous patterns of personality.[36] Instead of exhibiting independence of mind, they languished in an impoverished realm of "ticket thinking." These supposed realities provided Adorno with a compelling justification for studying the modern personality in terms of typologies, for, as he asserted, "the world in which we live is typed and 'produces' different 'types' of persons."[37]

In a manner consistent with broader currents in postwar social science, *The Authoritarian Personality* identified a psychological malaise on the basis of larger philosophical assumptions about the relationship between modernity and human psychology, but it had devoted comparatively little attention to underlying issues of social structure and the nature of modernity. As

---

[33] Ibid., 230.

[34] Ibid., 234.

[35] Ibid., 747.

[36] Ibid., 747.

[37] Ibid., 747.

Christopher Lasch has observed, the Adorno group worked backward from its pre-existent conception of contemporary social structure to its anticipated finding of psychological damage among contemporary individuals, thereby replacing "moral and political argument" over such matters as individual freedom and democratic practice with "reckless psychologizing" under the guise of scientific research and analysis.[38] More important, Lasch emphasizes, was the study's implication that the fascistic tendencies among ordinary people made the roles and techniques of social scientists all the more crucial to the maintenance of liberal democracy, which, in an age of widespread alienation and prejudice, required their "psychotherapeutic insights and practice" for the prevention of authoritarianism.[39] If the common person suffered from a dangerous pathology with sociological roots, it was up to the knowledge professional to diagnose and, hopefully, control the results.

Indeed, the apparent success of *The Authoritarian Personality* in revealing scientifically a "syndrome" of fascistic potential within the modern individual inspired subsequent efforts among American social scientists to scale and measure antidemocratic attitudes. In the years following the book's appearance, various academic journals, particularly those in the fields of public opinion and social psychology, published scores of studies investigating the possible existence of antidemocratic proclivities among average Americans.[40] Nevertheless, a significant number of American sociologists also entered this discussion, applying the F-scale to the exploration of problems as diverse as racism, anti-Semitism, and anticommunism in the United States.[41] These researchers found consistently that the prevalence and depth of authoritarian attitudes increased as their subjects' educational, occupational, and status levels decreased. Authoritarianism thus emerged not as a middle-class

---

[38] Christopher Lasch, *The True and Only Heaven* (New York: W. W. Norton, 1991), 452–53.

[39] Ibid., 453.

[40] Richard Christie and Peggy Cook provided an inventory of the various studies of authoritarianism and its various possible corollaries in "A Guide to Published Literature Relating to the Authoritarian Personality through 1956," *Journal of Psychology* 45, 2 (April 1958): 171–99. The overwhelming majority of studies Christie and Cook cited in their extensive bibliography were authored by psychologists.

[41] In a 1951 study of the possible connection between anomie and attitudes toward minority groups, Leo Srole introduced an abbreviated version of the F-scale to control for the presence of the authoritarian personality in prejudiced individuals. In "Authoritarianism and Political Behavior," *Public Opinion Quarterly* 17, 2 (Summer 1953): 185–201, Morris Janowitz and Dwaine Marvick used a modified, six-item version of the F-scale to examine the elements of submissive conformity and the "preoccupation with considerations of strength and weakness, domination and subservience, superiority and inferiority" that the Adorno group had argued were integral to the authoritarian personality. William J. MacKinnon and Richard Centers used a seven-item version of the F-scale in a study of the relationship between authoritarianism and class in Los Angeles County

phenomenon, as the Adorno group had asserted, but as a product of cultural alienation and the frustration of class aspirations, or the lower-class individual's exclusion from learning, occupational, and class opportunities. Although the studies provided a variegated pattern of results through the application of the F-scale, they nevertheless offered apparent evidence of a widespread intolerant, antidemocratic disposition among Americans of lesser social and educational status. Indeed, one pair of sociologists was so compelled by their discovery of so many "Happy Bigots" in American society that they speculated that "the tolerant person may well be the deviant and a legitimate subject for analysis in terms of abnormal psychology."[42]

These empirical studies thus provided a framework for subsequent theories of the fascist potential dwelling within the American psyche, exemplified by Seymour Martin Lipset's highly influential concept of "working-class authoritarianism." Lipset introduced this theory in a paper at a September 1955 conference on "The Future of Liberty," sponsored by the anti-communist Congress for Cultural Freedom. Among the conferees were the authors of some of the most influential mass-society critiques of totalitarianism, including Arendt, Ortega, and Karl Polanyi. Lipset's conference paper became the basis for his controversial 1959 article, "Democracy and Working-Class Authoritarianism," published in the *American Sociological Review* and again a year later in *Political Man*, a collection of Lipset's 1950s articles. By drawing upon an array of empirical studies of the relationship between working-class status

---

in "Authoritarianism and Urban Stratification," *American Journal of Sociology* 61, 6 (May 1956): 610–20. In a study of public attitudes toward U.S.-Soviet relations, "Authoritarianism and Internationalism," *Public Opinion Quarterly* 20, 4 (Winter 1956–1957): 621–30, MacKinnon and Centers used a modified, eight-item version of the F-scale to construct an "authoritarianism-equalitarianism scale" and concluded that the authoritarian disposition lent itself to an "ingroup-outgroup dichotomizing," which exacerbated existing rifts between the United States and the Soviet Union. Alan B. Roberts and Milton Rokeach, in "Anomie, Authoritarianism, and Prejudice: A Replication," *American Journal of Sociology* 51, 4 (January 1956): 355–58, borrowed Srole's abbreviation of the F-scale to replicate Srole's study and to test his conclusions as to the relationships between authoritarianism, anomie, and prejudice. Edward L. McDill, in "Anomie, Authoritarianism, Prejudice, and Socio-Economic Status: An Attempt at Clarification," *Social Forces* 39, 3 (March 1961): 239–45, also used Srole's version of the F-scale to replicate the Roberts-Rokeach study. Walter C. Kaufman, in "Status, Authoritarianism, and Anti-Semitism," *American Journal of Sociology* 62, 4 (January 1957): 379–82, constructed a "status-concern" scale, which he combined with the F-scale to explore a possible connection between the individual's concern with social status and his or her propensity to harbor anti-Semitic and fascist attitudes. James G. Martin and Frank R. Westie, in "The Tolerant Personality," *American Sociological Review* 24, 4 (August 1959): 521–28, applied the F-scale in a study of the relationship between educational and occupational status and prejudice.

[42]Martin and Westie, "The Tolerant Personality," 528.

and antidemocratic tendencies, Lipset asserted boldly that this connection amounted to an ideological crisis for left intellectuals who continued to place their faith in the historical agency of ordinary people and, most specifically, their capacity for initiating progressive change.

Like Selznick, Lipset had moved away from his youthful socialist ideas and toward a sociological perspective, a process that had begun even before he entered Columbia's graduate program in sociology. At the City College of New York, he and another future Columbia sociologist, Peter Rossi, had participated in leftist discussion groups, during which he and the other participants gravitated to a sociological consciousness. Abandoning the transformative ideas of the varieties of Marxism, they had adopted a pessimistic view of the futility of popular radical movements more in tune with the theories of Robert Michels, who had concluded that early twentieth-century European socialist political organizations were becoming, despite their egalitarian ethos, as bureaucratically ossified and as antidemocratic as the capitalist order they sought ostensibly to transform.[43] As a result, they gravitated to a faith in the sociological approach to the understanding of social phenomena, making Glazer's journey "from socialism to sociology."[44]

Lipset's Michelsian orientation amounted to a kind of bureaucratic fatalism which, when combined with his generation's loss of faith in the historical agency of workers, cast a suspicious eye on ordinary citizens as threats to institutional stability. Lipset introduced "Working-Class Authoritarianism" with the assertion that the presence of authoritarian predispositions within the Western working classes had called into question intellectuals' traditional faith in their role as agents of progressive or revolutionary change. The "gradual realization that authoritarian predispositions and ethnic prejudice flow more naturally from the situation of the lower classes than from that of the middle and upper classes in modern industrial society," Lipset proclaimed, "has posed a tragic dilemma for those intellectuals of the democratic left who once believed the proletariat necessarily to be a force for liberty, racial equality, and social progress."[45] Workers' historical commitment to the extension of political participation and progressive reform—its "non-economic

---

[43] Robert Michels, *Political Parties: A Sociological Study of the Oligarchical Tendencies of Modern Democracy* (New York: The Free Press, 1998).

[44] Lipset recounts his and others' transition from socialism to sociology in "Socialism and Sociology," in Irving Louis Horowitz, ed., *Sociological Self-Images: A Collective Portrait* (Beverly Hills, CA: Sage, 1969).

[45] Seymour Martin Lipset, "Democracy and Working-Class Authoritarianism," *American Sociological Review* 24, 4 (August 1959): 482.

liberalism"—had given way since 1914 to a narrow "economic liberalism" and a pernicious intolerance of democratic norms. The modern working class in many countries rejected multiparty politics, expressed an indifference to the protection of civil liberties, and possessed higher levels of nationalism and racial prejudice than did the middle and upper classes.

Lipset's article combined salient themes of the dozens of other sociological studies of mass society during the 1950s, identifying personal characteristics such as ignorance, alienation, anti-intellectualism, political apathy, and status insecurity as central to working-class authoritarianism. According to Lipset, the antidemocratic traits of lower-class people stemmed from what he characterized as their "general lack of sophistication," which consisted of their "greater suggestibility, absence of a sense of past and future, inability to take a complex view, difficulty in abstracting from concrete experience, and lack of imagination."[46] Those sympathetic to what Lipset called "extremist movements" suffered from a "lack of an adequate mental context," or the inability to grasp "the rich associations which provide a basis for critical evaluation of experience," and "a fixed mental context," or "the tendency to elevate whatever general principles are learned to absolutes," both of which left them vulnerable to mass suggestion.[47] These individuals, with their less-frequent participation in formal organizations, lower degrees of consumption of magazines and books, relative ignorance of public affairs, and political apathy, lived in the eternal present, unable to engage in the kinds of abstract thinking that would allow them to grasp significant long-term social and economic developments central to political discourse and therefore essential knowledge for political participation. Although middle-class individuals were raised to defer personal gratification so that they might pursue "long-term advantages," the sense of immediacy within individuals of low status created a susceptibility to extremist appeals for rapid, transformative change.

These common elements of 1950s studies of modernity—the adoption of the theory of mass society, the empirical focus on individuals' psychological states, as well as the exploration of mass alienation, apathy, and intolerance and their connections to the threat of mass fascism—became the basis for the Harvard and Columbia sociologists' interpretations of the phenomenon of McCarthyism. As Michael Rogin notes in The Intellectuals and McCarthy, his study of 1950s intellectual interpretations of right-wing radicalism, psychological explanations of radical-right political movements, rooted in the framework established by The Authoritarian Personality, asserted that these

---

[46] Ibid., 484, 492.

[47] Ibid., 492–93.

movements reflected deep transformations in American social structure that rendered ordinary people susceptible to extremist demagoguery.[48]

Moreover, McCarthyism's attack on the academy encouraged such conclusions among social scientists. As Ellen Schrecker explains in her study of the impact of McCarthyism on higher education, prestigious Ivy League schools such as Harvard and Columbia figured prominently among Senator McCarthy's targets as subversive bastions of effete intellectualism and arrogant elitism.[49] The impact of McCarthyism on social scientists became the subject of a major work of Columbia's Bureau of Applied Social Research, Paul Lazarsfeld and Wagner Thielens's *The Academic Mind,* which offered data on professors' levels of apprehension and self-censorship in the highly politicized academic environment of the early 1950s.[50] On a more theoretical level, sociologists at Harvard and Columbia interpreted McCarthyism within the context of the by-then-pervasive mass-society thesis, and they developed psychological explanations of radical-rightist movements that indicted masses of Americans as incapable of accepting democratic norms. In so doing, as Rogin demonstrates, they tended to minimize or even neglect McCarthyism's specific political and historical dimensions in favor of an abstract "mass-society" interpretation that considered popular attitudes, resentments, and anxiety over modernity to lie at the heart of the radical right's popular support.[51]

Indeed, these interpretations reflect assumptions about social structure continuous with the larger postwar mass-society critique. In the introduction to *The New American Right,* a collection of historians' and sociologists' interpretations of the resurgence of right-wing political and cultural sentiments in America, Daniel Bell asserted that McCarthyism reflected a long-standing

---

[48] Michael Rogin, *The Intellectuals and McCarthy: The Radical Specter* (Cambridge, MA: MIT Press, 1967).

[49] See Schrecker, *No Ivory Tower: McCarthyism and the Universities* (New York: Oxford University Press, 1986), especially pp. 255–59. Schrecker describes how the Columbia administration responded to harassment by such right-wing publications as *Counterattack* by disguising the firing of a controversial professor as a "bureaucratic reform" of its hiring and dismissal policies. At Harvard, a policy was instituted to screen out radical applicants for faculty positions by having them "purge themselves" by providing the FBI with names, thus protecting Harvard from future investigations or harassment. Noncommunists had to prove themselves free of any past or present connection to the Communist Party.

[50] Paul F. Lazarsfeld and Wagner Thielens, Jr., *The Academic Mind: A Report of the Bureau of Applied Social Research* (Glencoe, IL: Free Press, 1958).

[51] Rogin, *The Intellectuals and McCarthy.* According to Rogin, in the 1950s interpretations of McCarthyism, McCarthy "is said to have mobilized feelings of uneasiness over a sophisticated, cosmopolitan, urban, industrial society. He focused these vague discontents, the argument continues, on such specific symbols as intellectuals, striped-pants diplomats, homosexuals, and effete eastern aristocrats" (218).

and distinctly antimodernist outlook in America, noting a resemblance between modern right-wing extremism and the similarly moralistic and emotional movements of evangelical Protestantism, whose "egalitarian and antiintellectual" character had by the end of the nineteenth century placed them at odds not only with the emergent urban culture and its secularizing effects but also with its economic and political order. Bell therefore conceived of popular movements in American history as distinctly antimodern, extremist, moralistic, and irrational. American politics, in turn, had, since the days of Jefferson, assumed a "populist character," in which politicians necessarily appealed to the sentiments of the "common man," so that "skill in manipulating masses became the established feature of political life."[52]

In this interpretation, McCarthy's popular appeal rested not merely upon any intrinsic political ability, his populist pretensions in a traditionally progressive state, or even the class or ethnic makeup of his followers, but rather upon something larger and more pervasive: the predisposition of the multitudes to respond to appeals for morally transformative political action and their rejection of established patterns of deference to authority. Of McCarthy, Bell wrote, "He was the catalyst, not the explosive force. These forces still remain."[53] More than merely a political phenomenon, McCarthyism reflected "deeper-running social currents of a turbulent mid-century America," so that "conventional political analysis" could not but fail to explain it.[54] Such currents reflected Bell's acceptance of at least part of the mass-society theory: modernity had produced a kind of social "turbulence" that upset traditional patterns of political participation, and these conditions called for a rethinking of the relationship between the political structure and the polity.

Talcott Parsons concurred with Bell, citing in his contribution to the volume the politically corrosive "social strains" that had emerged within modern American society. Those whose lives or values were upset by the dramatic structural changes industrial society had wrought, he asserted, often succumbed to " 'irrational' behavior," as they groped for solutions to their discontent. They would tend to turn to solutions that promised a kind of magical release from their troubles, Parsons continued, solutions that reflected the sufferers' high degree of emotionalism and even superstition. "There will tend to be wishful patterns of belief with a strong 'regressive'

---

[52]Daniel Bell, "Interpretations of American Politics," in Daniel Bell, ed., *The New American Right* (New York: Criterion Books, 1955), 8.

[53]Ibid., 17.

[54]Ibid., 3.

flavor," he wrote, "whose chief function is to wish away the disturbing situation and establish a situation in phantasy where 'everything will be all right,' preferably as it was before the disturbing situation came about."[55] Like Bell, Parsons rejected discretely political interpretations of modern right-wing radicalism and instead cited such general conditions among the population at large as "anxiety, "aggression," "fear," and "frustration" borne of rapid social change.

As Rogin observes, these sociologists' conclusions regarding the high degrees of public anguish they perceived derived from contemporary interpretations of American political history, particularly that of Richard Hofstadter. In *The Age of Reform*, Hofstadter presented the thesis that pre-New Deal reform movements in the United States shared similarly emotional, moralistic, and backward-looking sentiments. In their resentment of rapid structural social change, these movements, epitomized by late nineteenth-century populism, struggled to defend the ideal of an individualistic, entrepreneurial America against the encroachments of the bureaucratized interests of high finance, industrialization, and elitist "big government." A movement like populism thus represented for Hofstadter the reaction of a rural, antimodern segment of American society to a perceived assault by urban, industrial values and institutions upon traditional morality, community life, and avenues to individual success.

Sociologists such as Bell and Lipset applied Hofstadter's thesis to contemporary social conditions, finding parallels between the grievances of these earlier movements and the social climate of postwar America, parallels that the growing body of empirical survey research of public attitudes about civil liberties, race relations, and authority seemed to confirm. So seductive was the notion of pervasive intolerance among the nation's newest generation of antimodernists that even David Riesman, an otherwise independent and rather judicious observer of American culture, echoed the case against the allegedly ignorant masses to Hofstadter, by declaring, "I think you know my feeling that America can't 'go fascist' because it is already in so many ways malleable to fascist thinking." He continued:

Throughout much of the world the middle class has been the nationalist class, responsible for nationalist revolutions from the French Revolution onward, including some of the countries of the Middle East or Asia today. Why is that not so in this country? Why is

---

[55]Talcott Parsons, "Social Strains in America" in Bell, ed., *The New American Right*, 127.

chauvinism so much more widespread among the uneducated? Or do we deal here with different kinds of nationalism?[56]

McCarthyism thus seemed to many social science observers to represent a powerful reprise of long-standing resentments whose roots lay in the unease created by industrial society's forces of rapid change, such as urbanization and immigration. Hofstadter's book therefore lent empirical credence to the idea of the United States as a society in the midst of a difficult transition, for it located moralistic, anti-elitist politics within segments of the population upon which modernity had imposed new expectations and pressures.

Hofstadter's conception of the Populist movement in particular resonated with mid-century critiques of mass society and its toll upon the individual, for it located rural discontent within the new, complex relationships and economic and social dislocations that industrialization had brought to the nation. Hofstadter's articulation of the concept of "status anxiety," the feeling of those who perceived modernity as a threat to either their maintenance or attainment of social prestige, became crucial to sociological interpretations of McCarthyite extremism. As Lipset wrote in *The New American Right*, this status anxiety could be experienced by both the "status insecure," those who had inherited their social status and feared for its survival amidst rapid social change, and the upwardly mobile, especially the "minority ethnic," whose immigrant status frustrated his pursuit of social acceptance.[57] In times of economic transition, extremist movements found that they could channel these anxieties into "status politics," articulating the frustrations of both groups and mobilizing them for anti-elitist crusades. For Lipset, then, the phenomenon of the 1950s radical right reflected long-standing tendencies for particular groups of Americans to gravitate to "irrational" movements that, in the absence of concrete solutions to their followers' troubles, sought to exploit status anxieties through the scapegoating of supposed "enemies."[58]

Rogin argues convincingly that such wholesale indictments of popular movements for their supposed irrationality, and, more crucially, for their primary role in building formidable threats to American democracy, over-emphasize the role of ordinary citizens and underplay that of elites. In his critique of the authors of *The New American Right*, he points out the 1950s sociologists' overemphasis on mass psychology in interpreting mass society

---

[56]Riesman to Hofstadter, October 30, 1958, David Riesman Papers, Harvard University Archive, HUG (FP) 99.12, Box 19.

[57]Seymour Martin Lipset, "The Sources of the 'Radical Right,'" in Bell, ed., *The New American Right*, 193–94.

[58]Ibid., 168.

and on its supposed counterparts of intolerance, alienation, and authoritarianism, all of which produced a relative neglect of the role of elites. McCarthy therefore seemed to represent something new and dangerous in mass society, a disrupter of traditional institutions and loyalties and a political renegade who operated outside the long-standing liberal-conservative divisions within American politics.[59] Rogin notes to the contrary, however, that McCarthy simply represented the traditional conservative, midwestern Republican values—"uneasiness about cosmopolitan values and styles of life, about large cities and big bureaucracies"—which had existed long before McCarthy, and which had simply become more virulent with the new perceived threat communism posed to the preservation of traditional values.[60]

More important, Rogin contends, the leading intellectual critics of McCarthyism failed to grasp the significance of existing empirical survey research on public attitudes toward McCarthy, especially Samuel Stouffer's *Communism, Conformity, and Civil Liberties*, which had revealed that only a tiny minority of Americans shared the political extremism so many sociologists and political scientists had connected to broader structural changes in American society. Stouffer's study, conducted from late May to July 1954, coincided with the Army–McCarthy hearings, by which time public awareness of radical-right politics had reached its peak. Nevertheless, Stouffer found that the issue of communist subversion within the United States had never been of more than very minor concern to the public. Gallup poll figures from the late 1940s and early 1950s had never found more than 10 percent of the public identifying that threat as the nation's foremost problem.[61] Even more surprising was Stouffer's citation of a Roper poll in which 30 percent of those surveyed could not even identify McCarthy as a participant in investigations of domestic communism.[62] Stouffer therefore concluded that

---

[59] Parsons argued in "Social Strains in America" that the radical right "profoundly splits apart the previously dominant groups," and that public opinion about McCarthyism "cuts clean across the traditional lines of distinction between conservatives and progressives" (136).

[60] Rogin, *The Intellectuals and McCarthy*, 221, 223.

[61] Stouffer, *Communism, Conformity, and Civil Liberties: A Cross-Section of the Nation Speaks Its Mind* (Garden City, NY: Doubleday, 1955). Stouffer cited polling figures from 1948 that indicated that less than 1 percent of those polled had expressed such fears. For 1949, that figure increased to 2 percent; for 1951, 4 percent; and 1953, 9 percent (86).

[62] Reactions to Stouffer's results took on a tautological air. For Lipset and Nathan Glazer, apathetic respondents who expressed indifference to the issue of domestic communist subversion became further evidence of authoritarianism within the public sphere. In their critique of Stouffer's methodology, Lipset and Glazer asserted that the fact that nearly a third of those surveyed couldn't identify McCarthy revealed the danger of a sizable "non-interested group" of Americans "with presumably little or no weight in the body politic," a group which "is actually much more anti-civil libertarian than those persons who are interested in the Communist problem, or in politics

intellectual suspicions of the presence of large measures of public hysteria over the communist issue were unfounded. "A picture of the average American as a person with the jitters, trembling lest he find a Red under the bed, is clearly nonsense," he wrote. "There may be such Americans, but they are very few in number."[63]

Rogin concludes that this disjuncture between 1950s intellectuals' fears of antidemocratic public attitudes and the rather unexceptional reality of those attitudes reflected their intellectual commitment to political pluralism, in which competing interests check the power of one another to the benefit of the society as a whole. After World War II, American intellectuals embraced pluralism as the solution to both the twentieth century's legacy of economic turmoil and totalitarian movements and, more broadly, the need for the application of bureaucratized expertise to social problems of increasing complexity. Mass politics, as recent history had shown, represented the antithesis of pluralism, for it disrupted those channels of political communication and decision making modernity required.

Indeed, abundant evidence exists that many leading sociologists of the 1950s accepted pluralist assumptions. Many supported their pluralist assertions with David Riesman's concept of "veto groups," the myriad private interests that vied for advantage in an open marketplace of social and political competition. Parsons affirmed a quasi-pluralist conception in a review of C. Wright Mills's *The Power Elite*, in which he contended that Mills's excessive focus on centralized power produced a "zero-sum" notion of power that neglected the creation of new forms thereof through the actions of individuals and groups.[64] Kornhauser accommodated both the centralization of power and the multiplication of public and private interest groups in his assessment of pluralism, conceiving of a political order in which concentrations of power failed to produce oligarchy by their lack of coordination.[65]

generally." See Glazer and Lipset, "The Polls on Communism and Conformity" in Bell, ed., *The New American Right*, 143–44.

[63] Stouffer, *Communism, Conformity, and Civil Liberties*, 87.

[64] Talcott Parsons, "The Distribution of Power in American Society," in G. William Domhoff, ed., *C. Wright Mills and the Power Elite* (New York: Free Press, 1960), 60–88. This essay appeared originally in *World Politics* 10, 1 (October 1957): 123–43. In *The New American Right*, Parsons remarked on the "fluid and unstructured character of the American elite," in which there is "no clear determination of where political leadership, in the sense including both 'politics' and 'administration,' is to center" (124).

[65] William Kornhauser, "'Power Elite' or 'Veto Groups?'" in Seymour M. Lipset and Leo Lowenthal, eds., *Culture and Social Character: Essays in Honor of David Riesman* (New York: Free Press, 1961).

However, in sociology, the theory of mass society had so attenuated the ideology of pluralism that it bore little resemblance to the ideal. In the absence of the healthy secondary groups—unions, churches, and other organizations—necessary for a pluralist order, sociological prescriptions for the sustaining of democratic institutions became more elitist in nature. As Edward Purcell explains, the experience of McCarthyite irrationalism fostered among intellectuals "a new admiration for elites, highly educated and socially prominent groups, as opposed to the psychologically discontented and poorly educated masses." The former, "with their sophisticated world views and stable social position," stood as "the most reliable source of democratic values."[66] An intellectual elite could perform the functions formerly fulfilled by communities and their secondary-group organizations.

Within postwar sociology, this identification with elitist outlooks placed sociology's nascent scientific identity solidly within professional circles, and it fostered among the Harvard-Columbia sociologists decidedly institutionalist formulae for the amelioration of intolerance and for the protection of civil liberties against public assaults. In his contribution to *The New American Right,* Parsons advocated the application of institutional leadership to the problem of popular irrationality and "regressive" patterns of belief in a manner that reflected his functionalist orientation to individual adherence to social norms: "In a normal process of learning in the individual, or of developmental change in the social system," he wrote, "such irrational phenomena are temporary, and tend to subside as capacity to deal with the new situation grows." This capacity improved as modernity's concomitant institutional maturation provided society with new, robust structures through which to mold and guide human thought and behavior. Thus, Parsons remained optimistic that, "under favorable circumstances these reactions are superseded by an increasingly realistic facing of the situation by institutionalized means."[67] For Parsons, then, institutional "realism" would replace the irrational search for fantastic political solutions, which, with their resemblance to "primitive magic," required the corrective of disenchantment that Weber observed in the processes of modernity itself. With proper

---

[66]Edward A. Purcell, Jr., *The Crisis of Democratic Theory: Scientific Naturalism and the Problem of Value* (Lexington: University Press of Kentucky, 1973), 242.

[67]Parsons, "Social Strains in America," 128.

indoctrination, the public's prescientific modes of perception would be neutralized though their acceptance of institutional norms.[68]

Lipset also contrasted the alleged irrationality of popular movements with the instrumental rationality of institutionally directed social and political change. In his analysis of working-class authoritarianism, he joined Parsons in asserting that the status anxious were "more likely than other strata to prefer extremist movements which suggest easy and quick solutions to social problems and have a rigid outlook." In contrast, appropriate and effectual political participation came from political elements "which view the problem of reform or change in complex and gradualist terms and which support rational values of tolerance"[69] Gradualism, an article of faith of knowledge experts and bureaucratic elites who desired moderate change that avoided the destabilizing and unpredictable political participation of non-elites, and norms of tolerance, which insured that such channels enjoyed public legitimation, constituted the basis for what Rogin describes as an elitist form of pluralism. This variety required the general acceptance of the rules of competition between groups, to be sure, but the groups themselves required direction by responsible and knowledgeable leaders. As Lipset wrote in *Political Man*, effective democracy in a "complex society" required "a value system allowing the peaceful 'play' of power," without which "democracy becomes chaotic."[70]

Lipset thereby advanced a Schumpeterian theory of democracy that privileged the role of institutionalized elites in preserving political continuity and stability. In *Capitalism, Socialism and Democracy*, Joseph Schumpeter had rejected what he termed the classical theory of democracy, for it assumed that the electorate played the primary role in influencing through rational discussion the decisions of their elected representatives, all of which then emerged as expressions of the "common good." Schumpeter wrote that such a "General

---

[68] Parsons had recommended precisely this approach ten years earlier on behalf of the de-Nazification effort in postwar Germany. In a 1945 article in the journal *Psychiatry*, Parsons asserted that the German people suffered from a peculiarly problematic "character structure," which included the predisposition "to define all human relations in terms of dominance, submission, and romantic revolt" (291). Because this character structure existed in a relationship of interdependence and mutual reinforcement with German institutions—a relationship of values and social system— a thorough retooling of those institutionalpatterns, particularly that of the German military, stood as a prerequisite for changing the character structure. Just as the Nazis had "harnessed" the dangerous elements within the German character, de-Nazification would require their institutional realignment toward the norms of "their counterparts in the democratic countries" (302). This article is reprinted in Uta Gerhardt, ed., *Talcott Parsons on National Socialism* (New York: Aldine de Gruyter, 1993).

[69] Lipset, "Working-Class Authoritarianism," 483.

[70] Lipset, "Economic Development and Democracy," in *Political Man: The Social Bases of Politics* (Baltimore: Johns Hopkins University Press, 1981), 27.

Will" remained a practical impossibility in any society, for it ignored conflicting value systems and the inherent limitations in the average person's capacity for identifying or understanding his or her own interests.[71] This political philosophy had thus erred in positing the very existence of a collective general will, and it "attributed to the electorate an altogether unrealistic degree of initiative which practically amounted to ignoring leadership."[72] In its place, Schumpeter advanced a theory of competitive leadership, in which political representation acted not to implement some articulated General Will but instead to vie for the people's acceptance in a "free competition for a free vote."[73]

Schumpeter's rejection of classical democratic theory in favor of a more limited conception, one that acknowledged modernity's exigencies of bureaucratic expertise and the manufacturing of consent, suited many leading postwar social scientists whose theoretical and philosophical influences, empirical researches, and practical political experiences had produced a similar gravitation to an attenuated form of representative rule. In the case of Lipset, for whom McCarthyism reflected deep underlying structural tendencies within American society that called into question the democratic integrity of the public sphere, an effective democracy became that which insulated elective bodies from outbursts of extrapolitical irrationality. The opinion surveys upon which Lipset relied in his 1950s articles—particularly his explorations of what he termed working-class authoritarianism and middle-class fascism—in turn provided a seemingly scientific foundation for understanding the nature of the masses and their proper role in a democratic society. Lipset's Schumpeterian conception of the relationship between public life and institutional activity therefore privileged the latter. A "stable" democracy became one that allowed not only for "the peaceful play of power," but also for "the adherence by the 'outs' to decisions made by 'ins' and the recognition by 'ins' of the rights of the 'outs.'"[74]

---

[71] Schumpeter, much like the other mid-century critics of mass society, characterized the "typical citizen" as prone to "irrational prejudice and impulse," and he charged that "simply because he is not 'all there,'" this mass individual remained susceptible to "dark urges." Such a conception rendered the classical democratic hopes utterly futile. Schumpeter concluded of the citizen that "if for once he does emerge from his usual vagueness and does display the definite will postulated by the classical doctrine of democracy, he is as likely to as not to become still more unintelligent and irresponsible than he usually is. At certain junctures, this may prove fatal to his nation." Joseph A. Schumpeter, *Capitalism, Socialism and Democracy* (New York: Harper & Row, 1950), 262.

[72] Ibid., 270.

[73] Ibid., 271.

[74] Lipset, "Some Social Requisites of Democracy: Economic Development and Political Legitimacy," *American Political Science Review* 53, 1 (March 1959): 71. A revised version of this article was published in *Political Man* as "Economic Development and Democracy" and "Social Conflict, Legitimacy, and Democracy."

Democracy involved the choosing of leaders, not the direct influence of the polity on the process of decision making itself.

More important, this theory of competitive leadership invalidated forms of political activity that failed to conform to established political practice, or what Lipset called "the rules of the political game."[75] In rejecting the concept of democracy as the identification and implementation of the "will of the people" or of the "common good," this theory implied the illegitimacy of political activity that lay outside of elective institutions or that violated established values. Just as the contributors to *The New American Right* had looked askance at the late nineteenth-century Populist movement for its alleged backward thinking, extreme moralism, and grassroots origins, the Harvard-Columbia sociologists perceived any modern forms of populism, of which they believed McCarthyism to be an example, to carry the same danger for democracy. Thus, Kornhauser contrasted the dangerous politics of mass society, in which the masses had "usurped" elite authority, intervening "directly and in an unrestrained manner" in the nation's affairs, with a pluralist order, in which elites enjoyed the authority that was traditionally theirs and in which "the population is not available for activistic modes of behavior."[76] If democracy involved the selection of those who would implement not some abstract conception of the common good but rather rationally determined courses of action, political activity outside of this relationship became by definition "extremist" and "irrational."

Philip Selznick applied this concept of leadership to the communist challenge to democracy. The social pathologies of public irrationality and aggression endemic to mass society that he believed threatened to draw individuals into the communist orbit called for institutional leadership that would mold public attitudes and channel them toward "democratic" norms. In his dissertation on the TVA, he had observed that mass society had made it necessary for governments to "attempt to manipulate the sentiments of the common man" with "new methods of control" in order to "change an undifferentiated and unreliable citizenry into a structured, readily accessible public."[77] Successful New Deal programs like the TVA had done so by incorporating citizen participation into their organizational structures in order to sustain legitimacy and remain consistent with democratic expectations. To maintain its political legitimacy in a democratic society, the TVA had "coöpted" regional and local institutions and individuals, reaching down to

---

[75] Ibid., 72.

[76] Kornhauser, *The Politics of Mass Society*, 59.

[77] Philip Selznick, *TVA and the Grass Roots: A Study in the Sociology of Formal Organization* (Berkeley: University of California Press, 1953), 219.

the "grass roots" and "absorbing new elements into the leadership or policy-determining structure of an organization."[78] This large, expansive federal program had thereby avoided a potential backlash from local communities, many of which might have rejected the program for imposing a more centralized authority upon them and eroding local political autonomy.[79]

Like the sociologist contributors to *The New American Right*, Selznick relied upon definitions of established political practice that proclaimed its incontestible legitimacy. Mass society's erosion of community and connectedness, its effect of "social disintegration," brought "the breakdown of normal restraints" and "internalized standards of right conduct." Without the "established channels of action" necessary for effective democracy, the masses acquired the opportunity to engage in "direct, unmediated efforts" to attain their perceived needs.[80] Selznick's characterization of these efforts bore a striking resemblance in its pejorative language to those of the sociologists who associated populism with the irrational, moralistic dispositions of the alienated. "Mass behavior" reflected "activist interpretations of democracy," which in turn carried the potential for "the increasing reliance on force to resolve social conflict."[81]

In a mass society, then, effective democracy required general public acceptance of established norms and modes of action in what Peter Bachrach termed a system of "democratic elitism." Postwar political theorists' disenchantment with the common citizen, Bachrach observed, led them to invert the classical conception of the relationship between the people and elite, so that the people themselves came to be understood as the chief threat to liberty.[82] Democracy therefore became a political practice in which effective legitimation of elite decision making superseded participatory democratic ideals of the past. The sustaining of this political legitimacy, which Lipset defined as "the capacity of a political system to engender and maintain the belief that existing political institutions are the most appropriate or proper ones for the society," demanded the kind of education that would nurture such a belief.[83]

---

[78] Ibid., 13.

[79] Selznick acknowledged that such co-optation tended toward the eventual dominance of administrative rather than participatory elements. "As the needs of the administration become dominant," he wrote, "the tendency for democratic participation to be reduced to mere involvement may be expected to increase. At the extreme, the democratic element drops out and the cooptative character of the organizational devices employed becomes identified with their entire meaning" (Ibid., 226).

[80] Selznick, *The Organizational Weapon*, 293.

[81] Ibid., 293.

[82] Peter Bachrach, *The Theory of Democratic Elitism* (Boston: Little, Brown, 1967), 32.

[83] Lipset, "Social Conflict, Legitimacy, and Democracy," in *Political Man*, 64.

Education itself hence became a means to a particular kind of democracy, one that addressed the individual's self-estrangement in a mass society. An alienative social structure called for palliatives that diminished that structure's impact on its alienated members, particularly its symptoms of intolerance and lack of respect for established political practice. "Education," Lipset wrote, "presumably broadens men's outlooks, enables them to understand the need for norms of tolerance, restrains them from adhering to extremist and monistic doctrines, and increases their capacity to make rational electoral choices."[84] Education socialized individuals into conformity with established political practice.

Lipset's professional colleagues concurred that this education would have to originate with intellectual elites. When Parsons called for "an increasingly realistic facing of the situation by institutionalized means," he envisioned an elite authority that would foster deferential public values and attitudes that would in turn support that authority's functioning. Political elites, he asserted, would specialize in "the management of public opinion," while "administrators" provided the necessary expertise.[85] Selznick similarly concluded that the protection of "established channels" and of "normal" and "right conduct" required the insulation of decision making from those who would attempt to undermine it. Because the "Stalinoids" in particular—middle-class individuals with pervasive organizational ties—possessed enough influence to wreak real damage upon important institutions, Selznick advocated aggressive institutional leadership that would ward off communist influences through particular educational efforts directed at protecting democratic values within American organizational life, insisting that "educational activities on the communist issue be *elite-oriented.*"[86] Elites would require access to information on past attempts of communist groups to

---

[84]Lipset, "Some Social Requisites of Democracy," 79.

[85]Parsons, "Social Strains in America," 228–29.

[86]Selznick, *The Organizational Weapon,* 329. This lack of faith in the reasoning capacities of ordinary people—and the consequent perceived need for the shaping of public consciousness by knowledge specialists—is reflected in Andrew Ross's analysis of the *Partisan Review* intellectuals' lack of faith in the masses' aesthetic sensibilities. Their writings, he argues in *No Respect* (New York: Routledge, Chapman and Hall, 1989), were "explicitly shot through with rhetoric about containment"(45). Just as the free world had a duty to stop the spread of the "disease" of communism—that is, to "disinfect" the democratic countries—writers at little magazines like *Partisan Review, Dissent,* and *Politics* perceived themselves as "cultural health professionals" who would determine the "acceptable levels of exposure to popular culture" (54). For Dwight Macdonald and Leslie Fiedler, this mission included the isolation of high culture from contamination by "midcult" through the establishment of a "lines of cultural demarcation that would still guarantee and preserve the channels of power through which intellectual authority is exercised" (Ross, 1989: 60). Midcult, like communism, called for effective containment.

manipulate particular segments of American society, so that they might tailor their educational efforts to their own unique organizational circumstances. The higher placed, those who enjoyed a more thorough integration within American society, would school those whose alienation rendered them vulnerable to manipulation by antidemocratic forces. Selznick remained particularly emphatic on the centrality of the middle-class "targets" of such subterfuge, and he went so far as to deny the legitimacy of their own opinions. "It is among these—especially professional and other groups who try to think for themselves and hence are accessible to ideological manipulation—that we find the fellow travelers of communism," he warned.[87] By implication, elites would have to do the thinking for everyone else.

Stouffer, similarly, advocated assertive elite leadership as the solution to the dangers of popular irrationality; however, his vision of the proper educative role of these elites differed significantly from that of the others. Where the other sociological interpreters of mass attitudes found fascist and communist proclivities, Stouffer's analysis of public opinion during the McCarthy era revealed only public apathy. Stouffer's Gallup and Roper poll data indicated not only that the public remained largely indifferent to McCarthy's appeals but that it was similarly indifferent to the importance of protecting basic civil liberties. Because few Americans had ever confronted threats to their constitutionally protected freedoms, Stouffer lamented, "they take freedom for granted. Only if the threat should come home to them in dramatic and personal ways are they likely to experience a deep concern."[88]

Stouffer nevertheless remained optimistic that, given the proper civic education, Americans would respect democratic norms. They were not proto-fascists, he argued; rather, they simply lacked awareness of the requisites of political liberty:

> Nobody could sit down and read through the filled-out questionnaire in this study without coming to the conclusion that most of the seemingly intolerant people in this study are good, wholesome Americans. Many of them, as we have seen in this book, are simply drawing quite normal and logical inferences from premises which are false because the information on which the premises are based is false. They have not been as yet sufficiently motivated by responsible leaders of public opinion to give "sober second thought" to the broader
> ~ and long-range consequences of specific limitations of freedom.[89]

---

[87] Ibid., 318.

[88] Stouffer, *Communism, Conformity, and Civil Liberties*, 87–88.

[89] Ibid., 223.

Stouffer, almost singularly among the critics of mass society, refuted the connection that others identified between the alienated modern personality and the threats of intolerance, populism, and extremist activism. He faulted intellectuals for their lack of faith in the public, asking whether in fact alienation prevailed among intellectuals more than among Americans at large. "To assume that most intolerant people among the rank and file are bad or sick would be to commit an error which, in the author's judgment, is all too common," he admonished. "This error is not unknown even among scholars, for a few of whom, incidentally, the 'native fascist' may fulfill the same psychological need of a target upon which to project personal anxieties as may the 'liberal' or the 'intellectual' for a few other citizens."[90]

For Stouffer, then, mass apathy did indeed afflict the public sphere, but there was more cause for optimism from his perspective because, significantly, poll data indicated that community leadership retained a faith in democracy. Stouffer's surveys of the opinions of community business leaders, city politicians, and newspaper editors sampled from cities of 10,000 to 150,000, indicated that these elites remained more supportive of civil liberties guarantees than did the general public. In general, he observed, they were more willing to "tolerate nonconformists," or to allow socialists, atheists, those "whose loyalty has been criticized by a Congressional investigating committee," or even avowed communists to express their views freely. The responsibility for inculcating tolerant, democratic values therefore lay with them. Clergy, school board members, teachers, librarians, superintendents, and other community leaders could generalize this tolerance within their communities. "Here at the grass roots—in their families, schools, and churches—is the place where children must learn to have faith in the Sermon on the Mount and the Bill of Rights," Stouffer concluded.[91] Moreover, mass society itself would facilitate this greater tolerance. Although many other sociological observers had lamented the threat of intolerance borne of increasing mass alienation, Stouffer, like Durkheim, found the forces of modernity to offer the promise of greater solidarity and democracy. "Great social, economic, and technological forces are operating slowly and imperceptibly on the side of spreading tolerance," he promised. Rising education levels, increasing geographic mobility, and "the vicarious experiences supplied by the magic of our ever-more powerful media of communications" had begun to expose people to other realms of human experience, making

---

[90] Ibid., 223.

[91] Ibid., 232.

them more inclined to accept the differences between people and thus less of a threat to democratic institutions.[92]

Nevertheless, despite his rejection of the alienation-authoritarianism perspective, Stouffer's advocacy of "education" resembled that of his peers in its elitism. Effective leadership would mold public attitudes and sentiments, winnowing out the negative elements while cultivating the proper ones. "A program of information and education," he wrote, should "correct false premises" and tap into the positive individual motivations "which await activation or need redirection."[93] Stouffer, like Parsons, Lipset, Kornhauser, and Selznick, therefore advocated a kind of education that concentrated more upon socialization than on creating active citizens. Whereas John Dewey had insisted that education for democracy required the preparation of individuals for full citizenship—that is, for participation in the ongoing clarification and pursuit of the public interest—the Harvard and Columbia sociologists presumed that in a pluralist order presided over by elites, no such thing as the public interest existed. Rather, politics involved discrete problem solving, in a gradual process of fine-tuning. Citizenship, therefore, meant deference to elected leaders, those who presided over decision making, and education should then merely promote the acceptance of that process among the masses. Like Dewey, they believed that the means of democracy remained crucial to its existence; however, unlike Dewey, the end of that democracy completely disappeared. For Dewey, a conception of the public good remained crucial to democracy, though that end remained eternally contingent. For these postwar sociologists, the process—the "rules of the game"—became an end in itself.

This political philosophy thereby protected the autonomy of scientific activity that scholars like Parsons and Merton had identified as the essence of modern sociology. Instead of wedding science to democratic discourse, as Dewey demanded, postwar sociology advanced a theory of democracy that excused the discipline from active participation in democratic discourse. Scientific discourse was to remain separate from public discourse. The American people were to be "educated," to be sure, but not in the nuances and meaning of modern social structure. Instead, they were to be trained in the "rules" that such a structure required, that the people would simply choose, and then abide by the decisions of, their elected representatives. As Weber had noted, rationalization and the disenchantment of the world had left only those possessed of the requisite fortitude with the capacity to carry on the

---

[92] Ibid., 236.

[93] Ibid., 236.

cause of scientific inquiry. The masses, living as they did in the prescientific realm of mystification, lacked the capacity to participate.[94]

These prescriptions for the protection of democratic values and practices, which remained calls for indoctrination far more than the cultivation of independence of mind, reflected their authors' wholesale internalization of mass society's postulates of alienation and intolerance. If the individual's "secondary" attachments—schools, churches, neighborhoods, and the like— had deteriorated under the corrosive influence of mass society, new secondary groups would have to arise to replace them. For these scholars, the appropriate source of modern moral leadership therefore became those with professional, scientific competence. Only those who could understand the social forces at work in the modern age could hope to mitigate their ill effects and foster appropriate values and attitudes.

In this sense, these writers departed significantly from the nineteenth-century conservative critique of direct democracy. That critique had postulated that the individual's political identity depended upon its roots within its community, class, and religious life, which guaranteed his or her respect for political continuity and deference to established authority. In a mass society, the absence of these institutions spelled for the conservatives the imperilment of not only the political order but of the ordinary individual as a political being. Mass democracy, an outgrowth of mass society, represented the destruction of "political man." However, unlike the classical conservatives, postwar sociologists like Parsons, Lipset, Selznick, and Kornhauser, for whom direct democracy portended similar consequences, exhibited nevertheless a new optimism over the prospects for political renewal. They envisioned a political order regulated not by the traditional Burkean social forces—the "little platoon" of local community to which the individual belonged—but by the new institutions wrought by the very processes of modernity that had abolished the old order. They interpreted the growing body of scholarly theoretical and empirical indictments of the alienated individual as supportive of their own assertion of a new kind of authority, that of the Weberian man of science, one who greeted the disenchantment of the world not with mass movements, racism, and calls for the radical reconstruction of political life but instead with a stolid realism and the assertion of his own discursive autonomy within a professionalized sphere of communication.

---

[94]Paradoxically, the civil rights movement coincided neatly with the emergence of these arguments for institutional leadership, so that American citizens had begun to practice direct action in order to force social change to take place even as sociologists recommended a greater separation between citizens and their political institutions. Thus, the most important renegotiation of public truth of this century in the United States escaped sociologists, as did the decisive roles ordinary Americans, far from elite circles, played in it.

The mass-society theory, then, when combined with postwar sociology's scientific self-conception, produced a profound contradiction. Sociology was seen to exist in a state of autonomy not only from the nonprofessional realm of lay discourse but also from the pressures of modern mass society itself. As Alvin Gouldner observed in 1970, postwar sociologists cloistered themselves in a realm of scientific detachment separated from the rest of humanity, believing that mass society dominated the masses' consciousness but not their own:

When sociologists stress the autonomy of sociology—that it should (and, therefore, that it can) be pursued entirely in terms of its own standards, free of the influences of the surrounding society—they are giving testimony of their loyalty to the rational credo of their profession. At the same time, however, they are also contradicting themselves as sociologists, for surely the strongest general assumption of sociology is that men are shaped in countless ways by the Press of their social surround... In large measure, this contradiction is hidden, in daily practice, by sociologists who premise a dualistic reality in which their own behavior is tacitly held to be different from the behavior of those they study. It is hidden by employing the focal sociological assumption, that men are shaped by culture and social structure, when sociologists study *others*, yet tacitly employing the assumption that men make their own cultures, when sociologists think about *themselves*. The *operating* premise of the sociologist claiming autonomy for his discipline is that he is free from the very social pressures whose importance he affirms when thinking about other men. In effect, the sociologist conjugates his basic domain assumptions by saying: *they* are bound by society; *I* am free of it... The sociologist thus resolves his contradictory assumptions by splitting them and applying each to different persons or groups: one for himself and his peers, another for his "subjects." Implicit in such a split is an image of self and other, in which the two are assumed to be deeply different and thus to be differentially evaluated, the "self" tacitly viewed as a kind of elite, the "other" as a kind of mass.[95]

Gouldner stood virtually alone among the 1950s graduates from Columbia's sociology program in confronting the antidemocratic implications of the mass-society thesis. In 1955, he criticized postwar sociologists' tendency toward a "metaphysical pathos," a profound pessimism about the prospects for democracy and an acceptance of the inevitability of impenetrable

---

[95]Alvin W. Gouldner, *The Coming Crisis of Western Sociology* (New York: Basic Books, 1970), 54–55.

bureaucratic authority that derived from their internalization of the bureaucratic fatalism of Weber and Michels. These scholars, he charged, had accepted Michels' "iron law of oligarchy" as the inevitable limit upon democratic agency much as nineteenth-century political economists had insisted upon the "iron law of wages" as the natural limit on workers' earnings. He singled out Selznick in particular for assuming in his TVA study that organizational realities placed immutable limits upon individuals' ability to achieve their goals, so that "if men persist in their ends, they are forced to satisfy the needs of their organizational instruments. They are, therefore, as much committed to their tools as to their ends."[96] Selznick's theory therefore implied an "icy stasis" for humanity, which ignored prospects for democratic human agency in determining and achieving social goals. Selznick and many others had become "morticians, all too eager to bury men's hopes" of controlling their own destinies.[97]

---

[96] Gouldner, "Metaphysical Pathos and the Theory of Bureaucracy," *The American Political Science Review* 49, 2 (June 1955): 504. Other critiques of the mass-society and alienation paradigms included those of Lewis Coser, Melvin Seeman, and Daniel Bell. Coser, a 1954 graduate of the Columbia program, repudiated the mass-society theory belatedly, publishing his misgivings a decade later in *Men of Ideas: A Sociologist's View* (New York: Free Press, 1965). During the 1950s, as the editor of *Dissent,* he shared the concern over mass culture's erosion of aesthetic standards shared by other New York intellectuals, but he distanced himself from the elitist implications of the mass-culture critique. See his response to Edward Shils's attack on the mass-culture theory in "Nightmares, Daydreams, and Prof. Shils," *Dissent* 5, 3 (Summer 1958): 268–73. Seeman, in "On the Meaning of Alienation," *American Sociological Review* 24, 6 (December 1959): 783–91, echoed Shils in advancing that the mass-society theorists had constructed an "ideal condition from which the individual is estranged" and that, therefore, to be alienated "means to be something less than one might ideally be if the circumstances in society were otherwise" (790). Bell offered several critiques of the mass culture and alienation paradigms. In addition to "The Theory of Mass Society," these included "In Search of Marxist Humanism: The Debate on Alienation," *Soviet Survey* 32, 2 (April–June 1960): 21–31. In a symposium paper on "The Nature and Value of Marxism Today" at the meeting of the American Philosophical Association, December 29, 1959, he connected the modern intellectual's fascination with such supposed conditions as alienation, anomie, bureaucratization, depersonalization, and isolation to "the disorientation of the radical intellectual in the mass society." He thus connected this fascination with his idea of the end of ideology, perceiving as crucial the alienation of the social observer living amidst the bankruptcy of ideologies of transformative social change. See his "The Debate on Alienation," in Leopold Labedz, ed., *Revisionism: Essays on the History of Marxist Ideas* (London: George Allen and Unwin, 1962), 210.

[97] Ibid., 507. Gouldner's philosophy regarding the social scientist's engagement with publics is elucidated in James J. Chriss's *Alvin W. Gouldner: Sociologist and Outlaw Marxist* (Brookfield, VT: Ashgate, 1999). Chriss locates Gouldner within the hermeneutical perspective of Wilhelm Dilthey and Charles S. Peirce, in which, *contra* Jürgen Habermas, it is insufficient for ordinary human actors to seek a communicative understanding of their social system, which changes and takes new directions all the time. In such a protean social system, the social scientist's role is therefore not to simply communicate in popularly accessible language but to create new, "extraordinary languages, and to help laypersons learn to speak them, in order to show people *themselves* how to use the 'liberating perspectives of the extraordinary languages of social theory' to create the good life" (11).

Ironically, the distance postwar sociologists placed between themselves and the larger community produced a strong counterattack from that very community. By the early 1950s, lay critics began to perceive in the profession's insularity—its cloistered professional stance, specialized language, obscure methodologies, and apparent reluctance to share its observations about society readily with that society—the potential for the very totalitarian proclivities that many sociologists believed existed among alienated workers and middle-class suburbanites. As sociologists wedded their scientific identity to classical theories of the malaise of the public sphere and the necessary attenuation of democratic practice, charges emerged from the public sphere that they themselves had succumbed to an alienated outlook that lent itself to totalitarian techniques of mass manipulation and undemocratic political administration. The defensive posture that Parsons, Merton, Lazarsfeld, and others had assumed in the face of skepticism and outright hostility from politicians, foundation administrators, and scientists shortly after the war therefore intensified, as the spectrum of detractors widened to include journalists, historians, philosophers, theologians, and, most immediately, recalcitrant sociologists, who feared the alienated social scientist far more than they did the alienated common citizen.

6
Fads, Foibles, and Autopsies
Unwelcome Publicity for Diffident Sociologists

E arly in 1946, Robert Lynd wrote a letter to Alfred McClung Lee, then the chairman of the Sociology and Anthropology departments at Wayne University, identifying what he perceived to be the source of American sociology's future disciplinary progress. Lynd observed that sociology possessed three salient "levels," each of which reflected a stage within its progress toward maturation. The first of these consisted of "non-quantitative, non-technically trained" scholars. The second included those who had had some exposure to modern empirical research techniques and therefore constituted "an intermediate group." The third level Lynd identified as "a terrific crop of youngsters trained by men like Stouffer [and] Lazarsfeld, with experience in group research in the war." It was this third group, trained in the vanguard research programs at Harvard and Columbia, which Lynd perceived to be the driving force behind sociology's maturation. "The future of sociology lies with the #3 [classification]," he declared, "and the steep rise in training, since the mid-[19]30s, means that people are combing the field for young men."[1] Indeed, Lynd, whose pioneering work in statistical sociology with his wife Helen, the *Middletown* studies, had demonstrated his confidence in

---

[1] Robert S. Lynd to Alfred McClung Lee, March 14, 1946, Alfred McClung Lee Papers, Brooklyn College Archive.

innovative quantitative research by sponsoring Paul Lazarsfeld's appointment at Columbia, which did much to solidify Columbia's leading role in postwar sociology.

Six years later, Lynd offered a strikingly different assessment of the ascendant empirical sociological research. In a letter to Lazarsfeld, he expressed grave concern over postwar sociology's direction. "There never was a time in which putting techniques in the hands of men devoid of a knowledge of history and human values, including sensitive knowledge of the trends in our time and knowledge of what things valuable to men are at stake, was so humanly dangerous," he warned. "We would all, I assume, agree that one does not hold back technical development because 'the times are not right,'" he continued. "But along with this goes, I believe, responsibility for seeing that the *meaning* of technical training and the *significance* of techniques *as we work at them and impart them to young social scientists* shall have a selected, definite orientation"[2] (emphasis in original).

Lynd's warning represented not a change of heart or loss of faith in the promise of social science but rather a reiteration of the central argument of his 1939 critique of American social science, *Knowledge for What?* in which he laid out his objections to the prevailing trends in social research and social theory. An overemphasis on research technique, he wrote, was converting social researchers into technicians who offered their services to anyone who would pay for them. Innovations in quantitative research methods tended all too often to define what could and could not be investigated, as social scientists limited their inquiries to that which could be counted or measured mathematically. Meanwhile, social theory withered under the pressures of small-scale, quantitative research that, he argued, failed to supply the basis for meaningful hypotheses about relevant social issues. At the heart of Lynd's argument lay his demand that social science provide society at large with useful observations about social issues that could form the basis for constructive, democratic action. "Social science will stand or fall on the basis of its serviceability to men as they struggle to live," he insisted. "If it plays safe and avoids risks, it will find itself ridden down and cast aside. For the one sure fact in the present confusions of our culture is that the issues will be confronted by some means of control in some fashion."[3]

---

[2] Robert S. Lynd to Paul F. Lazarsfeld, January 26, 1952, Paul Felix Lazarsfeld Papers, Rare Book and Manuscript Library, Columbia University.

[3] Robert S. Lynd, *Knowledge for What? The Place of Social Science in American Culture* (Middletown, CT: Wesleyan University Press, 1939), 177. Lynd's part in the debate over the role of the social scientist is analyzed in Chapter 4 of Mark C. Smith's *Social Science in the Crucible* (Durham, NC: Duke University Press, 1994). Smith explores Lynd's assertion of an activist social science that focused keenly upon social problems rather than the priorities of business and government and that

Lynd's praise of the evolving priorities of sociological research shortly after the conclusion of the war and his subsequent renewed criticism of them reflected American sociology's ambivalent position within postwar American society and its internecine struggle over its proper professional and public identities. As scholars like Parsons and Merton asserted that sociology was evolving steadily toward scientific maturation, as the refinement of its investigative techniques and the verifiability of its theoretical conclusions demonstrated its scientific status, their assertions called to the fore scholars well known both within and beyond the discipline who questioned both the validity of sociology's claims to scientific status and the implications such claims bore for the larger purpose of sociological work. The depth of professional ambivalence over the prospects for a science of society became manifest when Lynd and Pitirim Sorokin, both pioneers in the statistical study of society, themselves became harsh critics of this ideal and its quantitative methodological basis. These detractors' ambiguous intellectual and professional standing amongst their peers, as well as the manner in which they presented their objections, would provoke a response from the defenders of sociology-as-science that would serve to strengthen their original conception rather than encouraging its reevaluation.

Seventeen years after the publication of *Knowledge for What?* Sorokin published the profession's second book-length attack on the dominant trends in academic sociology. Sorokin confronted his peers' values from unique political and philosophical perspectives. Born in Russia, he came of age in the midst of the Russian Revolution. After earning his doctorate in sociology from the University of St. Petersburg, he immersed himself in the turbulent political life of revolutionary Russia, serving as the editor of a revolutionary newspaper and, ultimately, as secretary to the provisional parliamentary government of Alexander Kerensky. After his imprisonment by the Bolshevik government for counterrevolutionary activities, he was banished from Russia, arriving in the United States in 1922. From 1924 to 1930, he taught sociology at the University of Minnesota under the chairmanship of F. Stuart Chapin, a staunch advocate of scientific sociology.[4]

During the 1920s, Sorokin made crucial contributions to American sociology's empirical development with his use of statistical analysis in the study

---

helped foster alternative institutions through which ordinary people could express their creativity and exercise political influence. A good postwar example of Lynd's perspective here is his "Can Labor and Intellectuals Work Together?" in J.B.S. Hardman and Maurice F. Neufeld, eds., *The House of Labor: Internal Operations of American Unions* (New York: Prentice-Hall, 1951).

[4]Barry V. Johnston's *Pitirim A. Sorokin: An Intellectual Biography* (Lawrence: University Press of Kansas, 1995) traces Sorokin's personal, intellectual, and professional development.

of social mobility in peasant communities. His 1927 work, *Social Mobility*, a massive comparative study of numerous cultures and nations over a period of hundreds of years, introduced American scholars to the objective, quantitative techniques Sorokin believed needed to replace impressionistic, speculative forms of inquiry. Then, as if to balance his empirical emphasis in his first book, in 1928, he published *Contemporary Sociological Theories*, a summary of extant theoretical work in twentieth-century sociology. These accomplishments, as well as his subsequent publications, led to Harvard's offer of the chairmanship of its new Sociology Department, which he accepted in 1930.

Unlike Parsons, Sorokin lacked the personal, intellectual, and professional qualities necessary to forge a paradigm to compete with that of functionalism. His status as an émigré in a traditional, New England institution such as Harvard, his brusque, impatient manner with graduate students, and his lack of collaborative work with them meant that a "Sorokinian" school never materialized.[5] His scholarship, which by the 1930s exhibited pronounced macroscopic and historical emphases, in contrast to the small-scale and rather ahistorical studies that predominated in *The American Journal of Sociology* and *The American Sociological Review*, placed him outside of the Columbia-Harvard conception of scientific sociology. Thus, although his proficiency in and contributions to the empirical research techniques that leading postwar sociologists touted as the key to the construction of a scientific sociology appeared to ally him with his peers at Harvard and Columbia, Sorokin worked in relative professional and intellectual isolation from them.

Sorokin also demonstrated that his philosophy regarding the relevance and efficacy of postwar quantitative research methods differed profoundly from those contained within the 1950s scientific paradigm. In 1937, he had released the first three volumes of his monumental *Social and Cultural Dynamics*, a massive interpretation of the course of Western cultural and intellectual development. In it, he conceived of the history of the West as consisting of salient epochs, each with its own prevailing "system of truth." These systems shaped the fundamental dimensions of human existence in their respective epochs, for the *Weltanschauung* of each determined how humanity attempted to understand itself and conduct its affairs. Thus, the philosophy, religion, morality, art, literature, laws, and economic and political order of each period of human history necessarily conformed to its predominant system of truth.

Since the Renaissance, when church doctrine and revealed truth had given way to the authority of that which the senses could verify, Western

---

[5]Barry V. Johnston, "Sorokin and Parsons at Harvard: Institutional Conflict and the Origin of a Hegemonic Tradition," *Journal of the History of the Behavioral Sciences* 22 (April 1986): 119–22.

thought had embraced and internalized "Sensate" truth, or the truth of the senses. Unfortunately, Sorokin warned, sensate truth now threatened modern Western civilization with degeneration and, ultimately, chaos. Indeed, *Social and Cultural Dynamics* constituted a dire warning about modern man's unmitigated acceptance of sensate truth. "The organs of the senses," Sorokin proclaimed, "can give us but a chaotic mass of impressions, perceptions, sensations, incapable of supplying any integrated knowledge, anything except disorderly bits of pseudo observation and pseudo impression. They can give at the best but a mass of meaningless 'facts,' without any coherence."[6]

Thus, the very developments within Western thought that seemed to most observers—and certainly the leading voices within professional sociology—to be yielding a truer, more scientific understanding of existence were instead symptoms of a crippling historical malaise. In a shorter, more polemical extension of his arguments in *Dynamics*, entitled *The Crisis of Our Age*, Sorokin declared that modern culture's exclusive reliance on sensate truth had produced "a kind of *illusionism*," in which "mere impressions and artificial constructs relating to something unknowable" led civilization ever deeper into the abyss, "burying the truth, reality, and science itself."[7] Sensate culture's elevation of "a thin and narrow empiricism, divorced from other social values—religion, goodness, beauty, and the like" offered the false promise of the demystification of the human condition, while creating a morally and spiritually impoverished conception of humanity.[8]

In the absence of guiding principles and morals, Sorokin warned, civilization faced an era of ever-greater savagery and confusion. Sensate knowledge, with its concomitant emphasis on the purely instrumental value of knowledge and experience, fostered ever-more insidious and disguised forms of domination. Man the truth-seeker, debased by his relativism and his slavish commitment to the use-value of knowledge, was descending "to the level of an animal who tends, by means of various 'ideologies,' 'rationalizations,' and 'derivations,' to exalt his greed, his appetites, and his egoism."[9] The global events of the 1920s and 1930s, and especially the barbarity of Stalinism and Nazism, provided for Sorokin abundant evidence of these trends, as they demonstrated how dogma functioning in the service of the lust for power could fill the moral vacuum sensate culture had created. "This indifference of empirical science to goodness and beauty," Sorokin observed, "has rendered it

---

[6] Pitirim A. Sorokin, *Social and Cultural Dynamics*, vol. 1 (New York: American Book, 1937), 67.

[7] Pitirim A. Sorokin, *The Crisis of Our Age* (New York: E. P. Dutton, 1942), 98.

[8] Ibid., 124.

[9] Ibid., 123.

amoral, even cynical. It has thus become an instrumentality ready to serve any master, whether God or Mammon, and any purpose, whether socially beneficial or disastrous, constructive or destructive."[10] Tragically and inevitably, empiricism's damage far outweighed its blessings, for, he observed, "in few periods of human history have so many millions of persons been so unhappy, so insecure, so hungry and destitute, as at the present time, all the way from China to western Europe."[11]

Ironically then, according to Sorokin, sensate values had produced a deep malaise in which the epistemological principles of Bacon and Locke had proven incapable of maximizing the human happiness they had promised since the Enlightenment. "The practical failure of the decadent empiricism of contemporary culture," Sorokin proclaimed, "is demonstrated by our increasing inability to control mankind and the course of the socio-cultural processes."[12] Sorokin then provided a litany of the failures of economists, political scientists, sociologists, and psychologists to regulate economic forces, reform governments, reduce crime, and solve family problems. As knowledge became divorced from humanity's quest to control its destiny and to promote human values over expediency, civilization faced a calamitous drift. Social science, tragically, had succumbed to that drift precisely because it embraced unreservedly the scientistic principles of sensate culture.

With *Social and Cultural Dynamics,* Sorokin not only roundly rejected the prevailing "celebrationist" optimism that postwar scholarship evinced, but he also repudiated the linear view of intellectual development articulated by his sociological peers at Harvard and Columbia. Instead, Sorokin possessed a cyclical conception of historical development resembling those of Spengler and Toynbee, in which civilizations faced inevitable decline and ultimate disintegration. However, Sorokin's envisioned cultural rebirth stood in marked contrast to the pessimistic prophesies of his predecessors, and thus his theories presented a challenge to his generation of scholars to take up the cause of moral and spiritual transformation. Unfortunately, he contended, modern

---

[10] Ibid., 124–25.

[11] Ibid., 130. In his autobiography, Sorokin would declare that the outbreak of World War II came as no surprise to him, as he had been predicting such events since the 1920s "in great detail" and "had repeatedly warned the foolishly gaudy, optimistic, and decadent sensate society of the West about the imminent wars, bloody revolutions, destruction, misery, and 'liberation' in man of 'the worst of the beasts.'" He recalled rather smugly that his critics, after having ridiculed his predictions, were compelled to apologize to him for their failure to take seriously the decadence of their sensate civilization. See Pitirim A. Sorokin, *A Long Journey* (New Haven, CT: College and University Press, 1963), 265.

[12] Ibid., 130.

social thought remained mired in the residue of nineteenth-century positivism, attempting to sustain the dream of linear progress.[13]

Social and Cultural Dynamics, which was reissued in an abridged version
of over 700 pages in 1957, garnered substantial attention the world over,
receiving scores of reviews in scholarly and popular publications alike. In a
pattern that would become ever-more pronounced over the course of the
1950s, social scientists roundly condemned the work, whereas many nonprofessional reviewers praised it.[14] Years later, Sorokin would assess the
work's reception in terms that reflected his commitment to a sociology that
stimulated broad dialogue rather than devoting its energies to the scientific
precision of its findings. It was a measure of the success of Social and Cultural
Dynamics, he insisted, that so many reactions to the work were either strongly
favorable or unfavorable, rather than casually dismissive. "Whatever the vices
and virtues of the Dynamics," he would recall, "it seems to have had something that strongly 'hit' its proponents as well as its opponents. This 'something' was enough to make me satisfied with it." He likened its reception to
that proffered "an overwhelming majority of the great works in the history of
social thought. They also were enthusiastically praised as well as disdainfully
condemned."[15]

Sorokin's shrill indictment of the decadence of modern, sensate culture
provided the foundation in 1956 for the first of only two extended attacks on
scientific sociology proffered over the course of the 1950s, Fads and Foibles
in Modern Sociology.[16] Sorokin, then 66 years old and retired from teaching, attacked his peers as an outsider, isolated generationally, intellectually,
and professionally from a sociology he condemned as corrupted by "quantophrenia," "testomania," and "sham-scientific slang." He subjected these
pathologies to a series of exhaustive dissections in an attempt to resurrect

---

[13]In Social Philosophies of an Age of Crisis (London: Adam and Charles Black, 1952), Sorokin would
charge that his century's linear theories of progress had yet to approach those of the previous
century in originality of significance. He ridiculed them as "midget variations of Hegelian,
Comtean, Spencerian, or Marxian conceptions" (8).

[14]Robert Bierstedt, in American Sociology: A Critical History (New York: Academic Press, 1981),
summarizes the academic reviews of Social and Cultural Dynamics (341–45).

[15]Sorokin, A Long Journey, 260. Sorokin even contrasted Dynamics with his subsequent book, a
quantitative study of how the unemployed spend their time, a work which he characterized as
"probably . . . the most boring of all my boring works" (A Long Journey, 262).

[16]Sorokin had sounded his warning regarding sociology's future shortly after the publication of
Dynamics. In 1940, he delivered a paper at the annual meeting of the American Sociological
Society entitled "The Supreme Court of History," in which he reminded his critics that his
predictions of global crisis had proven accurate and demanded a sociology that repudiated the
natural science identification and narrow empiricism.

meaningful sociological investigation. Although *Social and Cultural Dynamics* remained vague as to the specific sins of sensate culture, *Fads and Foibles* contained meticulous criticisms of modern sociology and its prevailing linear conception of its own scientific development.

Sorokin began his treatise by challenging the assumption prevalent in postwar sociology that the "scientization" of the discipline represented a critical break with humanity's past attempts to understand itself. Rather than providing more accurate and meaningful conceptions of the human condition, he asserted, many professional scholars in the social sciences were self-deluded "New Columbuses" suffering from "discoverer's complex," as they believed themselves to be intellectual pioneers in formulating ideas that were in fact centuries old:

> The younger generation of sociologists and psychologists explicitly claims that nothing important has been discovered in their fields during all the preceding centuries; that there were only some vague "arm-chair philosophies"; and that the real scientific era in these disciplines began only in the last two or three decades with the publication of their own researches and those of members of their clique. Claiming to be particularly objective, precise, and scientific, our sociological and psychological Columbuses tirelessly repeat this delusion as a scientific truth. Accordingly, they rarely make any references to the social and psychological thinkers of the past. When they do, they hardly veil the sense of their own superiority over the unscientific old fogies.[17]

Whereas Robert Merton had contrasted the system-building social philosophers of previous centuries with their social science successors to demonstrate modern sociology's greater reliability and utility, Sorokin saw in the latter the arrogance and lack of historical perspective of the positivist and the technician. Sensate culture had produced a professional class with abundant optimism and technique but utterly devoid of humility or breadth of vision.

Thus, contemporary sociological theory simply reflected the modern scientific malaise, and Parsons and Shils stood as its "representative victims." Sorokin claimed to have found "absolutely nothing new" in Parsons's ideas, "excepting for a multitude of logically poor and empirically useless paradigms and neologisms." Psychologists, philosophers, and other sociologists,

---

[17]Pitirim A. Sorokin, *Fads and Foibles in Modern Sociology and Related Sciences* (Chicago: Henry Regnery, 1956), 3–4.

had developed such ideas with greater scientific integrity and precision.[18] Furthermore, Sorokin proclaimed, he himself had preceded Parsons and Shils with many of the very concepts included in their collaborative work, *Toward a General Theory of Action*. "Their basic definitions and concepts are practically identical with mine," he remarked. "Often they are identical even in wording."[19] Of course, Sorokin was careful to assert the greater cohesion and overall superiority of his own "humble analysis," the putatively greater empirical and analytical precision of which derived from its author's greater respect for the work of predecessors.

As for empiricist New Columbuses, Sorokin attacked Stouffer and the scientific aspirations Stouffer had conveyed in *The American Soldier*. Stouffer, too, suffered from "discoverer's complex." His research team had merely manipulated their questionnaire data, in "fallacious or quite arbitrary" ways. Their techniques, he proclaimed, "are mainly inept complications of the old techniques—complications, moreover, incapable of delivering the goods expected of them."[20] They had taken methodological precepts that had existed since the Enlightenment and declared them to be innovations. On the contrary, "the mathematical study of psychosocial phenomena," like that of natural and physical phenomena, had begun with the quantitative science of Spinoza, Descartes, Leibnitz, Newton, and others who believed in the scientific primacy of measurement. The Stouffer group's attempts to follow their example constituted mere "pseudomathematical imitations" that "misused and abused" their methods by applying them "to phenomena which, so far, do not lend themselves to quantification."[21]

Beyond his specific attacks upon quantitative social science, Sorokin assailed its scientific aspirations for their failure to acknowledge the implications of the monumental changes in scientific theory that had emerged by the

---

[18] Ibid., 15.

[19] Ibid., 14–15. Johnston, in "Sorokin and Parsons at Harvard," traces the theoretical and philosophical conflicts between Sorokin's and Parsons's sociology to their initial relationship at Harvard in the early 1930s, when Sorokin, as the department head, criticized harshly Parsons's draft of *The Structure of Social Action* for its conceptual vagueness and abstruse style, weaknesses he believed justified the postponement of Parsons's professional advancement (114–16).

[20] Ibid., 9.

[21] Ibid., 103. Sorokin attributed much of the fallibility of *The American Soldier's* methodology to the fact that the interview technique itself produced unreliable results. Respondents simply could not be counted upon to provide responses that would have any lasting scientific validity. Instead, they constituted "snapshots" of particular attitudes expressed at particular times, attitudes that not only carried the imprint of the researchers' scaling, but also the particular circumstances of the interview itself. Frontline conditions, Sorokin noted for example, would inevitably lead the respondents to formulate responses most likely to allow them "to escape the endless irritating questionnaires" (147).

middle of the twentieth century. In particular, Newtonian physics no longer provided an adequate model for scientific endeavor. Newton's well-ordered universe, with its detectable and predictable laws, no longer existed. In its place quantum physics had posited a universe in which subjectivity and uncertainty made an objective, scientific understanding of reality impossible. Sorokin cited Werner Heisenberg's uncertainty principle, which states the impossibility of determining the position or velocity of a subatomic particle, and Erwin Schrödinger's theory of wave mechanics as evidence that social scientists who saw in physics a model for their own identity were embracing a philosophy of science that physicists themselves had abandoned. Sociologists were therefore identifying with a world of physical science that no longer existed.[22] "The moral of this microphysics," Sorokin concluded, was that sociologists' and psychologists' search "for causal or statistical uniformities in the field of unique or rare psychosocial phenomena, is likely to be a search for something that really does not exist at all."[23]

Sorokin's indictment of the scientific aspirations of modern sociology and psychology constituted an application of his analysis of the historic sensate malaise to the culture of his own profession. "We seem to be a generation of competent technicians rather than of great discoverers and creators," he lamented. "With this change," he continued, "research itself would tend to become progressively narrower, shallower, and less and less significant for purposes of understanding the psychosocial universe, as well as for serving the daily mental, moral, and social needs of human beings."[24] Social science's fragmentation of empirical findings, the increasing relativization of experience, and the lack of compelling moral and spiritual principles that might guide the quest for new knowledge reflected the deepening crisis of sensate culture in general. Once again, Sorokin called for the adoption of an "integralist conception of reality," which would combine the insights obtained through sensory, rational, and intuitive activity. The synthesis of these different forms of knowing would ensure that "the knowledge obtained through one channel is supplemented and checked by the knowledge from the other two channels."[25]

Fads and Foibles provoked a hostile response from Sorokin's sociological peers in both The American Journal of Sociology and The American Sociological Review. Donald Horton, of the University of Chicago, charged Sorokin with

---

[22] Here, Sorokin assailed Lazarsfeld's theory of latent continuum structures, which "completely ignores the quantum theory and modern microphysics," for "the very essence of the quantum theory is the principle of discontinuity" (128).

[23] Ibid., 152.

[24] Ibid., 315.

[25] Ibid., 317.

selfishly and wrongfully undermining sociology's status as a cumulative project and attested to the professional marginalization that Sorokin had brought upon himself: "Professional isolation," he wrote, "is the fate invited by any man who builds private systems of thought outside the collaborative development of the science to which he is nominally attached."[26] Horton accused Sorokin of appealing to "third parties" in an attempt to discredit sociology as a profession rather than seeking to educate his peers, concluding that the book's charges "are a disservice to our discipline from which only the enemies of rational social inquiry can possibly benefit."[27]

It was appropriate that Robert K. Merton would issue one of the more sophisticated and extensive responses to *Fads and Foibles*. Indeed, Merton's response to the book stood as the most extensive and significant assessment of Sorokin's indictment, and it reflected Merton's continued commitment to the principles of scientific sociology as he had articulated them in *Social Theory and Social Structure*. Significantly, the profound disagreement between the two that *Fads and Foibles* was to catalyze was preceded four years earlier by a misunderstanding between them that stemmed from a bibliography of works on the sociology of science that Merton had assembled, in which he neglected to include works on the subject by Sorokin himself. After receiving an angry note from Sorokin on this matter, Merton pleaded for Sorokin's forgiveness:

> I have just received your note which disturbed and hurt me deeply because I believe that it is very unjust. True, the failure to include references to your relevant work in the sociology of science bibliography was an inexcusable oversight which succeeds only in damaging the value of that list of books. Nor can I explain how this happened. After all, I can scarcely have been unaware of the long chapters in the *Dynamics* which deal with the sociology of science, for you went out of your way to state in a footnote that I had assisted you in that part of your work. It would be pointless, therefore, for me to invent an explanation for an absurd oversight which does little credit to a bibliography on that subject. I simply don't know how it happened.

---

[26] Donald Horton, review of *Fads and Foibles* in *American Journal of Sociology* 62, 3 (November 1956): 339.

[27] Ibid., 339. Sorokin responded to such criticism by noting that the impact of his work upon the social science community persisted despite consistently unfavorable reviews such as these. In a letter to the editor of the *American Journal of Sociology*, he characterized Horton's negative review of *Fads and Foibles* as "a good omen for the book because of a high correlation between the damning of my books by the reviewers of the *American Journal of Sociology* and their subsequent career. The more strongly they have been damned (and practically all my books were damned by your reviewers), the more significant and successful were my damned works." Sorokin, letter to the editor, *American Journal of Sociology* 62, 5 (March 1957): 515.

My regret will do nothing to repair the error, but I do want you to know that I do deeply regret it.[28]

Significantly, Merton's apologetic letter indicated that Sorokin had responded to his omission with the charge that Merton intended to "obliterate" his name and contributions within that area of sociology. Merton's response thus contained more than a hint of resentment at Sorokin's overreaction. "It was, therefore, a great shock," Merton wrote, "in the midst of all this, to have your letter attacking my motives, rather than properly calling my attention to an oversight of which I am not proud."[29] Although the basic differences between Merton's and Sorokin's views on sociology's scientific viability—differences evident well before the publication of *Fads and Foibles*—provide the more compelling explanation for what would become a widening gulf between the two men on the promise of sociology, this misunderstanding nevertheless suggests a foreshadowing of the misgivings Merton would express about Sorokin's view of science.

In a contribution to a collection of essays on Sorokin's work, Merton and a co-author, Bernard Barber, defended the importance of a proper balance between theory and empirical investigation, research with modest, circumscribed objectives, and the faith that scientific sociology was an incremental endeavor that was gradually building a whole that was greater than the sum of its parts. Merton and Barber contended that Sorokin's macroscopic framework, in which huge epochs fell under the rubrics "sensate" and "idealistic," ignored profound variations in thinking within particular epochs and therefore failed to truly discredit the ambitions of sociologists and other scientists alike in their quest for knowledge.

Sorokin, Merton and Barber contended, had constructed a historical and sociological framework that depended entirely upon the power of ideas for its cohesion. Sorokin's was an "emanationist" theory of history, for it demanded that one accept that ideas constitute the driving force in a given civilization. Unlike Marx or Mannheim, who argued for the importance of the role of social structure in shaping ideas, Sorokin had posited that "ideas rule the world." Thus, Merton and Barber argued that, for Sorokin, "cultural mentality is regarded as fundamental; social structure and personality as producing, at most, minor variations on culturally embedded themes."[30] The problem with

---

[28] Robert K. Merton to Pitirim A. Sorokin, September 16, 1952, Pitirim A. Sorokin Papers, University of Saskatchewan Archives, Saskatoon, Saskatchewan.

[29] Ibid.

[30] Robert K. Merton and Bernard Barber, "Sorokin's Formulations in the Sociology of Science," in Phillip J. Allen, ed., *Pitirim A. Sorokin in Review* (Durham, NC: Duke University Press, 1963), 337.

such a cosmology, they insisted, was that it rendered Sorokin incapable of accounting for inconsistencies in his sensate model. What if a particular idea failed to reflect the supposedly predominant faith in sensate experience? Could not the complexity of a particular social structure allow for important ideas that deviated from the particular *Weltanschauung* Sorokin found there? Merton and Barber recognized that in the history of science it was precisely those exceptions to vulgar empiricism that had produced some of the greatest discoveries. "Sorokin largely shuts himself out from *analyzing* those variations which often make for the advancement of cumulative knowledge," they charged.[31] Scientific advancement did not simply reflect four centuries of a particular "fundamental orientation toward reality," because scientific activity did not proceed in a uniform fashion that would reflect such an orientation.

It was precisely this lack of uniformity in scientific work that Merton and Barber marshaled against Sorokin's indictments of social science. Sorokin had of course argued in *Fads and Foibles* that social scientists' collective ambition to build social science disciplines with the scientific integrity of the physical and natural sciences had proceeded without regard for the fact that mid-twentieth-century science had shifted away from the Newtonian universe; and scientific uncertainty now challenged scientific predictability, contingency replaced finality, and subjectivity placed new limits on the prospects for scientific objectivity. Merton and Barber, however, noted that if the history of science reflected such radical discontinuities, Sorokin himself had left them out of his theory of history. He had cast such a wide net in constructing his history of ideas and their corresponding social structures that he had ignored scientific developments that did not reflect the prevailing sensate values. Merton and Barber concluded:

> This is a perspective which, precisely because it is macroscopic, throws together, for all pertinent purposes, the work of a Galileo, Kepler, and Newton, on the one hand, and the work of a Rutherford, Einstein, and, shall we say, Yang and Lee on the other. It thus excludes from analysis the great differences that, for many human and intellectual purposes, are to be found in the science of the sixteenth or seventeenth century and the twentieth. It is a gross approximation that threatens to usurp the attention of those who have reason to regard the variability *within* the macroscopic sensate period as also fundamental.[32]

---

[31] Ibid., 338.

[32] Ibid., 339.

Sorokin, therefore, had performed only the preliminary work in assessing the true character of the cultures he had considered. The next step, according to Merton and Barber, required an investigation of the significant departures from each culture's predominant values and norms. "Even on Sorokin's own premises," they insisted, "the general characterizations of historical cultures as sensate, idealistic, or ideational constitute only a first step in the analysis, a step which must be followed by further detailed analyses of deviations from the central tendencies of the culture."[33] Without such investigations, Sorokin's analysis constituted a kind of reductive determinism.

Sorokin, of course, had not performed an investigation of deviating tendencies to the satisfaction of Merton and Barber. Thus, their reflections implied that Sorokin had demanded something of his fellow sociologists that he had failed to provide in his own analysis, namely the recognition that twentieth-century science had deviated markedly from the scientific assumptions of previous centuries. Although Sorokin had attacked scientific sociology for aspiring to a physical science model that had disintegrated in the face of revolutionary discoveries in theoretical physics, his theory of history seemed to deny that such a revolution had taken place. Twentieth-century science, like that of the previous four centuries, belonged to the sensate age. Thus, *Fads and Foibles* demanded that sociologists confront the uncertainty principle, while *Social and Cultural Dynamics* posited that both uncertainty and Newtonianism belonged to the sensate age. It appeared nonsensical to ask sociologists to repudiate an identity that was not only culturally determined, but also lacked clear epistemological choices.

Merton and Barber also took Sorokin to task for his seemingly equivocal position on the use of statistics. Sorokin had understood that to support his theoretical claims for the existence of discreet, integrated Sensate and Idealistic cultures, it would be necessary to use statistics. Thus, the critic of quantophrenia had himself seen fit to quantify his material. "Despite his vitriolic comments on the statisticians of our sensate age," Merton and Barber observed, Sorokin "recognized that to deal with the extent of integration implies some statistical measure."[34] Once again, Sorokin seemed to have contradicted himself. "Sorokin drenches us in quantitative facts," Merton and Barber noted, and rightly so, for his theory required thorough statistical

---

[33] Ibid., 353.

[34] Ibid., 351. Lazarsfeld cited similar equivocation on Sorokin's part, speculating, "Probably Sorokin's extreme criticism results from impatience with the slow progress of a field to which he contributed so much." Lazarsfeld, foreword to Rose K. Goldsen, Morris Rosenberg, Robin M. Williams, Jr., and Edward A. Suchman, eds., *What College Students Think* (Princeton, NJ: D. Van Nostrand, 1960), x.

substantiation. Thus, they declared, "Independently collected, systematic and quantitative data supply the most demanding test called for by such an empirically-connected theory. And that Sorokin also thinks this to be the case seems implied by the way in which he has gone about his task of conducting empirical inquiries in the sociology of science."[35]

Merton's and Barber's charges regarding Sorokin's attitude toward the use of statistics in sociology overdrew the extent of Sorokin's bias against quantification. In the 1920s, it had been Sorokin's *Social Mobility* that had introduced quantitative research methods to the subfield of rural sociology. Moreover, his critique of quantification and empirical sociology represented more an attempt to demystify the unexamined faith in statistics as a means to knowledge about society than a denial of the use of social statistics in general. He had accepted statistical research as vital but had simply decoupled it from linear scientific progress.

Nevertheless, Merton and Barber rose to defend the cumulative enterprise of scientific sociology against Sorokin's antiscientism. Sorokin's sociology of knowledge and, more important, his sociology of science, posited a cyclical intellectual universe, in which historically discrete systems of truth succeeded one another, seemingly without appropriating past intellectual and cultural achievements and integrating them into an ever-expanding whole.[36] Sorokin's system therefore denied altogether the validity of the arguments Merton, Lazarsfeld, Parsons, and others had been making regarding sociology's scientific evolution. If postwar sociology proceeded not in a linear trajectory, moving toward greater methodological precision, replicable results, and incremental progress, its status as a science would lack a firm foundation. Merton and Barber thus asserted again the incrementalist theory of scientific development. "The cycles of cultural change do not start anew," they agreed. "Particularly with regard to science, each succeeding historical phase makes use of antecedent knowledge on which it builds."[37]

---

[35]Ibid., 357.

[36]Sorokin's theoretical framework bore a strong similarity to Thomas Kuhn's use of the concept of paradigms to describe successive epochs of scientific thought. Sorokin, like Kuhn, posited the existence of historically and socioculturally autonomous systems of thought, each characterized by "the existence of some margin of choice or selection on its part with regard to the infinitely great number of varying external agents and objects which may influence it. It will ingest some of these and not others" (Sorokin, *Dynamics*, 1:50–51).

[37]Merton and Barber, "Sorokin's Formulations," 361. Where Sorokin had argued that cultures "selected" those elements that conformed to the prevailing *Weltanschauung*, thereby excluding experience that might allow for progress, Merton and Barber chose to view that selection process as part and parcel of progress. Even if humanity's accumulation of knowledge were not unilinear,

Sorokin's critique, although widely read and reviewed within sociological circles, did little to change sociologists' scientific aspirations and in fact hastened his marginalization within the discipline. Despite his standing by 1963 as the most widely translated and published sociologist in the history of the discipline, he remained isolated from the profession's broader currents.[38] Moreover, in the three years between *Fads and Foibles* and the publication of C. Wright Mills's more sweeping indictment of postwar sociology, few members of the profession followed Sorokin's example by producing comparable criticism of the fundamental assumption that sociology was a science. The absence of such thorough self-examination reinforced the perception that Sorokin was a renegade scholar whose iconoclasm, stridency, and inability to lay claim to any clear theoretical or conceptual contributions to the field diminished the impact of his critique. Such vulnerabilities characterized C. Wright Mills as well when in 1959 he presented his attack on his profession's prevailing assumptions and practices in *The Sociological Imagination*.

Well before the publication of *The Sociological Imagination*, Mills had noted the dangers of an irresponsible and unexamined preoccupation with scientific status within American sociology. In 1942, while still a graduate student at the University of Wisconsin, Mills produced a scathing review of the first volume of W. Lloyd Warner's *Yankee City* series, a statistical study of social stratification. Mills charged the Warner research group with allowing its research methods to control the study and its conclusions."[39] Mills's subsequent appointment to a research position in Columbia's Bureau of Applied Social Research under Lazarsfeld reinforced his opposition to the conception of science as the evolution of methods of measurement. Mills objected to the apolitical character of the bureau's studies of mass communications and public opinion polling and therefore attempted fruitlessly—and

---

they insisted, there still remained the fact of its dramatic scientific discoveries that, though certainly the products of selective perception and understanding, testified to its dynamism. It was these crucial differences between the scientific ideas and achievements of antiquity and those of the modern age, they concluded, that testified to the advances of the latter: they had selected those elements from the past that made sense, and they refined them or added new observations to produce more meaningful theories about the universe. Darwin, they observed, did not create the idea of biological evolution; rather, he absorbed past ruminations on it and applied them to his own concrete investigations into how it must have taken place. Such examples of "selective accumulation" testified to the existence of such a dynamic within science in general, including social science, in which new knowledge built continuously upon previous discoveries.

[38] See Don Martindale, "Pitirim A. Sorokin: Soldier of Fortune," in C. C. Hallen and R. Prasad, eds., *Sorokin and Sociology: Essays in Honour of Pitirim A. Sorokin* (Agra, India: Satish Book, 1972), 30–42.

[39] C. Wright Mills, "The Social Life of a Modern Community," *American Sociological Review* 7, 2 (April 1942): 263.

much to the frustration of Lazarsfeld—to integrate values and broad conceptual designs into the collection of questionnaire responses.[40]

By the early 1950s, Mills's opposition to quantitative work devoid of larger social significance, combined with his contentious disposition and his refusal to train graduate students, had led to his marginalization within the Columbia Sociology Department, a status best characterized by Seymour Martin Lipset, who would write in 1961 that Mills "has little importance for contemporary sociology."[41] Like Sorokin, Mills would, from this position of growing professional isolation, begin to construct a critique of academic sociology that would culminate at the end of the decade in the popularization of a set of specific perceptions of sociology and sociologists.[42] First, in *White Collar,* in which he explored the bureaucratic malaise afflicting the world of post-entrepreneurial work, he devoted a dozen pages to a denunciation of the culture of higher education. Under the pressures of organizational change on the professions, this culture had succumbed to the norms of all bureaucratized endeavors, subjecting professors and graduate students to rigid rules of conformity, hierarchy, and specialization. He lamented a "feudal" system of graduate training that, in its overspecialization and "vocationalizing" emphasis on career preparation, was "deadening to the mind." Thus, academia produced a "celibacy of the intellect" among the professoriate that forbade the cultivation of broad, imaginative temperaments or modes of inquiry. Such a culture therefore discouraged individual brilliance, nonconformity, and wide-ranging curiosity.[43]

---

[40]Irving Louis Horowitz, *C. Wright Mills: An American Utopian* (New York: Free Press, 1983), 78–80.

[41]Seymour Lipset and Neil Smelser, "Change and Controversy in Recent American Sociology," *British Journal of Sociology* 12, 1 (March 1961), especially pp. 50–51n. Horowitz describes Mills's professional maginalization in Chapter 5 of *C. Wright Mills* and includes this dismissal by Lipset and Smelser.

[42]Mills's earliest critiques of social science appeared in the *American Journal of Sociology.* The first, "Methodological Consequences of the Sociology of Knowledge," in the *American Journal of Sociology* 46, 3 (November 1940): 316–30, argued for the recognition of social influences upon methodological decisions and of the values choices inherent within them. In the second, "The Professional Ideology of Social Pathologists," in *American Journal of Sociology* 49, 2 (September 1943): 165–80, Mills found in widely used sociology textbooks a consistent lack of structural or conceptual frameworks and a rather atomizing conception of social problems.

[43]C. Wright Mills, *White Collar: The American Middle Classes* (New York: Oxford University Press, 1951), 130. Mills also perceived a proletarianization of the postwar professoriate to have embedded itself in the institutional culture of higher education, a prescient insight in light of the 21st-century university's adoption of employment and management practices previously associated with manufacturing and chainstore retailing, in which reserve armies of highly qualified professionals work under temporary and increasingly part-time contracts in order to free up resources for investment in other institutional endeavors. See Randy Martin, ed., *Chalk Lines: The Politics of Work in the Managed University* (Durham, NC: Duke University Press, 1998); and Cary Nelson, *Manifesto of a Tenured Radical* (New York University Press, 1997).

Turning then to the social sciences, Mills identified a connection between the pressure toward specialization and the desire for scientific status. "The attempt to imitate exact science," he wrote, "narrows the mind to microscopic fields of inquiry, rather than expanding it to embrace man and society as a whole."[44] Mills claimed that this insistence on science building sacrificed the kind of expansive perspective that true social science demanded. As a result, the social scientist "is not very likely to have as balanced an intellect as a top-flight journalist."[45] Mills's references to journalism and literature would increase over the course of his critiques of contemporary sociology, as he gradually constructed a vision of sociology that shared more in common with the humanities and the public world of letters than with the laboratory and the scientific method.

In 1953, Mills again addressed the question of the relationship between science and social science. In the journal *Philosophy of Science*, he wrote that the social science focus on subject matter amenable to statistical analysis and the supposedly cumulative construction of a body of knowledge that could then be labeled scientific had narrowed the focus of mainstream sociological research to a "molecular" level of investigation. Many sociologists had lost sight of the larger purposes of sociological work because they had "fetishized" what they perceived to be the techniques of hard science. "The supposed Method of Physical Science," he insisted, had elevated measurability over significance.[46] The sociological identity that Parsons, Merton, Lazarsfeld, and Stouffer had demanded became for Mills a capitulation to the intellectually debilitating pressure of the quest for professional status, which rendered sociological research sterile and trivial. Meaningful sociological work, he insisted, required instead a continuous "shuttling" back and forth between macroscopic and molecular perspectives, so that both hypotheses and analyses remained socially significant. These "levels" were mutually dependent: to neglect either of them would render analysis vague and unsubstantiated or narrow and inconsequential.

Significantly, Mills also noted in this article that the scientific desideratum meant that sociological work had removed itself from public discourse. Its microscopic orientation, along with the growing practical applications of such research in government and industry, completed the shift from a

---

[44]Ibid., 131.

[45]Ibid., 131.

[46]C. Wrigth Mills, "Two Styles of Social Science Research," in Irving Louis Horowitz, ed., *Power, Politics and People* (New York: Oxford University Press, 1963), 553. This essay appeared originally as "Two Styles of Research in Current Social Studies," in *Philosophy of Science* 20, 4 (October 1953): 266–75.

clientele of reformers and journalists to one of political and business elites. Mills described the molecular style of research as "a bureaucratization of reflection" compatible with larger patterns of institutional change in American life. As the provider of information to public and private decision makers, the sociologist "no longer addresses 'the public'; more usually he has specific clients with particular interests and perplexities."[47]

A year later, Mills brought his views of sociology's crisis to a lay readership. In a 1953 *Saturday Review* article with the inflammatory title, "IBM Plus Reality Plus Humanism = Sociology," he divided American sociology into the three fundamental "camps" that would become the basic categories of his analysis in his monumental assault on sociology, *The Sociological Imagination*, in which vulgar empiricism and abstruse and disembodied theory undermined the grand tradition of sociological work. Those who had internalized the scientific identity he labeled "The Scientists," and because this identity conferred status and social acceptance of their professional expertise, they were "very much concerned to be known as such." His characterization then descended somewhat to a tone befitting a popular magazine:

> Among them, I am sure, are those who would love to wear white coats with an I.B.M. symbol of some sort on the breast pocket. They are out to do with society and history what they believe physicists have done with nature. Such a view often seems to rest upon the hope that if only someone could invent for "the social sciences" some gadget like the atom bomb, all our human problems would suddenly come to an end.[48]

Mills's use of caricature, his linking of scientific sociology to the larger current of Western positivism, the fruits of the latter of which included the dubious blessing of atomic technology, demonstrated his skill in drawing stark characterizations of his subject for a readership of nonsociologists. As in *White Collar*, he employed vivid, encapsulatory images to unmask his targets. He identified among "The Scientists" a subcategory represented by "The Higher Statistician," who "breaks down truth and falsity into such fine particles that we cannot tell the difference between them." Images of highly organized enterprises devoted to the study of nothing in particular dominated the essay. "By the costly rigor of their methods," he charged, "The Scientists

---

[47] Ibid., 556.

[48] C. Wright Mills, "IBM Plus Reality Plus Humanism = Sociology," in Horowitz, ed., *Power, Politics and People*, 569. This article appeared originally in *The Saturday Review* (May 1, 1954): 22–24.

succeed in trivializing men and society, and in the process, their own minds as well."[49]

Mills thus addressed sociology's place within public discourse by noting how the discipline's focus upon sociological minutiae rendered it irrelevant to larger discussions and concerns within American society. Instead of a modest enterprise with a goal of incremental progress, it should be ambitious and confront large historical processes. Moreover, its conclusions required validation in the wider sphere of public discourse, and therefore remaining satisfied with narrow professional prestige constituted an abdication of sociology's public purpose. Unfortunately, Mills noted, despite American sociology's institutional and intellectual growth, it had failed to contribute any pathbreaking texts to Western discourse. "Several men in the social studies now enjoy enormous reputations," he noted, "but have not produced any enormous books, intellectually speaking, or in fact any contributions of note to the substantive knowledge of our time."[50] They had left ordinary educated people out of their discussions. Substantive knowledge necessarily consisted of that which possessed relevance outside of professional sociological circles, and yet, he lamented, "the social studies become an elaborate method of insuring that no one learns too much about man and society."[51] Even worse, sociology's quest for scientific certainty, and thereby, scientific prestige, had in fact impeded humanity's quest for enlightenment: "The span of time in which The Scientists say they think of their work is a billion man-hours of labor," Mills declared. "And in the meantime we should not expect much substantive knowledge; first there must be methodological inquiries into methods and inquiry."[52] The gradualist exhortations of Merton, Parsons, and others to exercise patience with sociology's inevitably slow scientific maturation became for Mills an excuse for avoiding the compelling problems of the age.

The "IBM" essay reflected Mills's growing alliance with nonsociological opinion against what he perceived to be his profession's descent into organized meaninglessness. If sociologists had abdicated their responsibility for facilitating public discourse about sociological issues, and if journalists had proven to serve such needs better than professional social researchers, the profession required a public unmasking. The quest for "science" had distracted sociologists from real social issues and had absorbed them instead with questions of theory and methodology, or, as he put it, "methodological

---

[49] Ibid., 569.

[50] Ibid., 569.

[51] Ibid., 570.

[52] Ibid., 570.

inquiries into methods and inquiry." Such distractions from the sociologist's true responsibilities, Mills charged, and he demanded, "Isn't it time for sociologists, especially eminent ones, to stop thinking about thinking and begin directly to study *something?*"[53] For his part, Mills had assumed the journalistic responsibility of informing the public of sociology's intellectual default. Lay readers, moreover, deserved positive examples of writing about society that would serve as models of meaningful analysis, so Mills devoted the remainder of the essay to a list of exemplary works on sociological topics, including those of the scholars of the Frankfurt School, Max Weber, Georg Simmel, Emile Durkheim, Gaetano Mosca, Robert Michels, Thorstein Veblen, Karl Mannheim, Gunnar Myrdal, and William H. Whyte. These authors, he asserted, reflected "the classic sociological endeavor" that represented the only alternative to the kinds of work he decried.

At the same time, the "IBM" essay lacked a strong integration of the rarefied scientific philosophy of empirical sociology with that of theoretical sociology. Despite Mills's effective use of concepts like The Higher Statistician and The Grand Theorist to render vivid characterizations of the two predominant trends within professional sociology, Mills's approach served to make them appear as separate phenomena with justifications more or less independent of one another. This dichotomization therefore provided little room for a consideration of the role of a scholar like Merton, who sought to reconcile Parsonian theory and quantitative methods in the name of science. Merton's justifications of both Parsonian theory building and small-scale empirical research as necessary components of sociology's maturation into a science lay outside of Mills's critique.

Nevertheless, Mills's treatment of the Scientists and Grand Theorists in the "IBM" essay provided the foundation for the crucial chapters of his 1959 work, *The Sociological Imagination*, his jeremiad against a profession he believed had forsaken its obligations to society. Mills intended the book, like the *Saturday Review* article, for a general audience. Irving Horowitz, then a fellow at Brandeis, later characterized the book, in a precise formulation of the traditional role of the public sociologist, as "written by an insider but it is for outsiders," a work for "ordinary people" whom the sociologist would serve as a "liberal educator," assisting them in conceptualizing and making sense of social structure.[54] The sociologist's public purpose lay in transforming phenomena experienced as "private troubles" into "issues." Whereas "the statement and resolution of troubles properly lie within the individual" and his or her immediate social milieu, Mills defined "issues" as "matters that transcend

---

[53] Ibid., 571.

[54] Horowitz, *C. Wright Mills*, 88.

these local environments of the individual and the range of his inner life." Issues were "public matters," in which "some value cherished by publics is felt to be threatened."[55] Issues required active debate within the public sphere because only through public debate would they come to be defined as issues at all.

These issues, however, remained inherently problematic because they escaped easy identification and understanding:

> Often there is a debate about what that value really is and about what it is that really threatens it. This debate is often without focus if only because it is the very nature of an issue, unlike even widespread trouble, that it cannot very well be defined in terms of the immediate and everyday environments of ordinary men.[56]

Social scientists, necessarily public individuals, bore the responsibility of clarifying that which escaped simple understanding, of seeking to transform "troubles" into "issues." It was their "foremost political and intellectual task" Mills insisted, "to make clear the elements of contemporary uneasiness and indifference."[57] Modern sociology had, however, abdicated this responsibility and had wrongfully left it to others, such as "critics and novelists, dramatists and poets," who, he insisted, "have been the major, and often the only, formulators of private troubles and even of public issues."[58]

Modern empirical sociology had performed this abdication through its confusion of science with the methods of investigation found in the natural sciences. In his chapter on "abstracted empiricism," Mills argued that postwar empirical research sought scientific legitimacy in its use of "The Method," which encouraged the production of studies for their own sake rather than to fulfill larger theoretical or social objectives. Its practitioners' failure to recognize this practice as a particular philosophical choice meant that they had confused science with the scientific method. This error, he contended, could be understood through a simple contrast with physics, which had matured as a science not because its methods alone produced valid scientific knowledge but because physicists exercised maximum creativity and imagination in their work. Empirical sociology, conversely, relied upon putatively scientific methods to define problems appropriate for research. Thus, in the absence of

---

[55]C. Wright Mills, *The Sociological Imagination* (New York: Grove Press, 1959), 8–9.

[56]Ibid., 9.

[57]Ibid., 13.

[58]Ibid., 18.

criteria other than measurability, Mills observed, "there is, in truth, no principle or theory that guides the selection of what is to be the subject of these studies... It is merely assumed that if only The Method is used, such studies as result—scattered from Elmira to Zagreb to Shanghai—will add up finally to a 'full-fledged, organized' science of man and society. The practice, in the meantime, is to get on with the next study."[59] Quantitative sociology's attenuated definition of science, one that confused science with the methods of scientific investigation, rendered it incapable of building a store of knowledge that would prepare it to address the pressing questions of modern life. "An empiricism as cautious and rigid as abstracted empiricism eliminates the great social problems and human issues of our time from inquiry," Mills wrote. "Men who would understand these problems and grapple with these issues will then turn for enlightenment to other ways of formulating beliefs."[60]

Although Mills connected empirical sociology's abandonment of public communication on fundamental social issues to its rarefied conception of science, he repudiated grand theory for reasons unrelated to science building. Grand theory, as elaborated by Parsons, suffered from a detachment from real sociological issues by virtue of its level of abstraction. Employing his infamous excerpting and "translating" of passages from Parsons's *The Social System* into simple sentences, Mills asserted that grand theory merely obscured simple sociological propositions with a morass of verbiage and long, complicated sentences. Moreover, in its "fetishizing" of overly abstract concepts, grand theory neglected to address questions of meaningful sociological import. Mills concluded, "The basic cause of grand theory is the initial choice of a level of thinking so general that its practitioners cannot logically get down to observation. They never, as grand theorists, get down from the higher generalities to problems in their historical and structural contexts."[61] Grand theory's error lay not in its pretensions to the status of a hard science but in its preoccupation with abstractions empty of concrete content.

Mills's critiques of prevailing theoretical and empirical patterns in 1950s sociology in *The Sociological Imagination* thus reflected the same dichotomization of sociology into the theoretical and empirical categories he had established in his *Saturday Review* essay. In his characterizations, grand theory and abstracted empiricism appeared to exist as separate entities with different philosophical premises. Mills failed to address the philosophical connection Parsons and Merton had articulated between them, in which small-scale

---

[59] Ibid., 67.

[60] Ibid., 73.

[61] Ibid., 33.

research and the construction of theory were to come together in the name of forging a scientific sociology. Instead, as Mills explained in the book's introductory chapter, highly abstract theorizing and narrow empiricism that avoided substantive social questions of the modern age represented discrete "tendencies" in sociology. Although Mills emphasized that grand theory abdicated any meaningful engagement with nonacademic publics, he neglected to identify its relationship to the project of creating a science of society. Parsonian sociology thereby became merely the practice of formulating theories without engaging in observational research. If grand theory legitimated anything, Mills asserted, it was society's prevailing "structure of power," a concept that he declined to develop so as to include professional sociology itself. By positing the existence of a "normative structure" to which a society's value system necessarily conformed, grand theory simply reified that structure and the values and institutions within it.[62] On its promotion of a "science of society," Mills was silent.

The Sociological Imagination, unlike Mills's earlier critiques of sociology, also contained a powerful personal dimension. By the late 1950s, Mills's estrangement from his professional peers was complete. His lack of graduate students and his declining influence over the Columbia Sociology Department's curriculum decisions, which Daniel Bell had come to dominate, encouraged his tendency to draw distinctions between sociological styles in terms of how significantly they differed from his own. Mills's focus on Lazarsfeld, for whom he had worked in the late 1940s on mass communications and public opinion polling projects, reflected his direct experience with the researcher who had exerted the greatest influence over postwar sociology's conception of its quantitative dimension. His attack on grand theory, similarly, distilled the object of his opposition to postwar theoretical trends into the person of Talcott Parsons, clearly the most significant representative of postwar theory. *The Sociological Imagination* thus represented, in Horowitz's words, Mills's "summing up of, and settling of accounts with, his Columbia colleagues—and a few from Harvard thrown in for good measure."[63]

By isolating Parsons and Lazarsfeld for consideration as the ultimate representatives of Grand Theory and Abstract Empiricism, respectively, Mills

---

[62] Ibid., 37, 40.

[63] Horowitz, *C. Wright Mills,* 87. Horowitz argues that Mills's Columbia milieu, including scholars such as Richard Hofstadter, Jacques Barzun, and Lionel Trilling, contributed to his emphasis on historically rooted scholarship, his antiscientism, and his demand for a more publicly engaged academic intellectual. Mills's intellectual relationships at Columbia are also the focus of Chapters 3 and 4 of David Walter Moore, "Liberalism and Liberal Education at Columbia University: The Columbia Careers of Jacques Barzun, Lionel Trilling, Richard Hofstadter, Daniel Bell, and C. Wright Mills," (Ph.D. diss., University of Maryland, 1978).

exacerbated the critique's appearance of having separated theory and methods into categories possessing separate, indeed independent, philosophical foundations. If Lazarsfeldian sociology's philosophical foundation existed as The Method, then that of Parsonian sociology was that of the fetishized "Concept." The way in which Parsons and Lazarsfeld had contributed vital arguments to postwar sociology's identity, however, remained unclear. Moreover, Mills's isolation of Parsons and Lazarsfeld for specific criticism, although clearly a strategy for illuminating sociology's larger identity, nevertheless rendered his argument vulnerable to the charge that he had unnecessarily personalized the debate over that identity, and that his hostility to their theoretical and empirical work signified his hostility to theory and empiricism in general. That the personal nature of his critique would detract from his broader argument about the proper role of sociology in contemporary America became clear as various of his friends and colleagues submitted their reflections on the draft version of the book.

In manuscript form, *The Sociological Imagination* existed as "An Autopsy of Social Science." Mills sent the manuscript to a number of scholars, among them Paul Sweezy, Ralph Miliband, Arthur K. Davis, Barrington Moore, Richard Hofstadter, Llewellyn Gross, Robert Dubin, and David Riesman. The responses of these sociologists, historians, economists, and political scientists revealed consistent patterns of praise, criticism, reservations, and outright objections.

Several of the manuscript readers with socialist perspectives criticized Mills's refusal to articulate a distinct ideological perspective through which to analyze the problems of sociology, much as would leftist reviewers of the published book itself.[64] Miliband, the British Marxist, political activist, and soon-to-be principal participant in the circles around the democratic-socialist journals *New Left Review* and *Socialist Register,* concluded that Mills, whom he saw as necessarily a socialist, needed to argue on behalf of an explicitly socialist perspective in sociology:

> Your point about a democracy of power (23) which you clearly deem desirable coupled with your general point about the centralisation of power clearly means that the social scientist's role must inevitably, and on your definitions be critical, unorthodox, attacking, subversive of existing concentrations of power. What you are saying right

---

[64]Horowitz notes this tendency among those who reviewed the published version, such as Sidney Peck, Arthur K. Davis, and Meyer Schapiro, the latter of whom read the manuscript. Horowitz, *C. Wright Mills*, 106–7.

through is that the good social scientist must in fact be a socialist and seek the renovation in a socialist-democratic direction of social structures. That's what it really means, doesn't it? But you don't quite say it, you imply.[65]

Davis, similarly, suggested that Mills make some kind of Marxian framework explicit in his argument. As a sociological scholar of the left, he too envisioned the kind of scholarship that would reach publics outside of sociology and admitted that when he sought "information about the basic structures and drifts of the present age and present nations," he rarely sought it in works by professional sociologists. Perceiving Mills as a kindred spirit, he suggested that Mills's radicalism be made manifest:

You move in this book quite a long way toward certain Marxian premises. One way to look at the one-sidedness of American academic social science is its separation from, and boycott of, the whole intellectual tradition associated with the Left side of modern industrialism. Why don't you give that tradition the same sort of broad and basic criticism you give to orthodox social science?[66]

For Davis, a critique of sociology's withdrawal from public life required an assertion of radical intent. "I draw the conclusion that academics need to be more politically active in radical [movements]," he declared, "or perhaps I merely would stress it more, for you also draw much the same conclusion . . . The sheeplike character of so many professors, where public issues are concerned, is disgusting."[67]

Barrington Moore, a Harvard sociologist, senior fellow at Harvard's Russian Research Center, and the author of a major critique of the ahistoricism and lack of the classical "critical spirit" in postwar sociological work,[68] nevertheless expressed concern over what he perceived as the manuscript's ideological ambiguity. In a memo to Mills's publisher, Oxford University Press, he

---

[65] Ralph Miliband to C. Wright Mills, April 26, 1958, C. Wright Mills Papers, Box 4B400, Center for American History, University of Texas at Austin.

[66] Arthur K. Davis to C. Wright Mills, June 19, 1958, C. Wright Mills Papers, Box 4B400.

[67] Ibid.

[68] Barrington Moore, Jr., *Political Power and Social Theory* (Cambridge: Harvard University Press, 1958), chap. 4. Another example of Moore's 1950s criticism of the discipline is "The New Scholasticism and the Study of Politics," *World Politics* 6, 1 (October 1953): 122–38.

insisted that Mills's lack of a true commitment to Marxism diminished his argument's impact:

He performs his task under peculiar handicaps—handicaps of a kind that have come up in his previous books. He espouses a residual and nostalgic Marxism and there is no intention of being funny in saying this. Were Mills an out-and-out Marxist his job would be infinitely simpler, no matter how much one might disagree with him. But he probably has strong reservations about Marxian economics and little belief in the Marxian metaphysics of history. His critique is thereby blunted and his positive recommendations become rather pale... Were he a thorough-going Marxist he would achieve a more synthetic or integrated result at the price of wide reputation. Since he is only a residual Marxist he cannot do more than take pot-shots, some of which are excellent, at the state of sociology.[69]

Moore, like Miliband and Davis, believed that Mills had given insufficient emphasis to a radical program for sociological research, and that he had weakened his critique by focusing on dominant trends in the discipline without demanding a specific kind of political responsibility of sociologists. Without a clear ideological foundation, Mills could not argue for a clear alternative identity for sociology, and thus his objections to particular sociological styles would inevitably appear as nothing more than personal attacks.

Moore therefore questioned Mills's identification of abstracted empiricism and grand theory as the primary enemies of meaningful social science, complaining that this distillation of sociology into two predominant trends constituted a dangerous oversimplification. That Mills had chosen to focus so thoroughly on Parsons and Lazarsfeld meant that he had obscured much of sociology's theoretical and methodological complexity. Thus, Moore complained to Oxford University Press, Mills "does not convey much of a notion of the richness and diversity in present-day work in sociology." The manuscript, he reported, exhibited an "over-sharpness of delineation, with an almost amusing neglect of nuances where it suits the argument to neglect them." Crucially, Moore then asked whether Mills should not have addressed the theoretical sociology of Merton, a scholar "perhaps equally eminent and far less willfully obscure" than Parsons. "Merton would have presented Mills with a far more difficult job than did Parsons," he asserted, "since he would have confronted him with a very seriously conceived effort to do appreciably

---

[69]Barrington Moore, Jr. to Oxford University Press, May 6, 1958, C. Wright Mills Papers, Box 4B400.

high level theoretical work that is yet informed by a strong empirical conscience and a marked awareness of academic ritualisms and stupidities."[70]

The more radical scholars, then, responded to the draft with nearly uniform misgivings regarding the ideological opacity of Mills's argument. Paul Sweezy, the Marxist professor of economics at Harvard, provided the only sympathetic assessment from a scholar of the left. He recognized that Mills intended more than simply a class analysis of ideas and practices in social science, as is suggested in his 1956 review of *The Power Elite:*

> There is a sort of contrived bloodlessness about American academic social science today. Its practitioners are much better trained than they used to be, but the consequence is not only technical competence. No less striking is the way they all fit into a few neat molds, like the models of an automobile coming off the factory assembly lines. They talk alike, deal in the same brand of trivialities, and take each other enormously seriously. Above all, there is a kind of tacit conspiracy to banish all really interesting and important issues from the universe of "scientific" discourse.[71]

Sweezy remained confident, however, that social scientists possessed the potential to overcome their timidity. In a letter to Mills, he ventured that the "academic underground" of scholars with more engagingly critical sensibilities and with similar contempt for "the fashionable trends" in their respective fields, was in fact much larger than it appeared. "Given a sufficient change in the general atmosphere—say, a return to a climate such as existed in the 30s," he promised, "they would come out into the open, and their prestige and influence would *overnight* be much greater than an unwary observer could possibly imagine"[72] (emphasis in original). Whether Sweezy understood a crisis of the Great Depression's magnitude to be a force for renewed public engagement within social science by virtue of its demystification of class relations under modern capitalism remained unclear. Nevertheless, he insisted that social science had not yet suffered complete self-estrangement, and he thus recommended that Mills abandon the use of the word "autopsy" in his work's tentative title.

---

[70] Barrington Moore, Jr. to Oxford University Press, May 6, 1958, C. Wright Mills Papers, Box 4B400.

[71] Paul Sweezy, "Power Elite or Ruling Class?" in G. William Domhoff and Hoyt B. Ballard, *C. Wright Mills and the Power Elite* (Boston: Beacon Press, 1968), 115–16. This review appeared originally in the September 1956 issue of *Monthly Review.*

[72] Paul Sweezy to C. Wright Mills, March 27, 1958, quoted in John Anson Warner, "The Critics of C. Wright Mills: Ideology and the Study of Political Power in America" (Ph.D. diss., Princeton University, 1973), 191.

David Riesman, who proved to be the most sensitive reviewer of the manuscript and who offered the most voluminous observations and suggestions, articulated his own concerns about Mills's focus on Parsons and Lazarsfeld. Despite his reservations about the trends in mainstream sociology, some of which had appeared in print, he refused to endorse Mills's efforts.[73] "It would seem that there are a great many far more significant people to talk about," he opined. "Your range of reference is characteristically wide but not your range of polemic." Riesman asserted that Mills had allowed the clarity of his objections to Parsonian and Lazarsfeldian sociology to elevate their examples to an unwarranted degree of emphasis in the manuscript. "The fact that a position could be stated, that it was interesting to you and possibly malignant," he warned, "made you pay disproportionate attention to it—just as any sectarian pays closest attention to those who are closest to him and yet a danger to his own hopes and influence."[74]

Riesman, like Merton, considered personal attacks on professional peers to be destructive to the evolution of the discipline. "I feel there is something curiously unhealthy about the tendency within sociology to spend so much time on criticism of relatively harmless or unimportant work so that in some fields there is at least as much criticism as there is work," he wrote. Such conflict, he continued, was "scaring away youngsters" who become reluctant to enter certain fields of research and instead chose "safer fields, less open to attack, including attack by you." Riesman admitted that Mills's emphases could do little to affect the reputations of such "established schools" as those of Parsons and Lazarsfeld, but he objected to sociology's contentious professional atmosphere, in which scholars spent much time attacking one another's methodologies rather than seeking to contribute new ideas and research to the discipline as a whole. "The atmosphere of sociology," he lamented, "is a little like that of literature today where the new critics wait for something to be written so that they can exercise their skill in interpretation or destruction."[75]

Most important, Riesman insisted, Mills had in his savaging of specific sociological shortcomings or detours squandered energy on issues that mattered little to American society at large. Sociology's internecine conflicts simply lacked the importance that could justify the kind of attention Mills had

---

[73]Riesman's own critiques of sociology include "The Meaning of Opinion," *Public Opinion Quarterly* 12, 4 (Winter 1948–1949): 633–48; and "Observations on Social Research," *Antioch Review* 11, 3 (September 1951): 259–78, reprinted in *Individualism Reconsidered* (Glencoe, IL: Free Press, 1954).

[74]David Riesman to C. Wright Mills, May 2, 1958, C. Wright Mills Papers, Box 4B400.

[75]Ibid.

given them. "Your work is useful as propounding another model," Riesman granted, "but it would be much more useful if it said more about your preoccupations with what is going on in the world and less about your preoccupations about what is going on in sociology. Surely you would agree that sociology is not *that* important." Mills's extended attack on reprehensible trends in sociology thus amounted to overkill. He had, Riesman charged, launched mere "elephant gun criticisms of the mosquitoes who ride on the back of American intellectual life," when instead he should have devoted his energies to the profound social questions he had explored so compellingly in his other writings. "There are so few people studying society and what goes on," Riesman wrote in conclusion, "—so few who even realize that it might be done and that it matters—that, as I have said, I hate to see you distracted."[76]

Other sociologists who read the manuscript recommended a similar retreat from the strong emphasis on sociology's empirical and theoretical flaws. Llewellyn Gross, who would soon challenge Parsonian theory himself in two important articles,[77] nevertheless warned Mills that his stark, personalized characterizations denied the presence of any valuable aspects in the kinds of scholarship he dismissed. "You use methodological terms quite frequently, you have your own logic or problematic inquiry, you even state at several points that some of the procedures of abstract empiricists may be useful," Gross noted. "It therefore seems to me that you could defend certain fundamentals of sound methodology without in any way altering your position."[78] Gross feared that Mills's harsh, wholesale judgments would solidify the position of those he criticized, for they could dismiss Mills for his having oversimplified their work. "I would not want you to give the reader the impression that you are opposed to all methodology because of the interpretations given to it by Grand Theorists and Abstract Empiricists," he wrote. Instead, Gross recommended a more sophisticated critique:

---

[76] Ibid.

[77] In Llewellyn Gross, "An Epistemological View of Sociological Theory," *American Journal of Sociology* 65, 5 (March 1960): 441–48, Gross questioned indirectly the validity of functionalist theory by asserting the inability of all "language schemes" to capture the essence of any objective reality, and he demanded a more pluralistic theoretical landscape. In "Preface to a Metatheoretical Framework for Sociology," *American Journal of Sociology* 67, 2 (September 1961): 125–43, he proposed a "neo-dialectical" framework for the evaluation of sociology's choice of words to combat the insularity of sociological discourse, which he believed was "alienating professionals and disenchanting the public mind" (125). This latter article challenged the hermeticism of the "system" approach to theory that functionalism promoted, calling for a more skeptical, critical perspective on sociology's language and a more active attention to discourses outside of sociology.

[78] Llewellyn Gross to C. Wright Mills, June 5, 1958, C. Wright Mills Papers, Box 4B400.

The weaknesses of the latter schools can be more clearly established if you prepare yourself against the possible rejoinder that their methodology is only an imperfect representation of some more suitable type toward which they are presently working... What you say about them is I feel quite correct. But I would add that they are poor methodologists because they are largely in the dark about what is going on in present day philosophy of science and mathematics, just as the latter are largely oblivious to the basic problems of man and his world.[79]

According to Gross, if Mills appeared to be attacking methodology in general, he risked losing many of those who might otherwise avoid the kinds of work he opposed and embrace meaningful sociology. Though he intended a reassessment of a particular way of thinking about methodology, as had Sorokin in *Fads and Foibles*, his approach threatened to give the impression of a wholesale repudiation of modern research techniques. Just as Merton had accused Sorokin of attacking quantitative methods even as he utilized them in his own studies, Mills too had left himself open to allegations that he had propounded a vulgarized case against modern sociological research.

Robert Dubin, an industrial sociologist and another critic of Parsons, joined the chorus of criticism of Mills's treatment of his adversaries. In a uniformly harsh judgment of the manuscript, he assessed Mills's chapter on grand theory as "very ill-tempered and thoroughly misleading." Although Mills had promised to explore grand theory as a whole, he had focused exclusively on Parsons, whom Dubin believed "hardly a representative sample." Dubin also disapproved of Mills's excerpting of Parsons's work, calling his "translations" of them "sophomoric" and indicating that they revealed only "his inability to write simple English" while avoiding the question of whether the passages possessed any scientific validity. Like Riesman and Gross, he suggested a more diplomatic treatment of the problems facing sociology, for to submit such a contentious, personalizing critique risked fomenting a backlash instead of a serious consideration of his argument. "Your general thesis is too good to be lost on the profession through dismissal by ascription of irrelevant motives to you," he wrote in conclusion.[80]

One prominent exception to these warnings of an unproductive counterreaction came from the historian and Columbia colleague of Mills, Richard Hofstadter. Unlike Moore, Riesman, Gross, and Dubin, Hofstadter praised Mills's assaults upon abstracted empiricism and grand theory, and he

---

[79] Ibid.

[80] Robert Dubin to C. Wright Mills, April 20, 1958, C. Wright Mills Papers, Box 4B400.

recommended that Mills devote even more of the manuscript to the specific examination of the disciplinary trends he opposed:

> It is courageous to attack the two leading tendencies in your field— Parsonianism and Lazarsfeldianism—but so much of your argument is developed with such generality that, despite its snarling tones, it seems reticent and genteel. One gets the feeling from the book that you are mightily dissatisfied with social science—and to all appearances usually on good grounds—but that what you are dissatisfied with remains excessively vague, especially since you have taken ten chapters to spell it out.[81]

Although Hofstadter ventured that Mills had offered a somewhat simplified picture of empirical work, particularly by ignoring the "playful aspects" that Mills himself had enjoyed, he agreed wholeheartedly with the section on Parsons and found Mills's "translations" of Parsons's prose "devastating." Nevertheless, he insisted that Mills had compromised his analysis with an indirectness that left the reader wondering what exactly was wrong with contemporary sociology and what could be done about it. Hofstadter, believing that Mills shared his own dark outlook, recommended a more forceful statement of the grim prospects for meaningful sociological discourse:

> In ch. 9, after all, you tell us that social scientists are pretty much a bunch of shits. Then in ch. 10 you tell us that there are no publics, movts., or organizations through which the few good guys among the social scientists can at present make themselves felt. All this seems persuasive enough (depending a little bit on the temperament of the reader). But then your few notes of hope and counsels of persistence on pp. 32–4 (e.g.) seem only pious gestures and don't really register very much with anyone who has taken seriously what you say elsewhere. I personally find you most persuasive when you are being bleakly pessimistic. It sounds: a) more like Mills; b) more like reality.[82]

Hofstadter, however, had in mind the kind of unmasking of "social engineers" that Robert Lynd had undertaken in *Knowledge for What?* Like Moore and Miliband, he perceived the sociologist's lack of autonomy from particular economic interests to be the root of sociology's problems, and he therefore devoted the remainder of his letter to his reflections on Mills's chapter on

---

[81] Richard Hofstadter to C. Wright Mills, July 3, 1958, C. Wright Mills Papers, Box 4B400.

[82] Ibid.

the application of sociology to problems of human relations, which in the published volume would become "The Bureaucratic Ethos." These "human relations boys," Hofstadter reminded Mills, corrupted social science by applying its research findings to narrow questions of workplace harmony and productivity at the expense of the larger social questions social science must rightly address. Instead of freeing the minds of citizens in a democracy, they sought to secure for management a tractable and complacent work force.

Much of the vagueness Hofstadter perceived in Mills's analysis thus stemmed from his sense that attacking unacceptable trends in sociology required not only a savaging of broad theoretical and empirical trends but also a condemnation of the discipline's capitulation to outside interests. Although he avoided recommending that Mills provide more forceful ideological statements of his radicalism in the book, he nevertheless questioned whether the book could have the intended impact without linking sociology more clearly to the interests of modern capitalism.

Mills, however, perceived the private recruitment of social science for purposes of human manipulation to represent only a part of deeper and more disturbing developments in the production and dissemination of knowledge in the Western world. Beyond the admittedly serious problem of the discipline's declining autonomy lay the less tangible issue Mills had termed the "bureaucratic ethos." As social science methods proved successful in solving problems for private clients, the social scientists involved in such work did indeed surrender their intellectual autonomy and internalize the values of those clients. However, according to Mills, the deeper dilemma this process presented lay not with the expanding cadre of "service intellectuals" but in the universalization of bureaucratic modes of thinking within professional scholarly work as a whole. Here, Mills's foundation lay not in Marxism but in Weber's theories on the bureaucratization of ideas. For Weber, "science" and the scientific ethos were products not simply of the class interests under capitalism but, more fundamentally, of the exigencies of modernity itself, which caused the "cultivated man" of past societies to give way to the modern, "specialist type of man."[83]

Most troubling to Mills, then, was an increasingly pervasive way of thinking about thinking, rather than simply the influence of class interests on the production of ideas. Even if social science's efforts in the realm of human relations proved ineffective, he warned, "they do serve to spread the ethos of bureaucracy into other spheres of cultural, moral, and intellectual life."[84] As

---

[83] Hans Gerth and C. Wright Mills, eds., *From Max Weber: Essays in Sociology* (New York: Oxford University Press, 1946), 243.

[84] Mills, *The Sociological Imagination*, 101.

troubling as was the private co-optation of social science to scholars like Miliband, Davis, Moore, and Hofstadter, the widespread diffusion of the values that accompanied such processes concerned Mills even more. Mills therefore rejected the argument, presented variously during the 1950s by Robert Lynd, William H. Whyte, Alvin Gouldner, and others that sociology's identity crisis reflected merely its growing subservience to a specific constellation of interests and incentives, particularly those of government, corporate, and foundation funding. In the published version of *The Sociological Imagination,* Mills noted that the "bureaucratic ethos" plagued sociology not simply because its adherents served specific outside interests as "human engineers" and adopted its "slogans" but rather because that ethos became generalized as sociologists as a whole appropriated a technocratic view of their social role and a rarefied conception of their expertise:

> The slogans of the human engineers serve to carry the bureaucratic ethos beyond the actual use of this style of thought and method of inquiry. To use these slogans as a statement of "what one is about" is to accept a bureaucratic role even when one is not enacting it. This role, in short, is very often assumed on an *as if* basis. Assuming the technocratic view, and as a social scientist trying to act upon it, is to act *as if* one were indeed a human engineer. It is within such a bureaucratic perspective that the public role of the social scientist is now frequently conceived.[85]

Mills thus asserted that sociology's bureaucratic ethos reflected not simply the discipline's bureaucratic role or its class interests but, more broadly, an identity that transcended practical pressures or interests of society and, at the same time, adopted their legitimating logic. Thus, "Science," as Mills had insisted most forcefully in the "IBM" essay, served as a means by which sociologists supported their claims to professional expertise and an autonomous realm of competence.[86]

---

[85] Ibid., 115.

[86] As for Marx, Mills perceived him as simply one of several exemplars of the practice of the sociological imagination, a perspective he would develop further in his subsequent work, *The Marxists.* Marx, along with Durkheim, Veblen, Schumpeter, Weber, and others whom Mills characterized as "classical social scientists," shared an historical and biographical approach to sociological interpretation. These thinkers, Mills argued, "have been concerned with the salient issues of their time—and the problem of how history is being made within it; with 'the nature of human nature'—and the variety of individuals that come to prevail within their periods" (165). Thus, Marx's writing represented merely one example of an orientation to social phenomena larger than Marx or any other thinker, radical or conservative. The common characterization of Mills as a

Mills therefore continued to believe in the importance of assessing contemporary sociology as he had. To Riesman's warning that he had allowed questions of relevance only to sociologists themselves to distract him from more important social issues, Mills responded that he agreed on the necessity of the sociologist's commitment to the latter, but he also defended the importance of writing about sociology itself. "Yes, of course you are correct," he conceded, "but this *is* about the social sciences or perhaps just about sociology and not about the world. Perhaps I shouldn't do such a housekeeping operation, but there it is."[87] In the published version of the work, then, the rather personal attacks on abstracted empiricism, grand theory, and their representatives remained as discrete chapters, and within the context of the book as a whole they contributed to a characterization of sociology that downplayed or even ignored the subtle variations within theory and research that Moore had insisted be acknowledged. Merton warranted merely a single casual reference, as the text retained its original focus on stark, almost monolithic trends.

Riesman, meanwhile, had reconsidered his earlier reservations about the manuscript. Less than a month after warning Mills about the likely and needlessly divisive consequences of his demolition of Parsons and Lazarsfeld, he admitted that his opinion on the matter now tended toward ambivalence or even grudging support. Not only was he now willing to admit the validity of a sociologist writing about sociology, but he also granted that a reconsideration of sociology's research priorities might be in order:

> I have been thinking a lot about your observations concerning writing about sociology rather than about the world. I am not entirely sure of my own views on this issue. But I am somewhat more inclined to accept the relevance of your own position and the correctness of it than I was when I wrote you, in part because I have since then been to the AAPOR [American Association for Public Opinion Research] meetings as well as to the meetings of our own Society for Social Research here, and been compelled to realize more fully the ways in which Paul Lazarsfeld's work captures too readily and too uncritically the adherence of many of the ablest young people . . . his younger

---

"transitional" figure between the Old Left and the New lay largely with this placement of Marx within a larger sociological tradition, rather than the elevation of Marx to a position above merely "ideological" scholarship. The published version of his manuscript therefore reflected the same ancillary role for Marxism that Mills had originally intended.

[87] C. Wright Mills to David Riesman, May 14, 1958, C. Wright Mills Papers, Box 4B400.

disciples have none of his own variety and complexity and they often see his way as the way to work.[88]

Over a year later, Riesman expressed similar misgivings to Helen Lynd:

When I gave a talk at the meeting on social policy of sociology in the Society for the Study of Social Problems, I began by saying that Robert Lynd had written a great book called *Knowledge for What?* in 1939, and now twenty years later, we were merely asking, "Sociology for what?"—meaning often by that simply what jobs and influence for sociologists. As you can imagine, I met violent opposition from the professionals who care more for sociology['s] standing than for its importance.[89]

Riesman, then, joined Hofstadter as one of only two reviewers of the manuscript who supported unreservedly Mills's assault on what he perceived to be the dominant postwar trends in sociology, particularly its neglect of its own public significance.

The fact that two nonsociologists supported Mills's case against Parsons and Lazarsfeld and against a nearly unanimous chorus of peers' objections foreshadowed the widening rift *The Sociological Imagination* would exacerbate between sociologists and both scholars and laypersons outside of sociology. Hofstadter's exhortations to Mills to sharpen his attack on sociology's transgressions against true intellectual work and its communication to the outside world reflected the larger hostile attitudes toward sociology that existed outside the profession. Although reviews of the book in sociology publications would reflect many sociologists' sense of betrayal over having their work simplified and condemned before a large readership outside the discipline, reviews in other publications would exhibit a sense of vindication, as the book seemed to have confirmed their suspicions about sociology's deliberate obscurantism, its preoccupation with trivia, and its reluctance to share its insights with larger communities of thoughtful people.

Sociological reviews of *The Sociological Imagination* indeed reflected a sense of betrayal, as sociologists expressed the same misgivings the reviewers of the manuscript version had shared with Mills. William Kolb wrote in the *American Sociological Review* that Mills had oversimplified the profession's

---

[88]David Riesman to C. Wright Mills, May 29, 1958, C. Wright Mills Papers, Box 4B400.

[89]David Riesman to Helen Lynd, September 10, 1959, David Riesman Papers, Harvard University Archive, HUG (FP) 99.12, Box 29.

character, especially in his assessment of empirical research and its alleged flaws. Mills's false dichotomy of valid and invalid sociological work caused him to miss the richness and diversity of that work, including the important small-scale empirical research that allowed the discipline to grow. Echoing Parsons, Merton, Stouffer, and Lazarsfeld, Kolb appealed to the incrementalist conception of sociology as a nascent science. "In any science," he asserted, "there are those who cannot develop to the full the imaginative sweep of that science, although it should be spread among as many as possible." Fortunately, sociology still depended upon small-scale research, he maintained, and thus "not all those who have the imagination of their science will wish or need to work in other than the more prosaic tasks of that science." Mills, however, had portrayed all such activity as inimical to the sociologist's true responsibilities, thereby denying the discipline the means for its maturation. "I cannot imagine any science past its infancy that will not give rise to some degree of expertise and the technical use of that expertise through organized expert activity," Kolb concluded.[90]

Harvard's George Homans expressed similar sentiments in his review in *The American Journal of Sociology*. Homans, whose emphasis on small-group interaction and exchange theory in his groundbreaking 1950 work, *The Human Group*, conflicted profoundly with the structural theories of his departmental peer Parsons, nevertheless criticized Mills for his lack of civility toward his adversaries. Although Homans agreed that grand theory "does not do what a theory ought to do," he denounced Mills's handling of his disagreements:

> Mills could perfectly well explain why he does not like something without describing it in terms calculated to prejudice the issue from the start. To say the very least, he is seldom generous to an opponent. Mills feels strongly that the value of reason is in danger in the modern world, but is his own example one we want men devoted to the life of reason to follow?[91]

Homans's review revealed that Mills's harsh treatment of his opponents produced precisely the backlash that many the reviewers of his manuscript had anticipated. Moreover, that Mills had also indicted small-group research, which he claimed lacked the necessary grand scope to transcend acceptance of society-as-is, aroused Homans's personal ire. To this charge, Homans

---

[90] Ibid., 967.

[91] George C. Homans, review of *The Sociological Imagination* in *The American Journal of Sociology* 65, 5 (March 1960): 517.

retorted, "Nonsense. This is like arguing that, if I do not study criminology, I am 'accepting' murder."[92]

Homans asserted in conclusion that Mills had proven himself an enemy of sociology's scientific maturation. Mills's insistence upon a sociology that attempted to grasp society's larger structure from a detached, critical vantage point constituted a dangerously attenuated, vulgarized conception of the discipline. "My full intellectual task," Homans declared in rebuttal, "is the advancement of science." Scientific work represented a broader endeavor than Mills could accept, one which embraced not only large questions of social structure but also those of immediate social milieus. "Any problems whatever, structural or other, within the whole field of social behavior are mine to investigate," Homans insisted. Mills, therefore, could not circumscribe the scope of sociology's problems for anyone, much less the discipline as a whole, for it was up to researchers as individuals to select the problems they deemed worthy of investigation. If Homans himself were mistaken in his own problem selection, he declared, "the verdict will be rendered by the future history of science: no contemporary has jurisdiction."[93] Sociology, a science in the making, evolved incrementally through the efforts of patient researchers, in an atmosphere of mutual respect, regardless of the immediate utility of their findings or the objects of their studies.

Lewis Coser, a University of Chicago sociologist, editor of *Dissent*, and a committed public intellectual, nevertheless expressed deep ambivalence about the book as well.[94] Despite Mills's many strong arguments, particularly his insistence on sociology's commitment to reason and freedom, his analysis nevertheless suffered from "a decided superficiality of approach." Mills, Coser insisted, proved "too much in a hurry, too eager to get at the 'big problems' to afford the patience for the painful compilation of detailed knowledge which is one of the marks of the major scholar." Although the scholars of the classical tradition, especially Weber, had accumulated massive quantities of information before constructing the theories and concepts that gave them renown, Mills displayed an unwillingness to engage in such work. "When Mills tackles the 'large issues,' one cannot but feel that he does so mainly because he just does not care for the small ones, is too impatient to concern himself with them," Coser wrote. Even worse, Mills's vulgar generalizing included a

---

[92] Ibid., 518.

[93] Ibid., 518.

[94] Coser outlined his concerns over the secession of sociology from public discourse in the introduction to *The Functions of Social Conflict* (New York: Free Press, 1956), in which he traced the profession's growing distance from its Progressive-Era audience of lawyers, reformers, radicals, and politicians, and its gravitation to an emerging clientele of public and private bureaucratic interests.

"temptation to substitute catchy sloganizing for real thinking" and a "meat axe" approach to reality.[95]

Worst of all, Mills refused to accept the validity of sociological styles that differed from his own. "He systematically denigrates all efforts to work in a different analytical vein," Coser charged. Like Mills's manuscript readers, Coser believed that Mills's stark delineations of meaningful and illegitimate sociological work were premature and therefore unwarranted, for, like Riesman, he perceived that such fractious criticism could only serve to stifle sociology's maturation. Joining Homans, he insisted that, "a new discipline requires for its growth the utmost openness, the maximum freedom for its practitioners to strike out in the most varied directions." Coser then appealed to the example of the history of science to demonstrate how "the most pregnant discoveries, the most fruitful breakthroughs, were often achieved in seemingly remote areas, in the explanation of what appeared at first peripheral phenomena."[96] Avoiding the question of whether or not sociology is a science, Coser nevertheless demanded that sociologists share the same modesty of purpose and patience with their discipline's unavoidably slow progress.

Coser avoided addressing Mills's assessments of Lazarsfeld and Parsons, but he did conclude that Mills had exalted his own approach at the expense of the discipline as a whole. While Coser shared Mills's suspicion of grand theory—he had challenged Parsonian functionalism directly in his 1956 work, *The Functions of Social Conflict*—he declared that Mills's oversimplification of the nuances of sociology nullified his argument. As Gross had predicted in his critique of the draft version of the book, even an otherwise sympathetic peer such as Coser could not countenance such an aggressive polemic. Mills's arrogance, Coser charged, served only to diminish the impact of what he had to say. "It is really hard to believe that, except for C. Wright Mills and perhaps a few others, American sociology is in the hands mostly of fools and knaves," he concluded.[97]

Edward Shils similarly rejected Mills's oversimplifications, concluding that his objections to abstract empiricism constituted a repudiation of empirical methods *in toto*. "Professor Mills is utterly fed up with research which is based on field-work and which exercises some statistical control over its collection and analysis of data," he wrote. Shils also dismissed Mills's condemnation of grand theory, remarking that Parsons's style constituted "a

---

[95] Lewis Coser, "The Uses of Sociology," review of *The Sociological Imagination* in *Partisan Review* 27, 1 (Winter 1960): 170.

[96] Ibid., 171.

[97] Ibid., 172.

notoriously easy target," and, at the same time, "where a steadier aim and a better discernment of the target is necessary, his performance is not so very creditable."[98] Once again, a repudiation of Mills's argument hinged upon his seeming oversimplification of sociology's empirical and theoretical styles.

Significantly, Shils also addressed the matter of public sociology, questioning Mills's basic premise that sociology was ready to adopt a broad commitment to enriching public discourse. "Professor Mills thinks that sociology is called by educated opinion, and the vacuum of the present cultural and political situation, to take the forefront of intellectual life," he wrote. "Journalism, literature, and art must make room for sociology, perhaps even become sociology, because only it is capable of depicting what is really important."[99] Unfortunately, he continued, a young discipline such as sociology could not hope to fulfill such grand expectations:

> There is not enough intellectual achievement in the sociological "diagnosis of our time" to allow it even to pretend to replace journalism, literature, art, etc., as interpretations of the contemporary situation, quite aside from the ultimate impossibility of its ever performing the expressive functions of these activities. . . . The fact is that in sociology as it exists to-day, in Professor Mills' kind of sociology no more than in that which he derogates—there is not available to instructed public opinion a reasonable picture of things as they really are. It would be fraudulent to claim that there is one.[100]

Shils's assessment of sociology resembled those of the proponents of the discipline's scientific identity in its assertion that sociology's engagement of publics in its current state of theoretical and empirical immaturity would offer a false promise of conclusive observations about society. As for the sociological imagination, Shils admitted that Mills's concept might have some validity, but in the vague state in which Mills had rendered it, it brought the discipline no closer to his desired ends. Mills had succeeded instead only in exalting his own perspective, apparent only as "the state of mind which will produce the results at which he himself has already arrived, through its use."[101]

---

[98] Edward Shils, "Imaginary Sociology," *Encounter* 14, 6 (June 1960): 78. In his biography of Mills, Irving Horowitz explores Mills's reaction to Shils's review, with its ad hominem characterization of Mills as a "burly cowpuncher" with a saddlebag of books by Kafka, Trotsky, and Weber, encountering for the first time his nemesis, Madison Avenue (101–3).

[99] Ibid., 78.

[100] Ibid., 78–9.

[101] Ibid., 79.

Lazarsfeld expressed similar misgivings toward Mills's demand for an immediately useful sociology and defended the relative insularity and lower expectations that he and Merton had counseled since the early 1950s. In the foreword to *What College Students Think*, a survey of students' political and cultural attitudes, he implied that Mills shared the same anti-empirical absolutism he perceived in Sorokin. Like Shils, Lazarsfeld demanded a more realistic understanding of sociology's social role than Mills seemed willing to accept, and he criticized Mills for his vague exhortations to its practitioners to engage in public dialogue with journalists, scientists, and others. "We sociologists would all like to have and to satisfy such a distinguished clientele," he admitted. "But how to do it? Unfortunately, Mills does not give very definite advice." Moreover, Mills's demands for sociological work that would ultimately illuminate personal milieus through a new understanding of social structure struck Lazarsfeld as naive: "Kings who have wanted the philosopher's stone or immediate cures for currently incurable diseases have usually advanced charlatanism not knowledge," he warned. Instead, sociology needed "sober and competent inquiry into particular problems of importance."[102]

Significantly, Lazarsfeld was the only critic of *The Sociological Imagination* to perceive a veiled attack on Merton in Mills's argument. Years later, he would note that although he and Parsons were clearly the book's "two explicit villains," Mills had also included "an anonymous statesman who tries to compromise on everything." "Of course," he offered, "everyone knows that it is Merton." Lazarsfeld considered Mills's subtle treatment of Merton to be a "vicious attack," made worse by the fact that he had avoided referring to him by name.[103]

However, Mills's failure to confront Merton's sociological values directly weakened his case against sociology's quest to emulate the other sciences. Moreover, to do so would have required a more sophisticated attack, for Merton stood as the crucial defender of contemporary theoretical and empirical work from a position between the two. He embodied a compelling combination of sensitivity to the value of the classical tradition, the limits of abstract theorizing, and the importance of theory grounded in empirical investigation. He had in his own work applied major theories of the classical tradition, such as Weber's theories on bureaucracy and Durkheim's anomie, to specific contemporary sociological problems. He had also argued most consistently for a scientific sociology that embraced eagerly the varied contributions of theorists and quantitative methodologists while eschewing the

---

[102]Paul F. Lazarsfeld, foreword to Rose K. Goldsen et al., *What College Students Think*, xi.

[103]Paul Lazarsfeld, Paul Lazarsfeld Oral History Project, Butler Library, Columbia University, New York, 3: 357.

kind of internecine conflict that would distract them from their cumulative scientific mission. That *The Sociological Imagination* lacked any substantive consideration of Merton's professional vision constituted an omission of significant consequence, as it allowed Merton to come to the defense of Mills's other targets from the vantage point of a bystander to the conflict and as a source of reconciliation. Merton could defend the scientific integrity of sociology from above the fray.

In 1959, shortly after the release of *The Sociological Imagination,* Merton delivered a paper before the Fourth World Congress of Sociology in which he denied that the controversies exemplified by Sorokin's and Mills's critiques reflected fundamental problems in sociology's identity. Rather, they simply revealed sociologists' differing views on which problems were most appropriate for study. "These polemics," he asserted, "have more to do with the allocation of intellectual resources among different kinds of sociological work than with a closely formulated opposition of sociological ideas."[104] Different research priorities simply, and inevitably, produced differences of opinion on the practical matter of what should be studied.

Sociology during the 1950s, however, had experienced contentious and often bitter disagreements over those priorities, disagreements that Merton believed to be wholly unnecessary and self-destructive. "These controversies follow the classically identified course of social conflict," he observed. "Attack is followed by counter-attack, with progressive alienation of each party to the conflict." Instead of illuminating the most pressing issues facing sociology, these attacks served merely to drive sociologists irreparably apart, thereby solidifying hostile camps of scholars who no longer perceived themselves as participants in a collective project of discovery. Merton lamented that "the consequent polarization leads each group of sociologists to respond largely to stereotyped versions of what is being done by the other." These stereotypes became "self-confirming" as the members of the different camps refused to test them against experience.[105]

Ultimately, sociology faced an impending fragmentation that would undermine the progress of its nascent identity. Merton warned:

All this tends to move towards the emergence of an all-or-none doctrine. Sociological orientations that are not substantively contradictory

---

[104] Robert K. Merton, "Social Conflict Over Styles of Sociological Work," in Larry T. and Janice M. Reynolds, eds., *The Sociology of Sociology* (New York: David McKay, 1970), 181. This paper was originally published in *Transactions of the Fourth World Congress of Sociology,* 3 (Louvain, Belgium: International Sociological Association, 1959): 21–44.

[105] Ibid., 182.

are regarded as if they were. Sociological inquiry, it is said, must be statistical in character *or* historical; only the great issues of the time must be the objects of study *or* these refractory issues of freedom or compulsion must be avoided because they are not amenable to scientific investigation; and so on.[106]

Merton contended that these polarizations subverted the kinds of meaningful "intellectual criticism" that allowed the discipline to grow. Just as Riesman had initially tried to discourage Mills from attacking his colleagues out of the fear that sociologists would redouble their efforts in defending their present approaches, Merton perceived that "polemics" that drove scholars apart served only to undermine the thoughtful analysis and assessment of ideas.

Merton's argument therefore constituted a call for civility in sociology's professional discourse, one that reflected his earlier optimistic statements on sociology's broad, cumulative mission. Although critics within sociology belabored the question of the discipline's proper identity and social role, Merton demanded that his peers recognize the broad compatibility and, more important, the scientific relevance of each other's work.

Merton then devoted the rest of his paper to the unwarranted criticisms that had arisen from within contemporary sociology. In his characteristically diplomatic manner, he addressed systematically each of the major criticisms Mills, Sorokin, and others had made without referring to these individuals by name. To avoid any appearance of advocacy of one side of a particular conflict over another, he simply presented the attacks and defenses in outwardly objective summaries and attributed them to third parties. Merton's presentation thus appeared as the reasoned reflections of one who refused to become embroiled in disputes he perceived to be unnecessary and divisive.

To the charge that much of what passed for sociological work was merely the belaboring of trivia, Merton replied that contemporary standards of relevance failed to appreciate the subtlety of scientific work and that its rewards often lay in the future. The complaint that sociology had neglected more significant problems in favor of trivia, he insisted, "typically assumes that it is the topic, the particular objects under study, that fixes the importance or triviality of the investigation." Scientists had always encountered this form of naysaying when, to the derision of their contemporaries, they studied simple phenomena like objects in motion or microorganisms, yet their observations had produced profound intellectual and practical results. Thus, in an aggressive defense of hard-science standards of objective topic selection in sociology, Merton declared boldly, "There is no *necessary* relation between

---

[106]Ibid., 182.

the socially ascribed importance of the object under examination and the scope of its implications for an understanding of how society or nature works." The very measurability of phenomena, rather than their perceived social relevance, made them appropriate for study, for "ideally that empirical object is selected for study which enables one to investigate a scientific problem to good advantage. Often, these intellectually strategic objects hold little intrinsic interest, either for the investigator or anyone else."[107]

As for the charge that questions of methodology had supplanted sociologists' attention to more substantive social issues, Merton argued that sociology had employed a sophisticated division of labor, in which methodologists supplied value-neutral research techniques to other scholars, whose responsibility lay in the different task of selecting problems to investigate. "The selection of substantive problems is not the task of specialists in methodology," Merton insisted. "Once the problem is selected, however, the question ensues of how to design an inquiry so that it can contribute to a solution of the problem. The effort to answer such questions of design is part of the business of methodology."[108] Merton's rejoinder thereby dismissed Sorokin's warning of the dangers of an empirical sociology uninformed by intuition, for methodologists could perform their role effectively without it. By separating issues of problem selection from those of technique, Merton defused the argument that the former had been sacrificed to the latter. Rather, they existed in a symbiotic relationship, sustained by the often separate efforts of theorizers and methodological innovators. Mills's indictment of Lazarsfeld as a mere technician then became irrelevant as well, for it was precisely Lazarsfeld's function to formulate techniques that others could then apply to a variety of specific problems.

Merton approached Mills's indictment of the "bureaucratic ethos," to which he referred without attribution as "the bureaucratization of the sociological mind," in a similar manner, contending that it simply failed to describe contemporary sociological research. The idea that "team research" threatened the classical tradition, in which the lone scholar supposedly selected both his research subjects and the means for studying them, ignored the long tradition of cooperation among scholars. Their use of research assistants and graduate students revealed as much, and the fact that research institutes could now "extend and deepen" forms of investigation that had lain beyond the reach of older generations of scholars should be seen as continuous with those earlier collaborative efforts.

---

[107] Ibid., 185–86.

[108] Ibid., 190.

Finally, Merton addressed the dissenters' demands for a public sociology. However, instead of addressing directly the question of whether scholars owed publics a regular accounting of sociology's findings and reflections, he approached the subject through the issues he had already considered in the paper, demonstrating that the detractors' arguments about specific socio-logical faults revealed their divergent views on sociology's proper audience. Arguing once again without the appearance of advocacy one way or the other, he observed:

> The recurrent noise about jargon, cults of unintelligibility, the overly-abundant use of statistics or of mathematical models is largely gen-erated by the sociologists who have the general public as their major reference-group. The work of these outer-oriented sociologists, in turn, is described by their academic critics as sociological journalism, useful more for arousing public interest in sociology than for ad-vancing sociological knowledge.[109]

Rather than comment on this professional schism, one that was so central to postwar sociology's identity struggles, he urged that the schism itself be studied: "It would be instructive to study the actual social roles and functions of these diversely oriented sociologists, rather than to remain content with offhand descriptions such as these, even though again we cannot expect that the results of such study would modify current alignments."[110] Merton thereby resolved the matter of an alleged conflict between public sociology and cumulative, scientific enterprise by transforming it into a problem for sociological research. The very question of science *versus* public discourse itself became an object for scientific investigation, one which need not exert any decisive influence on sociology's self-conception.

Merton's paper, presented in the guise of objectivity and impartiality, joined the other reactions of Mills's peers to form a rather cohesive body of similar objections to *The Sociological Imagination*. Believing that sociology stood unprepared for the kind of public role Mills demanded of it, they reiterated the argument from the scientific perspective that more time was needed for the profession to attain the level of certitude in its findings that would allow it to contribute meaningfully to scientific progress, much less public discourse. In the meantime, sociologists would have to content them-selves with the gathering of precise information on social phenomena of limited scope and of indeterminate short-term significance. They attacked

---

[109]Ibid., 195.

[110]Ibid., 195–96.

Mills for his polarizing characterization of sociology as dominated by hopelessly abstract theorizers and quantifiers, claiming that, in his arrogance, he had unfairly condemned his foes so as to elevate his own approach to sociology. Finally, beneath their objections to Mills's bile lay the Mertonian assumption that fractious, internecine conflict could only impede sociology's scientific progress. Especially in the case of Merton, the professional responses to *The Sociological Imagination* reflected widespread retrenchment rather than any rethinking of sociology's scientific self-conception.

Significantly, it was influential conservative reviewers of *The Sociological Imagination* who expressed the greatest enthusiasm for the book. Conservatives, for whom social science's arcane language and statistical complexity constituted a dangerous departure from traditional modes of inquiry and communication, commended Mills's appeal to a "classical tradition," particularly as it eschewed a wholesale endorsement of Marxism and instead embraced a pantheon of non-Marxists like Weber and Durkheim. The vigorously anticommunist and antiliberal statist John Chamberlain, a reviewer for *National Review* and the libertarian monthly journal *Freeman*, wrote in *The Wall Street Journal* that Mills represented a kind of conservative voice in sociology in his repudiation of the "barbaric jargonizing" of grand theory and the kind of obsessive quantitative research that tended to belabor the obvious rather than addressing "the big issues on which history pivots."[111] Thus, while Chamberlain expressed clear reservations over Mills's "power elite" theory, he could still accept Mills's brand of sociology as the basis for the kind of meaningful work necessary for refining it or any other theory.

Russell Kirk, the political scientist and ascendant intellectual voice in postwar American conservatism with his influential 1953 work of Burkean idealism, *The Conservative Mind*, also found Mills's book to be a welcome antidote to the liberal technocratic ethos he perceived both within the social sciences and American culture at large. Whereas the sociologists of the classical tradition had dealt with "the true problems of modern society," American sociologists tended to study tiny, unrelated fragments of social phenomena. "In a word," he mused, "they have tended to scatter their attention. According to the 'democratic theory of knowledge', they have assumed all facts are created equal." Like Chamberlain, Kirk celebrated Mills's repudiation of a sociology that lacked a moral foundation or guiding principles that would allow it to reach meaningful conclusions about matters of importance to society as a whole. Although necessarily critical of Mills's radicalism, Kirk appreciated his contempt for "the muddled liberalism that underlies most American sociological studies," which he perceived to be a

---

[111] John Chamberlain, "The Job and Jargon of Sociology," *Wall Street Journal* (May 14, 1959): 14.

consequence of the relativizing effects of overly abstract theorizing and quantification.[112]

Conservatives' responses to *The Sociological Imagination* reflected the degree to which the book validated their existing antipathies toward social science and its perceived partnership with a technocratic liberalism. Mills's repudiations of bureaucratic modes of thinking and willful obscurantism in particular resonated with conservatives' suspicion of social engineering, morally obtuse thinking, and, as Robert Nisbet theorized, the artificial separation of science from more organic avenues to intellectual discovery. Indeed, Nisbet, a Burkean sociological theorist and the author in 1953 of *The Quest for Community*, a study of the breakdown of community and authority under the pressures of modernity, demanded an expanded conception of sociology as a science. In 1962, in "Sociology as an Art Form," he advocated a holistic sociology that understood science and art to be "different manifestations of the same form of creative consciousness."[113] The unfortunate segregation of scientific and artistic pursuits, Nisbet observed, began during the industrial revolution, which absorbed and channeled scientific activity into the practical pursuit of technical and technological innovation, while Romanticism defined art as the search for beauty rather than reality or truth. Ultimately, technique, as the hallmark of modern science, had imprisoned sociology within the narrow realm of the testable and measurable, so that "free reflection, intuition, and imagination" had been sacrificed to "rigorous adherence to procedure."[114] Of this servitude to method as an end in itself, Nisbet lamented:

All too often in the history of thought we find techniques, methods, and doctrines becoming puny earthworks, hiding the view of the Olympian heights. How many mute, inglorious Simmels, how many village Cooleys lie today buried in required sequences of curriculum and in the computer rooms, their talents occupied not by development of ideas and insights but by the adaptation of trivial or well-worn ideas to the language of the machine or by the endless replication of studies that often shouldn't have been done in the first place? Such servitude is justified on the false and appalling ground that the student can thus be taught the "method" of science. One may observe cynically that he sees no Simmels and Durkheims walking the

---

[112]Russell Kirk, "Shewd Knocks at Sociological Theories," *Chicago Sunday Tribune* (May 24, 1959).

[113]Robert A. Nisbet, "Sociology as An Art Form," in Maurice Stein and Arthur Vidich, eds., *Sociology on Trial* (Englewood Cliffs, NJ: Prentice-Hall, 1963), 149. This essay originally appeared in *Pacific Sociological Review* 5, 2 (Fall 1962): 67–74.

[114]Ibid., 151.

campus today. I venture the statement that there would have been none in their day had certain curricular requirements and terminological fashions been then in existence.[115]

Nisbet's reaffirmation of the classical tradition, in its striking resemblance to that of Mills, demonstrates the powerful appeal such a position had for postwar conservatives as they confronted a science of society that in its narrowness of focus and complex methodologies contested the primacy of tradition and intuition. Nisbet's conception of community, defined by its members' shared sentiments and the value placed upon moral continuity, left no room for a professional class that adopted its own set of sentiments and its own separate community. Tocqueville, Tönnies, Durkheim, Weber, and Simmel were therefore exemplary for their commitment to confronting directly and intuitively the fundamental changes of their times. Their concepts of mass society, alienation, anomie, rationalization, community, and disorganization, Nisbet noted, were products not of technical innovation but of human imagination.

In its praise for Mills's critique, the conservative response to the book thus came closest to an appreciation of the implicit pragmatist foundation of Mills's sociology.[116] Conservatives understood that Mills's appeals to broad, public communication constituted a defense of a vital community life, in which not expert scientific opinion but rather the democratic communications of citizens—including social scientists—articulated the values appropriate to society. Although postwar conservatives hardly agreed with Dewey and George Herbert Mead that those values remained tentative and subject to constant reassessment, they nevertheless perceived with the pragmatists that a social science that, in the name of scientific accuracy, asserted its privileged possession of social awareness, separating its "facts" from their meaning within the context of community life and discourse, impoverished both democratic ideals and the search for truth itself.

The hostile reactions of Mills's colleagues, in turn, reflected the virtual absence of the pragmatist tradition from postwar sociology. After World War II, the social philosophies of Dewey and Mead declined in a trajectory

---

[115] Ibid., 158.

[116] For an exploration of Mills's foundation in the pragmatist tradition, see Horowitz, *C. Wright Mills*, chap. 6, especially pp. 117–31. Mills's master's thesis at the University of Texas also reflects his interest in Deweyan pragmatism and its insistence that true philosophy derives not simply from past events or ideas but from contemporary realities. See his "Reflection, Behavior, and Culture: An Essay in the Sociology of Knowledge" (master's thesis, University of Texas at Austin, 1939). Mills argued here that "a genuinely philosophic response" derived from "present thought and experience that is largely non-philosophic in nature" (8).

similar to that of the Chicago School of sociology itself.[117] Mills's exhortation that sociologists confront "big problems" and transform "private struggles" into public issues failed to resonate within a social science community that perceived new knowledge to be the product of expert inquiry rather than the communicative negotiations of American society conceived writ large.[118] Instead, as Merton and Homans had complained in their reviews, it seemed to demand more of the young science than the latter could hope to deliver. Whereas Dewey conceived of science as a democratic endeavor that placed the interests of society above disinterested scientific inquiry, Parsons in particular had made clear that a science of society could progress only if insulated from outside social pressures and prejudices. In the same manner, leftist critics in sociology refused to join Millsian pragmatism in a call for a more sophisticated indictment of sociology than that it had simply compromised its integrity and public function in its capitulation to powerful and

---

[117] See John P. Diggins, *The Promise of Pragmatism: Modernism and the Crisis of Knowledge and Authority* (Chicago: University of Chicago Press, 1994), chap. 10.

[118] A prominent exception to the indifference of 1950s sociology to the pragmatist critique can be found in the papers and articles of Herbert Blumer. Blumer, a Chicago sociologist, pupil of Mead, and the link between prewar and postwar symbolic interactionism, had since the 1930s advocated an empirical sociology that denied that sociology could become the kind of science that could produce facts with a validity independent of either the researcher or the subjects of investigation. In Herbert Blumer, "Public Opinion and Public Opinion Polling," *American Sociological Review* 13, 5 (October 1948): 542–54, he offered a decidedly pragmatist critique of public opinion polling, declaring that its techniques had blinded its practitioners to their flawed conception of how individuals formed their opinions. By assembling the responses of atomized individuals, survey researchers failed to recognize that opinion formation took place through the complex interaction of social groups, which made the determination of which opinions possessed sociological significance far more problematic than they had assumed. In Herbert Blumer, "What Is Wrong with Social Theory?" *American Sociological Review* 19, 1 (February 1954): 3–10, he criticized "operationalism," or theorists' goal of investing their concepts with precise and permanent meanings, insisting that the search for such "definitive" concepts had driven the discipline to value mathematical techniques over the creativity necessary to explore and truly understand social phenomena. In their place, he insisted upon "sensitizing" concepts that did not attempt to achieve eternally definitive status and instead simply provided the investigator with "a general sense of reference and guidance in approaching empirical instances" (7). In his 1955 presidential address before the Society for the Study of Social Problems, he assailed the survey movement's concept of social attitudes, which he argued abstracted individuals from their social milieux and therefore failed to consider the myriad of complex social interventions that made attitudes meaningful as precipitators to action. Whereas survey researchers assumed that the attitudes they measured provided insights into human action itself, Blumer countered that individuals never act simply on the basis of a particular attitude. Instead, they "piece together" their actions based upon a wide variety of intervening considerations. Meanwhile, the actions of others inevitably intervened between the attitude and the act, and thus the social context of attitudes and actions required the sociologist's attention as well. See Herbert Blumer, "Attitudes and the Social Act," *Social Problems* 3, 2 (October 1955): 59–65. Blumer's pragmatism, like Dewey's, required that values and attitudes be recognized as products of social interaction and that meanings were inevitably social in nature.

often manipulative interests. For Mills, of greater concern was the fact that sociology no longer attempted to tell the truth publicly about such interests and what he perceived as their strategies of manipulation. The knowledge specialist, more than merely a "servant of power," represented the postwar scholarly refusal to enlarge and enrich public discourse.

Until the paradigm shifts of the mid-1960s, which invested Mills's book in particular with new meaning and apparent applicability, leading sociologists dismissed *Fads and Foibles* and *The Sociological Imagination* as self-aggrandizing expressions of their authors' discontent with their own marginalization and their willingness to condemn the progress the discipline had made in order to elevate their own scholarly work. Their propensity to attack their peers by name and in a decidedly less-than-genteel manner appeared to indicate a lack of professionalism, a perception which both Sorokin's and Mills's professional isolation reinforced. Thus, the two critiques, rather than fostering a fresh debate over the meaning and purpose of sociology, produced a retrenchment.

Meanwhile, the markedly divergent journalistic reactions to both *Fads and Foibles* and *The Sociological Imagination* attest to the disproportionate impact Sorokin and Mills had upon lay perceptions of American sociology during the 1950s and early 1960s. The conservative praise for the latter reflected most closely the larger public conception of, and objections to, postwar sociology; conservative complaint that modern sociology had eroded the standards of traditional intellectual discourse without replacing them with anything morally meaningful found its companion in the broader lament that sociology's language and self-justifying methodologies had also encroached upon—and threatened to corrupt—public discourse. For sociology's lay detractors, *The Sociological Imagination* both validated their hostility and provided them with ample ammunition with which to attack the profession, and Sorokin and Mills had supplied lay observers with the additional material necessary with which to construct their own dismissals or, alternatively, warnings about professional social science, thus prompting the defenders of the scientific ideal to redouble their efforts to shield their advances against an emerging national climate of skepticism and hostility.

7

Pseudoscience and Social Engineering

American Sociology's Public Image in the Fifties

In November 1948, the American electorate returned President Harry Truman to office, confounding journalists, pundits, public opinion pollsters, and politicians who had expected Republican challenger Thomas Dewey to win the election. For social scientists in particular, the pollsters' failure to predict the election's outcome on the basis of their recent opinion sampling innovations proved deeply embarrassing at a critical moment in their struggle to forge a salutary public identity. In particular, this public relations crisis threatened to cast new and potentially more widespread doubt upon sociology's scientific integrity.

Once again, Merton spearheaded the effort to protect sociology's scientific legitimacy in the face of these latest grounds for lay skepticism. In 1949, he warned that the polls' inaccurate predictions threatened to produce a "radiation of effect," so that the public would not only look askance at pollsters and polling but question the entire social science enterprise as well, thereby impeding the young disciplines' scientific progress. "The growth and development of science is in part dependent upon the climate of social opinion regarding its nature, past achievements, and future prospects," he observed. In the case of social science in particular, a negative public image could "invite action which affects its basic support in society," such as that which occurred during the congressional debates over the inclusion of the social sciences in the National Science

Foundation.[1] Merton concluded that like the physical sciences, which attained widespread respect gradually through such practical successes as their contribution of new "comforts and conveniences deriving from technology," the social sciences would depend for their reputation upon the demonstration of practical utility within the larger community.

To gauge the impact the 1948 polls' failure might have had on the social sciences' public image, Merton examined National Opinion Research Center survey results of public perceptions of various professions. The data revealed that while the informants possessed a "sufficiently clear image" of the legal, medical, and clerical professions, the applied professions such as architecture and engineering, and the physical science professions, they lacked a clear conception of social science. Moreover, they ranked social scientists significantly lower than the other professions in terms of social prestige. Merton therefore turned to the "strategic groups" he deemed most responsible for conveying images of the professions, the editors and publishers of urban newspapers. It was they, after all, who had reported the pollsters' "dramatic and abundantly publicized" failure to the American people in 1948. As "strategic publics," the gatekeepers of information, perception, and opinion for the larger public, their coverage and treatments of opinion polling therefore reflected potentially upon the reputation of social science.[2]

Merton concluded from the survey data that the pollsters' failure had exerted but a negligible effect upon the social sciences' public image. The newspaper editors and publishers, like the general public, proved to possess either a sketchy image of the social sciences—one whose "fragmentary character" reflected a "prevailing lack of interest in the disciplines"—or no image at all.[3] The challenge for the social sciences, then, was not one of overcoming existing negative public perceptions but rather of establishing a positive image where little or no image yet existed. This challenge would, of course, tie social science's fate to the society's opinion leaders, those whose conceptions would in some form become those of wider publics. Merton concluded his article with a vision of an ideal atmosphere of public discourse on the nature of the professional social research, in which "prevailing images of social

---

[1] Robert K. Merton and Paul K. Hatt, "Election Polling Forecasts and Public Images of Social Science: A Case Study in the Shaping of Opinion Among a Strategic Public," *Public Opinion Quarterly* 13, 2 (Summer 1949): 185–86.

[2] Merton's focus on these "strategic groups" reflected his participation in the theory of "opinion leaders" formulated by Lazarsfeld, Bernard Berelson, and Hazel Gaudet in *The People's Choice* (New York: Columbia University Press, 1948), a study of the role of community leaders in influencing voter choices in the 1940 presidential election.

[3] Merton and Hatt, "Election Polling Forecasts," 222.

science among the decision-makers in our society" would be "thoroughly critical, moderately expectant, and slightly benevolent."[4] In other words, publicly aired discourse on social science among the nation's elites should reflect the same civility that science demanded of its practitioners, a decorum that Merton himself had always extended to critics and theoretical opponents.

Unfortunately for sociology, such civility failed to materialize. Instead, the profession entered the 1950s confronted by a deeply skeptical and often openly hostile army of detractors. As the first popular works of postwar sociology received attention outside the profession, and as peer and journalistic assessments of sociology proliferated, an image of the discipline took shape that contained two salient and apparently contradictory elements. First, sociology appeared to many of its detractors to be a pseudoscience preoccupied with trivia. These critics, often drawing upon the negative assessments of renegade sociologists themselves, conceived of the field as the province of a professionally ambitious cadre of newcomers to the intellectual discourse on society who, in their eagerness to demonstrate their proficiency, resorted to the superficially sophisticated "testing" of ostensibly sociological subjects that were already amenable to common-sense assessment. Sociologists oft-touted "objectivity," moreover, served simply to highlight for these critics the profession's lack of engagement with the pressing issues of the age. Like Robert Lynd, who in 1939 had declared that "research without an actively selective point of view becomes the ditty bag of an idiot, filled with bits of pebbles, straws, feathers, and other random hoardings,"[5] these skeptics questioned the scientific integrity of quantitative social research, airing similar objections to the discipline's arcane terminology and its preoccupation with social minutiae.

Other detractors expressed in various forms the concern that sociological work, as the sophisticated study of human association, posed a threat to democracy and individual autonomy. Although Merton had perceived within the ethos of postwar science the prospect for a democratic culture, one that would defeat fascist efforts to control and mold science for purposes of mass manipulation, these critics perceived in the social sciences in particular the means and intent for precisely that end. These professions' success in providing private clients with seemingly improved means of managing workplace discontent, shaping consumer preferences, and other techniques of human manipulation indicated to these detractors that social science threatened to

---

[4] Ibid., 222.

[5] Robert S. Lynd, *Knowledge for What? The Place of Social Science in American Culture* (Middletown, CT: Wesleyan University Press, 1939), 183.

encroach upon the sovereignty of the individual consciousness, turning people into willing participants in their own subjugation. While the first criticism of sociology as the investigation of trivia reflected a refusal to take sociology seriously as a window into the workings of industrial society, this latter critique indicted applied sociology and its contributions to marketing, personnel management, and public relations for introducing the means toward the forging of grave new threats to human freedom.[6] Together, these divergent critiques, one denying and the other decrying the efficacy of social science research, presented sociology with a profound public challenge to its scientific legitimacy.

A 1952 article by William H. Whyte in *Fortune* magazine typified the seemingly contradictory lay assessment of sociology as both pretentious and pernicious. In an analysis that would soon become part of his classic exploration of white-collar professional culture, *The Organization Man,* Whyte, then *Fortune*'s editor, bemoaned a growing "orthodoxy" within applied social science and its possible consequences for meaningful social inquiry. He observed that the business world had embraced social science with a religiosity that had pre-empted a critical evaluation of its actual utility, so that a poorly informed—and, in fact, baseless—consensus had emerged that social science possessed the techniques for the solution of modern managerial problems. "Few movements, Whyte observed, "have jumped so quickly from the laboratory and university to practical application in the world of commerce and everyday life."[7] This consensus threatened to solidify into orthodoxy, as skeptics became increasingly reluctant to object to their implementation for fear of being branded "unprogressive, if not downright heretical."[8] The appropriation of social science for business purposes offered the illusion of seemingly limitless progress in the quest for more effective public relations, advertising, and management techniques; and its scientific veneer, fortified with such concepts as "social physics" and the mathematical study of human activity, threatened to erode any critical perspective on its real applicability.

Social science's triumph in the realm of professional and technical prestige, Whyte insisted, belied its fundamental practical and philosophical flaws. Its claims to scientific authority denied the value of intuitive or common-sense thinking, sacrificing these to statistical analysis and the "objective" study of human interaction. "A machine for the engineering of mediocrity"

---

[6]In a recent analysis of these distorted views of sociology, Joel Best finds very similar attitudes to have persisted. See his "Killing the Messenger: The Social Problems of Sociology," *Social Problems* 50, 1 (February 2003): 1–13.

[7]Ibid., 89.

[8]William H. Whyte, Jr., "The Social Engineers," *Fortune* (January 1952): 89.

promised to be the dire consequence of such a repudiation of human intuition, Whyte warned, for by removing the human element from social observation, this social engineering replaced creative insight with the stultifying inertia of "groupthink," or the bogus consensus achieved when individuals subsumed their own ideas and goals to the misplaced ideal of group harmony.[9] The scientific claims then offered their blessing to this artificial consensus by providing it with a patina of "objectivity," as though the members of a given group had merely agreed upon what was scientifically correct in any given instance. The increasing mathematical complexity of the social engineer's techniques disguised their studies' coercive character, for through them the social engineer could use the mantle of "science" to justify the manipulation of human beings.

Whyte therefore declared that social engineering techniques and the assumptions that underlay them contained dangerously authoritarian implications not only for the business world but for the nation as a whole. In the field of mass communication in particular, it threatened to facilitate the wholesale manipulation of people's attitudes and motivations. "To people outside the Movement, 'mass communication' is merely an objective study of advertising, radio, movies, and other mass media," Whyte observed. "To the social engineer, however, it is a weapon."[10] Social engineering aspired to replace public debate over important social issues with expert "planning," which undermined democratic, public participation by virtue of its supposed scientific, and thus exclusive, character. "Individual moral grapplings, inclusive lay debate, are no longer in order," Whyte lamented, for social engineering supplied its findings not to the public at large but to elites in government, business, and the mass media, "the *de facto* thought leaders of the country."[11]

Although Whyte did distinguish between the social engineer and the "legitimate social scientist," his article contributed to a growing body of critical literature that took applied social science to task for its practitioners' failure to protect it from misappropriation. Social science, Whyte insisted, needed a forceful assertion of moral standards in research to prevent the scientific ethos from becoming an antidemocratic dogma:

> The more quickly our many bureaucracies grasp at the new "tools" of persuasion, the more will the legitimate social scientist be pressured

---

[9]Ibid., 88–89.

[10]Ibid., 90.

[11]Ibid., 91.

for "practical results." Those who would indulge in pure inquiry instead would find themselves "deviants" from the integrated society they helped to fashion; only as lackeys would they have a function. In sheer self-defense, if nothing else, the social scientist must keep an eye on ethics.[12]

Whyte elaborated on this ethical crisis in a subsequent issue of *Fortune*. In the absence of individuals with enough autonomy to make ethical commitments, he warned, "groupthink" would pre-empt the necessity of moral choice, producing a culture of endless "buck-passing," the denial of ethical complexity, and the "smothering of the individual."[13]

Whyte's polemic exhibited the two basic forms of opposition to the scientific identity that sociology would encounter both within and without the discipline throughout the 1950s and into the early 1960s. On one hand, Whyte's claim that applied social science fostered institutionalized mediocrity reflected the charge that social science, in its pursuit of scientific integrity, sacrificed meaningful inquiry to focus on those phenomena that could be measured readily and on investigative methods that could be easily quantified and repeated experimentally. On the other, he had articulated a more general postwar concern that the growing sophistication of techniques of analysis of social behavior could result in the denial of the integrity of the individual, that individual autonomy might succumb to the claimed scientific authority of experts and to their prescriptions for social harmony, while those same techniques provided decision- and opinion-making elites with ever-more effective means for securing conformity and obedience.

As such charges mounted, however, it became clear to professional sociologists seeking to defend their discipline's scientific integrity that their critics' contradictory arguments could be dismissed with a reassertion of the scientific ethos itself. That is, the very ideal of scientific status stood as the strongest defense against both those who perceived little of value in social science and those who imagined it to be producing results too volatile for a free society to withstand. If many considered social research to be an exercise in irrelevance, it was because they lacked the professional training to ascertain the significance of either its subject matter or the processes of its selection. Journalists, for example, simply lacked the expertise necessary for assessing sociology's technical integrity or practical utility. As for those who perceived in sociology the potential for the enlistment of techniques for the scientific manipulation of human beings, the profession's defenders rebutted that

---

[12]Ibid., 91.

[13]Whyte, "Groupthink," *Fortune* (March 1952): 117, 142.

while sociology was indeed scientific, the slow pace at which it accumulated verifiable, repeatable results forbade Machiavellian applications and prevented its wholesale appropriation for such purposes. Others simply asserted that sociology lacked such dangerous potential by virtue of its scientific immaturity, that a fledgling discipline lacked the means to produce anti-democratic results.

Lay anxieties over the dangers of a social science enlisted toward the goal of human manipulation reflected the growing anxieties over scientific progress itself that the monumental events and developments of the 1940s and 1950s engendered. The specter of global atomic destruction after Hiroshima and Nagasaki in particular served to complicate Western assumptions of the benevolence of scientific and technological progress, as new concerns emerged over the potential for their misuse. As Paul Boyer explains, many worried that atomic energy carried devastating social consequences, that it would accelerate the kinds of transformations allegedly wrought by mass society, producing even greater political centralization, technocratic usurpation of private decision-making authority, and disruptions of patterns of work and leisure.[14] Still others considered social science research to be of a piece with atomic technology, a partner in a common project of civilization's annihilation.

In addition to its unleashing of destructive new technologies, World War II had engendered a new science of mass psychological manipulation. American sociologists' and psychologists' wartime service in the U.S. Army's Division of Morale, the Office of War Information, the Army's Psychological Warfare Division, and the Office of Strategic Services tied social science to the wartime culture of morale building, mass mobilization, and social control.[15] Then, three years after the Axis surrender, B. F. Skinner's *Walden Two,* a utopian vision of a social order and harmony maintained through the application of behaviorist techniques of motivation direction, produced a storm of controversy in the mainstream press over professional psychology's perceived agenda of devising scientific techniques of social control to mold and direct human thought and behavior.[16] Joseph Wood

---

[14]See Paul Boyer, *By the Bomb's Early Light: American Thought and Culture at the Dawn of the Atomic Age* (New York: Pantheon Books, 1985), chap. 13.

[15]See Christopher Simpson, *The Science of Coercion: Communication Research and Psychological Warfare, 1945–1960* (New York: Oxford University Press, 1994).

[16]Profiles of Skinner and assessments of *Walden Two,* many of them negative, appeared in several mass-circulation magazines and newspapers, including *Fortune* (October 1948), *Time* (June 19, 1950), *New Yorker Magazine* (July 19, 1947), *Newsweek* (May 7, 1951), *Life* (November 3, 1947 and June 28, 1948), and the *New York Times* (June 14 and 18, 1950).

Krutch, the notable Columbia professor of dramatic literature, offered one of the more prominent responses to the book. In *The Measure of Man*, he attacked Skinner's vision as an "ignoble utopia," writing that the behaviorist assumption of an infinitely malleable human personality shaped by environmental influences produced "a creature who has fallen into the hands of an ideally competent dictator."[17] Krutch's indictment contributed to the vocabulary of denunciation of modern social science as a force for the destruction of humanistic values and the integrity of the individual, as he characterized social science theories and methods as "mechanistic, deterministic, and materialistic." "Many physicists have given 'free will' back to the individual, but many sociologists still seem to deny it to the human being," he lamented.[18] The theologian Reinhold Niebuhr warned in turn that Skinner represented the ascendant specter of a new, antidemocratic ideology of scientific elitism that held that "most men are creatures with simple determinate ends of life, and that their 'anti-social' tendencies are quasi-biological impulses and inheritances which an astute social and psychological science can overcome or 'redirect' to what are known as 'socially approved' goals."[19] Skinner, a "naïve psychologist," had envisioned not a humane, benevolent utopia, but rather a dystopia that sacrificed the "heroic and noble" elements of the human personality to the goals of harmony and order.

With the onset of the Cold War, these fears of psychological manipulation seemed to have been confirmed, as evidence surfaced in the early 1950s that the Chinese communists had employed mind-control techniques against American prisoners of war during the Korean War, allegedly "brainwashing" them as part of a program of "ideological conversion."[20] The specter of totalitarianism therefore meant for many observers that unregulated social

---

[17] Joseph Wood Krutch, *The Measure of Man: On Freedom, Human Values, Survival and the Modern Temper* (New York: Grosset & Dunlap, 1953), 61–62.

[18] Ibid., 191.

[19] Reinhold Niebuhr, *The Irony of American History* (New York: Charles Scribner, 1952), 80.

[20] As early as 1951, U.S. government-sponsored investigation was under way, as the U.S. Air Force commissioned Wilber Schramm, John W. Riley, and Frederick Williams to travel to Korea to study the psychological strategies employed by both the United States and the North Korean and Chinese communists. In addition to the production of a classified study for the Air Force and an academic article, the team released for public consumption a propaganda pamphlet, *The Reds Take a City: The Communist Occupation of Seoul* (New Brunswick, NJ: Rutgers University Press, 1951), to generate public support for the U.S. effort in Korea. See Simpson, *Science of Coercion*, 63–65, and Ellen Herman, *The Romance of American Psychology* (Berkeley: University of California Press, 1995), 126–30, on the military and intelligence sponsorship of such research. Other studies included Robert Jay Lifton's *Thought Reform and the Psychology of Totalism* (New York: W. W. Norton, 1961), which explored the implications of such psychological manipulation for human freedom.

science innovation might pose as grave a threat to civilization as nuclear fission. The stage was set for a public confrontation between social science's defenders and its detractors.

In 1951, *The American Scholar* sponsored a forum on the relationship between social science and the methods of science it professed to share with the other sciences. The forum's participants, prominent scholars from various academic disciplines, included Krutch, the historian Crane Brinton, the anthropologist A. L. Kroeber, and Skinner. Following what would become one of the leitmotifs of the postwar critiques of social science, the forum's theme centered upon its impact on "those values which most of us cherish in human beings," as if to establish at the outset that social science's coming-of-age had produced a struggle between scientific and humanistic ideals.[21]

In the midst of the panel's otherwise meandering discussion, Krutch took the opportunity to repeat his salvos against the kind of manipulative social science he associated with Skinner's work. He admonished that the social science professions had proved unwilling to acknowledge any public accountability as they entered society's circles of power, and that they had masked their growing social impact under the guise of scientific objectivity. "It seems to me," he announced, "that we are getting to a stage where the most powerful influence on society is exercised by a group of people who make all their value judgments casually, arbitrarily, without thought, without consideration, because they say—oh well, I am a scientist, and science is not concerned with those things."[22] Most important, these scientists failed to acknowledge the degree to which they adopted assumptions and techniques that pre-empted individual free will. Without referring to Skinner directly, Krutch anticipated a Skinnerian universe in which the social scientist sought to maximize human happiness but neglected to consult his supposed beneficiaries to find out what exactly they might consider happiness to be, opting instead to create a measurable, "scientific" index of happiness such as "production per man-hour." Such a social-engineering conception of the human condition, he charged, befit only a totalitarian society, in which the state set all social priorities and manipulated individuals toward their realization. "Both cultures against which we have waged war have been cultures which had developed further than we have the arts of applying experimental knowledge about human reaction to their populations," he reminded the panel.[23]

---

[21] Crane Brinton, A. L. Kroeber, Joseph Wood Krutch, and B. F. Skinner, "The Application of Scientific Method to the Study of Human Behavior," *American Scholar* 21, 2 (Spring 1952): 208.

[22] Ibid., 215.

[23] Ibid., 224.

The techniques of modern social science stood fundamentally at odds with the principles of individual autonomy and individual moral choice.

Krutch's warnings evoked the nineteenth-century Romantic fear that scientific and technological innovation would abolish human beauty, creativity, and uniqueness. Ultimately, he predicted, social engineering would produce the triumph of "unintelligent, uneducated people, at the expense of the heretic or simply the informed, independent and intelligent person."[24] To attempt to manage society scientifically could only involve the establishment of arbitrary and dangerously limiting conceptions of harmony and achievement. "My point is simply that I believe that the experience of living is the thing which for me has the greatest value," he declared, "and that all the social sciences which tend to manipulate and regularize and unify human conduct result in a general lowering of the intensity of the experience of living, and that, therefore, from my standpoint, they are bad."[25]

Skinner responded to Krutch's attacks by attempting to uphold the compatibility of social science and humanistic values. "If I had the power to design a successful state on the existing scientific knowledge—God forbid—then I would certainly not design a uniform sort of culture," he declared. "I should want great diversity, because I should want to make sure that all the various talents of the group should come to fruition in many different ways."[26] However, his defense convinced neither Krutch nor Brinton, both of whom perceived it as the recipe for a society with a scientifically formulated, controlling purpose that would defeat any ideal of diversity. Brinton objected that the talents Skinner valued "are all talents toward the end, and one end . . . an end which animates many social scientists—and that is to change things and other people."[27] Ultimately, the humanist arguments of Krutch and Brinton dominated the discussion. Krutch reiterated his argument from *The Measure of Man,* that the social scientist emphasized that which could be measured and predicted at the expense of other, more important dimensions of the human condition. When Skinner countered, "We cannot blame the social scientists for doing the things which they can do most successfully," he retorted, "No, I do not blame them, but I fear them."[28]

Krutch's emphasis on the dual critique of social science, that it both enforced a stultifying mediocrity and—as exemplified in his reference to Axis

---

[24] Ibid., 224.

[25] Ibid., 218.

[26] Ibid., 218.

[27] Ibid., 218.

[28] Ibid., 221.

tyranny—provided the techniques for dangerous new forms of coercion, provided the basis for an effective counterattack from professional sociologists. Once again, Merton assumed the role of sociology's spokesman, castigating the forum's participants in the subsequent issue of *The American Scholar* for their superficial, alarmist, and often contradictory musings about social science. So embarrassing were their mischaracterizations of social science, Merton charged, that they surely would have wished to edit the transcript of their discussion. Their most egregious error, however, remained the common tendency of social science's opponents to lambaste the professions for their innocuousness while cringing over the threat they posed to human freedom. Merton observed:

> It is affirmed in one breath, during this symposium, that social scientists cannot predict because they do not understand human behavior, and, in the next breath, that social scientists are truly dangerous creatures because they provide the knowledge of human behavior which enables men to be manipulated and managed for bad or stupid ends. Yet it would seem that knowledge will not provide this evil power unless it be true. (To choose one of the symposiasts' favorite analogies: evil intent is not enough to build an atom bomb; sound knowledge is also required.) If social science is unsound, it cannot be used to manage behavior, and if it is being used to manage behavior, it must, to that extent, be sound knowledge. Even Mr. Krutch cannot have it both ways.[29]

For Merton, the forum's more hostile participants shared one fundamental sentiment that lacked any connection to the true integrity of social science: that its various fields could be distilled into a single representation, a reified "social science" that called forth negative associations of the scientific ethos with organized frivolity and with inhuman techniques of domination. The symposium's participants from the humanities disciplines "simply do not *like* the social scientists," Merton complained, "and at this we cannot wonder, after seeing the horrific caricature of 'the' social scientist with which they live."[30]

---

[29] Robert K. Merton, "An Horrific Caricature," *American Scholar* 21, 3 (Summer 1952): 358.

[30] Ibid., 358. Merton himself downplayed the degree of Skinner's agreement with his own position. In fact, Skinner articulated in the symposium the very defense that Merton presented consistently on behalf of the social sciences, that they possessed neither the desire nor the capability to perform the kinds of manipulations upon the individual that the critics had alleged.

By the mid-1950s, critiques from a variety of quarters declared social science a recipe for domination, revealing among their authors a distinct pattern of political subtexts. Detractors on the left worried that the private sector would capitalize on new social science methods for purposes of molding Americans into passive, pliable workers and consumers. Conservatives, on the other hand, perceived in those methods the specter of coercive, and even totalitarian, government. Sociology thus found itself the target of ire from both ends of the political spectrum: although Merton's discovery of the frequent internal contradictions such arguments contained offered sociologists a line of defense, his promises of a benign, politically centrist, and disinterested profession offended those on the left who perceived in such an ethos a lack of moral or ideological resolve—fertile ground for co-optation by private interests—and those on the right who feared, for the same reason, a foundation for creeping socialism.

On the left, Cornell political scientist Andrew Hacker returned to the issue of sociology's vulnerability to misuse numerous times in the mid-1950s. A fierce anti-Skinnerian, Hacker posited the threat of social engineering more ably and with greater sophistication than had Krutch and Brinton in their more philosophical objections.[31] At the same time, he shared the widespread sense that social science's efforts in the realm of practical affairs stemmed precisely from a basic weakness, the "intellectual inferiority complex" it suffered relative to the status of the natural and physical sciences. As social scientists sought to demonstrate their respective fields' scientific validity by revealing their "practical applications" in industry and government, their good intentions inevitably succumbed to the exigencies of the particular institutional cultures in which they found themselves. Although they expressed an honest desire to solve society's problems, their participation in practical affairs necessarily reduced their outlook to the consideration of one overarching problem, that of the maintenance of order—as their clients defined and desired it. Hacker observed:

---

[31]Hacker attacked Skinner most forcefully in "Dostoevsky's Disciples," in *Journal of Politics* 17, 4 (November 1955): 390–413. His other forays into the subject of manipulative social science included "The Use and Abuse of Pareto in Industrial Sociology," *American Journal of Economics and Sociology* 14, 4 (July 1955): 321–34; "Utopia, Inc.," *Commonweal* 65, 9 (February 8, 1957): 479–81; and "Liberal Democracy and Social Control," *American Political Science Review* 51, 4 (December 1957): 1009–39. In "Utopia, Inc.," he argued that American intellectuals in general and social scientists in particular had forsaken visions of an ideal social order in favor of more limited aspirations that were compatible with perceived contemporary realities. Ironically, however, utopian ideals had then found a home in the corporate world. As its social engineers constructed "sophisticated plans for achieving the happiness of their subjects," it assumed responsibility for the Enlightenment cause that had motivated earlier generations of intellectuals (481). Hacker outlined his own justification of the active construction of utopian visions in "In Defense of Utopia," *Ethics* 65, 2 (January 1955): 135–40.

As the invited social scientist enters a factory or a prison or even a home for unmarried mothers, he has a set of *idées fixes* at the forefront of his mind. He must, he believes, adjust the maladjusted; he must make the unsociable sociable; he must redirect emotions from irrational to rational channels. However, one cannot speak of adjusting, socializing, and rationalizing in a vacuum. One is adjusted *to* a particular state of affairs; one is socialized *in* the context of a certain environment; and one's emotions are channelled according *to* a selected rationale. Hence, these processes which the social scientist undertakes must, of necessity, be based on predetermined ideas of what is a desirable state of affairs, social environment, or rationale. In this realm the social scientist is not free to pick up and choose as he likes. The assumptions that he will adopt will be those of the factory managers or the wardens or whoever it was that invited his aid.[32]

Hacker argued that social scientists' participation in business and governmental affairs compromised the very essence of the scientific work they promised to deliver, that of accurate prediction. In the natural sciences, prediction became possible when the scientist had formulated a controlled experiment, one in which he or she had accounted for the myriad of variables that might influence the result. In the case of the social sciences' participation in research for outside interests, however, a controlled experiment became that which fulfilled the ends of the client, such as higher productivity or the minimization of individual dissent. The result, which Hacker termed "Predictable Man," lacked independent will. His socialization into the organization was complete, and thus he no longer posed an obstacle to its smooth functioning. "Predictable Man cannot be a troublemaker because his troublemaking can be known beforehand, and measures to deal with it can be concocted," Hacker wrote. Therefore, "he is happy, loyal, cooperative, and respectful of authority."[33]

Hacker warned that such manipulative, order-driven social science denied the individual's humanity and capacity for autonomous agency. The social scientist's techniques for fostering individual adjustment replaced the individual personality with a group personality, one which abolished all "unsociable characteristics" that might impede organizational objectives. Organizations that abolished such characteristics ultimately abolished individual differences in general, so that individuals were rendered incapable of making indepen-

---

[32] Andrew Hacker, "The Specter of Predictable Man," *Antioch Review* 14, 2 (June 1954): 196–97.

[33] Ibid., 201.

dent choices. These circumstances constituted a grave threat to democracy, for the consent to the status quo that social science had engineered stemmed not from free debate but from the policies of the particular interests that employed the social scientist. Ultimately, the social scientist had abandoned the very ideal of a free society to serve narrow, practical ends. Hacker concluded:

> The modern social scientist has rejected the liberal-democratic conception of freedom. For the traditional notion of freedom presupposes alternative avenues of choice to be open to the individual. The social scientist would so adjust and socialize us that a single, predictable route would always be open to us whenever a decision had to be made. We would not, of course, be forced to take that road. But it would, once we were adjusted and socialized, be the only natural one for us to select.[34]

Hacker's critique constituted a frontal assault on the very idea of social science as a true science. Because it had tied its scientific aspirations to the demonstration of its practical utility, its success would depend inevitably upon its success in creating Predictable Man. "It is only if the conditions which surround our lives are 'altered, or otherwise controlled,'" he noted, appropriating the language of B. F. Skinner—"only if we will have been transformed into Predictable Man—that the science of human behavior will be able to call itself a true science and in that capacity to serve society."[35]

Perspectives like Hacker's regarding sociology's antidemocratic character also resonated within postwar American conservatism, to which the extreme and brutal social regimentation of Nazism and Stalinism appeared as manifestations of larger ideological and technical global trends. Conservatives, who had since the New Deal denounced social and economic planning as "creeping socialism" and had condemned the growing political authority of experts as invasive meddling, suspected modern social science of constructing piecemeal the totalitarian techniques that would abolish individual free will. Thus, like the congressional opponents of social science's inclusion within the National Science Foundation, who had expressed their misgivings about academic disciplines that seemed to them to be synonymous with socialism, conservative voices joined the clamor to denounce social scientists as officious transgressors against established moral authority.

---

[34] Ibid., 206.

[35] Ibid., 206.

This conservative critique found expression in a series of 1940s essays written by Friedrich A. von Hayek, the father of postwar conservatism.[36] Hayek's arguments, reproduced in his *The Counter-Revolution of Science* in 1955, ranged from philosophical repudiations of the idea of the social sciences' kinship with the natural sciences to shrill admonitions against social and economic planning, or the "conscious direction of social processes."[37] As Hayek expressed it, the conservative critique of social science reflected the conservative fear that liberal or "collectivist" efforts toward such ends threatened to impose upon the individual the will of a "specially favored class" or intellectual elite, ultimately rendering determinations of the true and the good inaccessible through the application of reason and empirical investigation. Scientism, then, produced a paradox of highly rationalized irrationality, in which "social engineers" imposed social consensus and techniques of social control upon masses of individuals, producing "a system in which all members of society become mere instruments of the single directing mind and in which all the spontaneous social forces to which the growth of the mind is due are destroyed."[38]

The postwar period witnessed the popularization of Hayek's perspective. A brief 1953 editorial in the *Saturday Evening Post* observed that many social scientists seemed to possess a disposition toward accepting uncritically "theories which are hostile to our form of social organization."[39] In 1956, in the wake of the Supreme Court's decision in *Brown v. the Board of Education of Topeka,* in which the Court relied upon the testimony of social scientists to establish segregation's harmful psychological effects, a *National Review* editorial found the "scientific investigation of society" in violation of natural law, for it replaced moral principles of justice with fraudulent, "objective" scientific rationales, ultimately producing a Skinnerian world which "would eliminate the individual completely from consideration." The editorial concluded with a repudiation of "the high priests of a 'science of man,' guided by nothing but their itch for control."[40] In another 1956 *National Review* piece,

---

[36]Friedrich A. von Hayek, "Scientism and the Study of Society," *Economica* 9, 35 (August 1942): 267–91; "Part II," *Economica* 10, 37 (February 1943): 34–63; "Part III," *Economica* 11, 41 (February 1944): 27–39.

[37]Hayek, *The Counter-Revolution of Science: Studies on the Abuse of Reason* (Glencoe, IL: Free Press, 1955).

[38]Ibid., 92. Robert Bannister, in *Sociology and Scientism* (Chapel Hill: The University of North Carolina Press, 1987), credits Hayek with having first used the term *scientism* in these articles to refer to the equation of social science with the other sciences.

[39]"How Scientific Are the Social Scientists?" *Saturday Evening Post* (June 13, 1953): 12.

[40]Frank S. Meyer, "Confusion in the Court," *National Review* 1, 8 (January 11, 1956): 22.

Richard M. Weaver accused social scientists of "scientific hubris," "materialistic monism," and of seeking "some millennial reconstruction of society" based on the assumption of "the infinite predictability and infinite manipulability of man."[41] As in the late-1940s National Science Foundation debate, sociology continued to conjure up impressions of a profession asserting a social-engineering ideology that violated the conservative conception of freedom and its foundation upon the thought and action of independent and freely competing individuals.

Moreover, the conservative condemnations of social science ran deeper than those of liberal or left-leaning critics. The latter simply objected to the misappropriation of social science expertise, whereas conservatives attacked the very validity of the claims to such expertise and the philosophical foundations of social science, asserting that its attempts to find sociological regularities in human behavior and relations threatened to overthrow the natural laws upon which civil society depended for a balance of both freedom and order. Thus, Albert Salomon, a German émigré historian of social thought at the New School for Social Research, asserted in 1955 that sociology's very origins lay in proto-totalitarian ideas. Comte and Saint-Simon, he argued, had made a "fatal mistake" in identifying their methods with those of the natural sciences, for they had elevated science to the status of an incontrovertible verity. Their scientific absolutism initiated the suppression of all "prescientific" thought, preparing the way for the totalitarianism of the twentieth-century. "The sociologists believed that a new world lay before them in which scientific planning, technical rationalization, and humanitarian education would be directed by anonymous social scientists who were subject to the laws of nature and of society, but not to the benighted authority of philosophers," Salomon wrote.[42] This optimism obscured a pernicious quest for absolute intellectual authority, for the science of society could not coexist with competing conceptions of social reality that would challenge its validity. Comte's and Saint-Simon's sociology therefore demanded "the total authority of their own school in administering its gospel—the pattern of total order," so that their scientific prescriptions for the rational transformation of society in the name of a humanitarian ideal" constituted to Salomon "a clearly articulated vision of a totalitarian society."[43]

---

[41] Richard M. Weaver, "Social Science in Excelsis," *National Review* 2, 19 (September 29, 1956): 18.

[42] Albert Salomon, *The Tyranny of Progress: Reflections on the Origins of Sociology* (New York: Noonday Press, 1955), 103. In an earlier essay in the regular column on social science issues in *Commentary*, Salomon had written of scientific sociology as a secular religion that advanced a spiritually impoverished vision of social perfectability. See his "Prophets, Priests, and Social Scientists," *Commentary* 7, 6 (June 1949): 594–600.

[43] Ibid., 104.

Although Salomon avoided indicting modern sociology for the sins of its fathers, he described the discipline as laboring under a poisonous patrimony that had demanded the absolute subordination of the individual to collective ends. This theme of social science's threat to the integrity of the individual also appeared in *Scientism and Values,* a 1960 collection of conservative attacks on sociological scientism edited by Helmut Schoeck, a sociologist at Emory University. Schoeck wrote that this scientism reflected a "cynical world view" that included a "doglike" or "ratlike" view of humanity. Reflecting the broader anti-Skinnerian backlash against scientific social control, he declared, "Man is best understood, so the scientistic expert holds, when seen from the level of a rodent eager to learn the ins and outs of a maze. He can be conditioned to put up with almost anything the few wise designers of the maze have mapped out for him."[44] Similarly, Murray N. Rothbard, a free-market economist and consultant, wrote that scientism created bogus analogies between human communities and organisms and between human beings and machines—or "servomechanisms"—thereby facilitating the manipulation of individuals, who could be "blueprinted and reshaped" in the name of mathematically rendered "models" of supposedly ideal social environments.[45] Henry S. Kariel, of Bennington College, charged that scientism's adherents stood at odds with humanism, that "there emerges a model indifferent to justice, indifferent to that indefinable human uniqueness that still makes it reasonable to speak of man's moral freedom and obliges us to keep the institution of politics in good repair."[46]

In 1961, Russell Kirk provided a distillation of these conservative salvos against social engineering in a more public forum. In *The New York Times Magazine,* the political scientist and regular *National Review* columnist cited Pitirim Sorokin's call in *Fads and Foibles* for a balancing of the scientific method with older humanistic modes of inquiry as evidence that mainstream sociologists had become scientistic "true believers," rejecting "humanitarian" models of inquiry in favor of that which could be measured and tabulated. Kirk characterized "the representative social scientist" as "an empiricist of the positivist variety," and asserted that, "emotionally, he is often a secular evangelist."[47] The scientization of sociology represented the discipline's desertion of democratic ideals and its descent into the realm of mass manipulation and

[44]Helmut Schoeck, introduction to Schoeck and James W. Higgins, eds., *Scientism and Values* (Princeton, NJ: D. Van Nostrand, 1960), x.

[45]Murray N. Rothbard, "The Mantle of Science," in Schoeck and Higgins, *Scientism and Values,* 165.

[46]Henry S. Kariel, "Social Science as Autonomous Activity," in Schoeck and Higgins, *Scientism and Values,* 258.

[47]Russell Kirk, "Is Social Science Scientific?" *New York Times Magazine* (June 25, 1961): 11.

social control. Kirk asked whether sociology's evolving methodological and technical refinements had engendered a philosophical withdrawal from ethical questions of concern to the American community as a whole, particularly that of the prospects for democratic culture. The sociologist, he declared, rather than enlarging the sphere of human freedom, sought more effective means of limiting that freedom through scientific manipulation: "His opinion polls, his analyses of out-groups, his indices of prejudice, his statistical computations of popular choice (and nowadays he is intoxicated with the computing machines), all are intended to convert mankind into a predictable and controllable species." The antidemocratic implications of such research, Kirk continued, thus placed the social scientists on the horns of a profound dilemma in a democratic society: "Today's humanitarian social scientist is discouraged by one hard fact," he asserted. "Only in totalitarian states have positivistic doctrines of social reconstruction on 'scientific' lines been applied thoroughly." In demanding legitimation for his scientific competence, the sociologist therefore risked encouraging a public perception of the social sciences as a training ground for antidemocratic techniques. Survey research, for example, provided not the basis for greater democratization of American life but rather a feeble legitimation of social scientists' scientific status. "So," Kirk concluded, the sociologist "is forced back upon studies in 'democratic behavior patterns'; but if 'democracy' is his ideal, how can he ever attain the status of priest-scientist that Comte ordained?"[48] Scientific sociology and democracy were not only incompatible but were inimical. Scientism in sociological work fostered intellectual elitism and a mere pretension to a healthier democracy.

Kirk concluded his polemic by demanding a return to time-honored approaches to the exploration of the nature of society. Enlightenment remained possible not through methodological and technical innovation in the name of "science" but rather though a renewed commitment to the Western intellectual tradition. "A large body of literature on the subject has long been available," he mused, "though often ignored by the novelty-seeking behavioral scientist. But the more important part of this literature is not 'scientific' in the strict modern sense. This knowledge is the work of poets, theologians, political theorists, moralists, jurists, and men of imagination generally."[49]

Once again, Merton rushed to his profession's defense, publishing his reply in *The New York Times Magazine* three weeks after Kirk's article appeared. By this time the pattern of the charges leveled against the profession had come to constitute a popular refrain, which compelled Merton to observe wearily that "the season of the antisociologists is upon us" and that,

---

[48] Ibid., 11.

[49] Ibid., 18.

this time, Kirk had merely "got in first."[50] As in his rebuttal to the *American Scholar* forum discussants, Merton upbraided the "anti-sociologists" collectively for their "grotesque" misrepresentation of the discipline and its methods. Significantly, he observed such stereotypes posed a danger to sociology largely because the public possessed little familiarity with the profession or what it did. Such charges, he asserted, imposed themselves upon "a public too busy to look for themselves," and they therefore required a response from sociologists themselves in the name of rescuing the profession's reputation.[51]

Merton's opening remark reflected again the relationship he and others conceived between scientific endeavor and the larger public sphere. Because the distractions of modern life hampered the lay person's understanding of this endeavor, sociological work necessarily proceeded with the tacit and minimally informed consent of the larger society. Redeeming sociology's public image therefore required demonstrating the relationship between its scientific integrity, its practical utility, and its benign—or, ideally, its salutary—effect on democratic practice. Merton set out first to call into question Kirk's sources and to reveal that once again sociology had been the victim of stereotyping. He began his rebuttal by noting Kirk's unfortunate reliance upon the authority of Sorokin to prove the fallacies of quantitative social research. Sorokin, Merton once again noted, had used statistics himself in each of his major works. Thus, each of Kirk's objections—to the statistics, the sociological jargon, and so on—constituted yet-another caricature of true sociology. All respectable sociologists resisted the kinds of transgressions against critical thinking Kirk claimed to find in the discipline as a whole. Sociologists could concur wholeheartedly with Kirk when he condemned jargon in sociology because they used not jargon but "technical language" to make the kinds of concise and efficient statements that everyday language could not convey. Jargon, Merton noted, was "a muddled and wordy imitation of technical language," and had no place in sociology.[52]

Merton then provided his now-standard counterattack to the antisociological position. Sociology's detractors wished to have it both ways, he claimed, for while they denied sociology's scientific legitimacy and the efficacy of its research methods, they also feared its antidemocratic potential.

---

[50]Robert K. Merton, "Now the Case *for* Sociology," *New York Times Magazine* (July 16, 1961): 14.

[51]Ibid., 19.

[52]Ibid., 14.

Clearly, the discipline could pose no threat to democracy if its methods lacked scientific integrity. Merton concluded:

> It would seem clear that, if there are no discoverable uniformities about man in society, there can be no sociological knowledge employed to regiment him. Should anti-sociologists admit that there are such uniformities, they can scarcely argue that these uniformities can be discovered by the defective sociology of today, with its inapplicable statistics, its tattered jargon, and its total misunderstanding of human nature.[53]

Conversely, if sociologists had indeed discovered such uniformities, Merton continued, the discipline's detractors would have to decide whether their alarm over the ends to which such discoveries would be put constituted a demand for intellectual repression. "Would they then propose to exorcise this knowledge for fear that it might be used to violate civilized values?" Merton asked. If so, "the anti-sociologists would join forces with the anti-intellectuals and totalitarian regimenters of thought they ostensibly combat."[54] Sociology's detractors had thus taken an intellectually indefensible position: either they had overreacted to a nonexistent threat or, if the threat did in fact exist, their opposition was tantamount to a plea for censorship.

Merton, characteristically, took a middle position between the two extremes. Sociology possessed scientific knowledge about social behavior, he declared, but that knowledge passed through the ethical filter of professionalism. "Today's sociology makes no attempt to substitute science for ethics and esthetics or to displace humanism with scientism," he promised. "Every responsible sociologist, and there are not a few, knows that his knowledge is no substitute for artistic thought."[55] Moreover, the antisociologists had overestimated the young discipline's potential not only for creating progress but for mischief as well. With the "exaggerated claims they make for our prowess and accomplishments," he concluded, "it is they, not we, who say that 'sociology is a power in the land.'"[56]

With his public reply to sociology's detractors, Merton again exploited the fundamental flaw in their combined position. Sociology could defend its scientific integrity by adopting a tone of modesty appropriate to the scientist.

---

[53] Ibid., 19.

[54] Ibid., 19.

[55] Ibid., 20.

[56] Ibid., 21.

Those who saw sociology as an exercise in irrelevance or a belaboring of the patently obvious had misunderstood sociology's incrementalist character, which required researchers' patient, methodical cooperation in the gradual accumulation of more knowledge about society. Sociology, a nascent science, could not yet offer society dramatic new discoveries or compelling, synthetic explanations of social phenomena.[57] On the contrary, like physics, it would have to slowly construct new knowledge out of the small building blocks of empirical and theoretical research. Moreover, as an immature science, sociology posed no threat to democracy, individual autonomy, or anything else, because it lacked the technical means to such ends. Merton's denial that sociology had become "a power in the land" reflected his faith in a disinterested sociology that embraced basic research.

Nevertheless, by the late 1950s, as the nation's confrontation with fascism receded and extremes of anticommunism subsided, the charge that social scientists too-often indulged in the explication of frivolous studies of trivial issues gained momentum, ultimately overshadowing the totalitarianism critique. Thus, in 1960, the year the National Science Foundation finally raised the social sciences to the divisional status enjoyed by the physical and biological sciences, August Heckscher, the director of the Twentieth Century Fund, would declare in a preface to the fund's annual report that sociological research, in its allegiance to standards of objective science and "nonutilitarian" ends, was becoming "increasingly divorced from deeds," so that it risked losing contact with the outside world. "It would be a tragedy," he warned, "if the modern foundation, under the false yoke of methodology or scientific objectivity, were to find itself cut off from the public it must serve."[58] The New York Times editors concurred with Heckscher, adding that "the catapulting need for intelligent action makes 'relevancy' and 'pertinence' more frighteningly urgent—often just for our continuing existence."[59] Although the editors emphasized that social research should remain "thorough and objective" and "truly scientific," and that scholars need not sacrifice these standards to purposive "programs of action," they urged that priority be

---

[57] Here, Merton reiterated his arguments of "Social Conflict Over Styles of Sociological Work," in Larry T. and Janice M. Reynolds, eds., The Sociology of Sociology (New York: David McKay, 1970), in which he contended that those who attacked sociologists for neglecting big problems in favor of trivia assumed that the research topic itself revealed the importance of a study. "There is no necessary relation between the socially ascribed importance of the object under examination and the scope of its implications for an understanding of how society or nature works," he had argued (186). Sociological knowledge possessed intrinsic value in this view, and thus, like the physicist, the sociologist worked in comfortable independence from the pressure for useful results.

[58] Quoted in New York Times (May 23, 1960): 31.

[59] NewYork Times (May 25, 1960).

given to projects "which will contribute the facts and projections thereof that wise policies demand—at the time when they are needed most."[60]

Although Merton's parries of the many barbs thrown at sociology by representatives across the political spectrum in the name of safeguarding democracy and individual will ably defended the profession's scientific credibility and its compatibility with democracy, the other arguments of the detractors proved more difficult to refute. Since Arthur Schlesinger's dismissive review of *The American Soldier* in 1949, journalists, historians, English professors, and others had exposed with great satisfaction sociology's alleged crimes against plain written expression, and defenses such as Merton's that sociology's obscure terminology constituted a kind of technical shorthand, an encapsulatory function that allowed for economy of expression, proved less than persuasive to those who perceived within it a professional elitism that undermined democratic discourse.

Indeed, Merton had importuned his professional peers quite explicitly to avoid the language of the public sphere in communicating their research findings and theoretical discoveries. In the 1949 edition of *Social Theory and Social Structure,* he had advised them to eschew lucid prose and literary stylings, for these threatened to undermine the scientific integrity of sociological scholarship. Instead, sociologists should construct "formal paradigms" that would codify and formalize sociological expression. This process would protect the scholar from lapsing into "highly discursive" language, in which "the logic of procedure, the key concepts, and the relationship between variables not uncommonly become lost in an avalanche of words." The authors of scientific work had to devote themselves assiduously to the maintenance of clarity in the concepts they used, avoiding the "unwitting employment of tacit concepts and assumptions."[61] Such a responsibility required that sociologists liberate themselves from generations of literary tradition to participate in the building of their science. Merton wrote:

Contributing to this tendency of the sociological exposition to become lengthy rather than lucid is the received tradition—inherited slightly from philosophy, substantially from history, and greatly from literature—which holds that sociological accounts should be written vividly and intensely, conveying all the rich fullness of the human scene with which they deal. The sociologist who does not disavow this handsome but alien heritage becomes more intent on expressing the

---

[60] Ibid.

[61] Robert K. Merton, *Social Theory and Social Structure: Toward the Codification of Theory and Research* (Glencoe, IL: Free Press, 1949), 13.

full individuality of his *response* to the sociological case in hand than on seeking out the generalizable, objective and readily transmissible concepts and relationships pertinent to that case. In place of using objective concepts—the very core of a science as distinct from the arts—the sociologist who depends on his heritage from the humanities searches for the exceptional constellation of words which will best express the particularity of his experience. Too often, he is confirmed in this misplaced use of his genuine artistic skills by the plaudits of a lay public, gratefully assuring him that he writes like a novelist and not like an overly-domesticated and academically henpecked Ph.D. On the other hand, as St. Augustine suggested in mild rebuttal long ago, "...a thing is not necessarily true because badly uttered, nor false because spoken magnificently."[62]

Graceful prose and public accolades therefore became for Merton a kind of seduction, luring the sociologist away from the scientific mission. Scientific writing suffered as its author aspired to literary grace, so that "the hard skeleton of fact, inference, and theoretic conclusion becomes overlaid with the soft flesh of stylistic ornamentation."[63]

Instead, Merton's sociologist would emulate the styles of expression characteristic of physics, chemistry, biology, geology, and statistics, which Merton observed to have "escaped this misplaced concern with the literary graces." Because each was "anchored to the purposes of science," it exhibited "brevity, precision and objectivity" and avoided "exquisitely rhythmic patterns of language, richness of connotation and deep-felt verbal imagery."[64] Moreover, that Merton's sentiments remained consistent throughout the fifties became clear with the publication nearly a decade later of the second edition of *Social Theory and Social Structure*, in which his warning acquired a new stridency. To his earlier admonition, he added that the sociologist who wrote like a novelist often sabotaged entirely the communication of his research results. "Not infrequently, and of course not always," he declared, such a scholar "pays for this popular applause, for the closer he approaches eloquence, the farther he retreats from sense."[65] As a form of scientific expression, then, Mertonian sociological writing defined itself by its independence from broader, more accessible forms of communication, a separation that Todd Gitlin has char-

---

[62]Ibid., 13–14.

[63]Ibid., 14.

[64]Ibid., 14.

[65]Robert K. Merton, *Social Theory and Social Structure*, 2nd ed. (Glencoe, IL: Free Press, 1957), 14.

acterized as the result of a deliberate process of "sanctification," in which the profession's identity depends upon "profaning what sociology is not." Sociology's "inward-turning, hard-to-decipher prose," Gitlin observes, constitutes "the mystery that enshrines the authority of the clerisy."[66]

However, if a style of expression appropriate only to sociology satisfied the requisites of scientific authority, it also served to proclaim to sociology's detractors that the profession had dedicated itself to intellectual irrelevance. The cultural historian and Columbia dean Jacques Barzun observed that those intellectual pursuits that existed as but "imitations" of physics and mathematics reflected a more general proliferation of "pseudo-jargon," which "gives routinized men satisfaction by being the easiest form of originality," so that "each violation" of common speech "re-enacts a small declaration of independence." Jargon offered an effortless route to discursive autonomy for those who would bestow upon their science "the superstition of mystery and omnipotence."[67] Other observers expressed similar disappointment with the recondite scholarship they encountered. In a disparaging review of books by Leonard Reissman, Seymour Lipset, William Kornhauser, and Pitirim Sorokin, George Lichtheim wrote sardonically in *Partisan Review* that sociology "offers the layman more entertainment, and a wider range of contrasts in tone and substance, than any other intellectual discipline, not excluding psychoanalysis."[68] William F. Buckley opined in *The National Review* that "an incredible amount of mischief goes on under the general franchise of sociology, much of it terribly elusive, windy and amorphous," and he cited specifically its "strange and terrifying and tirelessly abundant jargon."[69] John Pfeiffer, science editor for the *New York Times,* noted in the midst of a review of Sorokin's *Fads and Foibles* that Sorokin himself had committed the same sins against clear communication of which he had accused his professional peers.[70]

Malcolm Cowley, the literary critic and then-book review editor of *The New Republic,* offered one of the more comprehensive tirades against

---

[66]Todd Gitlin, "Sociology for Whom? Criticism for Whom?" in Herbert J. Gans, ed., *Sociology in America* (Newbury Park, CA: Sage, 1990), 216.

[67]Jacques Barzun, *The House of Intellect* (New York: Harper & Brothers, 1959), 237, 244. Barzun would attack the social sciences more directly in 1964, when he chastised them for using their "discoveries" of a multitude of supposed behavioral regularities to destroy the idea of selfhood and replace it with manipulation. See his *Science: The Glorious Entertainment* (New York: Harper & Row, 1964).

[68]George Lichtheim, "Is There a Sociologist in the House?" *Partisan Review* 27, 2 (Spring 1960): 309.

[69]William F. Buckley, *National Review* 1, 19 (March 28, 1956): 22.

[70]John Pfeiffer, "A Manner of Speaking," *New York Times Book Review* (October 21, 1956): 35.

sociology's abuses of language. In expression much like that of Schlesinger in his review of *The American Soldier*, Cowley excoriated the profession's "barbarous jargon," likening sociological expression to "a language that has to be learned almost like Esperanto." Sociologists exhibited a predilection for neologisms that they applied without sufficient justification to "the commonest actions, feelings, and circumstances."[71] Cowley singled out a particular sociologist and, three years before C. Wright Mills popularized the practice in *The Sociological Imagination*, castigated him for exemplifying the worst tendencies of the discipline as a whole. He chose as his sacrificial victim Norman E. Green, the deputy director of the Office of Social Science Progress at the Air Force's Personnel and Training Research Center.[72] In a 1956 article in the *American Sociological Review*, Green had, among other offenses, expended ninety-four words in advancing the common-sense proposition that "rich people lived in good neighborhoods." In another instance, Cowley found that Green had used one-hundred and sixty words to express what in lay language could have been conveyed in thirty-three. Cowley concluded that Green's "private language" constituted a deliberate communicative secession from lay discourse through a conscious effort to "inflate or transmogrify" the meaning of what had been written. "No less than forty-nine percent of Mr. Green's prose consists of words from foreign or classical languages," Cowley complained. "By this standard of measurement, his article is more abstruse than most textbooks of advanced chemistry and higher mathematics, which are said to contain only forty percent of such words."[73] Green's overwhelming reliance on arcane language and neologisms could only bewilder the reader, who "feels that he is picking his way through a field of huge boulders."[74]

Cowley then turned to the verbiage endemic to sociology as a whole. He noted the preponderance of nouns, which rendered sociological writing "gritty," like "sanded sugar." Pronouns, on the other hand, were sorely lacking, for sociologists flatly refused to announce their presence in their own research with the use of the first person. "On rare occasions," he observed, the sociologist "calls himself 'we,' like Queen Elizabeth speaking from the throne, but he usually avoids any personal form and writes as if he were a force

---

[71] Malcolm Cowley, "Sociological Habit Patterns of Linguistic Transmogrification," *The Reporter* 15, 4 (September 20, 1956): 41.

[72] Significantly, Cowley neglected to identify Green's position within the U.S. military. Green, a lieutenant colonel and Air Force systems analyst, hardly exemplified the detached professional obscurantist Cowley sought to identify as sociology's ideal type.

[73] Ibid., 42.

[74] Ibid., 42.

of nature."[75] In a similar manner, sociological language avoided second-person pronouns, ostensibly to confer an air of objectivity upon the author's assertions, so that "the sociologist pretends to be speaking not to living persons but merely for the record."[76] Finally, the prevalence of third-person, passive-voice expression in sociology articles facilitated their authors' seeming detachment from their own assertions. Cowley explained that this manner of writing rendered sociological discourse wholly impersonal: " 'It was hypothesized,' we read, or 'It was found to be the case.' Found by *whom?*" he asked.[77]

In 1960, Murray Kempton, the prominent journalist known for his iconoclasm and deep contempt for elitist arrogance, joined the clamor to harangue the sociological profession, reporting in a *New York Post* article on his visit to the annual meeting of the American Sociological Association. Kempton characterized the proceedings as an overwhelming Babel of separate researches, only a small fraction of which any single individual could hope to digest. "There are close to 500 different papers," Kempton reported, adding that "the press room where they are set out for the enlightenment of the journalist looks like a warehouse for the storage of telephone books."[78] Moreover, the quality of the papers left much to be desired. Kempton noted sociology's "remorseless pursuit of proof of what everyone knew all along," which made the profession "the most democratic of sciences," in which "a man need only write to publish and join his voice to a common gabble." Ultimately, sociological writing constituted merely "inferior journalism, or exposition of the perfectly obvious, or timidity about expressing what is not perfectly obvious or crocheting the irrelevant."[79]

Several months later, the journal *Sociological Inquiry* republished Kempton's observations and accompanied them with a rejoinder from Robert E. L. Faris, a 1930s Chicago graduate and the department head at the University of Washington. Faris argued that Kempton had failed to take sociology's evolution seriously and had neglected the growing significance of its contributions. "The truth is that we *are* adolescent, our voice is changing, and we *are* trying to be noticed," he wrote. "Even our most feeble papers feed a columnist in these times when thumb-sucking can give content to newspaper columns." However, sociology had failed to receive adequate credit for its

---

[75] Ibid., 43.

[76] Ibid., 43

[77] Ibid., 43.

[78] Murray Kempton, "Social Notes on the A.S.A. Meetings," *Sociological Inquiry* 31, 2 (Spring 1961): 180. This article originally appeared in *The New York Post* (August 31, 1960).

[79] Ibid., 181.

modest successes, for journalists like Kempton chose to emphasize formal aspects of the profession that lay observers could not hope to understand or appreciate. "The functions of a national meeting—such as: exchange of research discoveries, discussion and decision on problems of the profession, efficient allocation of persons to positions, and a variety of productive types of interstimulation—are understood by us but these do not entertain the subway reader," Faris asserted.[80] Such comments reflected once again the precept that the processes of professional sociology existed necessarily in isolation from popular understanding.

Significantly, Kempton returned to the fray shortly thereafter with another, larger lampoon of sociology in *Playboy* magazine. Like Cowley, he belittled the sociologists' use of a debased pseudo-language and provided a litany of examples of its preoccupation with time-tested truisms such as, "Homicide is more frequent among persons alienated and demoralized." More significant, however, was his perception of an ominous trend toward lay usage of sociological language. "Sociologese," he declared, had made inroads into public discourse and threatened to become public currency. "The sociologist both serves what he calls mass culture and infects it," he charged, for his "pervasive voice," now appeared in various mass publications such as *Redbook* and *Cosmopolitan,* in the form of trivial research results on subjects such as marriage and suburban life. As a consequence, nonsociologists had begun to use the language of sociology. "We can measure the awful new authority of the profession when we observe that its victims have begun to imitate their inquisitors," Kempton wrote.[81]

Kempton insisted that sociology's willful obscurantism and its paucity of meaningful discoveries rendered its new public presence wholly and irredeemably fraudulent. "Their intellectual aspirations appear to be all too humble," he lamented. "They aim low and what ducks they hit are sitting." Sociologists had, for example, "proven" such readily apparent truths as that "most students believe that getting good grades is a necessity they must take into account." Their research techniques, moreover, were "useless for problem-solving—so much so that sociologists have shown a general tendency in recent years to flee from the confrontation of practical problems."[82] Thus, their lack of real sophistication meant that they could not possibly replace more traditional sources of insight into the human condition. A novelist like Faulkner or a musician like W. C. Handy revealed American society's

---

[80]Robert E. L. Faris, "Anti-Social Notes on Social Notes," *Sociological Inquiry* 31, 2 (Spring 1961): 182.

[81]Murray Kempton, "Status-Ticians in Limbo," *Playboy* (September 1961): 117.

[82]Ibid., 118, 120.

richness with greater sensitivity than the results of any public opinion poll, Kempton promised.

Kempton's article reflected the degree to which the publication of Mills's *The Sociological Imagination* two years earlier had sharpened and helped to diffuse particular approaches to the public unmasking of sociology's scientific pretensions. To illustrate how sociologists, in the absence of meaningful results to show for their efforts, used obscure language simply to disguise the fraudulence of their claims to scientific status, Kempton appropriated Mills's technique of excerpting Parsons's abstruse prose. Noting only that "an unusually literate Columbia University sociologist" had unmasked his own profession's obscurantism in print, he duplicated Mills's reproduction of a passage of Parsonian theory and then provided his own translation in simple English. "Is this not inelegantly reducible to a simple proposition?" he asked.[83]

Kempton concluded that sociologists' abstruse manner of communication served the function of a calculated mystification in the name of promoting their scientific status. Such an evasion of responsibility for clear communication constituted a deliberate secession from public discourse:

> Sociology's more realistic professionals confess the inadequacies of their field and blame them on its adolescence as a science no further along in its progress than chemistry and physics were in the Seventeenth Century. If that is the case, then no science has ever rushed so precipitately toward a private speech isolated from the comprehension of the society around it. Persons innocent of physics can read Newton without particular pain or puzzlement, and the cultivated society of his time could do even better. The men who advanced the natural sciences seem, in fact, to have made a special effort to speak clearly; the charlatans and the deluded who hampered them had a monopoly on bizarre and incomprehensible language. Only the alchemists were arcane; it helped them in their business.[84]

Kempton's essay, contemptuous in tone and malicious in intent, exemplified the journalistic dismissal of academic claims to a scientific understanding of society. Like Schlesinger in his attack on *The American Soldier* over a decade earlier, Kempton insisted that obscurantist sociological scholarship would never supplant the insights of sensitive men of letters. Sociologists and their society," he concluded, "celebrate together the marriage

---

[83] Ibid., 120.

[84] Ibid., 122.

of pretension with bad journalism. And in both the heart dies in the bos-om."[85] Like Cowley, Kempton favored time-tested avenues to enlightenment, those which offered themselves as expressions of humanity rather than as products of obscure standards of academic professionalism.

Several sociologists responded to these charges that their scholarly pur-suits constituted exercises in banality and convoluted expression. In partic-ular, they attacked their critics for their backward thinking, asserting that their attacks constituted repudiations of science itself and its linear pro-gression toward ever-more reliable analysis and prediction. Sociologists, the heirs of the Enlightenment, faced a broad threat of retrenchment from the rest of society, from the reactionaries and skeptics who sought to arrest hu-manity's progression beyond prejudice and superstition. Significantly, their arguments, like Merton's, contained the assumption that sociologists' proper audiences remained other sociologists. After all, critics like Krutch, Kirk, and Kempton in particular, in their lack of professional social science training, displayed a willful ignorance about the systematic study of society and could therefore offer only uninformed and unsophisticated complaints about those who engaged in it.

Thus, Benett Berger would write in 1957 that the antisociologists' objec-tions constituted a misunderstanding of scientific authority. Berger, a sociol-ogy graduate student at Berkeley, asserted in "Sociology and the Intellectuals," a pivotal article on sociology's public reputation, that the sociologists' com-mitment to "the traditions of science" and the communication of their results not to "a general literate audience but to a community of their colleagues" negated the charges of triviality, obscurantism, and unintelligibility leveled at the profession throughout the 1950s. Such objections "cannot seem other than beside the point," he insisted, for scientific sociological work was not intended for the lay reader. "The continuing application of aesthetic criteria of judgment to a nonaesthetic pursuit" simply indicated the detractors' unwillingness to grant scientific status to sociology.[86] Berger's assessment demonstrates clearly how the professional sociological identity stood at odds with a public identity. The mantle of science functioned to cloister those pursuits that honored its standards, separating the sanctified from the spurious.

Other sociologists invoked Weber's concept of disenchantment to convey sociology's emergence from a prescientific social order into a scientific one, admitting that this transition involved an appreciable cost, but that such a

---

[85] Ibid., 122.

[86] Bennett Berger, "Sociology and the Intellectuals: An Analysis of a Stereotype," *Antioch Review* 17, 3 (September 1957): 280.

sacrifice remained necessary for knowledge to progress. Edward Shils therefore characterized sociology's naysayers as "intellectual reactionaries" and dismissed their complaints about sociology's "literary inelegance" as a "rearguard action."[87] Shils perceived in sociology's "enemies" a stubborn adherence to a prescientific worldview when it came to the study of society, which rendered them captives to the illusions of the past. Thus, he defended Parsons's theoretical constructions as evidence of the "*medicina forte*" required by modern theorizing, and he declared that despite the "grounds for ribaldry" it afforded so many, the progress of such valuable work remained inevitable. "The fact remains," he declared, "that inferiors, however much they scoff, know their betters; and the theory goes on imposing itself, even on those who believe they are rejecting it."[88] Science, an inexorable force, promised to overcome the cultural impediments before it, and Shils, like Weber, demanded a tough-minded, stoical resolve among those who would accept its difficult challenge.

Seymour Martin Lipset similarly invoked the theme of disenchantment when he observed that, in sociology's public struggles, individuals of "political sensitivity" and "broad moral concerns" contributed "most of the vitriol." When they applied these expectations to sociology, they inevitably saw a discipline "becoming less problem-oriented, less vital, less concerned, less committed, less historical, less humanistic, more sterile, and more conservative politically—and the worse for all these things."[89] For Lipset, these stalwart humanists represented the prescientific moralism that modern science sought to overcome. In language evocative of Weber, he concluded that sociology's scientific strivings produced "a sense of loss" in such individuals, as their traditional worldview succumbed to modernity's rationalization of thought and action. By contrast, the practitioners of science exhibited the kind of dispassionate temperament necessary for the progress of knowledge. They "tended more to 'go about their business,'" Lipset observed, and they had proved "much less defensive, aggressive, and vigorous on their side of the controversy."[90] Like Merton, Lipset asserted obliquely that history lay on the side of this latter group that, in the secularized modern world, possessed

---

[87] Edward Shils, "The Calling of Sociology," in Talcott Parsons, Edward Shils, Kaspar Naegele, and Jesse R. Pitts, eds., *Theories of Society: Foundations of Modern Sociological Theory* (New York: Free Press, 1961), 1409.

[88] Ibid., 1410.

[89] Seymour Martin Lipset, "The Setting of Sociology in the 1950's," in Lipset and Neil Smelser, eds., *Sociology: The Progress of a Decade* (Englewood Cliffs, NJ: Prentice-Hall, 1961), 8.

[90] Ibid., 8.

the values and professional civility necessary for progress. Much as the Enlightenment had deprived the individual of the comforts of absolute religious faith and divinely sanctioned authority, modern social inquiry required that people learn to live without their gods. In the age of the End of Ideology, society no longer needed—in fact, could no longer afford—the passion of the moralist.

8

The Perils of Popularity

Public Sociology and Its Antagonists

While scholars such as Merton, Lipset, and Berger struggled actively and publicly against their nonsociologist critics during the 1950s and early 1960s, other sociologists fought a rearguard battle against those who would trespass upon the scientific authority sociology had declared for itself, as well as against those from among their number who had attracted, willfully or unintentionally, a broad popular audience. Taking aim at popular journalists and the few scholars who had attained a high public profile, these defenders of disciplinary integrity lamented the alleged simplification of sociological research that such accessibility necessarily engendered, citing the potential for such popular work to foster public misperceptions of the very nature of sociological inquiry and warning of the danger it posed to the profession's scientific evolution. Thus, Arnold M. Rose, a University of Chicago graduate and a professor at the University of Minnesota, condemned "humanistic intellectuals who would be sociologists while rejecting the rigorous requirements of science," declaring that "they add nothing to the total of human achievement if they practice an amateur sociology for an uninformed audience when a more scientific sociology is available."[1]

---

[1] Arnold M. Rose, discussion of Berger's "Sociology and the Intellectuals," *Antioch Review* 17, 4 (December 1957): 505. As an example, Rose cited an advertisement for *Mass Culture*, the Bernard Rosenberg–edited collection of essays by prominent postwar intellectuals, which Rose repudiated as a trivialization of legitimate sociological work.

The example of Vance Packard reveals the degree to which the profession opposed the incursion of amateurism and moralistic humanism into its self-declared sphere of competence. Packard, a journalist, had by 1960 reached the best-seller lists three times in four years, with *The Hidden Persuaders* in 1957, *The Status Seekers* in 1959, and *The Waste Makers* in 1960. He explored a myriad of sociological issues in these books, including commercial interests' recent successes in exploiting people's anxieties to sell products, the intensi-fication of Americans' race for social status, and the wastefulness of consumer culture. In a direct affront to many sociologists, he had relied heavily on sociological research, including that of E. Digby Baltzell, Bernard Barber, Richard Centers, August Hollingshead, Joseph A. Kahl, W. Lloyd Warner, William F. Whyte, and Bevode C. McCall.

As Daniel Horowitz observes in his biography of Packard, the sociolo-gists who reviewed Packard's work continually berated him for asserting an old-fashioned, small-town conservatism that they insisted had no place in modern American life. William Peterson, an early-1950s Columbia Ph.D., attacked Packard's nostalgic representations of the satisfaction earlier gener-ations of Americans found in their work, and he ridiculed Packard's senti-mental recounting of the serenity of a Spanish fishing village he had visited.[2] Seymour Martin Lipset complained that Packard, an "old-fashioned con-servative," failed to propose "serious institutional reforms" to solve the prob-lems he described and that instead he fell back on empty appeals to traditional values, such as that American consumers insist upon quality goods to mitigate status competition and conspicuous consumption.[3] Lewis Coser similarly de-rided *The Status Seekers* as "*Kitsch* sociology," which was "anchored in nothing more substantial than a guilty nostalgia for a supposedly less status-conscious and hence less anxiety-ridden past."[4] Together, as Horowitz maintains, such criticisms evidenced sociologists' desire to preserve their scientific status against older forms of social criticism that remained "adversarial, humanistic, moral, or historical."[5]

Thus, even scholars like Coser, the editor of *Dissent* and clearly a critic of the liberal consensus of the 1950s, could find common ground with more

---

[2] William Peterson, review of *The Status Seekers*, in *American Sociological Review* 25, 1 (February 1960): 125.

[3] Seymour Martin Lipset, "The Conservatism of Vance Packard," *Commentary* 31, 1 (January 1961): 81–82.

[4] Lewis Coser, "Kitsch Sociology," *Partisan Review* 26, 3 (Summer 1959): 482.

[5] Daniel Horowitz, *Vance Packard and American Social Criticism* (Chapel Hill: University of North Carolina Press, 1994), 189.

liberal voices like that of Lipset, as together they sought to defend the Weberian project of dispassionate sociological analysis. As Horowitz admits, Packard's critics possessed some justification in objecting to Packard's appropriations and oversimplifications of extant sociological research, but he also notes how Packard's efforts to bring sociological issues to a public readership provoked an overreaction to the apparent threat he posed to sociology's scientific status. Horowitz reveals that the most vociferous attacks on Packard during the 1950s emanated not from the highly quantitative or theoretical camps of Lazarsfeld, Merton, Parsons and others, but rather from public-minded scholars such as Coser and Lipset. Horowitz explains this seeming paradox in terms of the public sociologists' desire to secure intellectual authority for the communication of sociological material to lay readers, and thus, "they were making it clear that professors could enter the arena of intellectual discourse from above but most journalists could not do so from below."[6] Indeed, Peterson had complained in his review of *The Status Seekers* that Packard, as a journalist, by definition possessed "no necessary competence to discuss America's social structure."[7] To sociologists who did desire a broader audience works like Packard's represented incursions upon their rightful sphere of expertise.

However, Packard's books did more than simply offer condensed versions of sociological studies in a framework of cultural conservatism. Packard also reinforced the existing negative image of social scientists forged by William H. Whyte, Joseph Wood Krutch, Andrew Hacker, and others, namely, that social scientists were busily constructing the means for the manipulation of humanity through insidious forms of "social engineering," aspects of social research that Merton and Berger had insisted were neither germane to, nor practicable within, sociology. In *The Hidden Persuaders,* for example, Packard documented how marketing agencies had enlisted "hundreds" of professional social scientists—ranging from "buck-happy" researchers to "very serious, competent" scholars—to refine the techniques of the burgeoning "motivation research" subindustry of modern advertising. Advertising companies had employed these social scientists to produce "M.R." studies that would enable them to reach into consumers' deep unconscious

---

[6]Ibid., 190. As Horowitz notes, the editors of the new journal *Trans-action,* co-published by Irving Louis Horowitz and Alvin Gouldner with the goal of popularizing sociology among lay readers, also took the offensive against Packard in one of its early issues. See "Is Vance Packard Necessary?" in *Trans-action* 2 (January–February 1965): 13–17.

[7]Peterson, review of *The Status Seekers,* 125. Peterson also characterized as "dubious" some of Packard's sources, such as Richard Centers and C. Wright Mills.

and subconscious motivations and to "precondition" them to consume particular goods and services.[8]

Packard's books thus publicized potentially damning evidence of the social sciences' active participation in mass manipulation for commercial purposes, which posed a challenge to those who would defend their work as disinterested, "scientific" sociology. Hence, in a review of *The Waste Makers*, Lipset rejected pointedly Packard's "Machiavellian" conception of modern mass marketing, claiming that the status seeking and conspicuous consumption he described, rather than being the work of "evil businessmen and advertisers," were more than likely "inherent in *institutions* based on American democratic values."[9] Although he avoided any mention of the role Packard ascribed to social scientists in the latter possibility, his review served to combat the broader conspiratorial climate of opinion regarding the nefarious applications of social science research. After all, he noted, Packard's books "are largely bought by those whose behavior they seem most violently to be attacking,"[10] as though Packard himself had as much or more to do with the spread of new methods of mass persuasion than did those interests he decried. Lipset's benign, Mertonian view of professional sociology demanded a defense of allied, modern institutions as equally benign.

Packard therefore contributed to sociology's ongoing legitimation crisis on not two, but three levels. He assumed the role of a modern philosophe, converting complex sociological concepts into readily accessible forms, which contrasted with professional sociologists' increasingly apparent refusal to do so themselves. His perspective, as Horowitz makes clear, resembled that of the antimodernist muckraker, one who remained willing to moralize about what he viewed as the pernicious aspects of modernity, despite the dispassionate, professionalized, and "scientific" temper of his age. Finally, like Andrew Hacker, he informed his readers repeatedly that a host of shady, manipulative sorts inhabited the world of professional social research. Unscrupulous sociologists, anthropologists, and psychologists, armed with the latest research techniques, assisted in the ongoing invasion of the individual subconscious, in the name of persuading people to buy things they didn't want or need, to invade their privacy, and to transform their lives into an endless round of status competition. Thus, he appeared in the role of the defender of the very public interests that, ironically, professional social scientists themselves often threatened to undermine.

---

[8] Vance Packard, *The Hidden Persuaders* (New York: David McKay, 1957), 29–30.

[9] Lipset, "The Conservatism of Vance Packard," 81.

[10] Ibid., 80.

Popularizers of sociology such as Packard exerted an additional effect on the struggle between the scientific identity and its critics. As Packard, David Riesman, and C. Wright Mills in particular introduced lay readers to sociological concepts, analysis, and styles of expression, sociology's detractors acquired concrete scholarly material that helped to crystallize and to define their own opinions of the profession. The "humanism" of Riesman and Mills seemed to contrast with the narrow, microscopic, and clinical perspectives of their colleagues. As Bennett Berger observed in "Sociology and the Intellectuals," the profession suffered under a pervasive "hostile stereotype" perpetuated by "humanistic intellectuals," a stereotype that popular works by professional social scientists and sociologists helped to reinforce. These humanistic critics found that they could point to such apparently more public-minded scholars as examples of what the rest of the field's practitioners should be doing.

Berger observed that, among the most widely influential works in sociology since the war, the "big books"—*The American Soldier, The Authoritarian Personality, The Lonely Crowd, White Collar,* and *The Power Elite*—differed profoundly in their authors' professed intent and in their actual content. He labeled the latter three books, those written by Riesman and Mills, "intellectual" works, for they "use data to illustrate a 'thesis.'" Although Berger neglected the larger question of the validity of works that lacked a thesis, his contrast nevertheless reflected his sense that popularization exacerbated the conflicted nature of sociology's public identity. Of Riesman's and Mills's works, he wrote:

They are clearly commentaries and interpretations of contemporary experience, and as such are grist for the intellectual's mill. It is this that makes them "interesting" and reviewable in the prominent periodicals of the intellectuals. *The American Soldier* and *The Authoritarian Personality* are less "interesting" to intellectuals because their primary intent is to report facts, not to diagnose, warn, or exhort. Nothing can kill an argument as quickly as a fact.[11]

Berger's dichotomies—"theses" versus facts, and interpretation versus objective reportage—reflect the discomfort with which many mainstream sociol-

---

[11] Bennett Berger, "Sociology and the Intellectuals: An Analysis of a Sterotype," *Antioch Review* 17, 3 (September 1957): 286n. Significantly, Berger was explicit about the public's comparatively favorable attitudes about social research. "Anyone who has done extensive interviewing of the 'popular mind' knows that ordinary people are generally naïvely interested as well as pleased and flattered to be interviewed by a social scientist; it takes considerable sophistication to feel disdainful of and superior to the poised pencil of the interviewer" (276).

ogists greeted popular sociological writing. Works that reflected advocacy and interpretation served to equip sociology's enemies with the means to condemn the profession. Although Berger conceded the value of such works, he feared that the "hostile stereotypes" that nonsociologist intellectuals had already popularized would discourage the production of the more scientific research upon which the discipline depended.

Indeed, that Berger's concerns were well-founded is evident in the professional and public experiences of David Riesman. Riesman's 1950s academic career illustrates clearly the ambiguous position of the social scientist as popularizer, one whose success in generalizing sociological concepts and ideas provided both ammunition for sociologists' critics and punishment in the form of professional antagonism and marginalization. Riesman's training in law rather than in social science research meant at the outset that his identity lay somewhat apart from that which mainstream sociologists internalized in their graduate work. Between 1939 and 1950, the majority of his published articles appeared in legal journals and dealt with juridical themes and issues that, although explored broadly, lay outside of social science discourse. Moreover, he entered professional social research as a professor in the University of Chicago's Department of Social Science rather than the Sociology Department. His professional relationship with Nathan Glazer, another scholar who engaged in both public and academic writing, grew out of his respect for the critical and often skeptical perspectives on social science research Glazer offered in his columns in *Commentary*, writings that left Riesman "impressed with [Glazer's] thoughtfulness and range," as well as the fact that Glazer "could write very well and had wide-angle curiosity."[12] Thus, in the second collaborative article the two published, Riesman and Glazer offered a critique of public opinion research, joining Merton in assessing the status of such research in the face of the embarrassing election predictions of 1948, and warning that effective polling required greater sensitivity to the social-structural foundations of opinions.[13]

Riesman expressed significant misgivings about the prevailing postwar trends in American social science even before the publication of *The Lonely Crowd* thrust them to the forefront of his professional concerns. In a 1949 letter to Lionel Trilling, he wrote:

I am so very glad that in your letter you took the chance to tell of your own work and life and of the fact that what I have written makes

---

[12] Author interview with David Riesman, Winchester, Massachusetts, September 3, 1995.

[13] See Riesman and Glazer, "The Meaning of Opinion," *Public Opinion Quarterly* 12, 4 (Winter 1948–1949): 633–48.

sense to you in these personal terms. I am, as you can well imagine, constantly challenged by my colleagues in the social sciences on account of my methods. They always ask me, "Where is the proof? How do we know you are not just establishing a cult?" (The latter was the charge Merton made over a year ago.)[14]

Riesman's conception of social research thus confronted directly the central issues of postwar debate over the nature of social research. Scientific verifiability militated against the kind of speculative, open-ended, and interdisciplinary inquiry he valued.

With the publication of *The Lonely Crowd* in 1950, Riesman presented professional sociology with a powerful counterexemplar to the kind of scientific work it professed to practice, one that came quickly to represent "good sociology" to nonprofessional readers. The book's journalistic and often speculative methodology, which featured freewheeling observations on popular culture and a dearth of statistical substantiation, made its insights, whatever their sociological validity, intelligible to masses of readers. In addition, as it addressed the contemporary human condition from a broad, humanistic perspective, it possessed an immediacy and a broad relevance that enhanced its appeal. As Herbert J. Gans notes in a study of sociological best sellers, the most popular works of sociology over the last four decades share this common objective of exploring American society at large in an interdisciplinary manner.[15] Moreover, *The Lonely Crowd* dealt in particular with large questions of concern to an increasingly introspective society.[16] As Canadian sociologist Dennis H. Wrong observed in 1956, the book's popularity stemmed from "its challenging assertion of a number of things about American society that many people were beginning to sense, but had not yet succeeded in articulating clearly."[17] Similarly, Eric Larabee, the former editor of *Harper's*, noted in a 1961 issue of the magazine that the release of *The Lonely Crowd* "coincided with an onset of national self-analysis," in which social dimensions of modern American life had stimulated a new interest among a

---

[14]David Riesman to Lionel Trilling, September 5, 1949, Lionel Trilling Papers, Box 5, Rare Books and Manuscripts Library, Columbia University.

[15]Herbert J. Gans, "Best-Sellers by Sociologists: An Exploratory Study," *Contemporary Sociology* 26, 2 (March 1997): 133. Gans cites works such as Philip Slater's *The Pursuit of Loneliness,* Richard Sennett's *The Fall of Public Man,* and Robert Bellah et al., *Habits of the Heart* as comparable examples of this wide-ranging, interdisciplinary approach.

[16]Wilfred McClay attributes some of the book's huge impact to "subterranean stream of doubt that ran beneath the triumphant surface of postwar American culture." See his *The Masterless: Self and Society in Modern America* (Chapel Hill: University of North Carolina Press, 1994), 240.

[17]Dennis H. Wrong, "Riesman and the Age of Sociology," *Commentary* 21, 4 (April 1956): 331.

nonprofessional readership, which could now turn to the insights of the "amateur anthropologists" who wrote about them.[18] Indeed, Riesman's files contain scores of letters from readers who expressed their appreciation for his insights into their lives. In a postwar age that, as Ellen Herman has observed, witnessed the ascendance of professional psychology and the growing cultural influence of psychological terms and concepts, Riesman's social-psychology orientation proved amenable to the national consciousness, and indeed, his central concept of "other-direction" became part of the popular vocabulary.[19]

According to Gans's statistics, *The Lonely Crowd* had by 1971 sold over a million copies, eclipsing the next-highest sellers in sociology by hundreds of thousands of sales. Moreover, Gans's figures reveal it to be one of only three works of sociology to sell more than 75,000 copies during the 1950s, a fact that imbues its high sales figures with added significance.[20] Its appearance, as Todd Gitlin notes, possessed additional historical fortuity for its having emerged near the beginning of the "paperback revolution" of the 1940s and 1950s.[21] Two years after its release, Riesman and Glazer contracted with Doubleday publishing company for an abridged Anchor paperback edition of the book. This edition promptly sold 55,000 copies within a year, placing Riesman in the unprecedented position of having produced a sociological best seller.[22]

Despite the book's widespread appeal, Riesman had not intended it for a general audience. In a response to one such reader's letter, he insisted that he had written it "specifically for academic people—not sociologists only but historians, students of population, anthropologists, etc.," and he explained

---

[18] Eric Larabee, "Riesman and His Readers," *Harper's* (June 1961): 59.

[19] Ellen Herman, *The Romance of American Psychology: Political Culture in the Age of Experts* (Berkeley: University of California Press, 1995).

[20] The other two 1950s best sellers Gans reports are Lewis Coser's *The Functions of Social Conflict* (1956) and Gresham Sykes's *Society of Captives* (1958). Gans was unable to obtain sales figures for the major works of C. Wright Mills or of Erving Goffman, which would undoubtedly add to the 1950s total. See Gans, "Best-Sellers by Sociologists," 131–35.

[21] Todd Gitlin, "Sociology for Whom? Criticism for Whom?" in Herbert J. Gans, ed., *Sociology in America* (Newbury Park, CA: Sage, 1990), 214–26. A helpful survey of this development in postwar paperback publishing is provided by Charles A. Madison in *Book Publishing in America* (New York: McGraw-Hill, 1966, especially pp. 547–56. For a history of paperback publishing, see Kenneth C. Davis, *Two-Bit Culture: The Paperbacking of America* (Boston: Houghton Mifflin, 1984). For an exhaustive history of the evolution of the major publishing houses after the war, see John Tebbel, *A History of Book Publishing in the United States*, vol. 4, *The Great Change, 1940–1980* (New York: R. R. Bowker, 1981), chap. 27. For a more critical analysis of modern publishing, see Lewis A. Coser, Charles Kadushin, and Walter W. Powell, *Books: The Culture and Commerce of Publishing* (New York: Basic Books, 1982).

[22] The October 9, 1954, issue of *Publisher's Weekly* reported the figure of 55,000, though a *Time* magazine profile of Riesman a month earlier reported only 40,000.

that his decision to give the manuscript to Yale University Press rather than a commercial publisher testified to that fact.[23] Years later, he asserted that he "really didn't think too much about the audience" when writing the book, and that he "was astonished that *The Lonely Crowd* won a nonacademic audience."[24] The wholly unanticipated public reception of the book therefore places it within the context of Riesman's professional efforts to expand the horizons of social scientists rather than those of nonprofessional readers, that is, to offer an alternative form of social science to other social scientists rather than an alternative perspective on American life to Americans at large.

Nevertheless, the popularity of *The Lonely Crowd* propelled Riesman to the unusual status of an academic celebrity, the heights of which included in 1954 a *Time* magazine cover story. Nonacademic reviewers reacted favorably to the book, noting in particular the accessibility of Riesman's prose. *The New Yorker* review of *The Lonely Crowd* observed that Riesman's style "is popular without condescension" and that it "holds jargon to a welcome minimum," and *Commonweal* praised his "sound literary instincts."[25] The *Time* profile proved remarkably sensitive to Riesman's work as well, eschewing stereotypes of pointed-headed professors and ivory-tower eccentricity in favor of a surprisingly lengthy exposition of the thesis of *The Lonely Crowd*. Altogether, the article provided nearly four pages on the book and only a small boxed inset on Riesman himself and his family life. The article noted approvingly that Riesman's writing remained "relatively free of academic jargon" and attributed this quality to his broad, interdisciplinary orientation to the study of society, which made it necessary for him to "use English" in addressing diverse audiences. Moreover, the profile lauded Riesman's research methodology, which showed a healthy respect for the techniques of good journalism. "He refuses to join the high-level theorists in their contempt for interviewers and other spade-workers," the profile noted with satisfaction, adding that he occupied a reasonable position between the extremes of theory and empiricism.[26]

---

[23] David Riesman to "Miss Shortridge," November 22, 1954, David Riesman Papers, Harvard University Archive, HUG (FP) 99.16, Box 40. See also David Riesman's "Innocence of *The Lonely Crowd*," *Society* 27, 2 (January–February 1990): 79.

[24] Author interview with David Riesman, Winchester, Massachusetts, September 3, 1995.

[25] *New Yorker* 26 (November 4, 1950): 166; Frank Getlein, review of *The Lonely Crowd*, by David Riesman, in *Commonweal* 54 (October 5, 1951): 621.

[26] "Freedom—New Style," *Time* (September 27, 1954): 24. Wilfred McClay assesses the *Time* profile as so laudatory and uncritical of Riesman "as to be embarrassing," so that "a thoughtful social scientist had been turned into mere grist for the journalist's mill." McClay, *The Masterless*, 238.

Meanwhile, the enthusiastic public reception of *The Lonely Crowd* exacted a toll on Riesman's professional image as a social scientist. In a letter to Glazer shortly before the release of the Anchor paperback edition of the book, he described a conversation with Mark Benney, a Chicago colleague, which reveals his mixed feelings about his newfound status as a public intellectual and its potentially damaging impact upon his reputation among his colleagues:

> Mark made the point—he knew nothing of the Doubleday issue—
> that we must be careful not to allow ourselves to be caught in the
> "unscientific" and popularizing position of Margaret Mead, if we
> wanted to protect the students we had attracted. He feels that there
> are such students everywhere, and I see increasing evidence just as
> you do, that this may be so. Consequently, while we ourselves feel that
> the academic snobbery against writing for a lay audience is ridiculous,
> we, I think, have to take account of those who might be injured
> by easy attacks. He feels therefore that anything we can do—and your
> census-oriented book would be a magnificent example—which
> would prevent us being ruled out of the fraternity of "science" is vital
> for the protection of these students who have enlisted under our
> banners.[27]

Riesman's letter, with its guarded dismissal of the narrow conception of scientific work that ruled the discipline, illustrates the dilemma of the first major postwar popularizer of sociology. The seriousness of his commitment to communicating outside his particular field had indeed affected his position within a professional culture that upheld scientific ideals that ruled out such "unscientific" communication. Such was Riesman's estrangement from the trends that the Lazarsfeld-Merton school of research had institutionalized that, at least for a time, even so likely a kindred spirit as C. Wright Mills seemed foreign to his brand of social science. In a 1951 letter to Trilling, Riesman wrote:

> I have great respect of [sic] Mills; in fact, [I] arranged for him to take
> my place at Chicago the second year I was at Yale, and hoped he'd stay
> on there. However, he was contemptuous, and my impression is that
> our group was neither 'scientific' enough or power-oriented enough
> for him—the same is true of my work in particular . . . I haven't read
> his white-collar study, but his New Men of Power and [Puerto] Rican

---

[27]Riesman to Nathan Glazer, April 23, 1952, David Riesman Papers, HUG (FP) 99.12, Box 13.

Journey suffer greatly from his being more impressed by far with Lazarsfeld's methods than the latter himself is; he thinks he has proved his points with sample surveys when in fact he has merely confused them. Lazarsfeld is, perhaps because he is more cynical, more worldly than Mills, well aware of the limitations of surveys, though he has contributed more than anyone to their improvement. Mills is greatly gifted, if only he could loosen up.[28]

Of course, Riesman's assessment of these early works by Mills cannot speak to the common ground the two would find by the late 1950s, yet it reveals the extent of Riesman's ambivalence toward the rest of the profession, so that not even Mills yet shared entirely his approach to social science research and writing, or the independence of these from conventional disciplinary standards.

During the early 1950s, Riesman continued to advocate a more creative, less narrowly "scientific" social science that would combine the best elements of modern theoretical and empirical advancements with a more traditional emphasis upon humanistic study and reflection. In 1951, he wrote in *The Antioch Review* that social science faced a profound new dilemma, in which its "new tools" enforced increasingly a "strict form," so that all generalizations required substantiation with objective data. He warned that this pressure for scientific accuracy "impoverished and hobbled" those generalizations, in that only those that proved statistically demonstrable could survive. Ultimately, social science "becomes less interesting, meaningful, and useful," as well as "less attractive altogether as an intellectual interprise."[29] Ideally, it should accept that no "royal road" existed that could provide objective social knowledge and that researchers should apply with caution the techniques offered by the "design engineers of social science." It was sheer folly for the profession to make large demands upon the nation's resources in the name of science when a more modest "handicraft" approach sufficed, one that could "shift and turn with the development of the thought of the researcher."[30]

Meanwhile, Riesman's popularity exacerbated his professional difficulties, for both his philosophy and his example stood in direct violation of Merton's exhortation to his professional peers in *Social Theory and Social*

---

[28] Riesman to Trilling, June 27, 1951, Lionel Trilling Papers, Box 5.

[29] David Riesman, "Observations on Social Science Research," in *Individualism Reconsidered and Other Essays* (Glencoe, IL: Free Press, 1954), 470. This essay originally appeared in *Antioch Review* 11, 3 (September 1951): 259–78.

[30] Ibid., 479–80.

Structure. The sociologist who aspired to elegant prose and poetic language attracted the attention of nonprofessionals, whose plaudits then exacerbated his or her estrangement from peers who had been trained to research and write like scientists. Riesman lamented this uncomfortable position in a letter to Robert Nisbet:

> As you can imagine, it has not been an unmixed blessing to have my work well received among some non-sociologists—who occasionally use it, most untactfully and unfairly, to tell my colleagues that they ought to be more like me! This reception means that some graduate students are scared off from using themes from me in their research in sociology and psychology, even while students in history, economics, or literature get kudos from becoming "interdisciplinary," through reference to me.[31]

As a successful public sociologist, then, Riesman confronted his profession's concern with demarcating discrete boundaries between itself and other social science disciplines, and the very attributes that made his work readable outside of sociology became liabilities in his relationships within a discipline committed to establishing its own uniqueness, a cause that required the privatization, not the democratization, of its written expression.

In 1958, Riesman accepted a position at Harvard as Henry Ford II Professor of Social Science. His move from the Chicago sociological milieu, with its no-longer dominant ethnographic research traditions of participatory observation and deeply contextualized interviews, to the ascendant Harvard culture seemed to suit him despite his misgivings about the state of the social sciences. Riesman wrote respectfully to Talcott Parsons shortly after arriving at Harvard that he had long thought of Parsons as "Mr. Sociology," and that he admired "the serious and eminently fair way" in which Parsons fulfilled this role.[32] At the same time, however, Riesman's estrangement from the dominant currents in 1950s sociology remained acute. A year earlier, in a letter to C. Wright Mills, he had observed of Harvard's Department of Social Relations—which Parsons had been instrumental in establishing—that the university's "best students" considered it an "intellectual slum" and avoided it in favor of history or literature. Faculty members from other departments

---

[31] Riesman to Robert Nisbet, no year indicated, David Riesman Papers, HUG (FP) 99.12, Box 34. This letter, dated September 16, contains a reference to the staffing then under way of the new campus of the University of California at Riverside, where Nisbet joined the Sociology Department in 1953.

[32] Riesman to Talcott Parsons, August 11, 1959, Talcott Parsons Papers, Harvard University Archive.

seemed to share the students' sentiments. Harvard historians, he lamented, asked nothing of the social scientists "other than that they drop dead."[33] Similarly, he would later recall his decision to go to Harvard as the product of larger patterns of overprofessionalization he had observed while at Chicago:

> I had the observation I made at Chicago, which was that people I had taught as undergraduates who were bright and alive, as graduate students in sociology they became much more intimidated and cautious... So I decided to teach undergraduates, and McGeorge Bundy, after one failed attempt to bring me to Harvard in 1954, came back with a program tailored for me, in which I would teach not sociology, but a general social science course in a general education program, only undergraduates. That just suited me fine.[34]

For Riesman, then, Harvard presented an opportunity not for integrating his scholarship and teaching into the Sociology Deparment's research culture, but rather for practicing his own variety of social investigation within a sphere of his own, without having to accept responsibility for transmitting the methods and articles of faith of the larger sociological profession to sociologists-in-training.

For their part, Riesman's new colleagues contributed their share to his reservations about the Harvard orientation to sociological work, for they seemed steadfastly committed to keeping weighty ideas out of the graduate curriculum in the name of inculcating incrementalist sociological inquiry. In 1961, Riesman lamented to Harvard professor of psychiatry Robert J. Lifton that his colleague Alex Inkeles had taken exception to his broad-minded teaching approach:

> Last winter he asked me to have lunch with him to upbraid me for the impact of Soc Sci 136 on students in Social Relations, saying that by presenting students early with such exciting ideas in an undisciplined way, our staff made it more difficult for the professional people in the Department later on to force students to do the serious work of sociology; we skimmed off the cream of ideas, so to speak, although in a superficial way, leaving him and his fellows to do the scrupulous cleaning up.[35]

---

[33] Riesman to C. Wright Mills, March 28, 1958, C. Wright Mills Papers, Box 4B400, Center for American History, University of Texas at Austin.

[34] Author interview with David Riesman, Winchester, Massachusetts, September 3, 1995.

[35] Riesman to Robert J. Lifton, August 22, 1961, David Riesman Papers, HUG (FP) 99.12, Box 28.

Riesman's wide-ranging, interdisciplinary orientation, the very attributes that made him engaging to so many outside of social science, therefore proved a source of frustration within his professional circle and even estrangement from it. Orlando Patterson goes so far as to assert that Riesman "died discarded and forgotten by his discipline," evidenced in part by the Harvard Sociology Department's decision to discontinue a lecture series named after him a mere two years into its existence. For Patterson, the gulf between Riesman's accessible, wide-ranging, and relevant scholarship and the "pseudo-scientific" preoccupations within the sociological mainstream spelled professional obscurity for his mentor.[36]

Riesman's Harvard experiences during the 1950s, in turn, saw his earlier attitudes acquire a new stridency. Privately, his opinions about contemporary sociological orthodoxy became more trenchant than the more diplomatic sentiments he had expressed in his early-1950s journal articles. In one installment of his series of responses to Mills's manuscript for *The Sociological Imagination,* he declared that sociology's scientific aspirations rendered it intellectually sterile and even antidemocratic. Sociologists received appointments for sheer productivity, measured in "foot pounds" or "BTUs." Their "ponderous" styles of scholarship negated the possibility of making meaningful judgments about society, as well as the opportunity for readers "to make a judgment on the mind and judgment of the writer."[37] This incrementalist formula produced a routine of insular communication over narrow issues of negligible significance. Lashing out at this culture of organized irrelevance, Riesman declared:

> I believe any idiot could be trained to pass on journal articles for review today. He would notice whether the writer begins by citing "the literature," then citing his "hypotheses" and experimental controls, then saying what he did, then repeating it all over again in the summary, all with tables of "significance." While there is the effort, as you point out, to fend off the non-academic public which of course couldn't be expected to understand—a comforting elitism—within the academy "democracy" rules and the patterns are set up so that "any number can play."[38]

Riesman therefore perceived a paradoxical state of affairs within sociology. In its elitist language and overly refined methods, it closed itself off from

---

[36] Orlando Patterson, "The Last Sociologist," *New York Times* (May 19, 2002).

[37] David Riesman to C. Wright Mills, April 16, 1958, C. Wright Mills Papers, Box 4B400.

[38] Ibid.

outside communication, even as it admitted any and all professionally sanctioned submissions to its own private conversation.

At the same time, Riesman found that his success with nonprofessional readers posed another intellectual challenge. As he continued to demand a more pluralistic, less orthodox social science, he recognized that the lay audiences for its work constituted an equally significant problem for the communication of meaningful ideas and observations. In the introduction to *Individualism Reconsidered,* a collection of his essays of the 1940s and 1950s, he admitted that he occasionally "regretted that *The Lonely Crowd* was not more inaccessible." Popularization, he observed, tended to diminish the sophistication of the ideas in the process, often to the detriment of the lay readers who consumed them. Inevitably, complex issues would be misunderstood and, in a society of other-directed individuals, imposed upon the rest of the group. Thus, those of Riesman's ideas that reached broader audiences, most of whom were of marginal social status and power—the "powerless," as he termed them—often produced precisely the kind of blind thought conformity he opposed.[39]

For Riesman, the mass media, the locus of any effort to popularize sociological issues, lay at the heart of the public intellectual's dilemma. Years later, he would recall of the *Time* magazine profile:

I did my best to avoid that. It was the last thing I wanted. I didn't want that kind of visibility. I tried to talk them out of it, saying, "You know, I'm just one worker among many, and you should have a story about studies, and not about me," but that isn't the way they work.[40]

Riesman, who had often expressed explicitly his commitment to the defeat of dogma and the challenging of orthodoxy and prejudice, recognized that the distillation of complex ideas for mass consumption jeopardized this important mission. In his contribution to *The New American Right,* Daniel Bell's edited collection of essays on McCarthyism, he echoed the *Partisan Review*

---

[39] David Riesman, introduction to *Individualism Reconsidered,* 10. On the other hand, it was precisely Riesman's elliptical, antideclarative style that chafed several reviewers. Norman Mailer complained in *Partisan Review* that Riesman "says so little in so many words and like so many sociologists gives little feel or sense of life itself." See *Advertisements for Myself* (New York: G. P. Putnam's Sons, 1959), 191. Similarly, Elizabeth Hardwick wrote in *Partisan Review* of Riesman's air of professional detachment: "It is hard to know how to judge a thinker whose intellectual positions are so profoundly modified by 'psychology,' who treats his own opinions as if they were those of a character in a novel he was writing." See her "Riesman Considered," *Partisan Review* 21, 5 (September–October 1954): 549.

[40] Riesman, David Riesman Oral History Project, Butler Library, Columbia University, New York, 20.

conception of mass culture, observing like Dwight Macdonald that the domination of public discourse by "middlebrows" meant that American intellectuals' ideas, "even where relevant to contemporary discontent, are quickly taken over by the mass media and transmuted into the common stock of middlebrow conceptions." Intellectuals lost control of the dissemination of their ideas at the hands of the media's formidable "pace of distribution," so that "what they produce soon becomes dissociated from them and their immediate coteries." Such a loss of control served only to exacerbate their already substantial alienation from the rest of society. "Even when they may reach a wider audience with more dispatch than ever before in history," he lamented, producers of ideas, estranged from their own "products," succumbed to "a feeling of impotence and isolation."[41] Riesman's bleak assessment of the very processes through which his own work had reached a large readership revealed the degree to which he had come to reassess his own popularity.

Meanwhile, the lay public, whose right of access to sociological perspectives Riesman had championed in *Individualism Reconsidered,* continued to receive unfavorable journalistic depictions of mainstream social science, which by 1960 included a lampoon of Riesman himself. That year, *Newsweek* magazine published a humorous report on an article on sociability Riesman had co-authored in the journal *Human Organization.* Riesman and his fellow researchers, accompanied by a staff of six others, had undertaken the "systematic study" of individuals at cocktail parties, the magazine reported with palpable sarcastic glee. As "participant observers," the team had attended eighty such events between 1955 and 1959, ostensibly to resolve such "nagging" questions as whether "some hosts are more genial than others," "some guests play charades only under pressure," and "the room in which the bar is situated tends to become crowded."[42] The team had attempted to assume the "conflicting roles" of both researchers and partiers, a feat that *Newsweek* mused could be accomplished only with difficulty due to the deleterious effects of cocktail parties on one's memory. To underline the frivolity of the project, the article concluded with the price tag of the group's research efforts, to be borne by the sponsoring National Institute of Mental Health and, therefore, the taxpayers.

In recounting the events surrounding the Sociability Project four years later, Riesman and Jeanne Watson, a social psychologist and member of the research team, recalled that *Newsweek* had from the beginning displayed no intention of taking the project seriously. After a phone call from the magazine to Riesman in the winter of 1959–1960, Riesman and Watson recalled,

---

[41] Riesman and Glazer, "Intellectuals and the Discontented Classes," in Daniel Bell, ed., *The New American Right* (New York: Criterion Books, 1955), 83.

[42] "Cocktail Parties—Are Hosts People?" *Newsweek* (May 2, 1960): 25.

"it was clear from the dialogue that they meant to ridicule the project as a waste of taxpayers' money, as well as presenting the amusing picture of a 'name' social scientist attending cocktail parties in pursuit of his dreary specialty."[43] The magazine had sought simply to reinforce existing stereotypes of social scientists that had been circulating since the early 1950s, that they tended to belabor the obvious, preoccupy themselves with trivia, and complicate ordinary social reality with their overspecialized methods and arcane language. Riesman's own celebrity had attracted their attention to the project, and thus the very energies that had popularized sociological work and ideas became a liability, as elements within a mass media that had annointed Riesman now exploited him for the purpose of ridiculing academic social research.

Moreover, the *Newsweek* article unleashed a small tempest of public criticism of the project. After the article appeared, the researchers received a barrage of phone calls from curious journalists and reporters, as well as angry letters from "self-styled taxpayers," many of whom had sent the researchers carbon copies of letters they had written to their congressional representatives "demanding in outraged terms an investigation of this immoral or inane waste of government funds." This brouhaha also activated several congressmen, who, as in the NSF debates of the late 1940s, demanded accountability for the researchers' use of public funds and questioned the conduct of alleged "snooping social scientists."[44]

As Riesman's experiences as a public scholar reveal, he labored under a set of profoundly conflicting constraints, those established by his own peers and others imposed by an ever-dubious national press that ridiculed professional sociological research even as it appropriated vulgarized versions of it for public consumption. The frustration he encountered in his efforts to break free of journalistic stereotypes and professional orthodoxy in his professional and public roles reveal the solidity of the rift between professional discourse and public-sphere communication. To address the public, as Packard did, was to invite charges such as that of William Peterson that journalists—and, by implication, journalistic treatments of sociology—were wholly unqualified to address sociological questions. To seek a healthy balance of professional and public communication, as Riesman attempted, invited derision, simplification, and a loss of control of one's own ideas.

Riesman therefore sought his audiences increasingly among more sharply defined groups by the late 1950s, particularly as he committed himself to the

---

[43] David Riesman and Jeanne Watson, "The Sociability Project: A Chronicle of Frustration and Achievement," in Phillip E. Hammond, ed., *Sociologists at Work: Essays on the Craft of Social Research* (New York: Basic Books, 1964), 317n.

[44] Ibid., 317n.

movement to halt the expansion of the nuclear arms race. Now, as a political activist, he doubted that intellectuals could hope to influence the national course of events by appealing to a broad spectrum of readers. In an article in the *Bulletin of the Atomic Scientists,* he wrote of his own "misgivings" about seeking an audience for nuclear policy issues "in the amorphous public at large." In any social order, even that of a "Utopian society," individuals would be "differentially interested in foreign affairs," and "even at moments of great crisis and danger not everyone would be mobilized." Current social and political conditions therefore required that intellectuals seek "small audiences" for their ideas. The ideas themselves, in turn, required the substance and complexity necessary for conveying the current dangers to those audiences. Intellectuals, he warned, must not allow them to be "immediately sloganized or sold."[45] While the concept of "other-direction" had taken on a life of its own in the public sphere, where it had been bandied about and applied haphazardly to a myriad of contemporary conditions, the stakes had become too high by the early 1960s for Riesman to risk such misinterpretation and misappropriation on the nuclear issue.

Riesman's relocation to Harvard coincided with this development in his personal and professional evolution in the form of a campaign to foster national awareness of the dangers of nuclear weapons and the deceptive and destabilizing civil defense campaign of the 1950s. Upon arriving at Harvard, Riesman and his friend and colleague H. Stuart Hughes founded the peace activist student group TOCSIN, for which Riesman served as faculty advisor.[46] Then, the collapse of the planned 1960 Paris summit on nuclear arms between President Eisenhower and Premier Khrushchev, and the Kennedy administration's subsequent authorization of a massive deployment of nuclear missiles, spurred Riesman to co-found with Glazer and Erich Fromm an antinuclear organization, the Committee of Correspondence, to publicize issues pertaining to the nuclear arms race and to call for a ban on nuclear testing.[47] The committee's newsletter, *The Correspondent,* would ultimately include statements by prominent American intellectuals of the period, including Lewis Mumford, Robert Heilbroner, and I. F. Stone. The committee, deriving its name of course from the colonial organizations of the American

---

[45] David Riesman, "Private People and Public Policy," *Bulletin of the Atomic Scientists* 25, 5 (May 1959): 207–08.

[46] David Riesman, "A Personal Memoir: My Political Journey," in Walter W. Powell and Richard Robbins, eds., *Conflict and Consensus: A Festschrift in Honor of Lewis A. Coser* (New York: Free Press, 1984); Todd Gitlin, "David Riesman, Thoughtful Pragmatist," *Chronicle of Higher Education* (24 May 2002), B5.

[47] Riesman describes his co-founding of the committee in "A Personal Memoir," 346–47.

Revolutionary era, was to publicize the nuclear issue, demystify the Cold War, and thereby, in Fromm's words, overcome "the iron wall of clichés of which we are prisoners."[48] At the outset, Fromm urged that the new organization reach out to a broad spectrum of public opinion, that it "try to represent people who think, whether they are policy makers, intellectuals, or ordinary people."[49] Nevertheless, Riesman perceived distinct limits to its communicative potential. In a letter to various members of the committee, he declared modestly that academic intellectuals' influence would inevitably remain small:

> I've felt throughout that those outside academic life, whether in journalism or in organizational life, tend to overestimate the importance and influence of those such as Erich Fromm or Stuart Hughes or myself whose names they know within academia: our professional colleagues know "better" and tend to devalue us precisely because we are known outside the profession or the guild, especially as some of us are also not firmly ensconced in the guild in the first place. Thus greater hopes are put on us than is warranted, even if we could spend full time on these activities.[50]

Riesman's assessment captures well his conflicted sense of the social scientist's potential for influencing either professional peers or public attitudes. Each sphere harbored too many limitations and punitive conventions to allow him the kind of communicative environment that would broaden satisfactorily the national conversation on vital social issues. To resolve this conflict, in the name of turning the nuclear states away from the path of annihilation, Riesman had, in Michael Burawoy's formulation, passed from a "traditional" public sociological role with *The Lonely Crowd*, in which he had shared sociological insights with an inchoate mass public—and in which, it is likely, only an elite segment of readers had truly digested his ideas—to an "organic" role, in which he could develop relationships with particular publics and engage in truly reciprocal dialogue with them.[51]

Like Riesman, C. Wright Mills experienced these dilemmas as his writings both targeted and reached more general audiences. Like Riesman, he faced

---

[48] Erich Fromm to David Riesman, March 4, 1961, David Riesman Papers, HUG (FP) 99.12, Box 11.

[49] Ibid.

[50] David Riesman to Jack Bollens, Robert Gilmore, Roger Hagan, H. Stuart Hughes, Stewart Meacham, Everett Mendelsohn, A. J. Muste, and Harold Taylor, May 17, 1961, David Riesman Papers, HUG (FP) 99.16, Box 11.

[51] Michael Burawoy conveys this distinction between "organic" and "traditional" public sociologists in his 2004 presidential address to the American Sociological Association, "For Public Sociology" (presidential address, annual meeting of the American Sociological Association, August 15, 2004);

the question of which audience he should address in a society that he, like most of the rest of his generation, perceived as in one way or another a mass society, in which publics became inert masses and ideas became empty slogans. To ignore the intellectual's responsibility to tell the truth publicly would be to abandon the cause of applying reason to human affairs altogether. The sociological imagination demanded that the sociologist transform private troubles into public issues, a task that only made sense if those for whom troubles remained private might understand their troubles' public essence. The "conservative mood" of postwar intellectual life meant for Mills that bearers of new knowledge had forsaken that mission, that they had been "giving up the old ideal of the public relevance of knowledge" and had done nothing to oppose "public mindlessness in all its forms."[52]

However, to leap into public discourse uncritically and without inhibition would be to subsume one's ideas to the rules of mass popularity and salability. Early in his career, Mills had published sentiments resembling Riesman's expressions of ambivalence over the popular success of The Lonely Crowd—though in Mills's case in more Marxian language—to the effect that "the means of effective communication are being expropriated from the intellectual worker. The material basis of his initiative and intellectual freedom is no longer in his hands."[53] He concluded that to submit to the prevailing means of communication of ideas constituted an act of intellectual capitulation. "When you sell the lies of others, you are also selling yourself," he wrote. "To sell your self is to turn your self into a commodity."[54] Independent communication therefore required the existence of "independent intellectuals," and, as Irving Louis Horowitz has observed, Mills therefore spent his career resolutely unaffiliated with institutions outside of Columbia, to which he remained but tenuously attached as well. As for the communication of sociological ideas, he drew simple dis-

published in the *American Sociological Review* 70, 1 (February 2005): 4–28. For the origins of these categories of intellectuals and intellectual roles, see Antonio Gramsci, *Selections from the Prison Notebooks* (New York: International Publishers, 1971). In Gramsci's radically egalitarian formulation, "all men are intellectuals" by virtue of their participation within productive social relations that in any and all cases necessarily include "a minimum of creative intellectual activity" (8–9), so that exchanges between individuals from different social groups becomes not only possible, in the form of "active participation in practical life," but essential for the pursuance of proletarian class interests (10).

[52] C. Wright Mills, "On Knowledge and Power," in Irving Louis Horowitz, ed., *Power, Politics and People: The Collected Essays of C. Wright Mills* (New York: Oxford University Press, 1963), 599, 604. This essay originally appeared in *Dissent* 2, 3 (Summer 1955), 201–12.

[53] C. Wright Mills, "The Social Role of the Intellectual," in Horowitz, ed., *Power, Politics and People*, 297. This essay originally appeared as "The Powerless People: The Role of the Intellectual in Society," in *Politics* 1, 3 (April 1944).

[54] Ibid., 300.

tinctions between appropriate and inappropriate forms of sociological popularization, condemning intellectuals who wrote for large audiences in mass-circulation commercial publications as having abdicated their responsibilities as independent thinkers. In an article in *Dissent* on the ways in which "men of knowledge" had capitulated to "men of power," Mills cited a Lionel Trilling essay in which Trilling had allegedly "written optimistically of the 'new intellectual classes,'" and had referred to the Luce publications as "samples of high 'intellectual talent.'" Mills charged that Trilling had succumbed to the common "celebrationist" tendency among contemporary intellectuals, which led them to associate their own rising fortunes with the general health of American society. Trilling had conflated the important differences between types of intellectual activity, especially the distinction between "knowledge as a goal" and "knowledge as a mere technique and instrument."[55] To praise popular journalists for their "intellectual talent," constituted for Mills the neglect of the important matter of their subservience to organs of mass communication that operated in the service of still higher circles of wealth and power.

Trilling, aware of course of the ideological divide between Mills's radicalism and his own liberal outlook, remained confused nevertheless as to Mills' intent in shaming him in print. He wrote to Mills that he had in his own essay made clear that his observation of the Luce employees' "intellectual talent" did not constitute "a favorable judgment of the intellectual quality of the Luce publications themselves." That Mills had received this erroneous impression surprised Trilling, for he had labored to avoid such a misinterpretation. "I'd much rather believe," he concluded, "that I did not succeed in this than that you wilfully [*sic*], for purposes of polemic, misrepresented what I said."[56]

Mills responded that he didn't intend to offend Trilling, but that the statement in which Trilling had written of the Luce publications' support of "intellectual talent" seemed to constitute an endorsement. In the essay as a whole Trilling had asserted that intellectuals had acquired a new influence over wealth and power in America, that, in Trilling's words, the latter "shows a tendency to submit itself, in some degree, to the rule of mind and imagination, to apologize for its existence by a show of taste and sensitivity." Trilling's use of the phrase therefore suggested his approval of the Luce publications, for their support of "intellectual talent" seemed part and parcel of the larger intellectual trends he perceived. Mills objected, "Why use the phrase 'intellectual talent'? No matter how it is qualified, 'the point of

---

[55] C. Wright Mills, "On Knowledge and Power," *Dissent* 2, 3 (Summer 1955): 207n.

[56] Lionel Trilling to C. Wright Mills, November 3, 1955, Lionel Trilling Papers, Box 4, Rare Books and Manuscripts Library, Columbia University. Also quoted in Horowitz, *C. Wright Mills: An American Utopian* (New York: Free Press, 1983), 85.

224 / Chapter 8

intellectual virtue' is bound to be taken up. About this I am certain that I am not alone." Trilling needed to acknowledge "the rise of the technician and consultant in all areas of modern America," so as "to make clear the difference between this type and the humanist type of intellect and rationality."[57]

As for the Luce journalists, Mills revealed his belief that they reflected the technocratic assault upon true intellectual activity and rational thought. To submit to the forces of popularization was to succumb to the larger celebrationist mindlessness of the age:

> The most important fact about the intelligence of those who live long with Luce is the ease with which their intelligence is used in the bright, clever pattern without any explicit ordering and forbidding being involved. That, it seems to me, is the beginning point for an analysis of the intellectual quality of the new technical intelligensia which you seem in some rather oblique, even opaque, way to be celebrating.[58]

The breadth of Mills's generalization about popular writing offended Trilling, who noted that not only had he and his wife been solicited to write for *Time* but that so had Irving Howe, whom he hardly considered "a bright and clever technician of the word and image."[59] Clearly, to Trilling, Mills had chosen to draw a line between independent writing and propaganda based solely on the writer's institutional affiliation.

At the same time, as if to confirm the irreconcilable divide between Mills's sociological vision and the laws of the marketplace, reviewers in the popular media often tarred Mills with the same characterizations their brethren had applied to sociology in general throughout the 1950s. *Time Magazine*'s review of *The Power Elite* attacked Mills's "sociological mumbo-jumbo," which it predicted "should discourage all but other sociologists," and it branded the book "dull" and "repetitious."[60] A *Harper's* review found the book "infuriating," "repetitious," and "interminable, or a little longer." Repeating the familiar charge of sociological writing's unintelligibility, the review observed that Mills's book "lapses into a language for which a reading knowledge of English will not

---

[57]Mills to Trilling, November 7, 1955, Lionel Trilling Papers, Box 4. Also quoted in Horowitz, *C. Wright Mills*, 85. In addition to Mills's "IBM Plus Humanism" essay, an important statement of his view of the role of the modern knowledge technician is "A Marx for the Managers," in *Ethics* 52, 2 (January 1942): 200–15. These arguments also appeared in Chapter 7 of *White Collar*, where Mills characterized the absorption of intellectuals into technical roles (156–60).

[58]Ibid. Also quoted in Horowitz, *C. Wright Mills*, 85.

[59]Trilling to Mills, November 22, 1955, Lionel Trilling Papers, Box 4.

[60]Review of *The Power Elite*, *Time* (April 30, 1956): 116.

prepare you." Mills also shared the professional affliction of belaboring the obvious: "Mills divulges far too many open secrets—at ponderous length and in a tone of shocked surprise he reveals that the rich send their children to private schools, that the managers of leading corporations live in large houses, and that if you want to be a captain of industry it is helpful to have a father in the captain-of-industry line, with statistics to prove it."[61] An *Atlantic Monthly* reviewer, C. J. Rolo, found it "exasperating," "crammed with the horrid jargon of sociology," and "inexcusably repetitious."[62] In language almost identical to that of the *Harper's* review, Rolo questioned Mills's "tone of outraged discovery" in his presentation of well-known facts such as "that tycoons ride in Cadillacs, send their children to expensive schools, and play golf with other tycoons."[63]

Despite this apparent gulf between Mills and the mass media, Mills was not averse to publishing essays and articles in larger-circulation magazines such as *Esquire, The New York Times Magazine, Saturday Review of Literature,* and *Harper's,* particularly by the late 1950s, as he began to leave the orbit of the New York intellectual circles represented by *Dissent* and *Partisan Review.* He also applauded the efforts of nonsociologists to popularize sociological perspectives, compensating for the venom his peers would direct at Vance Packard in a laudatory 1955 review of the fortuitously named journalist and editor Auguste Comte Spectorsky's best-selling study of the emergent postwar bedroom communities beyond ordinary suburbs, *The Exurbanites.* Consistent with the principles he would soon advance in *The Sociological Imagination,* he noted Spectorsky's exemplary approach of "sociological documentary," which combined the immediacy and personal perspective of journalism with some of the methods of "systematic observation" characteristic of the social sciences. He proclaimed that this approach was "tending to become the natural locus of bright ideas, of social discovery, of convincing explanation, and, in the largest and best sense, of social and moral criticism."[64] He compared it to the nineteenth-century novel,

---

[61] Paul Pickrel, "The Olympians," *Harper's Magazine* (April 1956): 88.

[62] C. J. Rolo, review of *The Power Elite* in *The Atlantic Monthly* (June 1956): 80. As Horowitz relates, the stridency of Mills's book-length philippics alienated many otherwise sympathetic intellectuals who knew Mills personally, including Dwight Macdonald, Richard Hofstadter, Riesman, and Trilling. In particular, Macdonald's devastating review of *White Collar* in *Partisan Review* moved Mills to solicit opinions from several colleagues as to the very integrity of his work. See Horowitz, *C. Wright Mills,* 248–53. Horowitz's claim that Hofstadter's criticisms of *White Collar* virtually terminated his relationship with Mills is contradicted by the former's extensive response to Mills's manuscript for *The Sociological Imagination* eight years later.

[63] Ibid., 80.

[64] C. Wright Mills, review of A. C. Spectorsky's *The Exurbanites,* in *Saturday Review* (October 29, 1955): 12.

which had also served as an important public source of broad perspectives on relevant social questions and, as the contemporary novel seemed to him to have abdicated that role, Spectorsky's example of popularized social science stood ready to fill it. Similarly, Mills approved of much of William H. Whyte's *The Organization Man*, especially its exposé of social science's "absurd pretensions" and "methodological preoccupations."[65] Such works, which confronted themes that Mills had developed more fully in his own work, constituted valuable illuminations of activities that might otherwise remain obscure to the lay reader.

Mills's embrace of popular sociological communication of a sort that extended beyond the limited readerships of such opinion organs as *Partisan Review, The Nation, The New Republic, Dissent, Monthly Review,* and *New Left Review* belied his statements about slick, empty Luce writers. As Irving Horowitz noted in 1963, Mills shared "the impulse to return sociology to the public from whence it emanated, to deprofessionalize it in fact," so that it "could provide that means by which man casts off an egoistic, sectarian and mythic pride and grows to maturity."[66] Ultimately, his commitment to this kind of communication of sociological ideas overcame his aversion to popularization. His last three books—*The Causes of World War III; Listen, Yankee;* and *The Marxists*—emerged in paperback editions upon first publication, and whereas Oxford University Press had published each of his earlier works, these last were released by major publishing houses, examples of the very organs of mass communication Mills had condemned earlier.[67] Moreover, portions of the first two books appeared in *The Nation* and *Harper's*, which, while hardly the mainstream, mass-circulation periodicals he decried to Trilling, nevertheless commanded substantial national readerships beyond narrow intellectual circles.[68]

These later works also reflected Mills's application of the journalistic techniques of sociological reportage he had advocated. In *The Causes*, he

---

[65]C. Wright Mills, review of *The Organization Man*, by William H. Whyte, *New York Times Book Review* (December 9, 1956): 6.

[66]Horowitz, ed., introduction to *Power, Politics and People* (New York: Oxford University Press, 1963), 16.

[67]In his history of paperback publishing, Kenneth C. Davis relates that *Listen, Yankee,* published by Ballantine Books, joined a host of other Ballantine titles addressing compelling contemporary issues, including John Hersey's *Hiroshima,* Seymour Melman's *The Peace Race,* Frank J. Donner's *The Un-Americans* on McCarthyism, Allan Guttmacher's anti-Comstock Law *The Complete Book of Birth Control,* and J. W. Schulte Nordholt's *The People That Walk in Darkness* on black American history. See Davis, *Two-Bit Culture,* 331.

[68]Portions of *The Causes of World War III* appeared initially as "Program for Peace" and "A Pagan Sermon to Christian Clergy" in the December 7, 1957, and March 8, 1958, issues of *The Nation.* Portions of "Listen, Yankee: The Cuban Case Against the United States" appeared in *Harper's Magazine* (December 1960): 31–37.

combined political, economic, and social analysis with journalistic advocacy, painting horrific scenarios of accidental nuclear strikes, exposing the criminality of political stasis in the face of the nuclear threat, and, in a "pagan sermon" to America's Christian clergy, demanding its active assertion of "moral conscience" in the political sphere. In *Listen, Yankee*, he fused sociological and journalistic elements to produce a "sociological documentary," using the interviews he had conducted in revolutionary Cuba not as the basis for a sociological interpretation of the revolution but to allow the revolutionaries themselves to present their experience to American readers. He claimed merely to be "organizing" the materials he had collected, providing "what Cubans in the middle of their revolution are now thinking about that revolution, about its place within their lives, and about its future."[69] Only in book's conclusion did he speak explicitly with his own authorial voice, admitting that he was "for" the revolution, though expressing concern that it might lead to another dictatorship, and insisting that wrongheaded U.S. policy forced the Cuban government to resort to more repressive rule.

In sum, Mills's output toward the end of his life reflects his concessions to the exigencies of popularizing sociological ideas in a mass society in the name of speaking truth to power publicly. Like Riesman, he attempted to find a middle path between choosing to accept the oversimplification of sociological communication in the mass media and remaining confined to small professional and intellectual readerships in sociology journals and New York's "little magazines." However, whereas Riesman experienced an abrupt and unplanned popularity that compelled him to reassess the efficacy of communicating complex sociological ideas to broad audiences, Mills followed the opposite trajectory, initially repudiating and then embracing ever-greater popularization. Whereas Riesman resisted commodification of his ideas in the name of preserving their sophistication and contingent status, Mills risked commodification in the name of publicizing his own. Nevertheless, as the dilemmas of popularization entered their lives from opposite directions, they produced the same varieties of professional estrangement and conflict.

Indeed, in the age of sociological interpretation of mass society, such a move undermined Mills's professional credibility as it had Riesman's, opening his work to the same charges lodged at Vance Packard, that the "packaging" of

---

[69] C. Wright Mills, *Listen, Yankee: The Revolution in Cuba* (New York: Ballantine, 1960), 8. "In writing this book," he explained, "I have thought the expression of my own views much less important than the statement of the Cuban revolutionaries' case. And that is why, insofar as I have been able, I have refrained from expressing a personal opinion. I have tried hard not to allow my own worries for Cuba, or for the United States, to intrude upon this presentation of the Cuban voice, nor have I attempted either to conceal or to underline such ambiguities as I happen to find in their argument" (12).

sociological concepts for broad consumption constituted an unacceptable intellectual sacrifice. Philip Rieff, a Chicago sociologist and close friend of Riesman, suggested this outcome well before the publication of Mills's polemical paperbacks. In a 1956 review of *The Power Elite*, he wrote, "Even Mills, the angry man of American social letters, may ultimately expect to hitch a ride on the American gravy train, against his personal will, as one of its most celebrated critics. For criticism too is a saleable commodity, as long as it remains professional and sharpens no movement of protest." In an oblique reference to Riesman's own media-celebrity status, Rieff declared wryly that "*Time* could render his face iconic for a week."[70] Rieff's comments reflected academic sociology's larger fear of co-optation by mass society, a reality with which Mills himself had struggled to come to terms. Mass society, Rieff warned, "can digest any virtuoso heretic striking blindly at where dogma used to be."[71]

Intellectual histories of Mills's career reflect a similar sense of his descent into the distortions and superficiality of mass culture. In his biography of Mills, Irving Louis Horowitz reconsiders his earlier devotion to Mills's radical sociology by characterizing the later Mills as a "captive" of mass culture who forsook responsible sociology for the public limelight, abandoned any semblance of scholarly standards and gentility, and imagined himself "the special bearer of mass beliefs."[72] Similarly, a more recent study of public-minded social scientists asserts that Mills's ideas indeed became "commodified," that by refusing to engage in the formulation of a political program, Mills indulged in "conspicuous criticism," leaving his writings open to "an infinite number of conflicting perspectives" that, like disposable consumer goods, become "obsolete upon formulation."[73] Such critiques adopt the postmodern position that to convey ideas within the broader marketplace of ideas reduces the

---

[70]Philip Rieff, review of *The Power Elite*, in *Partisan Review* 23, 2 (Summer 1956): 366.

[71]Ibid., 366.

[72]Horowitz, *C. Wright Mills*, 283.

[73]Christopher Shannon, *Conspicuous Criticism: Tradition, the Individual, and Culture in American Social Thought, from Veblen to Mills* (Baltimore: Johns Hopkins University Press, 1996), 175. Shannon argues that the critical tradition initiated by Thorstein Veblen and continued by such scholars as Robert and Helen Lynd, John Dewey, Ruth Benedict, and Mills, suffers from its adherents' lack of grounding in "received traditions" of inquiry. Their antitraditionalism, he argues, itself represents a tradition, one which has spawned endless permutations of criticism, each lacking a contextual basis for demonstrating its validity. He views Mills's sociological imagination, with its "constant shifting of perspective" as encouraging an endless variety of interpretations that ultimately fail to provide a normative guide for understanding. "If one imagines the sociological imagination practiced on a mass scale," he suggests, "one can see the relatively neutral 'facts' of abstracted empiricism giving way to the relatively neutral 'contexts' of the sociological imagination. Lacking a master context or a metanarrative, history becomes a smorgasbord of contingencies democratic/technocratic citizens/scientists choose from in constructing their preferred society" (165).

author to the humble status of the producer of "texts," each without essential validity, lasting significance, or foundation for action. Whereas John Dewey demanded the democratization of critical discourse and the intellectual's active engagement within it, this view perceives limits on sociological discourse as essential for protecting the sociological project from trivialization, from becoming merely another narrative in a congeries of other narratives.

Indeed, Mills's engagement with the public sphere with his later works failed to spur him to involvement in practical political activity, a fact that seems to corroborate these critics' assessments. Whereas Riesman immersed himself in the movement for nuclear disarmament, Mills remained detached from political activity despite the attention given *The Causes of World War III*. Ten years after Mills's death, Riesman complained that he "was never able concretely to involve him in anti-nuclear or any other anti-war activity":

> Mills' hope that his book, *The Causes of World War III*, could make a difference seems to me quite optimistic or vain . . . I invited Mills to a conference at Yaddo of American Friends Service Committee people and others, but he declined to attend, implying that all these pacifist people didn't amount to much and couldn't get anywhere.[74]

In recalling his late-1950s relationship with Mills, moreover, Riesman claimed that Mills "was less of an activist than many people believe."[75] Indeed, Mills repudiated a fundamental principle that the political activists and Mills disciples of the 1960s would uphold, the idea of participatory democracy. For Mills, the United States was a mass society that eviscerated the democratic potential of the public as it in turn co-opted the energies of intellectuals, rendering the latter ineffective in the kinds of relationships that Riesman and his fellow antinuclear activist-intellectuals sought to forge with concerned citizens of all sorts.

Mills therefore remained committed to engaging the public sphere from a distance, perceiving himself as a potential catalyst for the practical efforts of others. When Russell Johnson, an officer of the American Friends Service Committee, invited Mills in 1958 to speak at a conference in Boston on the arms race, Mills declined, explaining:

> I'd very much like to be with you in Boston in April but I cannot. My job is writing books: that is my action. (Sometimes I lecture publicly because I *must* for the money in it—my minimum fee as of now is

---

[74]Riesman to Robert Paul Jones, School of Social and Community Services, University of Missouri (December 11, 1972), David Riesman Papers, HUG (FP) 99.12, Box 32.

[75]Riesman to Richard Gillam, February 10, 1978, David Riesman Papers, HUG (FP).

$500 and expenses.) If I go out speaking as I am asked to do I could not do my proper, and I believe—for me—more important work. Meetings and speeches: that is your job; if I can help you in this by my books I am very glad indeed, for that is a major reason why I wrote the last one and the ones before that. But I have now to complete the next book and the one after that.[76]

That Mills's declining of the invitation indicates his lack of faith in political action and his commitment exclusively to the production of more texts seems to confirm the charge that he had indeed indulged in postmodern "conspicuous criticism." Indeed, Riesman later interpreted Mills's refusal to participate in the Committee of Correspondence as an indication of his steadfast refusal to affiliate himself with any cause outside himself. "He would have nothing to do with us," Riesman recalled, because "he had to do it all on his own... Even though we offered him a chance, he didn't take it, because it wouldn't have been *his*."[77] Whereas Riesman strove to assume the role of an organic intellectual, seeking out smaller communities of lawmakers, activists, and simply concerned citizens for dialogue about the imperiled planet, Mills chose to remain in the traditional intellectual role of circulating his ideas among unorganized, anonymous readers of opinion journals and nonfiction books.

Mills himself, however, invoked the Deweyan principle of publicizing ideas in the name of the democratization of communication, regardless of the present obstacles to actual political activity. As Jim Miller has argued, criticisms such as Horowitz's that Mills had forsaken sociology by indulging in facile sloganeering deny that his dissemination of a powerfully democratic message to whomever might pay attention possesses any compatibility with sociology. On the contrary, Miller argues, Mills "set out to bend the mass media to his own ends, urging intellectuals 'to make the mass media the means of liberal—which is to say, liberating—education.'"[78] That he declined to participate in

---

[76]Mills to Russell Johnson, December 15, 1958, published in Kathryn and Pamela Mills, eds., *C. Wright Mills: Letters and Autobiographical Writings* (Berkeley: University of California Press, 2000), 270. Significantly, Mills refused here to distinguish between *The Causes* and his earlier works. Although his books have often been divided into his more discretely "sociological" works and more polemical ones, Mills here conceived of them as parts of a continuous effort at national consciousness-raising.

[77]Author interview with David Riesman, Winchester, Massachusetts, September 3, 1995.

[78]Jim Miller, "C. Wright Mills Reconsidered," *Salmagundi* 70–71 (Spring–Summer, 1986): 89, 95. Miller finds Mills's most significant weaknesses not in his compromises with the intellectual sacrifices inherent in writing in a broader public forum but in his allegiance to sociology itself. In his reliance on ideal types, Miller asserts, he failed to provide a vision of democracy that transcended traditional, classical conceptions and could demonstrate its direct applicability to the new conditions of industrial society (97–98).

political movements confirms his long-standing refusal to join organizations in general, and thus, as Peter Clecak has explained, Mills labored under the "radical paradox" of the gulf between political ideals and prospects for political action, choosing to embrace and articulate those ideals in spite of the political quiescence he perceived within the larger society.[79]

Indeed, in *The Causes of World War III*, Mills wrote that, in the absence of a public organized behind the goal of peace, the intellectual nevertheless had to "retain the ideals, and hence by definition to hold them in a utopian way, while waiting."[80] Although one perspective understands Mills's position to contain the risk of languishing in the postmodern realm of commodified textual oblivion, Mills nevertheless had honored the pragmatist demand for acceptance of one's assertions as provisional—and perhaps ineffectual—and therefore valid first steps toward more fruitful, democratic communication.[81]

Within the context of sociology's larger professional struggles and the dilemmas of popular sociology during the 1950s, the experiences of Riesman and Mills show that their most fundamental dilemmas involved conflicts not so much between desires to communicate broadly and the limitations imposed by "mass society" as between sociology's scientific conservatism and its poor public image. Because mainstream sociologists tended to answer the profession's many critics—journalists, novelists, theologians, philosophers, and the like—with a Mertonian appeal for patience and for more time in which to overcome the scientific immaturity of professional social investigation, they left public sociologists such as Riesman and Mills in a no-man's land between an inhibiting professional definition of "science" and lay impatience with a profession that seemed neither "humanistic" in orientation nor readily intelligible or demonstrably useful. These tensions complicated Riesman's struggle to both participate in public discourse and to remain within the culture of professional social science. As a fervent antidogmatist who sought to participate but not pontificate, to promote fruitful

---

[79] Peter Clecak, *Radical Paradoxes: Dilemmas of the American Left: 1945–1970* (New York: Harper & Row, 1973). In his autobiographical writings, which he addressed to a fictitious Russian named "Tovarich," Mills opined on his commitment to personal autonomy and on how the life of the academician offered a greater degree of freedom than that afforded by other professions. See Kathryn and Pamela Mills, *C. Wright Mills: Letters*, 297.

[80] C. Wright Mills, *The Causes of World War III* (New York: Simon and Schuster, 1958), 93.

[81] A highly critical view of Mills's public commitments throughout his career can be found in Guy Oakes and Arthur J. Vidich, *Collaboration, Reputation, and Ethics in American Academic Life: Hans H. Gerth and C. Wright Mills* (Urbana: University of Illinois Press, 1999), in which the authors charge Mills with naked opportunism, reckless self-promotion, and deception, particularly over the course of his collaboration with Gerth on *From Max Weber* and *Character and Social Structure*.

conceptualization and to avoid vulgarization, his approach antagonized more orthodox peers, as well as public critics who roundly perceived sociology as a nebulous endeavor without a clear purpose or significance. Mills similarly severed his professional ties in the name of speaking truth to power, evincing the response from both former disciples and peers that he had sacrificed professional rigor and standards to expand his audience. Finally, not only were Mills's and Riesman's efforts insufficient to reorient public perceptions of sociology, they also stimulated a retrenchment within their profession. As such, they reveal the basic tension between sociology's scientific ideals and the perils and promise of democratic communication.

9

Conclusion

The Legacy of the Scientific Identity

The renowned French sociologist Pierre Bourdieu has characterized the period from the end of World War II to the beginning of the 1960s as a critical watershed in the evolution of sociology's professional identity, asserting that "it is only after 1945 that the ambition to give sociology full respectability by constituting it into a *profession* crystallized." Bourdieu cites disciplinary leaders' success during the 1950s in "imposing a true intellectual *orthodoxy*" upon sociology, one that served "to *mimic* what it took to be the major characteristic of a science worthy of the name—namely the surface consensus that was to bestow on sociology the respectability of a discipline at long last non-controversial."[1]

This consensus over a noncontroversial science of sociology, however, proved to be short-lived, as the professional ferment of the early 1960s in the United States initiated a growing diversity of theory, method, and opinion that seemed capable of overthrowing the scientific identity and its dichotomizing of scientific work and public discourse. In November 1963, a new sociological publication appeared that promised a new direction for academic sociology in the United States. Alvin Gouldner, the distinguished Washington University scholar of sociological theory and

---

[1]Pierre Bourdieu, epilogue to Bourdieu and James S. Coleman, eds., *Social Theory for a Changing Society* (Boulder, CO: Westview Press, 1991), 378–79.

organizational analysis and the magazine's founder, declared that *Trans-action* would strive to engineer "transactions" between sociology and the public sphere, "to span the communication gap between two communities now poorly connected: the social sciences—anthropology, economics, political science, psychology, sociology—and the general public." Sociology's "findings and ideas," he declared, would be presented in a readily intelligible form, thereby "facilitating their use in everyday life." *Trans-action* would avoid abstruse jargon, "translating technical terms into everyday language" to provide decision makers with easily accessible studies on "the major institutional problem areas of modern life," which Gouldner defined as those of "industry, medicine, housing, welfare, social service, law, religion, education, race relations, politics, and government." Modern sociologists possessed an ever-greater responsibility to assume this role, for their higher contemporary profile and the exigencies of modernity made public engagement essential to sociology's maintenance of legitimacy. "Like the physicist regarding the ruins of Hiroshima, the social scientist studying contemporary problems and the complex relationships among modern men knows that he can no longer discharge his social responsibilities by retreating from the world 'until more is known,'" Gouldner warned.[2]

The appearance of *Trans-action* did indeed seem to herald a new public-spiritedness within American sociology. By the early 1960s, scholars such as Irving Louis Horowitz, Norman Birnbaum, Ralf Dahrendorf, Stanley Aronowitz, G. William Domhoff, Maurice Zeitlin, and others had taken up C. Wright Mills's call for trenchant critiques of contemporary society, and in many cases their work communicated well beyond professional sociological discourse.[3] In addition, a proliferation of sociological best sellers appeared to undermine the Mertonian conception that sociological writing, as scientific work, differed qualitatively from popular writing. As Herbert Gans's evidence reveals, at least sixteen titles by sociologists sold more than 50,000 copies between 1962 and 1970, and half of these sold more than 100,000, including

---

[2] Alvin W. Gouldner, "About Trans-action," *Trans-action* 1, 1 (November 1963). For a history of *Trans-action*, see Irving Louis Horowitz, "On Entering the Tenth Year of Transaction: The Relationship of Social Science and Critical Journalism," *Society* 10, 1 (November–December 1972): 49–79.

[3] See Irving Louis Horowitz, ed., *The New Sociology: Essays in Social Science and Social Theory in Honor of C. Wright Mills* (New York: Oxford University Press, 1964); Steven E. Deutsch and John Howard, *Where It's At: Radical Perspectives in Sociology* (New York: Harper & Row, 1970); Martin Oppenheimer, Martin J. Murray, and Rhonda F. Levine, eds., *Radical Sociologists and the Movement: Experiences, Lessons, and Legacies* (Philadelphia: Temple University Press, 1991) is a collection of autobiographical essays on various expressions of radical sociological work and activity during the 1960s and 1970s, including the sociology liberation movement, Marxist and humanist sociologies, and the opening of new ASA sections on ethnic, gender, and world systems sociology.

Gans's own *The Urban Villagers* (1962), Howard Becker's *Outsiders* (1963), Irving Louis Horowitz's *War Games* (1963), and Kai Erikson's *Wayward Puritans* (1966). In addition, Eliot Liebow's *Tally's Corner* (1967), Richard Sennett's *The Fall of Public Man* (1967), and Philip Slater's *The Pursuit of Loneliness* (1970) sold half a million copies each.[4] Such works not only enjoyed lay popularity, but many exerted a profound influence upon professional sociology, thereby refuting Robert Merton's assertion in *Social Theory and Social Structure* that an emphasis on clarity and literary quality necessarily undermined a study's scholarly integrity.

In addition, between the latter half of the 1950s and early 1960s, a myriad of theoretical challenges to the Columbia-Harvard dominance emerged, as the perspectives of conflict theory and symbolic interactionism gained sufficient influence to compete with that of Parsonian functionalism.[5] In addition,

---

[4] Herbert Gans, "Best-Sellers by Sociologists: An Exploratory Study," *Contemporary Sociology* 26, 2 (March 1997): 134.

[5] Jeffrey Alexander provides an overview of the theoretical challenges to the Parsonian conception of action in *Twenty Lectures: Sociological Theory Since World War II* (New York: Columbia University Press, 1987). Lewis Coser and Ralf Dahrendorf criticized functionalism's overemphasis on social structure's order-producing essence and advocated more attention to the dynamics of social conflict. See Lewis Coser, *The Functions of Social Conflict* (New York: Free Press, 1956); Ralf Dahrendorf, "Out of Utopia: Toward a Reorientation of Sociological Analysis," *American Journal of Sociology* 64, 2 (September 1958): 115–27; and Dahrendorf, *Class and Class Conflict in an Industrial Society* (London: Routledge & Keegan Paul, 1959). In 1961, Dennis Wrong attacked functionalism for its minimizing of individual agency, questioning its suggestion that individuals assimilated or "internalized" social norms passively, and calling for a more dialectical view that appreciated the sociological importance of individual agency. Individuals, he argued, are "social, but not entirely socialized." See Dennis Wrong, "The Oversocialized Conception of Man in Modern Sociology," *American Sociological Review* 26, 2 (April 1962): 183–93. Symbolic interaction theorists derived from George Herbert Mead an appreciation of the role that interacting individuals played in the construction and exchange of symbols, concluding that individuals played a more active role in creating social meaning—and, therefore, in creating society itself—than functionalism had suggested. Erving Goffman, a student of Herbert Blumer and Everett Hughes, constructed a "sociology of everyday life," which sought to illuminate social interaction as an ever-changing process of role selection rather than the functionalist bias toward the overdetermination of norms and roles. Exchange theory, derived from the work of the French anthropologists Marcel Mauss and Claude Levi-Strauss, posited that individuals sought self-gratification through their interpersonal interactions, so that these interactions resembled economic transactions that produced "returns" for the individuals involved. George Homans pioneered the exchange-theory approach in *Social Behavior: Its Elementary Forms* (New York: Harcourt Brace, 1961). In his 1964 presidential address before the ASA, he challenged functionalism by replacing its emphasis on the equilibrium of social systems with the psychological study of "the behavior of men," claiming that functionalism's neglect of this approach rendered it incapable of explaining social phenomena. See George Homans, "Bringing Men Back In," *American Sociological Review* 29, 5 (December 1964): 809–18. Similarly, Harold Garfinkel's ethnomethodological approach to the study of human interaction challenged Parsonian functionalism by inquiring into how social actors assimilated the norms and values of their societies, fostering a new awareness of human agency in the processes by which individuals actively interpreted their social structures. By the 1970s, scholars had drawn upon the hermeneutical

within the context of the new political culture of the Kennedy era and the subsequent social and cultural changes of the 1960s, the expansion of sociology programs nationally combined with the emergent theoretical challenges to the Harvard–Columbia axis to stimulate a proliferation of new sociological subspecialties that also challenged disciplinary orthodoxies. The continued growth of the profession, the profound expansion of college and university student enrollments, and the rising prominence of programs at Wisconsin, Michigan, and Berkeley in particular, helped foster a greater diversity of theoretical orientations and research methods.[6] In empirical research, the study of race and gender ended the primacy of stratification research, whereas other new fields of the 1960s, such as the study of organizations and occupations, deviance, criminology, modernization, third world dependency, and human sexuality, also reshaped the character of sociological research.

The diversity these trends introduced to sociology eroded the paradigmatic unity the discipline had enjoyed from the end of World War II to the early 1960s, thereby complicating the goal of a discipline with a clear subject matter, precise methodological standards, and coherent theory building.[7] With this growing heterogeneity, the profession's claims to scientific status faced the dilemma of its own profoundly and increasingly diverse theoretical and methodological orientations, as well as divergent conceptions of sociol-

---

tradition of Wilhelm Dilthey and the more contemporary anthropological contributions of Clifford Geertz to assert the primacy of the cultural realm in determining what is understood to be reality, rejecting the idea of social structure as a Parsonian "system" in favor of the idea of society as a product of culture.

[6] The appearance in 1967 of Otis Dudley Duncan and Peter Blau's landmark stratification study, *The American Occupational Structure*, represented a watershed in the progression of quantitative survey research.

[7] Merton attempted to downplay the significance of the strains this growing diversity engendered. In 1959, he strove to demonstrate that it reflected not an erosion of sociology's core identity but rather simply "contrasting evaluations of the worth of one and another kind of sociological work," and thus it, too, constituted an appropriate subject for fruitful sociological study. Sociology could thereby assimilate its own diversity into a root consensus rather than allow it to undermine its scientific identity. See Robert K. Merton, "Social Conflict Over Styles of Sociological Work," in *Transactions of the Fourth World Congress of Sociology* 3 (Louvain, Belgium: International Sociological Association, 1959), 33. Edward Shils approached the problem of heterodoxy by repudiating the growing presence of service-intellectual activity and radical theory, terming them "manipulative" and "alienative" detours on the way to sociological findings "of universal validity." Instead, he advocated "consensual sociology," which, "built around the theory of action," would promote full publicity of sociological methods and ends. Sociologists would become "the contemporary equivalents of the *philosophes*," promoting a consensual society of toleration and mutual respect. Like Merton and like the theorists of liberal pluralism, Shils envisioned a sociology that would participate freely in a democratic marketplace of ideas. See Edward Shils, "The Calling of Sociology," in Talcott Parsons, Edward Shils, Kaspar D. Naegele, and Jesse R. Pitts, eds., *Theories of Society: Foundations of Modern Sociological Theory* (New York: Free Press, 1961), 1440–41.

ogy's subject matter. To many, the very idea of sociology then seemed to exist as merely a rubric accommodating rather uncomfortably a range of diverse and often unconnected researches that possessed but an obscure relation to a scientific whole. In such a state of affairs, as Bennet Berger lamented in the late 1950s, sociology could not embrace its own diversity in the manner of the humanities, for its various schools of thought served as "a constant reminder that not enough is *known*," a grave liability for any science, in which, inevitably, "opinion is tolerated only where facts are not available."[8]

Key developments since the early 1960s have facilitated the communication of sociological observations to nonsociologists. The emergent identity assertions and political movements of women, gays, and historically marginalized racial and ethnic groups during the 1960s and 1970s also encouraged scholarship that could now address interested and varied publics, rather than attempting to cater to the interests and satisfy the curiosities of a single amorphous, homogeneous public. Beginning with the publication of Mirra Komarovsky's *Blue-Collar Marriage* in 1962, women sociologists began to enjoy significant success in bringing gender issues to nonprofessional readers. Scholars such as Lillian Rubin, Carol Stack, Arlie Hochschild, Diane Vaughan, Rosabeth Kanter, Nancy Chodorow, Frances Fox Piven, and Ruth Sidel have produced widely read studies of marriage, poverty and social policy, the balancing of work and home life, relationships, and reproductive choice. Moreover, William Julius Wilson has authored widely influential works on issues of race and class, beginning with his groundbreaking *The Declining Significance of Race* in 1979 and culminating in *The Truly Disadvantaged* in 1987 and *When Work Disappears* in 1996.[9] Gans's statistics on these authors' public successes reveal a strong tendency among women and minority scholars to make their voices heard publicly, thus complementing those earlier popular works that addressed issues such as community life, political power, and the national cultural temper.

After 1963, the Johnson administration's Great Society further enhanced sociology's public role, as government established stronger ties with social scientists. Government agencies called upon sociologists to devise and assess the efficacy of the antipoverty programs of the 1960s, thereby establishing their authority over crucial areas of public policy. In particular, the Johnson administration's acceptance in 1965 of Daniel Patrick Moynihan's report on

---

[8]Bennett Berger, "Sociology and the Intellectuals: An Analysis of a Stereotype," *Antioch Review* 17, 3 (September 1957): 284.

[9]Orlando Patterson's comparative study of slavery from a global perspective and his work on freedom constitute another example of effective interdisciplinary sociology moving beyond the confines of sociological discourse to influence other fields of inquiry, as well as public discourse.

problems of poverty and social decay within black communities, as well as the conclusions Moynihan and Nathan Glazer reached in *Beyond the Melting Pot*, indicated that despite the controversy surrounding the studies—and also because of them—the social sciences had attained new measures of government endorsement and public awareness, both of which continued to develop with the release the following year of James S. Coleman's influential report on the state of the nation's public schools.[10] Furthermore, American political elites had by the late 1960s come to rely upon pollsters to construct effective campaigns, thereby enhancing the profile of survey research.[11]

Although these developments seemed to signal the disruption of the sociological identity of the 1940s and 1950s and its discouragement of communication outside professional social science circles, the preoccupation with scientific status nevertheless persisted. The enlarged scope and greater extent of government support for sociological research enhanced sociologists' status as "experts" in empirical investigation who would serve the public with their scientific—and, therefore, disinterested—techniques. Evaluation research into the effectiveness of Great Society programs, for example, meant that applied sociology had entered the mainstream of liberal policy making, which made such work central to the identity of a discipline that had sought for so long to demonstrate its broader social utility.

The scientific identity also continued to dominate the mainstream sociology journals throughout the 1960s. Charles Perrow, a late-1950s Berkeley graduate, finds evidence of its durability in the conservative character of professional sociological publishing, which exercised a decisive influence over sociologists-in-training in American graduate programs. He writes:

> Until perhaps the 1960s, mainline journals were more open to innovative and controversial work. Since then there has been more controversial work, but there has also been more "normal science" that develops established paradigms or reinterprets the classics in minor ways. The number of prestigious journals expanded very little, so they found less room for controversial articles, except in the occasional "special issue." The evidence for this view is that the

---

[10]Gans's statistics reveal that *Beyond the Melting Pot* has sold between 300,000 and 400,000 copies. For the political context and critical responses to the report, see Lee Rainwater and William L. Yancey, eds., *The Moynihan Report and the Politics of Controversy* (Cambridge, MA: MIT Press, 1967). On the Coleman Report, see Aage B. Sorensen and Seymour Spilerman, eds., *Social Theory and Social Policy: Essays in Honor of James S. Coleman* (Westport, CT: Praeger, 1993).

[11]Gideon Sjoberg and Ted R. Vaughan, "The Bureaucratization of Sociology: Its Impact on Theory and Research," in Ted R. Vaughan, Gideon Sjoberg, and Larry T. Reynolds, eds., *A Critique of Contemporary American Sociology* (Dix Hills, NY: General Hall, 1993), 78.

mainstream journals are filling up with the work of graduate students and new Ph.D.'s, mostly working in established paradigms, as perhaps they should, while those interested in more exploratory, unconventional, and reflective work have created new outlets.[12]

Perrow's observation suggests that important scholarly gatekeepers discouraged types of scholarship to which publics are particularly receptive and that what remained a professional desideratum among the leading lights of the profession after World War II had achieved a vital form of institutional sanction two decades later, in spite of growing heterogeneity in theory building and problem selection. Indeed, by the 1970s, as Steven Seidman observes, influential theorists such as Randall Collins and Peter Blau rejected Parsonian functionalism but nevertheless persisted in seeking the integration of their increasingly variegated discipline through the construction of a truly scientific approach that would unify sociological study.[13]

The scientific identity's durability in the midst of the political and intellectual ferment of the 1960s reveals how deeply rooted the discipline's professional aspirations to scientific status had been since 1945, such that even the radical scholarship of the 1960s and 1970s that challenged the social sciences' participation in the furtherance of governmental, corporate, and military objectives failed to erode its foundations.[14] Hence, to conceive of the scientific

---

[12]Charles Perrow, "journaling Careers," in L. L. Cummings and Peter J. Frost, eds., *Publishing in the Organizational Sciences* (Homewood, IL: Richard D. Irwin, 1985), 227.

[13]Steven Seidman, *Contested Knowledge: Social Theory in the Postmodern Era* (Cambridge, MA: Blackwell, 1994). Other observers, such as David Hollinger, have asserted that new ideological and theoretical developments in social science by the early 1960s sustained the scientific ideal by associating its norms and standards with the demands and pressures of modernity. Hollinger finds a "social scientific triumphalism" in 1960s social science, one sustained by the ascendant belief in the "end of ideology" and by the vogue of modernization theory. The end-of-ideology thesis, he indicates, "took for granted the political security of the enterprise of science," whereas modernization theory posited that Third World economic and social development could occur only where societies accepted "the scientific attitude," which was understood to be "the most important single motor of the modernization process." In this view, social science's scientific identity found legitimation in its relationship to larger political and cultural currents that suggested the necessity of a disinterested scientific outlook. See David Hollinger, "Science as a Weapon in *Kulturkämpfe* in the United States During and After World War II," in *Science, Jews, and Secular Culture: Studies in Mid-Twentieth Century American Intellectual History* (Princeton, NJ: Princeton University Press, 1996), 167.

[14]Conspicuous among these was the U.S. State Department program Operation Camelot, which enlisted sociologists and anthropologists in evaluating the revolutionary potential within Latin American societies with the intention of learning more about how to prevent radical insurgencies and preserve American influence in the region. See Irving Louis Horowitz, "The Life and Death of Project Camelot," *Trans-action* 3, 1 (November–December 1965).

ideal as primarily the product of Cold War ideology or of the machinations of interested institutionalized gatekeepers promoting applied research at the expense of more broadly critical or creative scholarship would be to deny the primacy of the more purely intellectual aspirations of those who forged it. Merton, Parsons, Lazarsfeld, Stouffer, and others embraced it not simply because they found it compatible or even synonymous with liberal-bureaucratic institutional values and goals, nor solely because it represented a formidable weapon against totalitarian ideologies, but because it transcended such temporal concerns and provided the practice of sociological work with the necessary autonomy from bureaucratic, economic, cultural, and political pressures for true knowledge to accumulate. That is, science existed as an end in itself, defining without outside interference the conditions necessary for its own realization.[15] In particular, science insulated sociology from the kinds of lay assaults upon its integrity that persisted throughout the late 1940s and 1950s, so that sociologists' measured and judicious responses to complaints about their own alleged obscurantism and otherworldly detachment proved that mainstream sociology remained impervious to attacks both from inside

---

[15]Indeed, the scientific ethos ultimately transcended postwar liberalism itself, crossing ideological boundaries so as to question Hollinger's claim of scientific idealism as an expression of political ideology. The contemporary Marxist sociologist Erik Olin Wright, in promoting his "analytical Marxism," demands a commitment to the empirical research methods in the name of "science" similar to that of ostensibly liberal sociologists. Although he distinguishes his science from the dogmatic rigidity of "scientific Marxism," he nevertheless adopts what he terms a "realist" view of science that shares much in common with that of mainstream sociology. In this view, he explains, "science attempts to identify the underlying *mechanisms* which generate empirical phenomena we experience in the world," and although he acknowledges that the observer's subjectivity and the sheer complexity and interdependence of that which is observed complicate such efforts, he nevertheless calls for the use of "statistically rigorous data analysis" to "construct explanations based on real mechanisms that exist in the world independently of our theories." Although he acknowledges that, like capitalist society itself, such methods can co-opt the radical scholar by "narrowing the field of legitimate questions to those that are tractable with these sophisticated tools," he sees them as the only legitimate means for the construction of "enclaves of radical scholarship." Like Merton, he hopes that, with enough dedication to the scientific effort, his sociology can create a larger, more comprehensive—and, most important, more generally credible—picture of the world "out there." Wright's epistemology reveals that the persistence of the faith in a true science of society had more to do with the momentum disciplinary leaders from Harvard and Columbia had generated in that direction during the 1950s, more than did the "liberal," "pluralist" political theories of Daniel Bell and Seymour Lipset, or the modernization theories of Alex Inkeles and others. See Wright's "Marxism as a Social Science," 202; and "What Is Analytical Marxism?" 197–98, in *Interrogating Inequality: Essays on Class Analysis, Socialism and Marxism* (New York: Verso, 1994). See also Sjoberg, Vaughan, and Reynolds, "The Bureaucratization of Sociology," 79, on Wright's epistemology. Russell Jacoby asserts, though without substantiation, that it is precisely the "Marxist" sociologists who are arguably most wedded to the scientific outlook, which makes them especially amenable to sociological work that enhances institutional leverage and prestige. See his *The Last Intellectuals: American Culture in the Age of Academe* (New York: Noonday Press, 1987), 185.

and out. For Merton in particular, criticisms of the scientific ideal demonstrated not that sociology had refused to perform its broader professional function but rather that much of American society remained trapped in prescientific modes of thinking that left those without sociological training unable to appreciate sociology's scientific mission. Thus, prominent critics within the profession—particularly Mills and Sorokin—and those outside of it—the Niebuhrs, Hackers, Buckleys, and Kemptons—failed to shake the profession's own sense of itself and its destiny. Their attacks simply reinforced sociology's sense of the rightness of internal communication and the impracticability of engagement with the broader public sphere. As Richard J. Bernstein has observed, critics' more specific objections to sociological methods as unscientific or compromised by their practitioners' participation in social engineering proved insufficient to call the whole scientific endeavor into question, so mainstream sociologists simply gave themselves the benefit of the doubt. Social science therefore entered a "slippery path," first by assuming its own practicability as a science and then by perceiving that no satisfactory arguments had been advanced to indicate otherwise, concluding "that one *ought* to adopt a properly scientific attitude."[16]

The endurance of the scientific identity meant that mainstream sociology continued to emphasize the kind of communicative separation from wider publics that had existed during the 1950s, notwithstanding the appearance of larger numbers of sociological best sellers. This rift, hardened within the crucible of the cultural and political trends and fissures of the 1960s, was also compounded by the fact that laypersons had received throughout the previous decade their impressions of sociology from dubious journalists, disgruntled scholars, and professional and nonprofessional popularizers.[17]

The reigning scientific paradigm has therefore confronted its most formidable challenge not in the tumult of practical politics and social and

---

[16] Richard J. Bernstein, *The Restructuring of Social and Political Theory* (Philadelphia: University of Pennsylvania Press, 1976), 42.

[17] As the 1960s witnessed professional sociology's continued exacerbation of its own low public profile, nonsociologists appropriated sociological concepts and methods, and sociological language entered the national vocabulary. In particular, the emergence by the early 1960s of what became "New Journalism" provided a mechanism for the popularization of sociological insights that traveled far beyond Vance Packard's conservative sociological reportage. Led by Tom Wolfe, its most fervent promoter and practitioner, New Journalism strove to wed literary devices to journalistic productions in what Wolfe described in a belated manifesto as an updating of the social realism of Dickens, Balzac, and Tolstoy. Like the great novelists of the nineteenth century, the journalist would seek to re-create a social world for the reader in all its complexity, including the devices of scene construction, elaboration of subjects' thoughts and feelings, sensitivity to authorial point of view, and the meticulous documentation of "everyday gestures, habits, manners, customs, styles of furniture, clothing," and other ephemera. See Tom Wolfe, "Seizing the

cultural pressures but instead in the philosophical turn toward postmodernism. This crisis for the profession had been anticipated in the early 1960s by Thomas Kuhn, who in *The Structure of Scientific Revolutions* challenged the conventional idea of linear, incrementalist scientific development with his conception of successive and discrete paradigms of scientific thought.[18] As Richard Bernstein observes, Kuhn's revisionism joined a wholesale attack on existing theories of science, so that "there was a growing sense that there was something artificial and distortive about the very way in which the problems in the philosophy of science were formulated," which fostered "a sensitivity to science as a historical, ongoing activity."[19] For American sociology and the Mertonian view of scientific development, Kuhn's paradigm theory meant that patient efforts toward the construction of a science of society were futile, in that they possessed neither essential validity nor any guarantee of lasting legitimacy. Thus, any science of society itself represented merely one of a multiplicity of possible sciences of society, each with its own internal logic and structures of inclusion and exclusion of particular ideas and discoveries.

This skepticism as to the efficacy of a science of society soon made its way into professional sociological discourse. Four years after Kuhn, Peter Berger and Thomas Luckmann published *The Social Construction of Reality*, in which they argued that social life lacked an essence independent of the knower, so that the perspective of any particular group of knowers reflected more the group's interests and perspective than an objective understanding of existence.[20] A year

---

Power," in *The New Journalism* (New York: Harper & Row, 1973), 31–32. It is noteworthy that virtually all of the writing that fell under that rubric remained profoundly sociological in both its perspectives and, most notably, in its subject matter. In *Esquire, Harper's, Rolling Stone, New York Magazine*, the *Village Voice*, and other popular magazines between 1962 to 1970, these articles and essays addressed such subjects as crime, deviance, subcultures, warfare, class, gender, sexuality, race relations, the culture of the professions, and the production and mass-marketing of culture. Moreover, the New Journalists adopted a research style that bore strong resemblances to the participant-observation technique of the 1920s Chicago School of Sociology—the very ethnographic methods that had fallen from favor during the 1950s—in which writers would immerse themselves within their subject matter, constructing deep contextualizations of events and extensive interviews with participants.

[18] David Hollinger cites Kuhn's contribution as the most prominent of a corpus of early 1960s works on the philosophy of science, including Fritz Machlup's *The Production and Distribution of Knowledge in the United States* (1962), Derek Price's *Big Science, Little Science* (1963), Don K. Price's *The Scientific Estate* (1965), Karl Hill's *The Management of Scientists* (1964), and Warren Hagstrom's *The Scientific Community* (1965). See Hollinger, "Free Enterprise and Free Inquiry: The Emergence of Laissez-Faire Communitarianism in the Ideology of Science in the United States," in *Science, Jews, and Secular Culture*.

[19] Richard J. Bernstein, *The New Constellation: The Ethical-Political Horizons of Modernity-Postmodernity* (Cambridge, MA: MIT Press, 1992), 23.

[20] Peter L. Berger and Thomas Luckmann, *The Social Construction of Reality: A Treatise in the Sociology of Knowledge* (Garden City, NY: Doubleday, 1966).

later, Harold Garfinkel published a collection of studies in ethnomethodology that posited that social meanings existed as the language creations of groups of individuals seeking to make sense of their world, thereby setting the stage for debates over the primacy of subjectivity in sociologists' attempts to make sense of society.[21] For a time, ethnomethodology seemed poised to make every sociologist his or her own methodologist, rendering a unifying scientific identity impossible.

With the profound impact of postmodernism on the humanities disciplines in the 1970s and 1980s and of Foucauldian denials of the existence of essential meanings independent of exernal circumstances, in particular, American sociology found itself confronted with the most compelling contemporary philosophical challenge to its scientific identity. Ironically, postmodernism's critique of sociology shared significant characteristics with the types of criticisms leveled at 1950s sociology by literary critics, philosophers, theologians, and journalists. Much as antisociologists such as Malcolm Cowley and Murray Kempton had blasted sociology for its belaboring of trivia and apparent detachment from the very social life it purported to study, postmodern assessments of social science have also encouraged the conclusion that sociology represents an exercise in futility. The postmodernist critique differs from the earlier humanistic critique, however, in its wholesale rejection of sociology's pursuit of social truth itself, insisting that its methodological and linguistic attempts to represent the social realm produce nothing but immediately replaceable "texts," none of which capture the essence of social reality.[22] Whereas the critics of the 1950s had insisted upon the humanistic study of society and appealed to time-honored criteria of morality and perspective, more recent philosophical arguments deny the validity of the entire project of approaching "society" as something amenable to representation.

The other postmodernist objection to a scientific sociology evidences another partial continuity with the 1950s critiques and appears simply to

---

[21] Harold Garfinkel, *Studies in Ethnomethodology* (Englewood Cliffs, NJ: Prentice-Hall, 1967).

[22] See Pauline Rosenau, *Postmodernism and the Social Sciences: Insights, Inroads, and Intrusions* (Princeton, NJ: Princeton University Press, 1992). The sociological debate over postmodernism is the feature of *Contemporary Sociology* 25, 1 (January 1996). Other discussions include Theda Skocpol, "The Dead End of Metatheory," *Contemporary Sociology* 16, 1 (January 1987): 10–12; Todd Gitlin, "Postmodernism: Roots and Politics," in Ian H. Angus and Sut Jhally, eds., *Cultural Politics in Contemporary America* (New York: Routledge, 1989), 347–60; Stanley Aronowitz, "Postmodernism and Politics," in Andrew Ross, ed., *Universal Abandon* (Minneapolis: University of Minnesota Press, 1988); Steven Seidman, "Theory as Social Narrative With a Moral Intent: A Postmodern Intervention," in *Postmodernism and Social Theory* (New York: Blackwell, 1991); Stephen Turner and Mark Wardell, eds., *The Transition in Sociological Theory: The Debate Over General Theory* (Boston: Allen & Unwin, 1986).

extend those earlier objections to a critical extreme. Much as antimodernists such as Joseph Wood Krutch and leftist anti-authoritarians such as Andrew Hacker indicted the social sciences for their complicity with powerful economic and political interests that sought to use them for purposes of mass persuasion and manipulation, the Foucauldian critique of sociology perceives the project of science building not as a process of fostering enlightenment but as the assembling of tools of domination. However, unlike the earlier argument that such abuses stemmed from the likelihood that social science techniques would continually fall into the wrong hands, the Foucauldian conception asserts that such techniques exist among larger constellations of language practices, all of which serve to circumscribe—and, therefore, to limit and control—human existence. Thus, inevitably, social science activity contributes to the mechanics of domination by sheer diffusion, impoverishing the known universe as it describes and defines it, thereby subjecting humanity to unseen structures of meaning that make "reality" itself a prison.

Just as Merton failed to address the 1950s critics of sociology forthrightly, defending the scientific project not by emphasizing sociology's broader social meaning and utility but by asserting its innocuousness and noting the contradictions in the critics' arguments that sociology could be at once trivial and dangerous, contemporary sociology lacks an adequate response to the postmodern critics and their charges of the fraudulence of sociology's efforts at representation and of the inhumane applications of its techniques. Instead, postmodernism appears to the practitioners of a science-minded discipline to reflect the intransigence of the humanists and their continued refusal to take up C. P. Snow's call for them to commit themselves to the bridging of the gap between themselves and the world of science. Like Merton, who questioned the very authority of nonsociologists to challenge sociology's scientific status, mainstream sociology has sought to excuse itself from "philosophical" discussions of its epistemological assumptions as irrelevant to science building.

Consequently, as Steven Seidman observes, sociological theorists have continued to adhere to the "metatheoretical" goal of constructing "foundations," or theories that seek to "uncover a logic of society" and to establish "the one true vocabulary that mirrors the social universe."[23] This mission, accompanied by the incrementalist empirical project of constructing small pieces of the whole of that social reality, means that sociology seeks to avoid the implications of postmodernity, protecting itself from antifoundationalist criticism with the kind of insularity Parsons, Merton, and others had deemed necessary for professional survival decades earlier. Consequently, Seidman and others

---

[23] Steven Seidman, "The End of Sociological Theory" in Seidman, ed., *The Postmodern Turn: New Perspectives on Social Theory* (Cambridge: Cambridge University Press, 1994), 120.

warn, sociology not only exacerbates its own delegitimation as a means of understanding social life, but it also leaves itself vulnerable to charges that its "science," as a specialized discourse, "is tied to the project of Western modernity and to a multiplicity of more local, more specific struggles around class, status, gender, sexuality, race, and so on." In other words, a sociology that isolates itself from community life can be easily charged with ethnocentrism, androcentrism, heterocentrism, and a host of other subterfuges that function in the service of its own normative discourse on society.[24]

The postmodern turn has also threatened to lead sociology down the path of epistemological solipsism.[25] If in the face of philosophical objections to its methods and theoretical categories the discipline fails to offer a firm basis for the validity of its observations, it stands to lose any basis for demonstrating the superiority of particular theories and methods over others. Garfinkel's ethnomethodological approach, in particular, advanced the primacy of individual assessments of experience through language, including that of the individual sociological researcher, leading some scholars to declare independence from research standards imposed from outside themselves.[26] Postmodernism thus presents the possibility of professional breakdown, as fragile and arguably arbitrary standards of research and publication lose any basis for authority other than that of inclusion and of exclusion of particular points of view.

Those seeking to defend sociology against postmodernism have indicated that sociology stands poorly equipped to answer its philosophical charges because it tends to accept the postmodernist criticisms passively rather than subjecting them to critical scrutiny. One veteran sociologist complains that many sociologists "consider philosophy to be superordinate to sociology," and in this deferential atmosphere, "philosophers' critiques of sociology can be uninhibited and invidious." "In essence," he concludes, "philosophers' role is to

---

[24] Ibid., 124.

[25] Zygmunt Bauman makes this point in "Is There a Postmodern Sociology," in Seidman, ed., *The Postmodern Turn*, 199: "The recognition of futility of universal standards, brought along by postmodernity, allows that self-centered concerns treat lightly everything outside criticism. There is nothing to stop one from coming as close as possible to the sociological equivalent of *l'art pour l'art*."

[26] In *Culture and Truth* (Boston: Beacon Press, 1989), Renato Rosaldo describes the example of anthropologist Jean Briggs's *Never in Anger: Portrait of an Eskimo Family*, in which Briggs dispensed with any semblance of ethnographic "objectivity" and incorporated her own feelings into her study—especially those of "depression, frustration, rage, and humiliation"—to illuminate the stoicism at the core of Eskimo life. Rosaldo sees Briggs's "going native" as a constructive repudiation of Weber's "manly" scientific ethic of disinterested, dispassionate scholarship, in which the explicit inclusion of the researcher's feelings and experiences reveals more fully the nature of the subject of research. In sociology, Carolyn Ellis's works, which incorporate highly personal feelings and experiences into studies in "auto-ethnography" or "emotional sociology," represent a methodological innovation of a similar sort.

decree and criticize, sociologists' role is to accept," and meanwhile, "the practice of philosophy goes unexamined."[27] Others worry that the sheer size of the discipline and the multiplicity of its subspecialties render it vulnerable to the kinds of fragmentation characteristic of postmodernity, which deepen its existing identity crisis. Randall Collins suggests that "sociology may have grown too big" and that the breadth of social material for which it is responsible yields "more knowledge than can be digested," so that "it has fragmented in substance and purpose." Such a state of affairs "facilitates raids," he observes, "because most sociologists know little and care less about what is happening in distant specialties."[28] Sociology's very diversity and its cross-fertilization of other disciplinary pursuits make it more likely that philosophical objections to it would go unchallenged, for the defenders of something called "sociology" would inevitably encounter the problem of defining what exactly distinguishes sociological work from other forms of social inquiry, many of which borrow from and contribute to sociology's many subfields.

For Seidman, the responsibility to communicate sociological ideas publicly stands as the only reliable form of legitimation and relevance open to sociology. Like Richard Rorty, he advocates the "pragmatic turn" as the way out of the postmodern dilemma, for this commitment abandons the quest for sociological "truth" in favor of a discourse that opens itself to nonprofessional audiences and to their practical and moral concerns. He demands the replacement of sociological theory with "social theory," declaring the difference to lie in the latter's embrace of "broad social narratives" and involvement in "contemporary social conflicts and public debates."[29] Sociologists would serve as facilitators of democratic discourse, promoting open communication rather than attempting to resolve social questions once and for all in the name of building scientific edifices. They "would become defenders of an elaborated reason against the partisans of closure and orthodoxy, and of all those who try to circumvent open public moral debate by partisan or foundationalist appeals."[30]

From this perspective, sociology has languished in protracted "crisis" because its practitioners have argued over how best to obtain "valid" or "true" results from research rather than seeking the democratization of truth seeking

---

[27] Joel Smith, "Emancipating Sociology: Postmodernism and Mainstream Sociological Practice," *Social Forces* 74, 1 (September 1995): 64, 66–67.

[28] Randall Collins, "The Confusion of the Modes of Sociology," in Steven Seidman and David G. Wagner, eds., *Postmodernism and Social Theory*, 187–88.

[29] Ibid., 120.

[30] Ibid., 135. A debate along these lines of postmodernism *versus* pragmatism occurs between Seidman and Patricia Ticineto Clough, Laurel Richardson, and Norman K. Denzin in *The Sociological Quarterly* 37, 4 (Fall 1996): 721–59.

itself. Richard Bernstein refers to the latter position as "fallibilism," or the acceptance that all propositions are provisional and that in any philosophical or empirical endeavor, the pragmatist must, in Charles Sanders Peirce's words, "trust rather to the multitude and variety of its arguments than to the conclusiveness of any one."[31] As a democratic community of inquiry presents the only environment in which such a fallibilistic ideal could be realized, sociology as a form of democratic practice must therefore adhere less to self-definitions that emphasize its distinctiveness and separate sphere of communicative competence and instead embrace whatever means of communication lie at its disposal. Sociology then comes to share elements of journalism, literature, and other forms of expression. As Rorty promises, "When the notion of knowledge as representation goes, then the notion of inquiry as split into discrete sectors with discrete subject matters goes. The lines between novels, newspaper articles, and sociological research get blurred. The lines between subject matters are drawn by reference to current practical concerns, rather than putative ontological status."[32]

This role of publicizing sociological work also provides sociology with at least a modicum of protection against charges of social and psychological manipulation. In his assessment of postmodern sociology, Zygmunt Bauman posits two types of sociological knowledge: one "meliorative," involving applied work in the service of private and (especially) public clients, and the other "emancipatory," or work performed in the name of equipping citizens for the democratic confrontation of social problems. Support for the first type, he asserts, is "drying up," as the state reduces its use of sociology to such ends as "the management of 'law and order,'" and as administrative interests lose faith in using social science to "complete the promise of modernity." Thus, Bauman anticipates the end of sociological positivism and its "grand designs," "cultural crusades," and "legitimizing visions," so that sociology will no longer need to provide the state with "models of centrally administered rational society."[33] Happily, sociology would then be left with its emancipatory function, that "the shifting of attention to the kind of knowledge which

---

[31] Charles Sanders Peirce, quoted in Bernstein, *The New Constellation*, 327.

[32] Richard Rorty, "Method, Social Science, and Social Hope," in *Consequences of Pragmatism* (Minneapolis: University of Minnesota Press, 1982), 203. Clearly, many, if not most, sociologists would be less than comfortable with such an outcome. Jonathan Turner writes that "if the programs of the critics were followed, sociology would be a mixed bag of rather pedestrian philosophizing, historical and empirical description, ideological debate and commentary, vague scheme-building, commentary on current (and past) events, extreme relativism, and a general doubt that we can know or do anything." See his "The Promise of Positivism," in Seidman and Wagner, eds., *Postmodernism and Social Theory*, 167.

[33] Zygmunt Bauman, "Is There a Postmodern Sociology?" in Seidman, ed., *The Postmodern Turn*, 201.

may be used by human individuals in their efforts to enlarge the sphere of autonomy and solidarity."[34] In this view, as Rorty observes, both the pragmatist and Foucauldian conceptions of social knowledge are correct: such knowledge possesses the potential both for liberation and domination, and only in sharing such knowledge does the former triumph over the latter.

The pragmatist vision asks a great deal of a highly bureaucratized discipline dependent upon foundation grants, corporate contracts, and other forms of outside sustenance for survival and always under pressure to demonstrate within an increasingly privatized and commercialized university culture an often vulgarized practical utility. Nevertheless, American Sociological Association (ASA) presidents have called for the fulfillment of public sociological roles for decades and often rather presciently, it turns out. In his 1976 presidential address before the ASA, Alfred McClung Lee advocated a "social science news service" to promote clearer communication between professional sociology and the organs of the mass media, "to give sociology its full public image."[35] In his 1988 ASA presidential address, Herbert Gans demanded a renewed commitment to social criticism, calling it the "revitalizing of an old mode of public sociology." Noting that journalists, essayists, literary critics, and philosophers rather than sociologists had come to assume this role, he asserted not that sociologists should become journalists or "humanistic critics" but that sociologists might enjoy a fruitful cooperation and collaboration with them in making sociological issues public assets.[36]

Gans's call for cooperation across professional and disciplinary boundaries requires the abandonment of scientific competence as a measure of professional status, a move that would repudiate the insularity and defensiveness which 1950s sociology helped solidify within the postwar profession. Sociologists' long-standing resentments of popularizers such as Vance Packard would have to give way to an atmosphere of mutual encouragement. As Gans warns, arrogant rejections of "pop sociology" threaten to "turn off members of the lay public otherwise ready to pay attention to our work. Worse yet, wholesale

---

[34]Ibid., 201.

[35]Alfred McClung Lee, "Sociology for Whom?" (presidential address, annual meeting of the American Sociological Association, New York, NY, August 30, 1976); American Sociological Review 41, 6 (December 1976): 934.

[36]Herbert J. Gans, "Sociology in America: The Discipline and the Public" (presidential address, annual meeting of the American Sociological Association, Atlanta, GA, 1988); American Sociological Review 54, 1 (February 1989): 8–9. More recently, Gans has advocated the strengthening of public sociology through sociologists' communication of research findings in "clear, nontechnical English, especially when they study topics that the public wants or needs to understand better," as well as the selection of research problems "that most concern, and vex, Americans." See his "Wishes for the Discipline's Future," in Chronicle of Higher Education 51, 49 (August 12, 2005), B9.

rejection of sociologies other than ours may end up by biting the public hand that feeds us."[37] Effective popularization, on the other hand, "will increase public interest in sociology" and thereby benefit everyone. Sociologists must therefore not only adopt a more pluralistic perspective but also abandon the use of "Sociologese" in favor of comprehensible English. Ultimately, Gans asserts, an opening up of sociology to public communication would prevent further "scholarly insulation and a correlative lack of reality checks, which can disconnect our work from what is generally referred to as the real world."[38]

More recently, scholars have called for a more-expansive public sociology that transcends publication in such nonacademic forums as opinion magazines and major urban newspapers to reach a broader range of publics. In his 2004 ASA presidential address, Michael Burawoy distinguishes between this "traditional" form of public participation and an "organic" one that engages publics at the community level and reaches those with limited or negligible access to elite forms of media and opinion.[39] In the case of the former, he argues, "the publics being addressed are generally invisible in that they cannot be seen, thin in that they do not generate much internal interaction, passive in that they do not constitute a movement or organization, and they are usually mainstream." In the case of the latter, the organic sociologist "works in close connection with a visible, thick, active, local and often counter-public."[40] Although Burawoy acknowledges the indispensability of the traditional public sociological role of addressing a broad readership, he insists that organic public sociology fosters reciprocal relationships, in which meaningful dialogue fosters "mutual education" that not only strengthens such publics as labor organizations, neighborhood groups, religious communities, immigrant groups and organizations, and activist networks—and indeed often helps to define them and makes their members conscious of themselves as publics—but also enriches sociological work itself.[41] Moreover, as Social Science Research Council president Craig Calhoun asserts, this engagement with a wide range of publics would not only

---

[37] Ibid., 8.

[38] Ibid., 11.

[39] Michael Burawoy, introduction to "Public Sociologies: A Symposium from Boston College," *Social Problems* 51, 1 (February 2004): 104, 128.

[40] Michael Burawoy, "For Public Sociology" (presidential address, annual meeting of the American Sociological Association, San Francisco, CA, August 15, 2004); *American Sociological Review* 70, 1 (February 2005), 7.

[41] Such interaction, Burawoy notes, can give "normative and political valence" to social groups and that "to fail to do so is to give carte blanche to state and market to fill the vacuum." See his "The Critical Turn to Public Sociology," in Rhonda F. Levine, ed., *Enriching the Sociological Imagination: How Radical Sociology Changed the Discipline* (Leiden, The Netherlands: Koninkijke Brill, 2004), 319.

increase the opportunities for communication between sociologists and wider communities but also foster more effective problem identification and the setting of research agendas.[42] In particular, such an opening of dialogue with various publics suggests the importance of sociological research "from the bottom-up."

Auspiciously, some current public-spirited sociologists have connected this conception of myriad publics to the oft-underemphasized dimensions of professional sociological work. They have, for example, championed ethnographic methods as a means of reducing the distance between the researcher and his or her subjects and, Gans argues, to produce scholarship that is more widely accessible.[43] Others have called for a greater emphasis on the sociologist's public role as professional educator: Stephen Pfohl of Boston College characterizes the college classroom as an essential environment for raising critical questions about "the common sense of the dominant culture," particularly to "counter the dominant cultural narratives spun by those who profit most from the exploitation of others."[44] Indeed, as Burawoy notes, students are the sociologist's "first public" and are thus an essential partner in the creation of the kinds of reciprocally educative relationships demanded of the public sociologist, as they bring their experience to the classroom and educate the educator.[45]

The character of contemporary public discourse on social issues demonstrates amply that where professional sociological participation in public communication has remained insufficiently assertive, other voices have proven adept at entering the void. The postwar history of professional psychology, for example, exhibits the effective substitution of a therapeutic outlook for public issues of a more sociological nature. As Ellen Herman has shown, postwar American psychology successfully sold itself and its faith in personality-adjustment to public and private clients as the source of solutions to such diverse problems as Cold War containment, suburban alienation, workplace discontent, and even women's demands for social equality.[46] More

---

[42] Craig Calhoun, "Toward a More Public Social Science" (president's report, Social Science Research Council, 2004), 13–17. Available at http://www.ssrc.org/programs/publications_editors/publications/PresReport/SSRC_PresReport.pdf.

[43] Herbert J. Gans, "Wishes for the Discipline's Future," *Chronicle of Higher Education* 51, 49 (August 12, 2005), B9.

[44] Stephen Pfohl, "Blessings and Curses in the Sociology Classroom," quoted in "Public Sociologies: A Symposium from Boston College," 113.

[45] Michael Burawoy, "Public Sociologies: Contradictions, Dilemmas, and Possibilities," *Social Forces* 82, 4 (June 2004), 1608.

[46] Ellen Herman, *The Romance of American Psychology: Political Culture in the Age of Experts* (Berkeley: University of California Press, 1995).

ominously, conservative think tanks have since the 1970s adapted sociological methods to the promotion of antistatist, free-market economic policy making, rollbacks of social programs for the underprivileged, draconian immigration policies, and such dubious propositions as that the United States has "resolved" its most pressing racial problems. Such examples not only indicate the efficacy of the efforts of those who have capitalized on sociology's public default, but they also reveal that a demand for meaningful sociological perspectives exists at many social levels, from individual self-reflection and decision making to governmental policy making.

A public sociology informed by pragmatism therefore represents an assertion of democratic idealism that rejects the culture of professional isolation and distrust of the public sphere characteristic of 1950s sociology. In particular, the postwar supposition that ordinary citizens had become too alienated or inert civically to participate in the reflexive interpretation and shaping of their lives and that the conditions of mass society necessarily undermined meaningful public communication is even less tenable in a digital age in which publics constitute themselves and share information through virtual networks. Whereas online communication certainly undermines older forms of publics, by turning masses into specialized niches much as modernity turned publics into masses, the recent successes of online grassroots organizing and political campaigning, the breaking of important news stories by bloggers and independent journalists working outside of the mainstream media, and, most relevantly, professional sociologists' assertions of public roles in generating online clearinghouses for sociological research demonstrate the new possibilities afforded by the Web.

Such a turn in professional priorities hardly constitutes a radical repudiation of professional sociology's heritage, which reflects a commitment initiated by scholars in the classical tradition to a public-spirited focus upon issues and problems that lie at the heart of the discourse on modernity. As Edward Shils observes:

> [Weber] regarded it as one of his tasks to clarify the issues of policy and to make the educated lay public and university students, university teachers, and publicists and politicians "face the facts." In general, most German, French, and British sociologists of the end of the last century and the first decades of the present century wrote with the intention of instructing a larger public beyond the boundaries of academic sociology, insofar as it existed.[47]

---

[47] Edward Shils, *The Calling of Sociology and Other Essays on the Pursuit of Learning* (Chicago: University of Chicago Press, 1980), 81.

Indeed, Weber's public commitments speak to his adherence to the Enlightenment faith in the application of reason to public affairs. His role as an adviser in the Versailles peace treaty, his involvement in the German Democratic Party after the war, and his writings as a columnist for the *Frankfurter Zeitung* reveal a more complex relationship between his scientific scholarly pursuits and his wider commitments than the postwar generation of American sociologists generally conceived to exist.[48] Robert Park's early career presents another example of such public engagement. Shortly after obtaining his doctorate, Park wrote a series of articles on the monstrous Belgian colonial atrocities in the Congo in an effort to mobilize public opinion against Leopold II's imperialist brutality.[49] Even Talcott Parsons, Uta Gerhardt has shown, addressed the lay public assertively in the early 1940s—albeit under the direction of the War Department—using radio broadcasts, lectures, speeches, and newspaper articles to encourage public support for the Allied war effort.[50]

Public sociology therefore requires simply a reassessment of the discipline's postwar priorities and a reconnection to its late-nineteenth-century origins, when Albion Small wrote in the inaugural issue of *The American Journal of Sociology* that the new journal would "attempt to translate sociology into the language of ordinary life." "The aim of science," Small declared, "should be to show the meaning of familiar things, not to construct a kingdom for itself in which, if familiar things are admitted, they are obscured under an impenetrable disguise of artificial expression."[51]

---

[48]In 1962, Alvin Gouldner questioned this tendency among postwar sociologists to draw from Weber's call for value-free sociology that they should avoid political involvements. By contrasting the highly politicized German academy of the turn-of-the-century with the rather quiescent postwar American academic culture, Gouldner proposed that the latter required more vigorous public debate to integrate itself into society. "Social science," he insisted, "can never be fully accepted in a society, or be a part of it, without paying its way" by addressing before the larger community "the contemporary human predicament" (205). See his "Anti-Minotaur: The Myth of a Value-Free Sociology," *Social Problems* 9, 3 (Winter 1962): 199–213. Wolfgang Mommsen's *Max Weber and German Politics, 1890–1920*, trans. Michael S. Steinberg (Chicago: University of Chicago Press, 1984) remains the definitive work on Weber's political involvements. In *Max Weber and Political Commitment* (Philadelphia: Temple University Press, 1986), Edward Bryan Portis explores the conflict between Weber's scientific and political commitments.

[49]See Stanford M. Lyman, *Militarism, Imperialism, and Racial Accommodation: An Analysis and Interpretation of the Early Writings of Robert E. Park* (Fayetteville: University of Arkansas Press, 1992).

[50]See Uta Gerhardt, ed., introduction to *Talcott Parsons on National Socialism* (New York: Aldine de Gruyter, 1993).

[51]Albion Small, "The Era of Sociology," *American Journal of Sociology* 1, 1 (July, 1895): 13–14.

Bibliography

ARCHIVAL SOURCES

Paul F. Lazarsfeld Papers. Rare Book and Manuscript Library, Columbia University, New York.
Paul Lazarsfeld Oral History Project. Butler Library, Columbia University, New York.
Alfred McClung Lee Papers. Brooklyn College Archive, Brooklyn, New York.
C. Wright Mills Papers. Center for American History, University of Texas at Austin.
Talcott Parsons Papers. Harvard University Archive, Cambridge, Massachusetts.
David Riesman Oral History Project. Butler Library, Columbia University, New York.
David Riesman Papers. Harvard University Archive, Cambridge, Massachusetts.
Pitirim A. Sorokin Papers, University of Saskatchewan, Saskatoon, Saskatchewan, Canada
Lionel Trilling Papers. Rare Book and Manuscript Library, Columbia University, New York.

SECONDARY AND PUBLISHED SOURCES

Abbott, Andrew. *Department and Discipline: Chicago Sociology at One Hundred.* Chicago: University of Chicago Press, 1999.
Adorno, Theodor. "On Popular Music." *Studies in Philosophy and Social Sciences* 9, no. 1 (1941): 17–48.
———. "A Social Critique of Radio Music." *Kenyon Review* 7, no. 2 (Spring 1945): 208–17.

Adorno, Theodor, Else Frenkel-Brunswick, Daniel J. Levinson, and R. Nevitt Sanford, eds. *The Authoritarian Personality*. New York: W. W. Norton, 1950.

Alexander, Jeffrey. *Twenty Lectures: Sociological Theory Since World War II*. New York: Columbia University Press, 1987.

Arendt, Hannah. *The Human Condition*. Chicago: University of Chicago Press, 1958.

———. *The Origins of Totalitarianism*. Cleveland: World Publishing, 1958.

Arnove, Robert F., ed. *Philanthropy and Cultural Imperialism: The Foundations at Home and Abroad*. Boston: G. K. Hall, 1980.

Aronowitz, Stanley. "Postmodernism and Politics." In *Universal Abandon*, ed. Andrew Ross. Minneapolis: University of Minnesota Press, 1988.

———. *Science as Power: Discourse and Ideology in Modern Society*. Minneapolis: University of Minnesota Press, 1988.

Bachrach, Peter. *The Theory of Democratic Elitism*. Boston: Little, Brown, 1967.

Bain, Read. "Sociology as a Natural Science." *American Journal of Sociology* 53, no. 1 (July 1947): 9–16.

Bannister, Robert C. "Principle, Politics, Profession: American Sociologists and Fascism, 1930–1950." In *Sociology Responds to Fascism*, ed. Stephen P. Turner and Dirk Kasler, 172–213. New York: Routledge, 1992.

———. *Sociology and Scientism: The American Quest for Objectivity, 1890–1940*. Chapel Hill: University of North Carolina Press, 1987.

Barber, Bernard. *Science and the Social Order*. New York: Free Press, 1952.

———. "Sociological Aspects of Anti-Intellectualism." *The Journal of Social Issues* 11, no. 3 (1955): 25–30.

Baritz, Loren. *Servants of Power: A History of the Use of Social Science in American Industry*. Middletown, CT: Wesleyan University Press, 1960.

Barton, Allen H. "Paul Lazarsfeld and Applied Social Research." *Social Science History* 3, no. 3 (October 1979): 4–44.

Barzun, Jacques. *The House of Intellect*. New York: Harper, 1959.

———. *Science: The Glorious Entertainment*. New York: Harper & Row, 1964.

Bauman, Zygmunt. "Is There a Postmodern Sociology?" In *The Postmodern Turn: New Perspectives on Social Theory*, ed. Steven Seidman, 187–204. Cambridge: Cambridge University Press, 1994.

Bell, Daniel. "Adjusting Men to Machines: Social Scientists Explore the World of the Factory." *Commentary* 3, no. 1 (January 1947): 79–88.

———. "The Debate on Alienation." In *Revisionism: Essays on the History of Marxist Ideas*, ed. Leopold Labedz, 195–211. London: Allen & Unwin, 1962.

———. "In Search of Marxist Humanism: The Debate on Alienation." *Soviet Survey* 32, no. 2 (April–June 1960): 21–31.

———. "Interpretations of American Politics." In *The New American Right*, ed. Daniel Bell, 3–32. New York: Criterion Books, 1955.

———. *The New American Right*. New York: Criterion Books, 1955.

———. "'Screening' Leaders in a Democracy: How Scientific is Personnel Testing?" *Commentary* 5, no. 4 (April 1948): 368–75.

———. "The Theory of Mass Society: A Critique." *Commentary* 22, no. 1 (July 1956): 75–83.

———. "Vulgar Sociology." Review of *The Sociological Imagination*, by C. Wright Mills. *Encounter* 15, no. 6 (December 1960): 54–56.

Bell, Wendell. "Anomie, Social Isolation, and the Class Structure." *Sociometry* 20, no. 2 (June 1957): 105–16.

Bellah, Robert. *Beyond Belief.* New York: Harper & Row, 1970.

Bender, Thomas. "Academic Knowledge and Political Democracy in the Age of the University." In *Intellect and Public Life: Essays on the Social History of Academic Intellectuals in the United States*, ed. Thomas Bender, 127–39. Baltimore: Johns Hopkins University Press, 1993.

———. "The Erosion of Public Culture: Cities, Discourses, and Professional Disciplines." In *Intellect and Public Life: Essays on the Social History of Academic Intellectuals in the United States*, ed. Thomas Bender, 30–46. Baltimore: Johns Hopkins University Press, 1993.

Bendix, Reinhard. "The Image of Man in the Social Sciences: The Basic Assumptions of Present-Day Research." *Commentary* 11, no. 2 (February 1951): 187–92.

Berger, Bennett, ed. *Authors of Their Own Lives: Intellectual Autobiographies of Twenty American Sociologists.* Berkeley: University of California Press, 1990.

———. "Sociology and the Intellectuals: An Analysis of a Stereotype." *Antioch Review* 17, no. 3 (September 1957): 275–90.

Berger, Peter L., and Thomas Luckmann. *The Social Construction of Reality: A Treatise in the Sociology of Knowlege.* Garden City, NY: Doubleday, 1966.

Bernstein, Richard J. *The New Constellation: The Ethical-Political Horizons of Modernity/Postmodernity.* Cambridge, MA: MIT Press, 1992.

———. *The Restructuring of Social and Political Theory.* Philadelphia: University of Pennsylvania Press, 1976.

Besnard, Philippe. "The Americanization of Anomie at Harvard." *Knowledge and Society: Studies in the Sociology of Culture Past and Present* 6 (1986): 41–53.

Best, Joel. "Killing the Messenger: The Social Problems of Sociology." *Social Problems* 50, 1 (February 2003): 1–13.

Bierstedt, Robert. *American Sociology: A Critical History.* New York: Academic Press, 1981.

Blumer, Herbert. "Attitudes and the Social Act." *Social Problems* 3, no. 2 (October 1955): 59–65.

———. "Public Opinion and Public Opinion Polling." *American Sociological Review* 13, no. 5 (October 1948): 542–54.

———. "What is Wrong With Social Theory?" *American Sociological Review* 19, no. 1 (February 1954): 3–10.

Bourdieu, Pierre, and James S. Coleman, eds. *Social Theory for a Changing Society.* Boulder, CO: Westview Press, 1991.

Boyer, Paul. *By the Bomb' Early Light: American Thought and Culture at the Dawn of the Atomic Age.* New York: Pantheon Books, 1985.

Brady, David. "Why Public Sociology May Fail." *Social Forces* 82, no. 4 (June 2004): 1629–38.

Bramson, Leon. *The Political Context of Sociology.* Princeton, NJ: Princeton University Press, 1961.

Brewer, Rose M. "Response to Michael Burawoy's Commentary: 'The Critical Turn to Public Sociology.'" *Critical Sociology* 31, no. 3 (2005).

Brick, Howard. *Age of Contradiction: American Thought and Culture in the 1960s.* Ithaca, NY: Cornell University Press, 2001.

———. *Daniel Bell and the Decline of Intellectual Radicalism: Social Theory and Political Reconciliation in the 1940s.* Madison: University of Wisconsin Press, 1986.

Brinton, Crane, A. L. Kroeber, Joseph Wood Krutch, and B. F. Skinner. "The Application of Scientific Method to the Study of Human Behavior." *American Scholar* 21, no. 2 (Spring 1952): 208–25.

Brown, J. David. "Elaboration, Revision, Polemic, and Progress in the Second Chicago School." In *A Second Chicago School? The Development of a Postwar American Sociology,* ed. Gary Alan Fine. Chicago: University of Chicago Press, 1995.

Bryan, Edward. *Max Weber and Political Commitment.* Philadelphia: Temple University Press, 1986.

Bryant, Christopher G. A. *Positivism in Social Theory and Research.* London: Macmillan Publishers, 1985.

Bulmer, Martin. "The Growth of Applied Sociology After 1945: The Prewar Establishment of the Postwar Infrastructure." In *Sociology and Its Publics: The Forms and Fates of Disciplinary Organization,* ed. Terence C. Halliday and Morris Janowitz. Chicago: University of Chicago Press, 1992.

Burawoy, Michael. "The Critical Turn to Public Sociology." In *Enriching the Sociological Imagination: How Radical Sociology Changed the Discipline,* ed. Rhonda F. Levine, 309–22. Leiden, The Netherlands: Koninkijke Brill, 2004.

———. "For Public Sociology." Address to the American Sociological Association, San Francisco, 15 August 2004. *American Sociological Review* 70, no. 1. (February 2005): 4–28

———. "Public Sociologies: Contradictions, Dilemmas, and Possibilities." *Social Forces* 82, no. 4 (June 2004): 1603–18.

Burawoy, Michael, William Gamson, Charlotte Ryan, Stephen Pfohl, Diane Vaughan, Charles Derber, and Juliet Schor. "Public Sociologies: A Symposium from Boston College." *Social Problems* 51, no. 1 (February 2004): 103–30.

Buxton, William. "Snakes and Ladders: Parsons and Sorokin at Harvard." In *Sorokin and Civilization,* ed. Joseph B. Ford, Michel P. Richard, and Talbutt Palmer C. Talbutt., 31–43. New Brunswick, NJ: Transaction, 1996.

Buxton, William, and Stephen P. Turner. "From Education to Expertise: Sociology as a 'Profession.'" In *Sociology and Its Publics: The Forms and Fates of Disciplinary Organization,* ed. Terence C. Halliday and Morris Janowitz, 373–407. Chicago: University of Chicago Press, 1992.

Calhoun, Craig. "Toward a More Public Social Science." Presidents Report, Social Science Research Council, 2004, 13–17. Available at http://www.ssrc.org/programs/ publications_editors/publications/PresReport/SSRC_PresReport.pdf (accessed 15 September, 2005).

Chamberlain, John. "The Job and Jargon of Sociology." *Wall Street Journal,* 14 May 1959, 14.

Chriss, James J. *Alvin W. Gouldner: Sociologist and Outlaw Marxist.* Brookfield, VT: Ashgate, 1999.

Christie, Richard, and Peggy Cook. "A Guide to Published Literature Relating to the Authoritarian Personality Through 1956." *Journal of Psychology* 45, no. 2 (April 1958): 171–99.

Clecak, Peter. *Radical Paradoxes: Dilemmas of the American Left, 1945–1970.* New York: Harper & Row, 1973.

Cloward, Richard A. "Illegitimate Means, Anomie, and Deviant Behavior." *American Sociological Review* 24, no. 2 (April 1959): 164–76.

"Cocktail Parties—Are Hosts People?" *Newsweek,* 2 May 1960, 25.

Coleman, James S. "Columbia in the 1950s." In *Authors of Their Own Lives: Intellectual Biographies of Twenty American Sociologists,* ed. Bennet M. Berger, 75–103. Berkeley: University of California Press, 1990.

———. *Community Conflict.* New York: Free Press, 1957.

Collins, Randall. "The Confusion of the Modes of Sociology." In *Postmodernism and Social Theory: The Debate Over General Theory,* ed. Steven Seidman and David G. Wagner. New York: Blackwell, 1991.

———. *Sociology Since Midcentury.* New York: Academic Press, 1981.

———. *Three Sociological Traditions.* New York: Oxford University Press, 1985.

Converse, Jean M. *Survey Research in the United States: Roots and Emergence, 1890–1960.* Berkeley: University of California Press, 1987.

Cooley, Charles Horton. *Social Organization: A Study of the Larger Mind.* New York: Schocken Books, 1962.

Coser, Lewis A. *The Functions of Social Conflict.* New York: Free Press, 1956.

———. "Kitsch Sociology." *Partisan Review* 26, no. 3 (Summer 1959): 480–83.

———. *Men of Ideas: A Sociologist's View.* New York: Free Press, 1965.

———. "Nightmares, Daydreams, and Professor Shils." *Dissent* 5, no. 3 (Summer 1958): 268–73.

———. "The Uses of Sociology." Review of *The Sociological Imagination,* by C. Wright Mills. *Partisan Review* 27, no. 1 (Winter 1960): 166–73.

Coser, Lewis A., Charles Kadushin, and Walter W. Powell. *The Culture and Commerce of Publishing.* New York: Basic Books, 1982.

Cowley, Malcolm. "Sociological Habit Patterns of Linguistic Transmogrification." *The Reporter* 15, no. 4 (20 September 1956): 41–43.

Dahrendorf, Ralf. *Class and Class Conflict in an Industrial Society.* Stanford, CA: Stanford University Press, 1958.

———. "Out of Utopia: Toward a Reorientation of Sociological Analysis." *American Journal of Sociology* 64, no. 2 (September 1958): 115–27.

Davis, Arthur K. "Sociology Without Clothes." *Monthly Review* 11, no. 7 (November 1959): 256–63.

Davis, Kenneth C. *Two-Bit Culture: The Paperbacking of America.* Boston: Houghton-Mifflin Company, 1984.

Dean, Dwight G. "Alienation: Its Meaning and Measurement." *American Sociological Review* 26, no. 5 (October 1961): 753–58.

Degler, Carl N. "The Sociologist as Historian: Riesman's *The Lonely Crowd.*" *American Quarterly* 15, no. 4 (Winter 1963): 483–97.

Deutsch, Steven E., and John Howard. *Where It's At: Radical Perspectives in Sociology.* New York: Harper & Row, 1970.

Dewey, John. "Liberating the Social Scientist: A Plea to Unshackle the Study of Man." *Commentary* 4, no. 4 (October 1947): 378–85.

———. *The Public and Its Problems.* Athens, OH: Swallow Press, 1954.

Diggins, John Patrick. *The Promise of Pragmatism: Modernism and the Crisis of Knowledge and Authority.* Chicago: University of Chicago Press, 1994.

Dubin, Robert. "Deviant Behavior and Social Structure: Continuities in Social Theory." *American Sociological Review* 24, no. 2 (April 1959): 147–64.

Durkheim, Emile. *The Division of Labor in Society,* trans. George Simpson. New York: Free Press, 1956.

———. *The Rules of Sociological Method,* trans. W. D. Halls. New York: Free Press, 1982.

———. *Suicide: A Study in Sociology,* trans. John A. Spaulding and George Simpson. New York: Free Press, 1997.

England, J. Merton. *A Patron For Pure Science: The National Science Foundation's Formative Years, 1945–1957.* Washington, DC: National Science Foundation, 1982.

Faris, Robert E. L. "Anti-Social Notes on Social Notes." *Sociological Inquiry* 31, no. 2 (Spring 1961): 182.

Fine, Gary Alan, ed. *A Second Chicago School? The Development of a Postwar American Sociology.* Chicago: University of Chicago Press, 1995.

Fisher, Donald. "American Philanthropy and Cultural Imperialism: The Reconstruction of a Conservative Ideology." In *Philanthropy and Cultural Imperialism: The Foundations at Home and Abroad,* ed. Robert F. Arnove, 233–68. Boston: G. K. Hall, 1980.

———. "The Role of Philanthropic Foundations in the Reproduction and Production of Hegemony." *Sociology* 17, no. 2 (May 1983): 206–33.

"Freedom—New Style." *Time,* 27 September 1954, 22–25.

Friedrichs, Robert W. *A Sociology of Sociology.* New York: Free Press, 1970.

Fromm, Erich. *Escape from Freedom.* New York: Farrar and Rinehart, 1941.

———. "Individual and Social Origins of Neurosis." *American Sociological Review* 9, no. 4 (August 1944): 380–84.

———. *The Sane Society.* New York: Henry Holt, 1955.

Furner, Mary O. *Advocacy and Objectivity: A Crisis in the Professionalization of American Social Science, 1865–1905.* Lexington: University Press of Kentucky, 1977.

Gans, Herbert J. "Best-Sellers by Sociologists." *Contemporary Sociology* 26, no. 2 (March 1997): 131–35.

———. "Sociology in America: The Discipline and the Public." *American Sociological Review* 54, no. 1 (February 1989): 1–16.

———. "Wishes for the Discipline's Future." *Chronicle of Higher Education* 51, no. 49 (12 August 2005): B9.

Garfinkel, Harold. *Studies in Ethnomethodology.* Englewood Cliffs, NJ: Prentice-Hall, 1967.

Gellner, Ernest. "The Alchemists of Sociology." *Inquiry* 2, no. 2 (Summer 1959): 126–35.

Gerhardt, Uta, ed. *Talcott Parsons on National Socialism.* New York: Aldine de Gruyter, 1993.

Gerth, Hans. "The Relevance of History to the Sociological Ethos." *Studies on the Left* 1, no. 1 (Fall 1959): 7–13.

Getlein, Frank. Review of *The Lonely Crowd,* by David Riesman. *Commonweal* 54, no. 26 (5 October 1951): 621–23.

Gillin, John L. "The Development of Sociology in the United States." *Publications of the American Sociological Society* 21 (1927): 1–25.

Gitlin, Todd. "Postmodernism: Roots and Politics." In *Cultural Politics in Contemporary America*, ed. Ian H. Angus and Sut Jhally, 347–60. New York: Routledge, 1989.

———. "Sociology for Whom? Criticism for Whom?" In *Sociology in America*, ed. Herbert J. Gans, 214–26. Newbury Park, CA: Sage, 1990.

Glazer, Nathan. "The 'Alienation' of Modern Man: Some Diagnoses of the Malady." *Commentary* 3, no. 4 (April 1947): 378–85.

———. "*The American Soldier* as Science: Can Sociology Fulfill Its Ambitions?" *Commentary* 8, no. 5 (November 1949): 487–96.

———. "From Socialism to Sociology." In *Authors of Their Own Lives: Intellectual Autobiographies of Twenty American Sociologists*, ed. Bennett M. Berger, 190–209. Berkeley: University of California Press, 1990.

———. "The Polls on Communism and Conformity." In *The New American Right*, ed. Daniel Bell, 141–65. New York: Criterion Books, 1955.

———. "The Rise of Social Research in Europe." In *The Human Meaning of the Social Sciences*, ed. Daniel Lerner, 43–72. New York: Meridian Books, 1959.

———. "The Study of Man." *Commentary* 1, no. 2 (December 1945): 84–87.

———. "What Is Sociology's Job? A Report of a Conference." *Commentary* 3, no. 2 (February 1947): 181–86.

———. "What Public Opinion Polls Can and Can't Do." *Commentary* 12, no. 2 (August 1951): 181–84.

Gorman, Paul R. *Left Intellectuals and Popular Culture in Twentieth-Century America*. Chapel Hill: University of North Carolina Press, 1996.

Gouldner, Alvin W. "About Trans-action." *Trans-action* 1, no. 1 (November 1963), back and inside covers.

———. "Anti-Minotaur: The Myth of a Value-Free Sociology." *Social Problems* 9, no. 3 (Winter 1962): 199–213.

———. *The Coming Crisis of Western Sociology*. New York: Basic Books 1970.

———. *The Future of Intellectuals and the Rise of the New Class*. New York: Seabury Press, 1979.

———. "Metaphysical Pathos and the Theory of Bureaucracy." *American Political Science Review* 49, no. 2 (June 1955): 496–507.

———. "Reciprocity and Autonomy in Functional Theory." In *Symposium on Sociological Theory*, ed. Llewellyn Gross, 241–70. New York: Harper & Row, 1959.

———. "Some Observations on Systematic Theory, 1945–1955." In *Sociology in the United States of America: A Trend Report*, ed. Hans L. Zetterberg, 34–42. Paris: United Nations Educational, Scientific, and Cultural Organization, 1956.

Gramsci, Antonio. "The Intellectuals." In *Selections from the Prison Notebooks*, trans. Quintin Hoare and Geoffrey Nowell Smith. New York: International Publishers, 1971.

Gross, Llewellyn. "An Epistemological View of Sociological Theory." *American Journal of Sociology* 65, no. 5 (March 1960): 441–48.

———. "Preface to a Metatheoretical Framework for Sociology." *American Journal of Sociology* 67, no. 2 (September 1961): 125–43.

———. *Symposium on Sociological Theory*. New York: Harper & Row, 1959.

Hacker, Andrew. "Dostoevsky's Disciples." *The Journal of Politics* 17, no. 4 (November 1955): 390–413.

———. "In Defense of Utopia." *Ethics* 65, no. 2 (January 1955): 135–40.

————. "Liberal Democracy and Social Control." *American Political Science Review* 51, no. 4 (December 1957): 1009–39.

————. "The Specter of Predictable Man." *The Antioch Review* 14, no. 2 (June 1954): 195–207.

————. "The Use and Abuse of Pareto in Industrial Sociology." *American Journal of Economics and Sociology* 14, no. 4 (July 1955): 321–34.

————. "Utopia, Inc." *Commonweal* 65, no. 9 (8 February 1957): 479–81.

Halliday, Terence C. "Sociology's Fragile Professionalism." In *Sociology and Its Publics: The Forms and Fates of Disciplinary Organization*, ed. Terence C. Halliday and Morris Janowitz, 3–42. Chicago: University of Chicago Press, 1992.

Halliday, Terence C., and Morris Janowitz, eds. *Sociology and Its Publics: The Forms and Fates of Disciplinary Organization*. Chicago: University of Chicago Press, 1992.

Hammond, Phillip E., ed. *Sociologists at Work: Essays on the Craft of Social Research*. New York: Basic Books, 1964.

Hardwick, Elizabeth. "Riesman Considered." *Partisan Review* 21, no. 5 (September–October 1954): 548–56.

Haskell, Thomas. *The Authority of Experts: Studies in History and Theory*. Bloomington: Indiana University Press, 1984.

————. *The Emergence of Professional Social Science: The American Social Science Association and the Nineteenth Century Crisis of Authority*. Chicago: University of Chicago Press, 1977.

Herman, Ellen. *The Romance of American Psychology: Political Culture in the Age of Experts*. Berkeley: University of California Press, 1995.

Hofstadter, Richard. *The Age of Reform*. New York: Vintage, 1960.

Hollinger, David. "The Defense of Democracy and Robert K. Merton's Formulation of the Scientific Ethos." In *Science, Jews, and Secular Culture: Studies in Mid-Twentieth Century American Intellectual History*, ed. David A. Hollinger, 80–96. Princeton, NJ: Princeton University Press, 1996.

————. "Free Enterprise and Free Enquiry: The Emergence of Laissez-Faire Communitarianism in the Ideology of Science in the United States." In *Science, Jews, and Secular Culture: Studies in Mid-Twentieth Century American Intellectual History*, ed. David A. Hollinger, 97–120. Princeton, NJ: Princeton University Press, 1996.

————, ed. "Inquiry and Uplift: Late Nineteenth-Century American Academics and the Moral Efficacy of Scientific Practice." In *The Authority of Experts: Studies in History and Theory*, ed. Thomas Haskell, 142–56. Bloomington: Indiana University Press, 1984.

————. "Science as a Weapon in *Kulturkämpfe* in the United States During and After World War II." In *Science, Jews, and Secular Culture: Studies in Mid-Twentieth Century American Intellectual History*, ed. David A. Hollinger, ed. 155–74. Princeton, NJ: Princeton University Press, 1996.

————. *Science, Jews, and Secular Culture: Studies in Mid-Twentieth Century American Intellectual History*. Princeton, NJ: Princeton University Press, 1996.

Hollingshead, August B. *Elmtown's Youth: The Impact of Social Classes on Adolescents*. New York: Wiley, 1949.

Homans, George. "Bringing Men Back In." *American Sociological Review* 29, no. 5 (December 1964): 809–18.

――――. Review of *The Sociological Imagination,* by C. Wright Mills. *American Journal of Sociology* 65, no. 5 (March 1960): 517–18.

――――. *Social Behavior: Its Elementary Forms.* New York: Harcourt Brace, 1961.

Horkheimer, Max. "Art and Mass Culture." *Studies in Philosophy and Social Sciences* 9, no. 2 (1941): 290–304.

Horney, Karen. "Culture and Neurosis." *American Sociological Review* 1, no. 2 (April 1936): 221–35.

――――. *The Neurotic Personality in Our Time.* New York: W. W. Norton, 1937.

――――. "What Is a Neurosis?" *American Journal of Sociology* 45, no. 3 (November 1939): 426–32.

Horowitz, Daniel. *Vance Packard and American Social Criticism.* Chapel Hill: University of North Carolina Press, 1994.

Horowitz, Irving Louis. *C. Wright Mills: An American Utopian.* New York: Free Press, 1983.

――――. "The Life and Death of Project Camelot." *Trans-action* 3, no. 1. (November–December 1965).

――――. *The New Sociology: Essays in Social Science and Social Theory in Honor of C. Wright Mills.* New York: Oxford University Press, 1964.

――――. "On Entering the Tenth Year of Transaction: The Relationship of Social Science and Critical Journalism." *Society* 10, no. 1 (November/December 1972): 49–79.

Horton, Donald. Review of *Fads and Foibles in Modern Sociology and Related Sciences,* by Pitirim A. Sorokin. *American Journal of Sociology* 62, no. 3 (November 1956): 338–39.

Hovland, Carl Iver, Arthur A. Lumsdaine, and Fred D. Sheffield. *Experiments on Mass Communication.* Studies in Social Psychology in World War II. Vol. 3. Princeton, NJ: Princeton University Press, 1949.

"How Scientific Are the Social Scientists?" *Saturday Evening Post,* 13 June 1953, 12.

Hughes, Everett C. "Can History Be Made?" Review of *The Sociological Imagination,* by C. Wright Mills. *The New Republic* 140, no. 25 (22 June 1959): 19.

Hunt, Morton M. "How Does It Come to Be So?" *New Yorker,* 28 January 1961, 39–62.

Inkeles, Alex. "Industrial Man: The Relation of Status to Experience, Perception, and Value." *American Journal of Sociology* 66, no. 1 (July 1960): 1–31.

Jacoby, Russell. *The Last Intellectuals: American Culture in the Age of Academe.* New York: Noonday Press, 1987.

Janowitz, Morris, and Dwaine Marvick. "Authoritarianism and Political Behavior." *Public Opinion Quarterly* 17, no. 2 (Summer 1953): 185–201.

Johnston, Barry V. *Pitirim A. Sorokin: An Intellectual Biography.* Lawrence: University Press of Kansas, 1995.

――――. "Sorokin and Parsons at Harvard: Institutional Conflict and the Origin of a Hegemonic Tradition." *Journal of the History of the Behavioral Sciences* 22 (April 1986): 107–27.

Kariel, Henry S. "Social Science as Autonomous Activity." In *Scientism and Values,* ed. Helmut Schoeck and James W. Higgins, 235–60. Princeton, NJ: D. Van Nostrand, 1960.

Katz, Elihu, and Paul F. Lazarsfeld. *Personal Influence: The Part Played by People in the Flow of Mass Communications.* New York: Free Press, 1955.

Kaufman, Walter C. "Status, Authoritarianism, and Anti-Semitism." *American Journal of Sociology* 62, no. 4 (January 1957): 379–82.

Kempton, Murray. "Social Notes on the A.S.A. Meetings." *Sociological Inquiry* 31, no. 2 (Spring 1961): 180–81.

———. "Status-Ticians in Limbo." *Playboy*, September 1961, 117–22.

Kirk, Russell. "The Battle of Sociology (Continued)." *New York Times Magazine*, 23 July 1961.

———. "Is Social Science Scientific?" *New York Times Magazine*, 25 June 1961.

———. "Shrewd Knocks at Sociological Theories." *Chicago Sunday Tribune*, 24 May 1959.

Klausner, Samuel Z. "The Bid to Nationalize American Social Science." In *The Nationalization of the Social Sciences*, ed. Samuel Z. Klausner and Victor M. Lidz, 3–39. Philadelphia: University of Philadelphia Press, 1986.

Klausner, Samuel Z., and Victor M. Lidz, eds. *The Nationalization of the Social Sciences.* Philadelphia: University of Pennsylvania Press, 1986.

Kloppenberg, James T. "Pragmatism: An Old Name for Some New Ways of Thinking." *Journal of American History* 83, no. 1 (June 1996): 100–38.

Kolb, William L. "The Impingement of Moral Values on Sociology." *Social Problems* 2, no. 2 (October 1954): 66–70.

———. "Values, Politics, and Sociology." Review of *The Sociological Imagination*, by C. Wright Mills. *American Sociological Review* 25, no. 6 (December 1960): 966–69.

Kornhauser, William. *The Politics of Mass Society.* Glencoe, IL: Free Press, 1959.

———. " 'Power Elite' or 'Veto Groups?' " In *Culture and Social Character: Essays in Honor of David Riesman*, ed. Seymour Martin Lipset and Leo Lowenthal. New York: Free Press, 1961.

Krugman, Herbert E. "The Appeal of Communism to American Middle Class Intellectuals and Trade Unionists." *Public Opinion Quarterly* 16, no. 3 (Fall 1952): 331–55.

Krutch, Joseph Wood. *The Measure of Man: On Freedom, Human Values, Survival and the Modern Temper.* New York: Grosset & Dunlap, 1953.

Kuhn, Thomas S. *The Structure of Scientific Revolutions.* Chicago: University of Chicago Press, 1962.

Larabee, Eric. "Riesman and His Readers." *Harper's*, June 1961, 59–65.

Lasch, Christopher. *The True and Only Heaven: Progress and Its Critics.* New York: W. W. Norton, 1991.

Lasswell, Harold. *World Politics and Personal Insecurity.* Glencoe, IL: Free Press, 1950.

Lazarsfeld, Paul F. "The American Soldier—An Expository Review." *Public Opinion Quarterly* 13, no. 3 (Fall 1949): 377–404.

———. "An Episode in the History of Social Research: A Memoir." In *The Intellectual Migration: Europe and America, 1930–1960*, ed. Donald Fleming and Bernard Bailyn, 270–337. Cambridge. MA: Belknap Press, 1969.

———. "Evidence and Inference in Social Research." *Daedalus* 87, no. 4 (Fall 1958): 99–130.

———. Foreword to *What College Students Think*, ed. Rose K. Goldsen, Morris Rosenberg, Robin A. Williams, Jr., and Edward A. Suchman, iii–xi. Princeton, NJ: D. Van Nostrand, 1960.

———. Introduction to *Social Research to Test Ideas*, by Samuel A. Stouffer, xv–xxxi. New York: Free Press, 1962.

———. "The Obligations of the 1950 Pollster to the 1984 Historian." *Public Opinion Quarterly* (Winter 1950–1951): 617–38.

———. "Problems in Methodology." In *Sociology Today: Problems and Prospects*, ed. Robert K. Merton, Leonard Broom, and Leonard S. Cottrell, Jr., 39–78. New York: Basic Books, 1959.

———. "The Sociology of Empirical Social Research." *American Sociological Review* 27, no. 6 (December 1962): 757–67.

———. "Working With Merton." In *The Idea of Social Structure: Papers in Honor of Robert K. Merton*, ed. Lewis Coser, 35–66. New York: Harcourt Brace Jovanovich, 1975.

Lazarfeld, Paul F., and Morris Rosenberg. *The Language of Social Research*. Glencoe, IL: Free Press, 1955.

Lazarfeld, Paul F., and Robert K. Merton. "Mass Communication, Popular Taste and Organized Social Action." In *The Communication of Ideas*, ed. Lyman Bryson, 95–118. New York: Harper, 1948.

Lazarfeld, Paul F., and Wagner Thielens, Jr. *The Academic Mind: A Report of the Bureau of Applied Social Research*. Glencoe, IL: The Free Press, 1958.

Lazarfeld, Paul F., Bernard Berelson, and Hazel Gaudet. *The People's Choice*. New York: Columbia University Press, 1948.

Le Bon, Gustave. *The Crowd*. New York: Viking Press, 1960.

Lederer, Emil. *The State of the Masses: The Threat of the Classless Society*. New York: Norton, 1940.

Lee, Alfred McClung. Letter to the Editor. *The Annals of the American Academy of Political and Social Science* 267 (January 1959): 252.

———. Review of *The American Soldier*, vols. 1 and 2. *The Annals of the American Academy of Political and Social Science* 265 (September 1949): 173–75.

———. "Sociology for Whom." *American Sociological Review* 41, no. 6 (December 1976): 925–36.

Lerner, Daniel. "*The American Soldier* and the Public." In *Continuities in Social Research: Studies in the Scope and Method of "The American Soldier,"* edited by Robert K. Merton and Paul F. Lazarsfeld, 212–51. New York: Free Press, 1950.

———. *The Human Meaning of the Social Sciences*. New York: Meridian Books, 1959.

Levine, Rhonda, ed. *Enriching the Sociological Imagination: How Radical Sociology Changed the Discipline*. Leiden, The Netherlands: Koninklijke Brill, 2004.

Lichtheim, George. "Is There a Sociologist in the House?" *Partisan Review* 27, no. 2 (Spring 1960): 295–310.

Lifton, Robert Jay. *Thought Reform and the Psychology of Totalism*. New York: W. W. Norton, 1961.

Lipset, Seymour Martin. *Agrarian Socialism: The Cooperative Commonwealth Federation in Saskatchewan*. Berkeley: University of California Press, 1950.

———. "The Biography of a Research Project: *Union Democracy*." In *Sociologists at Work: Essays on the Craft of Social Research*, ed. Phillip E. Hammond, 96–120. New York: Basic Books, 1964.

———. "The Conservatism of Vance Packard." *Commentary* 31, no. 1 (January 1961): 80–83.

———. "Democracy and Working-Class Authoritarianism." *American Sociological Review* 24, no. 4 (August 1959): 482–501.

———. "The Department of Sociology." In *A History of the Faculty of Political Science, Columbia University*, 284–303. New York: Columbia University Press, 1955.

————. *Political Man: The Social Bases of Politics.* Baltimore: Johns Hopkins University Press, 1981. First published in 1960.

————. "The Setting of Sociology in the 1950's." In *Sociology: The Progress of a Decade,* ed. Seymour Martin Lipset and Neil Smelser, 1–13. Englewood Cliffs, NJ: Prentice-Hall, 1961.

————. "Socialism and Sociology." In *Sociological Self-Images: A Collective Portrait,* ed. Irving Louis Horowitz, 143–75. Beverly Hills: Sage, 1969.

————. "Some Social Requisites of Democracy: Economic Development and Political Legitimacy." *American Political Science Review* 53, no. 1 (March 1959): 69–105.

————. "The Sources of the 'Radical Right.'" In *The New American Right,* ed. Daniel Bell, 166–233. New York: Criterion Books, 1955.

————. "Vance Packard Discovers America." *The Reporter* 21, no. 1 (9 July 1959): 31–33.

Lipset, Seymour Martin, and Leo Lowenthal, eds. *Culture and Social Character: Culture and Social Character: The Work of David Riesman Reviewed.* New York: Free Press, 1961.

Lipset, Seymour Martin, and Neil Smelser. "Change and Controversy in Recent American Sociology." *British Journal of Sociology* 12, no. 1 (March 1961): 41–51.

————. *Sociology: The Progress of a Decade.* Englewood Cliffs, NJ: Prentice-Hall, 1961.

Lipset, Seymour Martin, Martin Trow, and James S. Coleman. *Union Democracy: The Internal Politics of the International Typographical Union.* Garden City, NY: Anchor Books, 1956.

Lowenthal, Leo. "Historical Perspectives of Popular Culture." In *Mass Culture: The Popular Arts in America,* ed. Bernard Rosenberg and David Manning White, 46–58. Glencoe, IL: Free Press, 1957.

Lundberg, George. *Can Science Save Us?* 2nd ed. New York: Longmans, Green, 1961.

————. "The Proximate Future of American Sociology: The Growth of Scientific Method." *American Journal of Sociology* 50, no. 6 (May 1945): 502–13.

————. *The Scientific Monthly* 64 (May 1947).

————. "Sociology Versus Dialectical Immaterialism." *American Journal of Sociology* 53, no. 2 (September 1947): 85–95.

Lyman, Stanford M. *Militarism, Imperialism, and Racial Accommodation: An Analysis and Interpretation of the Early Writings of Robert E. Park.* Fayetteville: University of Arkansas Press, 1992.

Lyman, Stanford M., and Arthur Vidich. *Social Order and the Public Philosophy: An Analysis and Interpretation of the Work of Herbert Blumer.* Fayetteville: University of Arkansas Press, 1988.

Lynd, Robert S. "Can Labor and Intellectuals Work Together?" In *The House of Labor: Internal Operations of American Unions,* ed. J.B.S. Hardman and Maurice F. Neufeld, 511–15. New York: Prentice-Hall, 1951.

————. Foreword to *Agrarian Socialism,* by Seymour Martin Lipset, vii–xvii. Berkeley: University of California Press, 1950.

————. *Knowledge for What? The Place of Social Science in American Culture.* Middletown, CT: Wesleyan University Press, 1939.

————. "The Science of Inhuman Relations." Review of *The American Soldier. New Republic,* 29 August 1949, 22–25.

Lynd, Robert S., and Helen Merrell Lynd. *Middletown: A Study in Modern American Culture*. New York: Harcourt Brace, 1929.

———. *Middletown in Transition*. New York: Harcourt Brace Jovanovich, 1937.

Lyons, Gene. *The Uneasy Partnership: Social Science and the Federal Government in the Twentieth Century*. New York: Russell Sage Foundation, 1969.

Macdonald, Dwight. "Abstractio Ad Absurdum." Review of *White Collar*, by C. Wright Mills. *Partisan Review* 19, no. 1 (January–February 1952): 110–14.

MacIver, Robert M. *The Ramparts We Guard*. New York: Macmillan, 1950.

MacKinnon, William J., and Richard Centers. "Authoritarianism and Internationalism." *Public Opinion Quarterly* 20, no. 4 (Winter 1956–1957): 621–30.

———. "Authoritarianism and Urban Stratification." *American Journal of Sociology* 61, no. 6 (May 1956): 610–20.

Madge, John. *The Origins of Scientific Sociology*. London: Tavistock Publications, 1963.

Madison, Charles A. *Book Publishing in America*. New York: McGraw-Hill, 1966.

Mailer, Norman. "David Riesman Reconsidered." In *Advertisements for Myself*, 190–204. New York: G. P. Putnam's Sons, 1959.

Mannheim, Karl. *Man and Society in an Age of Reconstruction*. London: Kegan Paul, Trench, Trubner, 1940.

Marchand, Roland. *Creating the Corporate Soul: The Rise of Public Relations and Corporate Imagery in American Big Business*. Berkeley: University of California Press, 1998.

Marcuse, Herbert. "Some Social Implications of Modern Technology." *Studies in Philosophy and Social Sciences* 9, no. 3 (1941): 414–39.

Martin, James G., and Frank R. Westie. "The Tolerant Personality." *American Sociological Review* 24, no. 4 (August 1959): 521–28.

Martindale, Don. *The Nature and Types of Sociological Theory*. Boston: Houghton Mifflin, 1960.

———. "Pitirim A. Sorokin: Soldier of Fortune." In *Sorokin and Sociology: Essays in Honour of Pitirim A. Sorokin*, ed. C. C. Hallen and R. Prasad, 30–42. Agra, India: Satish Book, 1972.

———. "The Roles of Humanism and Scientism in the Evolution of Sociology." In *Explorations in Social Change*, ed. George K. Zollschan, 452–90. Boston: Houghton-Mifflin, 1964.

Mattson, Kevin. *Intellectuals in Action: The Origins of the New Left and Radical Liberalism, 1945–1970*. University Park: Pennsylvania State Press, 2002.

Mazlish, Bruce. *A New Science: The Breakdown of Connections and the Birth of Sociology*. University Park: Pennsylvania State University Press, 1989.

McClay, Wilfred M. *The Masterless: Self and Society in Modern America*. Chapel Hill: University of North Carolina Press, 1994.

McDill, Edward L. "Anomie, Authoritarianism, Prejudice, and Socio-Economic Status: An Attempt at Clarification." *Social Forces* 39, no. 3 (March 1961): 239–45.

Meier, Dorothy L., and Wendell Bell. "Anomia and Differential Access to the Achievement of Life Goals." *American Sociological Review* 24, no. 2 (April 1959): 189–202.

Merton, Robert K. "An Horrific Caricature." *American Scholar* 21, no. 3 (Summer 1952): 356–58.

—. *A Life of Learning.* Charles Homer Haskins Lecture. American Council of Learned Societies, 1994.

—. *Mass Persuasion: The Social Psychology of a War Bond Drive.* New York: Harper, 1946.

—. "A Note on Science and Democracy." *Journal of Legal and Political Sociology* 1, no. 1 (October 1942): 115–26.

—. "Now the Case *for* Sociology." *New York Times Magazine,* 16 July 1961.

—. "Priorities in Scientific Discovery: A Chapter in the Sociology of Science." *American Sociological Review* 22, no. 6 (December 1957): 635–59.

—. "Science and the Social Order." *Philosophy of Science* 5, no. 3 (July 1938): 321–34.

—. "Social Conflict Over Styles of Sociological Work." In *Transactions of the Fourth World Congress of Sociology,* 21–44. Louvain, Belgium: International Sociological Association, 1959.

—. "Social Structure and Anomie." *American Sociological Review* 3, no. 6 (October 1938): 672–82.

—. *Social Theory and Social Structure.* Glencoe, IL: Free Press, 1949.

—. *Social Theory and Social Structure.* 2nd ed. Glencoe, IL: Free Press, 1957.

—. *Social Theory and Social Structure.* 3rd ed. Glencoe, IL: Free Press, 1968.

—. "Sociological Theory." *American Journal of Sociology* 50, no. 6 (May 1945): 462–73.

—. "Some Preliminaries to a Sociology of Medical Education." In *The Student-Physician,* ed. Robert K. Merton, George G. Reader and Patricia L. Kendall, 3–79. Cambridge, MA: Harvard University Press, 1957.

Merton, Robert K., and Bernard Barber. "Sorokin's Formulations in the Sociology of Science." In *Pitirim A. Sorokin in Review,* ed. Phillip J. Allen, 332–68. Durham, NC: Duke University Press, 1963.

Merton, Robert K., and Paul K. Hatt. "Election Polling Forecasts and Public Images of Social Science: A Case Study in the Shaping of Opinion Among a Strategic Public." *Public Opinion Quarterly* 13, no. 2 (Summer 1949): 185–222.

Merton, Robert K., and Patricia L. Kendall, eds. *The Focused Interview: A Manual of Problems and Procedures.* Glencoe, IL: Free Press, 1956.

Merton, Robert K., and Paul F. Lazarsfeld. *Continuities in Social Research: Studies in the Scope and Method of "The American Soldier."* Glencoe, IL: Free Press, 1950.

Merton, Robert K., Leonard Broom, and Leonard Cottrell, Jr. *Sociology Today: Problems and Prospects.* New York: Basic Books, 1959.

Meyer, Frank S. "Confusion in the Court." *National Review* 1, no. 8 (11 January 1956): 22–23.

Michels, Robert. *Political Parties: A Sociological Study of the Oligarchical Tendencies of Modern Democracy.* (New York: Free Press, 1998).

Miller, Jim. "C. Wright Mills Reconsidered." *Salmagundi* 70–71 (Spring–Summer 1986): 82–101.

Mills, C. Wright. *The Causes of World War Three.* New York: Simon & Schuster, 1958.

—. "IBM Plus Reality Plus Humanism = Sociology." *The Saturday Review,* 1 May 1954, 22–24.

—. *Listen, Yankee: The Revolution in Cuba.* New York: Ballantine, 1960.

—. "A Marx for the Managers." *Ethics* 52, no. 2 (January 1942): 200–15.

—. *The Marxists.* New York: Dell, 1962.

——. "Methodological Consequences of the Sociology of Knowledge." *American Journal of Sociology* 46, no. 3 (November 1940): 316–30.

——. "On Knowledge and Power." *Dissent* 2, no. 3 (Summer 1955): 201–12.

——. *The Power Elite.* New York: Oxford University Press, 1956.

——. "The Professional Ideology of Social Pathologists." *American Journal of Sociology* 49, no. 2 (September 1943): 165–80.

——. "Reflection, Behavior, and Culture: An Essay in the Sociology of Knowledge." Master's thesis, University of Texas at Austin, 1939.

——. Review of *The Exurbanites*, by A. C. Spectorsky. *Saturday Review*, 29 October 1955, 11–12.

——. Review of *The Organization Man*, by William H. Whyte. *New York Times Book Review*, 9 December 1956, 6, 26.

——. "The Social Life of a Modern Community." Review of *The Social Life of a Modern Community*, by W. Lloyd Warner. *American Sociological Review* 7, no. 2 (April 1942): 263–71.

——. *The Sociological Imagination.* New York: Grove Press, 1959.

——. "Two Styles of Research in Current Social Studies." *Philosophy of Science* 20, no. 4 (October 1953): 266–75.

——. *White Collar: The American Middle Classes.* New York: Oxford University Press, 1951.

Mills, Kathryn, and Pamela Mills. *C. Wright Mills: Letters and Autobiographical Writings.* Berkeley: University of California Press, 2000.

Mommsen, Wolfgang. *Max Weber and German Politics, 1890–1920*, trans. Michael S. Steinberg. Chicago: University of Chicago Press, 1984.

Moore, Barrington. "The New Scholasticism and the Study of Politics." *World Politics* 6, no. 1 (October 1953): 122–38.

——. *Political Power and Social Theory.* Cambridge, MA: Harvard University Press, 1958.

Moore, David Walter. "Liberalism and Liberal Education at Columbia University: The Columbia Careers of Jacques Barzun, Lionel Trilling, Richard Hofstadter, Daniel Bell, and C. Wright Mills." Ph.D. diss. University of Maryland, 1978.

Mullins, Nicholas C. *Theories and Theory Groups in Contemporary American Sociology.* New York: Harper & Row, 1973.

Nettler, Gwynn. "Antisocial Sentiment and Criminality." *American Sociological Review* 24, no. 2 (April 1959): 202–08.

——. "A Measure of Alienation." *American Sociological Review* 22, no. 6 (December 1957): 670–77.

Niebuhr, Reinhold. *The Irony of American History.* New York: Charles Scribner's Sons, 1952.

Nielsen, François. "The Vacant 'We': Remarks on Public Sociology." *Social Forces* 82, no. 4 (June 2004): 1619–27.

Nisbet, Robert A. "Conservatism and Sociology." *American Journal of Sociology* 58, no. 2 (September 1952): 167–75.

——. *The Quest for Community: A Study of the Ethics of Order and Freedom.* New York: Oxford University Press, 1953.

——. *The Sociological Tradition.* New York: Basic Books, 1966.

——. "Sociology as an Art Form." *Pacific Sociological Review* 5, no. 2 (Fall 1962): 67–74.

Oakes, Guy, and Arthur Vidich. *Collaboration, Reputation, and Ethics in American Academic Life: Hans H. Gerth and C. Wright Mills* (Urbana: University of Illinois Press, 1999).

Ogburn, William F. "The Folkways of a Scientific Sociology." *Publications of the American Sociological Society* 24, no. 2 (1929): 1–11.

Oppenheimer, Martin, Martin J. Murray, and Rhonda F. Levine, eds. *Radical Sociologists and the Movement: Experiences, Lessons, and Legacies.* Philadelphia: Temple University Press, 1991.

Oromaner, Mark Jay. "The Most Cited Sociologists: An Analysis of Introductory Text Citations." *The American Sociologist* 3, no. 2 (May 1968): 124–26.

Ortega y Gasset, José. *The Revolt of the Masses.* New York: W. W. Norton, 1932.

Packard, Vance. *The Hidden Persuaders.* New York: David McKay, 1957.

———. *The Status Seekers.* New York: David McKay, 1959.

———. *The Waste Makers.* New York: David McKay, 1960.

Park, Robert Ezra. "The City as Social Laboratory." In *On Social Control and Collective Behavior.* Chicago: University of Chicago Press, 1967.

———. "The City: Suggestions for the Investigation of Human Behavior in the Urban Environment." In *Classic Essays on the Culture of Cities,* ed. Richard Sennett. New York: Appleton-Century-Crofts, 1969.

———. "Human Migration and the Marginal Man." In *Classic Essays on the Culture of Cities,* ed. Richard Sennett. New York: Appleton-Century-Crofts, 1969.

Parsons, Talcott. "The Distribution of Power in American Society." In *C. Wright Mills and the Power Elite,* ed. G. William Domhoff and Hoyt B. Ballard, 60–88. Boston: Beacon Press, 1968.

———. *Essays in Sociological Theory.* Glencoe, IL: Free Press, 1954.

———. "Nazis Destroy Learning, Challenge Religion." In *Talcott Parsons on National Socialism,* ed. Uta Gerhardt. New York: Aldine de Gruyter, 1993.

———. "The Position of Sociological Theory." *American Sociological Review* 13, no. 2 (April 1948): 156–64.

———. "The Prospects of Sociological Theory." *American Sociological Review* 15, no. 1 (February 1950): 3–16.

———. "The Science Legislation and the Role of the Social Sciences." *American Sociological Review* 11, no. 6 (December 1946): 653–66.

———. "Science Legislation and the Social Sciences." *Political Science Quarterly* 62, no. 2 (June 1947): 241–49.

———. "Social Science: A Basic National Resource." In *The Nationalization of the Social Sciences,* ed. Samuel Z. Klausner and Victor M. Lidz, 41–112. Philadelphia: University of Pennsylvania Press, 1986.

———. "Social Strains in America." In *The New American Right,* ed. Daniel Bell, 117–40. New York: Criterion Books, 1955.

———. *The Social System.* Glencoe, IL: Free Press, 1951.

———. "Some Sociological Aspects of the Fascist Movements." *Social Forces* 21, no. 2 (December 1942): 138–47.

———. *The Structure of Social Action.* New York: McGraw Hill, 1937.

Parsons, Talcott, and Bernard Barber. "Sociology, 1941–1946." *American Journal of Sociology* 53, no. 4 (January 1948): 245–57.

Parsons, Talcott, and Edward Shils. *Toward a General Theory of Action.* Cambridge: Harvard University Press, 1951.

Parsons, Talcott, Edward Shils, Kaspar Naegele, and Jesse Pitts, eds. *Theories of Society: Foundations of Modern Sociological Theory.* New York: Free Press, 1961.

Patterson, Orlando, "The Last Sociologist." *New York Times,* 19 May 2002.

Peck, Sidney M. "Post-Modern Sociology." *Studies on the Left* 1, no. 1 (Fall 1959): 71–74.

Perrow, Charles. "Journaling Careers." In *Publishing in the Organizational Sciences,* ed. L. L. Cummings and Peter J. Frost, 220–30. Homewood, IL: Richard D. Irwin, 1985.

Peterson, William. Review of *The Status Seekers,* by Vance Packard. *American Sociological Review* 25, no. 1 (February 1960): 124–26.

Pfeiffer, John. "A Manner of Speaking." Review of *Fads and Foibles,* by Pitirim A. Sorokin. *New York Times Book Review,* 21 October 1956, 35.

Phillips, Bernard. *Beyond Sociology's Tower of Babel: Reconstructing the Scientific Method.* New York: Aldine de Gruyter, 2001.

Phillips, Bernard, Harold Kincaid, and Thomas J. Scheff, eds. *Toward a Sociological Imagination: Bridging Specialized Fields.* Lanham, MD: University Press of America, 2002.

Pickrel, Paul. "The Olympians." *Harper's,* April 1956, 88–90.

Poser, Richard. *Public Intellectuals: A Study of Decline.* Cambridge, MA: Harvard University Press, 2001.

Purcell, Edward A., Jr. *The Crisis of Democratic Theory: Scientific Naturalism and the Problem of Value.* Lexington: University Press of Kentucky, 1973.

Riecken, Henry W. "Underdogging." In *The Nationalization of the Social Sciences,* ed. Samuel Z. Klausner and Victor M. Lidz, 209–25. Philadelphia: Philadelphia University Press, 1986.

Reynolds, Larry T., and Janice M. Reynolds. *The Sociology of Sociology.* New York: David McKay, 1970.

Rieff, Philip. "Socialism and Sociology." Review of *The Power Elite,* by C. Wright Mills. *Partisan Review* 23, no. 3 (Summer 1956): 365–69.

Riesman, David. *Abundance for What? And Other Essays.* Garden City, NY: Doubleday, 1964.

———. *Individualism Reconsidered and Other Essays.* Glencoe, IL: Free Press, 1954.

———. "Innocence of *The Lonely Crowd.*" *Society* 27, no. 2 (January–February 1990): 76–79.

———. *The Lonely Crowd: A Study of the Changing American Character.* New Haven, CT: Yale University Press, 1961.

———. "Observations on Social Science Research." *Antioch Review* 11, no. 3 (September 1951): 259–78.

———. "A Personal Memoir: My Political Journey." In *Conflict and Consensus: A Festschrift in Honor of Lewis A. Coser,* ed. Walter W. Powell and Richard Robbins, 327–64. New York: Free Press, 1984.

———. "Private People and Public Policy." *Bulletin of the Atomic Scientists* 25, no. 5 (May 1959): 203–08.

———. "The Suburban Sadness." In *The Suburban Community,* ed. William Dobriner, 375–408. New York: G. P. Putnam's Sons, 1958.

Riesman, David, and Nathan Glazer. "Intellectuals and the Discontented Classes." In *The New American Right,* ed. Daniel Bell, 137–59. New York: Criterion Books, 1955.

————. "The Meaning of Opinion." *Public Opinion Quarterly* 12, no. 4 (Winter 1948–1949): 633–48.

Riesman, David, and Jeanne Watson. "The Sociability Project: A Chronicle of Frustration and Achievement." In *Sociologists at Work: Essays on the Craft of Social Research*, ed. Phillip E. Hammond, 235–321. New York: Basic Books, 1964.

Riley, John W., Jr. Review of *The American Soldier*. *American Sociological Review* 14, no. 4 (August 1949): 557–59.

Riley, Matilda White. "Membership in the American Sociological Association, 1950–1959." *American Sociological Review* 25, no. 6 (December 1960): 914–26.

Roberts, Alan B., and Milton Rokeach. "Anomie, Authoritarianism, and Prejudice: A Replication." *American Journal of Sociology* 51, no. 4 (January 1961): 355–58.

Rogin, Michael. *The Intellectuals and McCarthy: The Radical Specter*. Cambridge, MA: M.I.T. Press, 1967.

Rolo, C. J. Review of *The Power Elite*, by C. Wright Mills. *Atlantic Monthly*, June 1956.

Rorty, Richard. "Method, Social Science, and Social Hope." In *Consequences of Pragmatism*, ed. Richard Rorty, 191–210. Minneapolis: University of Minnesota Press, 1982.

————. *Philosophy and the Mirror of Nature*. Princeton, NJ: Princeton University Press, 1979.

Rosaldo, Renato. *Culture and Truth*. Boston: Beacon Press, 1989.

Rose, Arnold M. "Discussion of Bennett Berger's 'Sociology and the Intellectuals.'" *Antioch Review* 17, no. 4 (December 1957): 502–06.

Rose, David. "David Riesman Reconsidered." *Society* 19, no. 3 (March–April, 1982): 52–61.

Rosenau, Pauline. *Postmodernism and the Social Sciences: Insights, Inroads, and Intrusions*. Princeton, NJ: Princeton University Press, 1992.

Rosenberg, Bernard. "Rebellious Orgmen & Tame Intellectuals." *Dissent* 5, no. 2 (Spring 1958): 119–24.

Rosenberg, Bernard, and David Manning White, eds. *Mass Culture: The Popular Arts in America*. Glencoe, IL: Free Press, 1957.

Rosenberg, Harold. *The Tradition of the New*. New York: McGraw Hill, 1959.

Ross, Andrew. *No Respect: Intellectuals and Popular Culture*. New York: Routledge, Chapman and Hall, 1989.

Ross, Dorothy. *The Origins of American Social Science*. Cambridge: Cambridge University Press, 1991.

Rothbard, Murray N. "The Mantle of Science." In *Scientism and Values*, ed. Helmut Schoeck and James W. Higgins, 159–80. Princeton, NJ: D. Van Nostrand, 1960.

Salomon, Albert. "Prophets, Priests, and Social Scientists." *Commentary* 7, no. 6 (June 1949): 594–600.

————. *The Tyranny of Progress: Reflections on the Origins of Sociology*. New York: Noonday Press, 1955.

Saxton, Stanley L. "Sociologist as Citizen-Scholar: A Symbolic Interactionist Alternative to Normal Sociology." In *A Critique of Contemporary American Sociology*, ed. Ted R. Vaughan, Gideon Sjoberg, and Larry T. Reynolds, 232–51. Dix Hills, NY: General Hall, 1993.

Schlesinger, Arthur, Jr. "The Humanist Looks at Empirical Social Research." *American Sociological Review* 27, no. 6 (December 1962): 768–71.

————. "The Statistical Soldier." *Partisan Review* 16, no. 8 (August 1949): 852–56.

Schoeck, Helmut. Introduction to *Scientism and Values*, ed. Helmut Schoeck and James W. Higgins, ix–xvi. Princeton, NJ: D. Van Nostrand, 1960.

Schrecker, Ellen. *No Ivory Tower: McCarthyism and the Universities*. New York: Oxford University Press, 1986.

Schumpeter, Joseph A. *Capitalism, Socialism and Democracy*. New York: Harper & Row, 1950.

Seeman, Melvin. "The Intellectual and the Language of Minorities." *American Journal of Sociology* 64, no. 1 (July 1958): 25–35.

———. "On the Meaning of Alienation." *American Sociological Review* 24, no. 6 (December 1959): 783–91.

Seidman, Steven. *Contested Knowledge: Social Theory in the Postmodern Age*. Cambridge, MA: Blackwell, 1994.

———. "The End of Sociological Theory." In *The Postmodern Turn: New Perspectives on Social Theory*, 119–39. Cambridge: Cambridge University Press, 1994.

———. *Postmodernism and Social Theory: The Debate Over General Theory*. New York: Blackwell, 1991.

———. "Theory as Social Narrative With a Moral Intent." In *Postmodernism and Social Theory: The Debate Over General Theory*, ed. Steven Seidman and David G. Wagner. New York: Blackwell, 1991.

Seidman, Steven, Laurel Richardson, and Norman K. Denzin. "Discussion." *The Sociological Quarterly* 37, no. 4 (Fall 1996): 721–59.

Selznick, Philip. "Dilemmas of Leadership and Doctrine in Democratic Planning." In *Studies in Leadership*, ed. Alvin W. Gouldner, 560–91. New York: Harper, 1950.

———. "Institutional Vulnerability in Mass Society." *American Journal of Sociology* 51, no. 4 (January 1951): 320–31.

———. *The Organizational Weapon: A Study of Bolshevick Strategy and Tactics*. Glencoe, IL: Free Press, 1952.

———. *TVA and the Grass Roots: A Study in the Sociology of Formal Organization*. Berkeley: University of California Press, 1953.

Shanas, Ethel. Review of *Measurement and Prediction*, by Stouffer, et al. *American Journal of Sociology* 57, no. 4 (January 1952): 388.

Shannon, Christopher. *Conspicuous Criticism: Tradition, the Individual, and Culture in American Social Thought from Veblen to Mills*. Baltimore: Johns Hopkins University Press, 1996.

Shils, Edward. "Authoritarianism: 'Right' and 'Left.'" In *Studies in the Scope and Method of "The Authoritarian Personality,"* edited by Richard Christie and Marie Jahoda, 24–49. Glencoe, IL: Free Press, 1954.

———. "The Calling of Sociology." In *Theories of Society: Foundations of Modern Sociological Theory*, ed. Talcott Parsons, Edward Shils, Kaspar Naegele, and Jesse R. Pitts, 1405–48. New York: Free Press, 1961.

———. *The Calling of Sociology and Other Essays on the Pursuit of Learning*. Chicago: University of Chicago Press, 1980.

———, ed. "Daydreams and Nightmares: Reflections on the Criticism of Mass Culture." *Sewanee Review* 65, no. 4 (October 1957): 586–608.

———. "Imaginary Sociology." Review of *The Sociological Imagination*, by C. Wright Mills. *Encounter* 14, no. 6 (June 1960): 77–79.

————. "The Theory of Mass Society." *Diogenes* 39 (Fall 1962): 45–66.

Sica, Alan, and Stephen Turner, eds. *The Disobedient Generation: Social Theorists in the Sixties.* Chicago: University of Chicago Press, 2006.

————. "The Rhetoric of Sociology and Its Audience." In *Sociology and Its Publics: The Forms and Fates of Disciplinary Organization,* ed. Terence C. Halliday and Morris Janowitz, 347–72. Chicago: University of Chicago Press, 1992.

Simmel, Georg. *On Individuality and Social Forms.* Chicago: University of Chicago Press, 1971.

Simpson, Christopher. *Science of Coercion: Communication Research and Psychological Warfare.* New York: Oxford University Press, 1994.

Sjoberg, Gideon, and Ted R. Vaughan. "The Bureaucratization of Sociology: Its Impact on Theory and Research." In *A Critique of Contemporary American Sociology,* ed. Ted R. Vaughan, Gideon Sjoberg, and Larry T. Reynolds, 54–113. Dix Hills, NY: General Hall, 1993.

Skocpol, Theda. "The Dead End of Metatheory." *Contemporary Sociology* 25, no. 1 (January 1987): 10–12.

Small, Albion. "The Era of Sociology." *American Journal of Sociology* 1, no. 1 (July 1895): 1–15.

Smith, Bruce L. R. *American Science Policy Since World War II.* Washington, DC: Brookings Institution, 1990.

Smith, Joel. "Emancipating Sociology: Postmodernism and Mainstream Sociological Practice." *Social Forces* 74, no. 1 (September 1995): 53–79.

Smith, Mark C. *Social Science in the Crucible: The Debate Over Objectivity and Purpose, 1918–1941.* Durham, NC: Duke University Press, 1994.

Snizek, William E., Ellsworth R. Fuhrman, and Michael K. Miller, eds. *Contemporary Issues in Theory and Research: A Metatheoretical Perspective.* Westport, CT: Greenwood Press, 1979.

Snow, C. P. *The Two Cultures.* Cambridge: Cambridge University Press, 1959.

Sorensen, Aage B., and Seymour Spilerman, eds. *Social Theory and Social Policy: Essays in Honor of James S. Coleman.* Westport, CT: Praeger, 1993.

Sorokin, Pitirim A. *Contemporary Sociological Theories.* New York: London, Harper & Brothers, 1928.

————. *The Crisis of Our Age.* New York: E. P. Dutton, 1942.

————. *Fads and Foibles in Modern Sociology and Related Sciences.* Chicago: Henry Regnery, 1956.

————. Letter to the Editor. *American Journal of Sociology* 62, no. 5 (March 1957): 515.

————. *A Long Journey.* New Haven, CT: College and University Press, 1963.

————. *Social and Cultural Dynamics,* vol 1. New York: American Book, 1937.

————. *Social Mobility.* New York: Harper, 1927.

————. *Social Philosophies of an Age of Crisis.* London: Adam and Charles Black, 1952.

————. "Sociology as a Science." *Social Forces* 10, no. 1 (October 1931): 21–27.

Spectorsky, Auguste Comte. *The Exurbanites.* Philadelphia: Lippincott, 1955.

Srole, Leo. "Social Integration and Certain Corollaries: An Exploratory Study." *American Sociological Review* 21, no. 6 (December 1956): 709–16.

Stein, Maurice R. *The Eclipse of Community: An Interpretation of American Studies.* Princeton: Princeton University Press, 1960.

————. "The Eclipse of Community: Some Glances at the Education of a Sociologist." In *Reflections on Community Studies*, ed. Arthur J. Vidich, Joseph Bensman and Maurice R. Stein, 207–32. New York: John Wiley, 1964.

————. "The Poetic Metaphors of Sociology." In *Sociology on Trial*, ed. Arthur Vidich and Maurice R. Stein, 173–82. Englewood Cliffs, NJ: Prentice-Hall, 1963.

Stein, Maurice R., Arthur J. Vidich, and David Manning White, eds. *Identity and Anxiety: Survival of the Person in Mass Society*. Glencoe, IL: Free Press, 1960.

Stouffer, Samuel A. *Communism, Conformity, and Civil Liberties: A Cross-Section of the Nation Speaks Its Mind*. Garden City, NY: Doubleday, 1955.

————. "Measurement in Sociology." *American Sociological Review* 18, no. 6 (December 1953): 591–97.

————. *Social Research to Test Ideas*. Glencoe, IL: Free Press, 1962.

————. "Some Afterthoughts of a Contributor to 'The American Soldier.' " In *Continuities in Social Research: Studies in the Scope and Method of "The American Soldier,"* edited by Robert K. Merton and Paul F. Lazarsfeld, 197–211. Glencoe, IL: Free Press, 1950.

Stouffer, Samuel A., Louis Guttman, Edward A. Suchman, Paul F. Lazarsfeld, Shirley A. Star, and John A. Clausen, eds. *Measurement and Prediction*. Studies in Social Psychology in World War II, vol. 4. Princeton, NJ: Princeton University Press, 1949.

Stouffer, Samuel A., Arthur A. Lumsdaine, Marion Harper Lumsdaine, Robin M. Williams, Jr., M. Brewster Smith, Irving L. Janis, Shirley A. Star, and Leonard S. Cottrell, Jr. *The American Soldier: Combat and Its Aftermath*. Studies in Social Psychology in World War II, vol. 2. Princeton, NJ: Princeton University Press, 1949.

Stouffer, Samuel, Edward A. Suchman, Leland C. DeVinney, Shirley A. Star, and Robin M. Williams, Jr. *The American Soldier: Adjustment During Army Life*. Studies in Social Psychology in World War II, vol. 1. Princeton, NJ: Princeton University Press, 1949.

Summers, John H. "The Big Discourse." *The Nation*, 9 October 2000.

————. "The Deciders." *New York Times Book Review*, 14 May 2006.

Sweezy, Paul. "Power Elite or Ruling Class?" In *C. Wright Mills and the Power Elite*, ed. G. William Domhoff and Hoyt B. Ballard, 115–32. Boston: Beacon Press, 1968.

Taylor, Carl C. "The Social Survey and the Science of Sociology." *American Journal of Sociology* 25, no. 6 (May 1920): 731–56.

Tebbel, John. *A History of Book Publishing in the United States*, vol. 4. *The Great Change, 1940–1980*. New York: R. R. Bowker, 1981.

Tiryakian, Edward A. "The Significance of Schools in the Development of Sociology." In *Contemporary Issues in Theory and Research: A Metatheoretical Perspective*, ed. William E. Snizek, Ellsworth R. Fuhrman and Michael K. Miller. Westport, CT: Greenwood Press, 1979.

Tittle, Charles R. "The Arrogance of Public Sociology." *Social Forces* 82, no. 4 (1 June 2004): 1639–44.

Tönnies, Ferdinand. *Community and Civil Society*. Cambridge: Cambridge University Press, 2001.

Tucker, Robert C., ed. *The Marx-Engels Reader*. New York: W. W. Norton, 1978.

Turner, Jonathan. "The Promise of Positivism." In *Postmodernism and Social Theory: The Debate Over General Theory*, ed. Steven Seidman and David G. Wagner. New York: Blackwell, 1991.

Turner, Stephen P. "The Maturity of Social Theory. " In *The Dialogical Turn: New Roles for Sociology in the Postdisciplinary Age*, ed. Charles Camic and Hans Joas. Lanham, MD: Rowman & Littlefield, 2004.

Turner, Stephen P., and Jonathan H. Turner. *The Impossible Science: An Institutional Analysis of American Sociology*. Newbury Park, CA: Sage, 1990.

Turner, Stephen P., and Mark Wardell, eds. *The Transition in Sociological Theory*. Boston: Allen & Unwin, 1986.

U.S. President's Research Committee on Social Trends. *Recent Social Trends in the United States*, 3 vols. New York: McGraw-Hill, 1933.

Vaughan, Ted R., Gideon Sjoberg, and Larry T. Reynolds, eds. *A Critique of Contemporary American Sociology*. Dix Hills, NY: General Hall, 1993.

Vidich, Arthur, and Maurice Stein, eds. *Sociology on Trial*. Englewood Cliffs, NJ: Prentice-Hall, 1963.

von Hayek, Friedrich A. *The Counter-Revolution of Science: Studies on the Abuse of Reason*. Glencoe, IL: Free Press, 1955.

———. "Scientism and the Study of Society." *Economica* 9, no. 35 (August 1942): 267–91.

———. "Scientism and the Study of Society, Part II." *Economica* 10, no. 37 (February 1943): 34–63.

———. "Scientism and the Study of Society, Part III." *Economica* 11, no. 41 (February 1944): 27–39.

Warner, John Anson. "The Critics of C. Wright Mills." Ph.D. diss. Princeton University, 1973.

Warner, W. Lloyd, and Paul S. Lunt. *The Social Life of a Modern Community*. New Haven: Yale University Press, 1941.

———. *The Status System of a Modern Community*. New Haven: Yale University Press, 1942.

Weaver, Richard M. "Social Science in Excelsis." *National Review* 2, 19 (29 September 1956): 18–19.

Weber, Max. "Science as a Vocation." In *From Max Weber: Essays in Sociology*, ed. Hans Gerth and C. Wright Mills, 129–56. New York: Oxford University Press, 1946.

Wells, Richard H., and Steven J. Picou. *American Sociology: Theoretical and Methodological Structure*. Washington, DC: University Press of America, 1981.

Westbrook, Robert. *John Dewey and American Democracy*. Ithaca, NY: Cornell University Press, 1991.

Whyte, William H. "Groupthink." *Fortune*, March 1952, 114–117, 142, 146.

———. "The Social Engineers." *Fortune*, January 1952, 88–91, 108.

Wiley, Norbert. "The Rise and Fall of Dominating Theories in American Sociology." In *Contemporary Issues in Theory and Research: A Metatheoretical Perspective*, ed. William E. Snizek, Ellsworth R. Fuhrman, and Michael K. Miller, 47–79. Westport, CT: Greewood Press, 1979.

Wilner, Patricia. "The Main Drift of Sociology Between 1936 and 1982." *History of Sociology* 5, no. 2 (Spring 1985): 1–20.

Wirth, Lewis. *On Cities and Social Life*. Chicago: University of Chicago Press, 1964.

Wolfe, Alan. *Whose Keeper? Social Science and Moral Obligation*. Berkeley: University of California Press, 1989.

Wolfe, Tom. "Seizing the Power." In *The New Journalism*, ed. Tom Wolfe, 23–36. New York: Harper & Row, 1973.

Wright, Erik Olin. *Interrogating Inequality: Essays on Class Analysis, Socialism and Marxism*. New York: Verso, 1994.

Wrong, Dennis. "The Failure of Sociology." *Commentary* 28, no. 5 (November 1959): 375–80.

———. "Human Nature and the Perspective of Sociology." *Social Research* 30, no. 3 (Autumn 1963): 300–18.

———. "The Oversocialized Conception of Man in Modern Sociology." *American Sociological Review* 26, no. 2 (April 1962): 183–93.

———. "Riesman and the Age of Sociology." *Commentary* 21, no. 4 (April 1956): 331–38.

———. *Skeptical Sociology*. New York: Columbia University Press, 1976.

Znaniecki, Florian. "The Proximate Future of Sociology: Controversies in Doctrine and Method." *American Journal of Sociology* 50, no. 6 (May 1945): 514–21.

Index

David Paul Haney is an Adjunct Professor at Austin Community College and St. Edward's University.